Web Application Development with PHP 4.0

New Riders

Other Books by New Riders Publishing

MySQL
Paul DuBois, 0-7357-0921-1

A UML Pattern Language
Paul Evitts, 1-57870-118-X

Constructing Superior Software
Paul Clements, 1-57870-147-3

Python Essential Reference
David Beazley, 0-7357-0901-7

KDE Application Development
Uwe Thiem, 1-57870-201-1

Developing Linux Applications with
GTK+ and GDK
Eric Harlow, 0-7357-0021-4

GTK+/Gnome Application
Development
Havoc Pennington, 0-7357-0078-8

DCE/RPC over SMB: Samba and
Windows NT Domain Internals
Luke Leighton, 1-57870-150-3

Linux Firewalls
Robert Ziegler, 0-7357-0900-9

Linux Essential Reference
Ed Petron, 0-7357-0852-5

Linux System Administration
*Jim Dennis, M. Carling, et al,
1-556205-934-3*

Web Application Development with PHP 4.0

Tobias Ratschiller
Till Gerken
With contributions by
Zend Technologies, LTD
Zeev Suraski
Andi Gutmans

New Riders

201 West 103rd Street,
Indianapolis, Indiana 46290

Web Application Development with PHP 4.0

By: Tobias Ratschiller and Till Gerken

International Standard Book Number: 0-7357-0997-1

Library of Congress Catalog Card Number: 00-100402

04 03 02 01 00   7 6 5 4 3 2 1

Interpretation of the printing code: The rightmost double-digit number is the year of the book's printing; the right-most single-digit number is the number of the book's printing. For example, the printing code 00-1 shows that the first printing of the book occurred in 2000.

Composed in Bembo and MCPdigital by New Riders Publishing

Printed in the United States of America

Trademarks

Warning and Disclaimer

Publisher
David Dwyer

Executive Editor
Al Valvano

Managing Editor
Gina Brown

Product Marketing Manager
Stephanie Layton

Publicity Manager
Susan Petro

Acquisitions Editors
Ann Quinn
Alan Bower
Stacey Beheler
Nancy Maragioglio

Editor
Robin Drake

Indexer
Cheryl Lenser

Manufacturing Coordinator
Chris Moos

Book Designer
Louisa Klucznik

Cover Designer
Aren Howell

Composition
Amy Parker

Proofreader
Jessica McCarty

Contents

About the Authors

Tobias Ratschiller is a new media consultant based in Italy. With extensive knowledge of software development, database design, and content-management systems, he specializes in the creation of large-scale, dynamic Web sites. He has provided consulting and implementation services for some of the world's largest Web sites and has contributed to several books and articles on PHP. He teaches at seminars throughout Europe and is a frequent speaker at leading conferences.

Till Gerken is a freelance developer and consultant for various companies, focusing on the creation of Web applications for Internet-based services. His background ranges from using C/C++, Pascal, and x86 Assembler to create such high-performance multimedia systems as 3D engines and real-time sound mixers, to using PHP and its associated tools to create medium- to large-scale, dynamic Web sites.

About the Technical Reviewer

Graeme Merrall contributed his considerable hands-on expertise to the entire development process for *Web Application Development with PHP 4.0*. As the book was being written, he reviewed all the material for technical content, organization, and flow. His feedback was critical to ensuring that *Web Application Development with PHP 4.0* fits our readers' need for the highest quality technical information.

Graeme originally graduated in 1993 with a degree in biochemistry. During his university studies, he discovered the Internet while it was still very much in its infancy. This led him away from biochemistry into employment with an ISP and later with a leading Web design firm in New Zealand, where he developed his skills in PHP and ASP.

As well as programming, Graeme has written for the local newspaper in his former home town in New Zealand and has produced several tutorials and articles on PHP for Wired Digital's Web Monkey.

Born and raised in New Zealand, Graeme currently resides in Sydney, where he runs his own consultancy, specializing in e-commerce and business integration with the Internet. In his spare time, he enjoys modern literature, music, and crocodile wrestling.

About Zend Technologies, LTD.

The Zend Engine is the basic scripting engine that drives PHP. Owned by Zend Technologies, LTD, the engine is licensed to PHP for free use under the Q Public license. The Zend engine brings to PHP performance, reliability, and an easy-to-use scripting interface.

The history of the Zend Engine began four years ago when the company founders, Zeev Suraski and Andi Gutmans, joined the core development team of PHP and wrote the scripting engine of PHP, which is installed on over a million hosts today. Now, with the introduction of PHP 4.0, the Zend Engine has matured into a versatile scripting engine, and Andi Gutmans and Zeev Suraski are engaged in developing a host of products for enhancing PHP's performance and commercial value.

Acknowledgments

We'd like to say "thank you" to the staff at New Riders: You've probably had a hard time with us, and we appreciate your friendliness and professional handling. Robin Drake, our editor, deserves special thanks for her patience with us. Thanks as well to our technical editor, Graeme Merrall, and acquisitions editor, Ann Quinn.

The following people have helped us during various stages of this book, and we'd like to thank them as well: Alan Bower, Nancy Maragioglio, Jakob Nielsen, Kristian Koehntopp, Zeev Suraski, Andi Gutmans, Leon Atkinson, Alexander Aulbach, Uwe Steinmann, Boaz Yahav, and Rafi Ton. We'd also like to thank the authors of our case studies. Finally, thanks to SoftQuad for providing their excellent XMetaL XML editor for use in writing and editing the text.

Acknowledgments from Tobias

The person who deserves the most thanks is Till Gerken, of course, who was a great coauthor. We've spent thousands (or so) of hours on IRC, reviewing chapters, writing and fixing code—and having fun. It was hard work, but we had a great time.

Thanks to all folks on Efnet's #php—they're a great community, and it's fun hanging out there. If you have the chance, stop by and say hello to tigloo (Till) and Yapa (that's me). Everyone on IRC was helpful, and Zeev was especially patient in answering our questions.

Thanks to Robert Finazzer, who has provided valuable business advice over the last few years, and has always been understanding when I've written articles or books instead of working with him on multimillion-dollar ventures. Greetings to the rest of the team at Profi Online Service, and of course Joachim Marangoni.

Acknowledgments from Till

I hardly thought that I would ever get to the point of writing this section, but now it's here. With it, I am finishing a project on which I spent a lot of time and energy during the past year. I must admit that I sometimes thought that we wouldn't make it, and I'm proud now at seeing it on the shelf.

Because of this, the first person I have to mention is Tobias Ratschiller, who originally pulled me into the PHP business. From the very start he had an overwhelming faith in me and showed endless patience while working with me. He was a five-star coauthor and I'm glad I had the opportunity to write this book with him. Even when I was sometimes unhappy with my material, he never had a lack of good suggestions. As he already said, we spent endless hours on IRC, criticizing and fixing up each other's text and code, not to mention all the emails. It was definitely a lot of fun!

In addition to the acknowledgments above, I have to thank my friends, both those who supported me in my work and those who didn't. Even though I always hated it when other authors said "too many to mention them all here," I must admit that I feel the same and that it would do more harm to leave someone out. After all, you know who you are!

Last, but not least, I want to thank my family for putting up with me and my workaholic attitude, and for providing a home for me when I had to find a quiet place.

Tell Us What You Think

As the reader of this book, you are the most important critic and commentator. We value your opinion and want to know what we're doing right, what we could do better, what areas you'd like to see us publish in, and any other words of wisdom you're willing to pass our way.

As the Executive Editor at New Riders Publishing, I welcome your comments. You can fax, email, or write me directly to let me know what you did or didn't like about this book—as well as what we can do to make our books stronger.

Please note that I cannot help you with technical problems related to the topic of this book, and that due to the high volume of mail I receive, I might not be able to reply to every message.

When you write, please be sure to include this book's title and author as well as your name and phone or fax number. I will carefully review your comments and share them with the author and editors who worked on the book.

Fax: 317-581-4663
Email: nrfeedback@newriders.com
Mail: Al Valvano
          Executive Editor
          New Riders Publishing
          201 West 103rd Street
          Indianapolis, IN 46290 USA

Foreword by Zeev Suraski

When I first came across PHP about three years ago, I never imagined that one day I'd be writing a foreword for a PHP book. As a matter of fact, back then, the possibility that there would actually ever be any PHP books seemed a bit far-fetched. Looking back at what made PHP grow to be one of the most widely used scripting languages for Web development is no less than astonishing. My involvement in the PHP project started, like many things, by accident. As an end user, I'd stumbled on a bug in PHP/FI 2.0—something that was weird enough to get colleague Andi Gutmans and me to look under the hood. When we saw the code that made PHP/FI 2.0 tick, we weren't too pleased with it. On the other hand, we really liked the idea of an HTML-embedded, server-embedded server-side scripting language. So, like good to-be software engineers, we decided it'd be cool to write it from scratch, but this time, the "right way."

Our rewrite of the language, and the huge amount of cooperative work that was put into a wide variety of function modules and sample code, pushed PHP beyond our wildest dreams and expectations. PHP is being used today on well over a million domains on the Internet, and is the tool of choice for server-side scripting in UNIX environments. PHP 4.0 is the next step in ensuring that PHP remains on the cutting edge of Web scripting technologies for years to come. The Zend engine (www.zend.com) revolutionizes the performance and scalability of PHP-based Web sites. Its integrated session support; built-in XML, Java, and COM support; as well as a bundle of additional features enable the Web developer to develop more powerful dynamic sites, more easily than ever before.

With the continued development and integration of leading-edge technologies, PHP stays up to date. The new Java and DCOM support, the advanced XML features, and the improved OOP features further increase PHP's acceptance in business environments and make PHP a viable tool for enterprise computing. The commercial add-ons from Zend Technologies—for example, the debugger, IDE, and compiler—will lead to a further leap. Also, the insides of PHP 4.0 have gone through architectural revolutions that will be largely unnoticed by the end user. For example, the Web server interface has been completely abstracted, allowing the support of Web servers other than Apache. Books like the one you're reading right now provide you with the necessary background to utilize these new technologies successfully.

In my opinion, the future looks bright for Open Source in general and PHP in particular. In 1997, you had to jump through hoops just to convince your manager that Linux was at least as stable as Windows NT, and using Open Source in large companies wasn't even considered. The world has changed. Companies that took the mission to back Linux-based solutions, such as RedHat, SuSE, and VA Linux, have not only become commercial giants, but also positioned Linux and Open Source in general as an acceptable solution in every company today. Luckily, these companies were smart enough to do that while keeping the Open Source spirit and a strong relationship with the community. The Open Source development model on one hand, and the firm commercial backing on the other, brought Linux to unimaginable heights. I'm sure that commercial companies that take the mission to back PHP, such as Zend Technologies, will help in making PHP an even more widely used solution, especially in the highest-end Web sites.

I would like to take this opportunity to thank Prof. Michael Rodeh of IBM Haifa and the Technion Institute of Technology, who encouraged Andi and me to cooperate with Rasmus Lerdorf, the author of PHP/FI 1.0 and 2.0; Rasmus Lerdorf, who was very happy to cooperate with us to make PHP 3.0 the official PHP/FI 2.0 successor; The PHP Group and the entire team of PHP developers, without which PHP wouldn't have been the excellent tool it is today; and finally, the PHP community, which has proven to be an endless resource for ideas and support.

I'm sure you'll find this book helpful when learning about advanced PHP and the development of Web applications. This is one of the few books covering more than the mere syntax of a language—it introduces you to the concepts behind the language, and can help you to enhance your problem-solving skills in Web programming.

Good luck!
Zeev Suraski

Introduction

*The ancient Masters
didn't try to educate the people,
but kindly taught them to not-know.*

While the success of Open Source software like Linux or Apache has been documented extensively throughout all mainstream media, the rise of PHP has gone largely unnoticed. Still, the Web scripting language PHP is the most popular module for the Apache Web server, according to an E-Soft survey (www.e-softinc.com/survey/). Netcraft studies have found that PHP is in use on over 6% of all Web domains in the world (see www.netcraft.com/survey). That's an incredible market penetration for a rather specialized product. This popularity continues to rise exponentially. Increasingly, this is being reflected in traditional media: As of May, 2000, more than 20 books about PHP have been published in different languages, with more in the pipeline.

Commercial players are beginning to join the bandwagon: PHP is included with Web servers, for example C2's Stronghold, and Linux distributions. A new company, Zend Technologies, has been formed to provide commercial add-ons and support for PHP. A long list of large-scale Web sites employ PHP, as well as hundreds of thousands of small to medium Web sites.

For the authors, this book began in June of 1999, when we were approached by New Riders Publishing to write a book about advanced PHP. The idea of writing a PHP book had been in our heads since some time prior, and the New Riders proposal was very welcome.

About 1,500 emails, 500 CVS commits, and countless hours on IRC later, we're finally done. It was a bear of a job, but we think we succeeded in writing a book that's different from pure reference manuals. We have tried to explain the concepts of Web application development, rather than giving you just a dry overview of PHP's features.

The evolution from a novice programmer with no or little formal education to a software development expert happens in different stages. The programmer begins the career as an apprentice. At this time, the programmer usually doesn't worry about coding styles, planning, or testing—unreadable code, missing security, and long hacker nights are typical for this stage. While the programmer may know all the tricks and hidden features of a language, he or she will encounter difficulties in team development, maintenance, and larger development projects. At this point, you can easily spot those who will be expert developers later. They start to ask questions:

- How can I avoid implementing the same functionality over and over?

- What provisions do I have to put into effect to make my application secure and stable?

- What does it take to make my application easier to maintain?

- How can multiple people work together efficiently on a team?

This is where our book comes into play. We hope to provide software developers with some guidelines on better PHP and Web application software development. Many technologies are available today, and you can only fully utilize them if you understand the fundamental principles behind the development process, and if you develop problem-solving skills. Typical reference manuals don't help with those issues.

Target Audience

If you're new to programming, this book is not for you. You'll find a helpful resource, however, in the following cases:

- You have already developed applications with PHP, and want to take your skills to the next level.
- You have experience with other programming languages and want to develop Web applications with PHP.
- You're an expert with PHP and want to extend PHP's feature set on your own.

You don't need to be a PHP wizard to read this book, but you should be familiar with PHP's syntax, or have good knowledge of programming principles.

Prerequisites

This book assumes that you have a working PHP setup, preferably PHP 4.0 or later. Because of its popularity, we use MySQL as the database system where one is required. Because platform independence is one of PHP's strongest features, however, our examples should run on UNIX as well as on Windows.

Organization of This Book

This book is divided into three parts. The first part, "Advanced PHP," covers the advanced syntax of PHP; for example, object orientation, dynamic functions and variables, and self-modifying code. It also gives you an overview of project planning principles, coding styles, and application design. This part provides the necessary base for fast, productive development of industry-quality Web applications.

Part II, "Web Applications," focuses on building the software: It explains why sessions are important, what security guidelines you need to keep in mind, why usability matters, and how to use the PHPLib for session management and database access. You'll also find three case studies of successful PHP projects here, to help you convince your IT managers.

The third part of the book, "Beyond PHP," is for readers who want to go beyond what's currently available with PHP, and explains how to extend PHP with C. This is the official documentation on extending PHP, as approved by Zend Technologies.

In detail, the following topics are covered.

Chapter 1—Development Concepts

Having to deal with advanced projects makes the usage of coding conventions, proper planning, and advanced syntax unavoidable requirements. This chapter covers general coding conventions that are a requirement for all industry-quality projects—naming and comment conventions, as well as how to break up the source into logical modules.

Chapter 2—Advanced Syntax

This chapter covers PHP's advanced syntax, for example multidimensional arrays, classes, variable variables, self-modifying code, and the like.

Chapter 3—Application Design: A Real-Life Example

In this chapter, we walk you through the entire process of planning a complete Web application: phpChat, a Web-based chat client interface to IRC. This chapter shows planning fundamentals, gives guidelines on project organization, and shows how to realize modular, plug-in-enabled applications.

Chapter 4—Web Application Concepts

Session management, security considerations and authentication, and usability form the base of every Web application. Web applications aren't possible without proper session management. You have to find a way to recognize users during multiple page requests if you want to associate variables like a shopping cart with one specific user. And this identification had better be secure if you don't want to have one user seeing another's credit card information. Indeed, special considerations are necessary for improving security in your applications. Even if PHP is less prone to crackers' attacks than other CGI environments, it's easy to write totally exposed applications when you don't keep in mind certain important principles covered in this chapter.

This chapter also introduces basic usability concepts. As soon as we begin to talk about applications instead of stand-alone scripts, the user's role becomes more important. After all, it's users who finally determine the success or failure of a project—and this chapter shows some guidelines to achieve better user satisfaction.

Chapter 5—Basic Web Application Strategies

This chapter discusses more fundamentals of Web applications. All Web applications process form input, for example, or deal with separation of layout and code. Moving on from these topics, this chapter also introduces you to effective team development by giving an overview of version control with CVS. Finally, it discusses multi-tier applications, COM, and Java from a PHP point of view.

Chapter 6—Database Access with PHP

Without databases, Web applications are not possible. Chapter 6 presents the PHPLib as a tool for vendor-independent database access, and gives an overview about its other features, such as session management, user authentication, and permission management.

Chapter 7—Cutting-Edge Applications

By developing a complete knowledge repository using PHPLib, this chapter familiarizes you with PHPLib's template class, self-references in SQL, and other advanced topics. Then the chapter presents an overview of XML and how applications can benefit from this exciting technology. The chapter also describes PHP's interfaces for XML parsing and its WDDX functions.

Chapter 8—Case Studies

Success stories can help tremendously when introducing a new technology into a corporate environment. In Chapter 8, we present case studies featuring Six Open Systems, BizChek, and Marketplayer.com—three great examples among hundreds of companies using PHP successfully in high-demand scenarios.

Chapter 9—Extending PHP 4.0: Hacking the Core of PHP

Are more than 1,200 functions still not enough for you? No problem, because this chapter is the official documentation on extending PHP. If you know some C, Chapter 9 gives you some condensed insight into the internals of PHP 4.0, and shows you how to write your own modules to extend PHP's functionality.

Conventions Used in this Book

The following conventions are used in this book:

Convention	Usage
italic	New terms being defined.
`monospace text`	Commands, syntax lines, and so on, as well as Internet addresses such as `www.phpwizard.net`.
➥	Code-continuation characters are inserted into code when a line shouldn't be broken, but we simply ran out of room on the page.

I

Advanced PHP

1

Development Concepts

Naming is the origin of all particular things.

To TRULY MASTER A LANGUAGE, IT'S CRUCIAL TO understand not just the syntax and semantics of the language, but its philosophy, background, and design characteristics.

PHP for Me?

Have you ever asked yourself why there are so many programming languages? Apart from such "mainstream" languages as C, C++, Pascal, and the like, there are others such as Logo, Cobol, Fortran, Simula, and many more exotic languages. Most software developers don't really think about alternative programming languages when outlining a project; they have their preferred language (maybe a corporate-dictated language), know its advantages as well as its drawbacks, and adapt the project according to the language's specific strengths and weaknesses. But this might impose unnecessary additional workload to level out flaws in the chosen language.

Knowing how to use a language but lacking the knowledge of its specific concepts is like a truck driver wanting to participate in a cart race. Of course, he knows generally how to drive the cart—he might even place well at the finish line—but he'll never be an outstanding driver until he's familiar with the specialties of his new vehicle.

Similarly, when asked to write an application, the OOP programmer will try to fit it into objects, and the procedural programmer will handle the same task differently. Which approach is better? Each programmer will say that his or her method is best, but only someone who's familiar with both concepts—OOP and procedural programming—will be able to judge.

Each language mentioned earlier represents a different approach of solving problems in a specific way—mostly only problems of a specific kind, with special requirements. Because these languages focus on a very limited field of use, their success is limited to these fields as well. Languages like C and Pascal probably became so popular because of their broad focus, leaving out special features for specific problems but satisfying the need for a tool that solves common problems.

How does PHP fit into this scheme? Although it's called a language, PHP isn't really a language of its own, but instead is a mixture of different languages. It mainly uses the syntax most programmers know from C, but still is substantially different; it's interpreted. PHP also knows different variable types, but does no strict type checking. PHP knows classes but no structured types. There are a lot of examples like this, but you probably get the point already: PHP melts a lot of different conceptual approaches into a completely new, unique approach.

To be successful in creating Web applications using PHP, we encourage you to answer the following question first: *Is PHP the ideal language for my project?* Good question. But we would be dumb to say no. (Who would be writing a book about something they think is bad?) Let's rephrase the question: *Is there a better language than PHP for my project?* This is safe to answer. If you're doing Web application development, PHP is the language for you.

The Importance of Planning

Why You Should Read This Section

Even if you're already a professional programmer familiar with PHP, we encourage you to read the following sections, as they cover the basics for successful development. If you're already familiar with the discussed topics, take the time to browse through the text anyway; you might discover new information—new views of problems, new approaches, new solutions. The more you know about approaching different aspects of your future projects, the better you'll be at nailing down the critical fragments and handling them in a superior way. Many of the following sections also discuss topics that are more questions of belief than commonly accepted rules. We'd like you to trust us as professional developers and rely on our experience before abandoning the content—it will pay later on.

Before diving into PHP-specific issues, let's start from a wider point of view. Some issues apply to application development in general, regardless of which language you're using and on what platform you're developing.

When working on a professional project, it's very important that you think about what you're doing. *Know your enemy—never underestimate him.* Although your project isn't really an enemy, the point still applies. Know all your project's specifications, its target platform(s), its users, and never underestimate the significance of small problems that you haven't evaluated *completely* before moving on to other topics.

Judging from our experience, planning takes at least 50% of the development time; the bigger the project, the more thoroughly you should develop its outlines. This principle applies to contacting your customers and working closely with them on defining an overall project outline, as well as talking with your developers about defining a coding outline. The less effort you spend on consistency and maintainability, the sooner you'll run into problems when reopening old files and trying to fix bugs or add new features.

Planning time isn't necessarily proportional to a project's size. As an example, think about a search algorithm that you have to design. The application doesn't have to do more than basically crawl through a heap of information, extracting data according to a set of rules. Let's say that the data is already there, so setup and output won't require a lot of effort. The application will spend most of its execution time in its main searching loop. The loop probably won't even take more than 100 lines of code, but choosing or designing an optimal algorithm for an optimal loop could easily take a whole day. This little loop might be the most substantial part in your design phase, while on the other hand you may create projects with a few thousand lines that have been thoroughly planned in less than a day.

Similarly, let's say you need a little script that lists all files in a directory. You could hack it quickly so it would perform just this specific task, listing all files in a specified directory. You wouldn't have to worry about it anymore—the problem's solved and you can move on to other tasks, leaving your snippet behind. But another strategy might be to take into consideration that at a later point—maybe even in a completely different project—you'll probably need a similar tool again. Just hacking directory listers over and over when you need one, each for its specific task, would be a waste of time. Thus, when first encountering such a situation, you should think about it. You could create a separate module from the directory lister, allowing it to list different directories, optionally recursing subdirectories, eventually even accepting wildcards. You might create a bulletproof little function that would handle most special cases and also handle everyday demands to a directory lister just perfectly. With this latter method, after a few projects you would have a library of solid tool functions that you could reuse safely and rely on, and that sometimes might strip down development time significantly.

Of course, an ever-increasing number of freely available tool function libraries exist, but these will hardly satisfy all your needs, nor will they be optimized for your special demands. Some libraries are also just too heavy to carry around—having to parse a few hundred kilobytes of extra code every hit might significantly decrease the performance of your site. In this situation, it pays to be able to replace a sub-optimal solution with a 100% optimal solution that you created.

Larger projects offer even more opportunities for problems due to lack of planning. Late in development, you might encounter difficulties that you didn't or couldn't foresee because of the lack of work and time spent on the design. These difficulties might be so severe that they require you to completely restructure the entire project. Imagine a database-backed application that relies on an additional database abstraction layer. The database abstraction layer accepts only textual data, but at a later point you notice that you also need it to accept numeric data. You might enable it to accept numeric data by workaround conversions, but at a later point discover that the workarounds don't satisfy your needs. The only thing you can do at this point is change the database interface, which requires a rework of the abstraction layer as well as a check of all calls to it in the main code—and of course the removal of the previously created workarounds.

Hours or days of work spent on something that could have been avoided from the very beginning—problems that often decide between success or failure, because *time is the most valuable resource that you will never have enough of.*

The following sections guide you through most of the very basic, yet very important practical issues of development: improving your code quality as well as basic design and documentation issues. After covering these, we create an application programming interface (API), taking the naïve, practical approach to familiarize you with the new concepts, followed directly by an API creation from scratch, developing it theoretically "on paper" and then nailing down a few practical principles to help you implement your next API—matters of style, do's and don'ts, as well as a few tricks of the trade.

Coding Conventions

What's the difference between good code and bad code? Actually, it's very simple. Good code—really good code—can be read almost like a book. You can start anywhere and at once you know what the lines you're reading are used for, under which circumstances they're executed, and any setup they might require. Even if you lack background knowledge and encounter a sophisticated and complicated algorithm, you'll at least be able to see quickly which tasks it performs, and under which aspects it performs them.

It would be easy to simply show examples and say, "Do as they did," but we'd like this chapter to impart a solid basis for writing professional code—a basis that makes the difference between truly well-crafted code and an everyday hack. Unfortunately, space restrictions prevent us from discussing all aspects of good code-writing style as elaborately as we'd like, but this chapter will give you a good head start. We urge you to acquire dedicated material, in order to familiarize yourself with every little bit of software design and engineering. This broad field is almost a science of its own, on which a lot of treatises exist—mostly very dry and theoretical, but unrenounceable in practice. We've compressed the most important issues into the following sections, discussing the very elementary questions.

Choosing Names

Choosing variable names is probably the task that programmers do most often but think about the least. With the number of different variable names that can appear in larger projects, if you'd construct a listing of the name, type, and declaration point of each you could create something very similar to a small phone directory. How would you like your directory to look? Different naming schemes have evolved over time, with different philosophies, each with its own advantages and disadvantages. The schemes generally fall into two extremes: short and simple variable and function names, versus "speaking" variable and function names—longer names that tell about the variable's type and intention.

The "phone directory" might look like this:

Name	Address	Phone
J. D.	382 W. S.	-3951
M. S.	204 E. R.	-8382

Very informative. You know that it has two entries, but not much more. You know the person's initials, but not the full name. You know the house number, but not the exact street name. You know only part of the phone number.

Let's look at another example:

Name	Address	Phone
ht5ft9in_age32_John Doe_male_married	386 West Street, Los Angeles, California, USA, Earth	+1-555-304-3951
ht5ft6in_age27_Mary Smith_female_single	204 East Road, Los Angeles, California, USA, Earth	+1-555-306-8382

In this example, the individual's name includes height, age, gender, and marital status; the address tells you not only street and city but also state, country, and even planet; and the phone number appends country and area codes.

Is the second solution better than the first? Neither is optimal. People teach both approaches in programming lectures, but neither is really satisfying. Defining a type tpIntMyIntegerCounter and then declaring a variable instMyIntegerCounterInstance for a simple for loop seems too much when you only need to traverse an array and set all elements to zero (see Listing 1.1).

Listing 1.1 **An overdose of exactness.**

```
for ( $instMyIntegerCounterInstance = 0;
      $instMyIntegerCounterInstance < MAXPINTEGERCOUNTERRANGE;
      $instMyIntegerCounterInstance++)
          $instMyArrayInstance[$instMyCounterInstance] = 0;
```

On the other hand, working with indices called i, j, k (instead of long ones like $instMyIntegerCounterInstance) is also unacceptable when doing complicated buffer operations such as compression or the like.

This is just one example of the misuse of a common concept. What to do? The solution is to choose a good overall concept and make exceptions at the right places. When you're writing an application, you know what's going on in your code and can quickly maneuver from one point to another—but other people may not find this so easy. If you get a source file from someone else on your team and need to add a list of features to it, you first have to get an overall impression and identify the code's different sections. Ideally, this process will take place parallel to reading the source. But because this is impossible to do without hints and common patterns to help you structure the source code for reading, it's very important to pack as much additional information into the source code as possible, *while not obscuring the obvious facts*. So how can you perceive this information and integrate it into your own code?

- Make your code easy to read.
- Add comments wherever possible.
- Choose speaking variable names wherever appropriate.
- Keep clear and consistent function interfaces.
- Structure your code into logical function groups.
- Abstract separate chunks of code.
- Use files to group your functions not only logically but physically.
- Write documentation.

The following sections discuss each of these issues.

Making Your Code Easy to Read

To be able to understand text when reading, your brain must analyze the information it receives from your eyes, identify the important parts, and then translate these parts into correct order. Analysis is performed in two steps: physical analysis and logical analysis. *Physical analysis* is performed first, by examining the visual structure of the text; for example, paragraphs, rows, columns, and even spaces between words. This process breaks up the perception of the text as a whole (for example, the sheet of paper or the window on your desktop containing the text) into a tree-like structure of smaller chunks. Assuming a top-down tree with the tree node at the top and leaves at the bottom, the top of the tree contains the most generic information; for example, the order of paragraphs that you have to read. At the bottom of the tree is something like the order of words in a line, or even the order of characters in a word.

The *logical analysis* process takes this physical information, traverses the tree in order, and tries to translate the information into a meaningful result. Whether this is a grammatical translation (what structure does the sentence have?) or a contextual translation (what does the sentence mean?) doesn't matter for this discussion; the important thing is that the better the results of the physical analysis, the easier, faster, and better the results of the logical analysis.

Logical analysis can compensate for missing information from physical analysis, but only to a limited extent.

```
Asanexampletakethissentenceifyoucanreadityourlogicalanalyzerworksverywell.
```

You probably can read the preceding sentence, but it takes much longer and requires much more concentration than the rest of the sentences in this book. Important information is missing (the spaces) for the first step in analysis, and you're not used to that.

We could make it easier by adding a bit of punctuation:

```
Asanexample, takethissentence--ifyoucanreadit, yourlogicalanalyzerworksverywell.
```

The punctuation is useful information for your physical analyzer. Notice that it's much easier to read this version, as well as to refocus at any point of your choice. On to the next step:

```
As an example, take this sentence--if you can read it, your logical analyzer
works very well.
```

This is the regular way you read a sentence, your native way of perceiving text. But we could delineate the structure of the sentence *even more*:

```
As an example,
take this sentence--
if you can read it,
your logical analyzer
works very well.
```

This is an extreme method for using physical means to aid you in understanding the sentence as quickly as possible. Note that the separation in this case hinders the natural reading flow because you're not used to seeing a sentence split up into syntactical units—but for source code it's an advantage. Because source code often contains complicated constructs, formulas, and the like, it's very important to support the reader by giving the source a clear physical structure. This can be achieved by using indentation and placing special keywords of your programming language at exposed positions.

Let's take a look at a short PHP program:

```
<?function myfunc($myvar){$somevar=$myvar*2;return($somevar+1);}print myfunc(1);?>
```

The code itself is probably not an intellectual masterpiece, but let's look only at its *structure*. Without having read this snippet previously, would you be able to point instantly to the start of the main code? Would you be able to mark the first and last instruction of the function in it? Notice that even if you're fast at finding the desired places, your eyes will inevitably start at the beginning of the line, passing through the source from left to right, stopping where you assume the target will be. Unconsciously, your brain rereads the whole line because it's missing information from the physical analysis. To compensate for the lack of information from the first step, your logical analyzer will take over this step as well and will be stressed twice as much. Just as with a computer, your brain has limited power, so the additional workload for the logical analyzer takes the form of a lack of capacity when your brain actually tries to *understand and memorize* the source code. But understanding and memorizing is exactly what you want people to achieve when reading *your* source code, and what you want to do when reading other people's sources.

So, this was almost a scientific approach to explain why formatting source code is useful. Is there another reason? Oh, yes: Well-formatted source code just looks good.

Following are a few guidelines for what we think is the optimal style to use in formatting source code. Please note that these are not mandated, but are regarded as common style. Many industrial and Open Source projects have been formatted this way, and it often pays to write in this style.

- Put all block tags (<?, ?>, <?php, <%, %>, {, }, etc.) on separate lines.
- Indent all blocks with tabs (ideally, set the tab width to no less than 4).
- Leave spaces between keywords and key characters, especially when doing calculations.
- Group logical chunks of code within a block by placing them on consecutive lines, and leave a blank line between all others.
- Separate blocks from each other using a blank line.
- Separate function headers and eventual function footers from the rest of the code using a blank line (importing globals is treated as a part of the function header).
- Integrate block comments into the code, using the same indentation as the code block to which each refers.
- Put all line comments into the same column throughout a block.

As an example, Listing 1.2 shows the earlier code snippet, reformatted.

Listing 1.2   **Reformatted code snippet.**

```
<?

function myfunc($myvar)
{

    $somevar = $myvar * 2;

    return($somevar + 1);

}

print(myfunc(1));

?>
```

Notice that this piece of code has fewer difficulties to navigate.

The use of spaces in the snippet can be exaggerated even more by also separating parentheses from keywords:

```
<?

function myfunc ( $myvar )
{

    $somevar = $myvar * 2;

    return ( $somevar + 1 );

}

print ( myfunc ( 1 ) );

?>
```

It may seem somewhat excessive here, but imagine this code embedded into a few thousand other lines of code, and you might change your opinion. Some people say that the spaces between parentheses are more disturbing and irritating than helpful in structuring the text—we must confess that sometimes that's true. The examples in this book don't always use this kind of formatting; we're leaving the decision to you as to whether to use this method. The most important thing is this: *Be consistent*. Once you've decided to use a certain style, keep it at least throughout a project. If you're modifying other people's sources, follow their style as well as you can. Consistency is one of the most important aspects in professional development.

Try reading all example sources attentively and then try to imitate their style, adapting your own style until you've reached something very close to the original. As soon as you're feeling familiar with it, you'll see that it wasn't a worthless effort.

To motivate you before going further, two examples.

The code in Figure 1.1 is meant to create an SQL statement. Except for the last line assigning a string containing `"select *"` to a variable named $query, we don't think that anything in Figure 1.1 indicates the code's purpose. In the code in Figure 1.2, on the other hand, it's easy to understand what's going on.

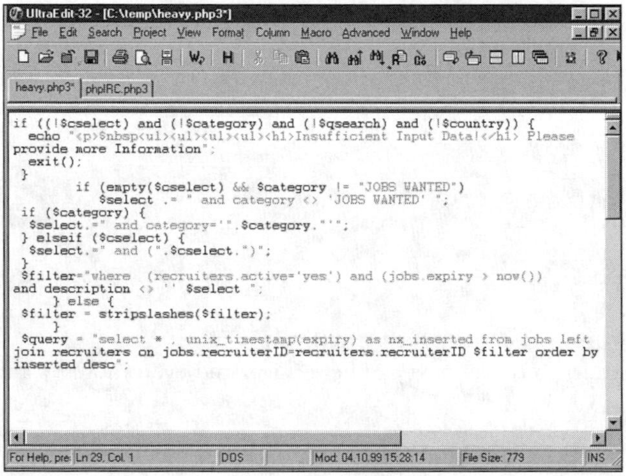

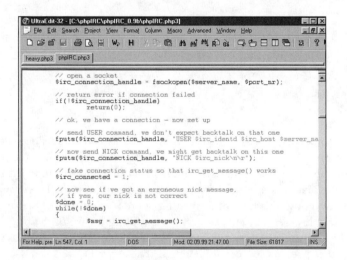

Figure 1.1   Bad code.

Figure 1.2   Better code.

We believe that this is what code should look like, at least approximately. It shows a clear structure, is well commented, and is easy to understand.

Adding Comments

We can't stress it enough—even though while programming you may think it's the dumbest thing to do—commenting *is* substantial when producing high-quality code. When solving complicated problems, seldom do two people think the same way. What may be totally obvious to one is obscure to the other. Comments are very helpful in these situations, and they should be added to your code wherever possible.

There are two main kinds of comments: *header comments* (such as comments in file headers, module headers, or function headers) and *inline comments*. Header comments should be used for purposes of introduction; to inform the reader about generic things in a file; or about the next, larger piece of code. Inline comments should be used within functions, embedded into the code, to explain what a certain line or block of code is actually doing.

The following sections should give you an idea of the look of these comments and the information that they should contain. These days, such comments are usually produced by Rapid Application Development (RAD) tools or other authoring aids, but since no similar systems are available for PHP at the time of this writing, the comments should be handcrafted, in spite of the additional workload.

In the following sections, the comment types are discussed in order of abstraction, from most abstract to most concrete.

Keeping Comments Up to Date

Remember to create comments *before* or *while* working on the module/function they describe; it's a very annoying job to rework a file just to add this information afterward. Also, take great care when modifying functions at a later point—always update your comments appropriately! For example, if you add or remove global variables, update their usage indication in the comment header as well; the same goes for changes in parameter ordering, parameter types, and so on.

Use Macros to Speed Up Your Commenting

In your favorite editor, create macros for each comment type and assign them to a hotkey (for example, Ctrl+Alt+F1 for file headers, Ctrl+Alt+F2 for module headers, and so on). Include variables in these comments if the editor supports this feature, so that creating an elaborate and informative comment becomes just a matter of a short Q&A dialogue.

File Header Comments

File header comments should look something like those in Listing 1.3.

Listing 1.3 **File header comment.**

```
//////////////////////////////////////////////////////////////////////////////
//
// phpIRC.php3 - IRC client module for PHP3 IRC clients
//
//////////////////////////////////////////////////////////////////////////////
//
// This module will handle all major interfacing with the IRC server, making
// all IRC commands easily available by a predefined API.
//
// See phpIRC.inc.php3 for configuration options.
//
// Author: Till Gerken  Last modified: 09/17/99
//
// Copyright (c) 1999 by Till Gerken
//
//////////////////////////////////////////////////////////////////////////////
```

You might prefer to use a bounding box created by multiline comments, which some people tend to find more aesthetic (see Listing 1.4).

Listing 1.4 **File header comment using multiline comments.**

```
*******************************************************************************
 *                                                                           *
 * phpIRC.php3 - IRC client module for PHP3 IRC clients                       *
 *                                                                           *
 *******************************************************************************
 *                                                                           *
 * This module will handle all major interfacing with the IRC server, making *
 * all IRC commands easily available by a predefined API.                    *
 *                                                                           *
 * See phpIRC.inc.php3 for configuration options.                            *
 *                                                                           *
 * Author: Till Gerken  Last modified: 09/17/99                              *
 *                                                                           *
 * Copyright (c) 1999 by Till Gerken                                         *
 *                                                                           *
 *******************************************************************************/
```

Extracting Block Comments in UNIX

On UNIX systems, the following `grep` command extracts such block comments from the source:

```
grep '^[\\\/ ]*\*' source.php3
```

Which style you choose for formatting your headers isn't crucial, but the information you choose to include in the file header *is* important. As shown in this example, headers should include such general information as details about the module, author, and so on. Items should be placed in a meaningful order (for example, it makes no sense to include a long description and then a short description—by the time you've read the long description you don't need the short one anymore). The following list shows suggested information as well as order:

1. Module filename.
2. Short module description (one line).
3. Long module description.
4. Notes about usage, requirements, warnings, and so on.
5. Author's name and contact information.
6. Creation and last modification date of the module.
7. Copyright notice.
8. License notice.
9. Pointers to change log, home page, distribution file, and so on.
10. Eventually, excerpts from the change log, if needed.

If this sounds like too much information, remember that it's better to have redundant information rather than a lack of information. Of course, not all fields are appropriate under all circumstances; we didn't include all the fields in the earlier example. However, you should try to put as much data as you can into your headers—it's good style, and the worst that can happen is that some people just won't read it. Others might be grateful for it—maybe even you, since neglecting copyright and licensing information in a commercial project can result in headaches later on, when other programmers are recycling your code for free.

Module Header Comments

If you have more than one module in a file (for example, when a module only consists of three functions to abstract functionality from a larger procedure of a bounding module), you should place an informative header before the very first function.

A module header looks like Listing 1.5.

Listing 1.5 **Module header comment.**

```
///////////////////////////////////////////////////////////////////////////////
//
// Submodule for file access from main()
//
///////////////////////////////////////////////////////////////////////////////
//
// This submodule will provide functionality for easy file access,
```

continues

Listing 1.5   **Continued**

```
// and includes error checking and reporting.
//
// Functions:
//
//    int file_open(string $file_name)
//    bool file_close(int $file_handle)
//    int file_read(int $file_handle, $nr_bytes)
//
// Remarks:
//
//    - provides no seek function
//    - does not allow write access
//
///////////////////////////////////////////////////////////////////////////////
```

These headers might include the following items, in order:

1. Short module description.

2. Detailed module description.

3. Function prototype list.

4. Remarks/notes.

Again, multiline comments work as well.

Function Header Comments

Function headers should describe the syntax, purpose, and necessary caller information in enough detail for each function (see Listing 1.6). These kind of comments are secondary in importance only to inline comments. Function header comments serve the purpose of quickly informing the programmer about the requirements and specialties of each function during development and extension of a module, mainly needed by "foreign" developers who didn't create the functions originally. A lack of function header comments usually requires a developer to dive into the code itself to find out the required information, which often results in mistakes because not all hidden traps (sometimes very well hidden) are seen.

Listing 1.6   **Typical function header comment.**

```
///////////////////////////////////////////////////////////////////////////////
//
// int irc_get_channel_by_name(string $name)
//
///////////////////////////////////////////////////////////////////////////////
//
// Searches a channel by its name in the internal channel table and returns
// its handle.
//
```

```
//////////////////////////////////////////////////////////////////////////
//
// Parameter:
//    $name - name of channel to search for
//
//////////////////////////////////////////////////////////////////////////
//
// Return value:
//    Channel handle (numeric), 0 on error
//
//////////////////////////////////////////////////////////////////////////
//
// Global references:
//    $irc_channel_array
//
//////////////////////////////////////////////////////////////////////////
```

A function header comment should contain a collection of the following items, in order:

1. Function prototype.
2. Detailed function description.
3. Remarks/notes.
4. Parameter description.
5. Return value description.
6. Global references.
7. Author and date of last change.

Inline Comments

Inline comments are placed directly into the code and should explain all questions directly where they arise. Note that while you're programming, it's natural that everything is perfectly clear to you as you type it. This is usually the cause for too few comments. When you reopen this file at a later point, maybe even after a year, you'll have forgotten about all the structures you used and why you used them. We've encountered this problem too often, in our own code and that of other people. The rule for inline comments is that you can hardly use *too* many. The only exception to this rule is when comments are overused to the point that they obscure the code they're meant to describe. Also, you should be careful not to comment obvious things. See Listing 1.7 for a few examples.

Listing 1.7   **Bad inline comments.**

```
function calculate_next_index ( $base_index )
{

    $base_index = $base_index + 1;          // increase $base_index by one

    //
    //
    // Table of contents
    //
    // 1. Introduction
    // 2. About the authors
    [LOTS of lines cut out]
    //
    //
    $new_index = $base_index * COMPLICATED_NUMBER / 3.14 + sin($base_index);


}
```

$base_index is increased by 1 in the first line of code—is that something to comment? We doubt it. Everyone can see that $base_index is being incremented, but why is it incremented, and why is it incremented by 1 exactly? A better comment would be something like Jump to the next ordinal index we want to point to; it's exactly one element away.

The same kind of problem is introduced with the second comment, but with a different cause. The programmer has pasted the complete reference for the algorithm into the code, including lots of inappropriate junk. Of course, it's good to describe in detail what you're doing, but you have to filter what's really important and what isn't.

Ask yourself these questions when commenting code:

- What are you doing?
- Why are you doing it?
- Why are you doing it this way?
- Why are you doing it at this point?
- How does this code affect the other code?
- What does this code require?
- Are there any drawbacks to your method?

For example, when you're parsing strings, document the format of the input strings, the tolerances of your parser (its reactions to errors and mistakes in the input), and its output. If all this information is too heavy to include it directly into your code, keep at least a pointer to external documentation where the reader can inform himself about all aspects of the parser. Also, remember to update your function header comments by placing a link to the documentation there as well.

Choosing Speaking Names

As mentioned earlier, choosing appropriate names for functions and variables is an essential issue in programming. Generally, when selecting a name for a variable, it's important to first determine whether the variable is local or global. If the variable is only visible in the local scope of a function, choose a short, precise name that states the content or meaning of this variable. The variable name should consist of a maximum of two words, separated either by an underscore or by capital letters, as shown in Listing 1.8.

Listing 1.8 **Examples of local variable names.**

```
$counter
$next_index
$nrOptions
$cookieName
```

Remember not to mix naming schemes! Either use all lowercase variable names, separating words with an underscore, or use capital letters to separate the words. You can also use both capital letters and underscores to separate words, but never use capital letters for one variable and underscores for another. This leads to mistakes and exhibits poor style. After you've found your own style, keep it consistent throughout the project.

Each global variable should have a prefix that identifies the module to which it belongs. This scheme helps to assign globals to their modules, as well as to avoid conflicts when there are two variables of the same name from different modules in the global scope. The prefix should be separated from the variable name using an underscore. The prefix should consist of a single word, most likely an abbreviation (see Listing 1.9).

Listing 1.9 **Examples of global variable names.**

```
$phpPolls_setCookies
$phpPolls_lastIP
$db_session_id
$freakmod_last_known_user
```

The (Small) Size Advantage

Create smaller projects, each with a different naming style, for these reasons:

- You can find your preferred style.

- You'll be practiced whenever you have to adapt to someone else's style.

As this example shows, global variable names tend to be longer than local variable names. This is due not only to the module prefix but also to clarification practices. When the definition and initialization point of a variable are unknown because they're hidden in a module to which you don't have access, it's very important to reflect the variable's meaning and contents in its name. There's a practical limit to this, of course—nobody would want to remember names of 40+ characters—but this is more a limit of common sense.

Basically, you should name global variables just as you would describe them to someone. For example, how would you describe the variable `$phpPolls_lastIP`? You might not know what phpPolls does, but the name suggests that it has something to do with polls. `lastIP` says that it's the last IP... Which IP? You don't know. Obviously, the name for this global isn't very well chosen, because it doesn't describe its contents exactly. Now suppose that you ask the purpose for this variable, and get the answer, "It contains the IP of the last user who submitted a vote." Think about a name for it now. How does `$phpPolls_last_voters_IP` sound? Better, isn't it? But although the name itself might be good, it's still not suitable because you've also seen two other globals from phpPolls, both prefixed with `phpPolls_` and then written in one word. For consistency, you decide to separate different words within the name only by capitals: `$phpPolls_lastVotersIP`.

Function names should be treated in the same elaborate style as global variables, but with a few differences. Function names should describe their functionality and fit into the flow of the language. Fitting names into the language flow is achieved by determining the actions that a function performs and choosing a name that will be the most suitable in the majority of all occurrences of that name.

If a function determines whether a user is currently online, for example, it might have one of the following names:

```
function get_online_status($user_name);
function check_online_status($user_name);
function user_status($user_name);
function user_online($user_name);
function is_user_online($user_name);
```

Depending on the return type, only the first and the last name in this list are suitable. Assuming that the function would return a Boolean value, it would usually be used in conjunction with an `if()` clause, where it would look like this:

- Choice 1:
    ```
    if(user_status($user_name))
    {
        // do something
    }
    ```

- Choice 2:
```
if(is_user_online($user_name))
{
    // do something
}
```

In the first choice, the function name looks kind of displaced: "If the user status of John then do something." Check this against the second possibility, "If user John is online then do something." The second option doesn't break the language flow and makes much more sense when taking a first look. The first choice leaves questions open: What status is being referred to and how is that status being returned? The second function name clearly indicates that this function will check the online status of someone and return this as a Boolean value.

What if the result of the check would be returned in a variable parameter of the function?

- Choice 1:
```
function user_status($user_name, &$status)
{
    // retrieve status and return in $status
}

$success = user_status($user_name, $user_online);
```

- Choice 2:
```
function get_online_status($user_name, &$status)
{
    // retrieve status and return in $status
}

$success = get_online_status($user_name, $user_online);
```

Although `user_status()` isn't a bad choice for a name for this purpose, `get_online_status()` suits it better. The word `get` clearly indicates that the function retrieves the online status and saves it somewhere—either in a global variable or in a variable function argument.

For functions that simply do data processing, use active names instead of passive names. Don't use nouns such as `huffman_encoder()` or `database_checker()`—name the functions `huffman_encode()` and `check_database()` or switch the words into the opposite order, whichever will best fit your module prefix.

Is Your Code Bilingual? Trilingual?

One of the most common criticisms of code involves "nationalization," the sprinkling of the programming language (which usually has an anglophonic origin) with another language. In our case (Tobias being from Italy, Till being from Germany), when we reviewed projects from local programmers, people liked to use German and Italian variable and function names instead of English names, which resulted in a strange mix. As you probably don't use a mixture of English, French, Spanish, or whatever in your daily correspondence, please also show consistency while programming and use English names with PHP. It also helps foreign people to understand what you have written.

Keeping Clear and Consistent Interfaces

You may hate seeing the word *consistency* again, but for designing interfaces it's a critical piece in the mosaic of programming.

Unfortunately, an example of how *not* to do it can be found in PHP itself.

When you're driving a car, the gas pedal is on the right and the brake is on the left. When you change cars, you expect this setup to stay the same. You expect that wherever you go, a red traffic light means *stop* and green means *go*. Similarly, when you use a library to access files and have to pass a file handle to every function, it would be very strange if the function to read from a file would expect the file handle as first parameter, the write function would expect it as last parameter, and a third function would expect it somewhere in the middle of its parameter list.

When designing an interface, you should first think about these things:

- What data will be exchanged using the interface?
- Which parameters do I really need?
- What are the common parameters that most (or all) interface functions share?
- What would be the most logical order for these parameters?

Keeping this in mind, once you've decided to do it in a certain way you should make no exceptions to this rule in your module. Even internal functions should conform to the rule. This strategy will enable you to make internal functions available in the interface later on. Plus, your team members will thank you when they have to integrate new code into your module.

If you look at the string functions in the PHP manual, you'll find `strpos()`, `strchr()`, `strrchr()`, and so on. All these functions take as parameters `string haystack`, `string needle`, with `haystack` being the string in which to search and `needle` being the string to search for. Now take a look at `str_replace()`. Not only does this function suddenly introduce a different naming scheme, its arguments are also the exact opposite of the rest of the functions: it accepts `string needle`, `string haystack`.

When we asked the reason for this discrepancy, we got the answer that `str_replace()` would be a fast replacement for `ereg_replace()` and that most people would change their calls from `ereg_replace()` (accepting the reverse order arguments) to `str_replace()`. Of course, this argument has a point. But why do the regex functions accept their arguments in an order opposite to that of the string functions? Because the regex functions in PHP reflect the ones in C. When developing an application, it's always annoying to see `str_replace()` sticking out from the rest of the function group. When outlining the interfaces of your next libraries, take great care that this situation doesn't happen to you.

Structuring Code into Logical Groups

Applications usually consist of different function groups, each handling a special task and/or area of the application. For example, when writing a database-backed application, a function group should be responsible solely for handling database access. This code builds an entity of its own and can safely be detached from the rest of the program—if you designed it well. Function groups that logically perform only a certain task should be designed in such a way that they can be treated independently from the rest of the code. These functions should also be physically separated from the main code, building a *module*.

Before implementing an application, you should create a list of all functions that can be grouped together, forming a module, and create a separate design plan for each module. Take great care to create detailed data flowcharts in order to make the modules capable of handling all demands of the application. The importance of outlining on paper shouldn't be underestimated. Space restrictions prevent us from going into detail on this topic, but we encourage you to educate yourself with some of the very good books available on design methods.

Abstracting Separate Chunks of Code

Abstracting blocks of code is a task that should be done during both planning and implementation. Let's say that a function will perform the following jobs:

1. Open a file.
2. Read a block of data from the file.
3. Validate the data.
4. Correct any errors in the data.
5. Write the data back to the file.
6. Close the file.

Each step can be packed into a separate block of code. It's good style to abstract these blocks and create separate functions out of them. Not only will this enable you to reuse each code block in other functions (you'll probably need file operation support somewhere else as well), but it will also make the code much easier to read and debug. You can make the abstracted parts bulletproof, equip them with error-handling support, and much more. If you tried to do this inline, your code would quickly grow beyond manageable size and become very clumsy. Plus, if you use the same code blocks in other functions and notice an error or need to change something, you'd have to make the same corrections over and over in every other function using this block. By abstracting, you centralize the critical points; by correcting a single line, you can change the behavior of all related functions.

Using Files to Group Functions

We've shown that it pays to use multiple files for source code, but we encourage you to also use files for most other resources, such as configuration data; custom headers, footers, or other templates; and anything else that can be extracted from your project as a separate entity.

Using multiple files for a single project offers quite a few advantages:

- You get smaller source code files that are easier to maintain.
- You can create different revisions for each file instead of having to check in the whole project for a small modification.
- You can detach resources from the project and reuse them in other projects.
- Different team members can work on the project simultaneously, without having the trouble of merging when checking all files into the revision control system.

These issues apply to most resources that can be present in a project.

Files should be named according to their contents, optionally with a prefix if a bunch of files belong to a larger group and should be placed into subdirectories from the project root. For example, in a database abstraction layer with modules for accessing different databases packed into single files, each should be prefixed with dba_ (where dba stands for *database abstraction*), so that you'd get dba_mysql, dba_odbc, dba_oracle, and so on.

Make sure that you can vary subdirectories later on by using configurable module directories in your includes. For example (note that dba in this example doesn't refer to the PHP dba_* functions):

```
<?
require("config.php3");

require("$dba_root/dba.php3");
require("$socket_root/socket.php3");
require("$phpPolls_root/phpPollUI.php3");

// [...]
?>
```

The variables $dba_root, $socket_root, and $phpPolls_root in this example should be contained in a central configuration file with global options for the whole project. This configuration file should only contain options that are needed by every source file independently, and thus have to be made globally available. Such options might include environmental options such as the site name, file system locations, and so on.

> ### Stay on the (Generic) Path
> When including the configuration file from a subdirectory, always use relative paths to ensure that your project is mobile on your filesystem and on your customers' systems as well—never rely on special conditions of your developing environment being present in all deployment environments as well. Whatever you can keep generic should be kept generic.

Writing Documentation

In addition to commenting and structuring, it's important to pay attention to documenting. The documentation for a project is probably the first part of the project that your customers will see, and the first impression is the one that counts.

Professionally laid out documentation that contains more than the obligatory "Follow the installation instructions in the README" should be a routine step in your development process. Just as you expect a well-written manual for your cell phone, new monitor, or other technical item purchased in even the smallest store, your customers expect good documentation from you (not to mention that they're probably paying you a lot of money for it).

As with comments, extensive documentation is usually produced with the help of RAD tools. Unfortunately, no tools exist yet that are designed especially for PHP, so writing a manual is an unaided and thankless—yet required—job. However, this shouldn't do harm to your productivity. A complete manual should be designed very much like a small book, featuring the following items:

- Introduction
- Table of contents
- User's guide
- Technical documentation
- Developer's guide
- Complete function reference

The user's guide should describe in detail all features of your application's interface (if it has one) for a standard user. Don't get too technical in this section, as it should only be a "how to" kind of description. Be sure to cover every aspect elaborately. The technical documentation should be written for technically interested users and administrators and should contain technical requirements of your application, used and introduced standards, as well as information about internal data processing if it would be of any interest to the reader—and of course as your licenses permit. If you're allowing customers to see and/or modify the source code, include a developer's guide to explain the project's structure, data flow, and internal relationships, as well as a function reference listing *all* functions (including internal functions) along with a complete description.

If you're working on a team, professional technical writers are a great addition to the crew—they have experience in creating in-depth technical documentation, as well as enough time for writing it. Having a team member who's occupied with development also write the documentation creates a lot of additional stress, since developers are usually busy enough trying to keep the deadlines.

An API Design Example

In the midst of all this theory, let's design an application program interface (API) from the ground up to familiarize you with the conventions and concepts discussed earlier. Please note that this is a practical approach, not a theoretical approach. We've chosen to do it in a practical manner to let you memorize each step; in future projects, you'll have to design APIs on a mere theoretical basis, without having seen a line of code first. For hints, tips, and tricks about the theoretical approach, see Chapter 3, "Application Design: A Real-Life Example."

The module for which we'll be creating an API is meant to handle a simple scheduler. The actual implementation of the scheduler functions isn't of any importance; remember that this is exactly what has to be obscured to the user. The user just wants to manage a set of appointments, so the API has to present itself as *just that*, namely providing an interface for appointment management. It's not necessary to inform the user of the underlying system, whether you're using Julian or Gregorian dates or maybe even your own format—at some point, you might want to provide an extra set of such features to the user (for example, date format conversion), but it's completely unnecessary when all you need initially is simply to enable someone to manage appointments.

On the other hand, this doesn't mean *preventing* or even *disabling* a future implementation of these features. The trick when designing an API is to meet your requirements exactly, while being able to extend the API to any eventual needed functionality. This requires in-depth planning and thoughtful definitions, as discussed throughout this chapter.

The API has to present itself to the user as the only way of accessing the functionality of the module it represents. No functionality can be missing, nor can any unnecessary functionality be available—or even functionality that doesn't belong directly to this module.

The list of requirements for a simple scheduler may be as follows:

- Add an event.
- Delete an event.
- Retrieve a list of upcoming events.

Let's define prototypes for the add and delete functions first, as shown in Listing 1.10. What might these functions need as information and what could they provide as return values?

Listing 1.10   **Prototypes for the first two functions.**

```
void add_an_event(int day, int month, int year, int hour, int minutes,
➥int seconds, string description);
void delete_an_event(int day, int month, int year, int hour, int minutes,
➥int seconds);
```

This is probably what comes to mind first: an interface that accepts a "common sense" list of parameters, namely the date in day/month/year variables and the time in hours/minutes/seconds, as well as a string for the description of an appointment. The functions don't return anything; their names are speaking.

Speaking, yes—but well-speaking? add_an_event() is speaking for sure, but nevertheless a bad choice for a function like this. First of all, the function will be meant for global access; that is, it's a main element for the API. As such, it should identify itself clearly as belonging to this API as well, by using a name prefix.

What could this prefix be called? calendar and scheduler are good choices; in this example, we'll use calendar (see Listing 1.11).

Listing 1.11   **Renamed function prototypes.**

```
void calendar_add_an_event(int day, int month, int year, int hour, int minutes,
➥int seconds, string description);
void calendar_delete_an_event(int day, int month, int year, int hour, int minutes,
➥int seconds);
```

Now we've got a prefix, but the names are still unsatisfactory. The an in calendar_add_an_event() and similarly in calendar_delete_an_event() isn't really needed; it's a relic from choosing names that are "too speaking." Leaving out words such as *a*, *an*, and *the* is a good practice when choosing function names; most of the time such words use up space in the name but don't make a big difference because they have no explanatory function. Moreover, they should definitely be avoided when choosing variable names; in variable names, it makes absolutely no sense to choose a name such as $a_key or $the_key, since the fact that it's a key is obvious. It makes more sense to select a name that explains *what* key; for example, $last_user_key.

Listing 1.12 shows the newly renamed functions.

Listing 1.12   **Final function names.**

```
void calendar_add_event(int day, int month, int year, int hour, int minutes,
➥int seconds, string description);
void calendar_delete_event(int day, int month, int year, int hour, int minutes,
➥int seconds);
```

On to the next question. These functions carry a *huge* parameter list. Is this necessary? The parameters as they are now have been chosen intuitively, according to the common date format that separates day, month, year, hour, minute, and second. However, interchanging information with such an interface is a kludge. Functions should hardly ever need to accept more than five parameters. If there are more parameters to be passed, you should think about passing them using a structure. Structures help to keep the interface clean, which is sometimes a much more worthwhile goal than avoiding the extra overhead that structures impose when initializing and/or modifying them.

Before trying to fit all parameters into a structure, there's still the possibility of alternative data formats. To encode date and time data, for example, you might use BCD (Binary Coded Digits) format or UNIX timestamp format, to name just two possibilities. Both formats pack all these required variables into a single one. BCD is partly still very widespread, but when it comes to PHP, which originates from a UNIX-like platform, timestamps dominate (see Listing 1.13). In case you haven't encountered timestamps yet, they count the number of seconds since midnight UTC, January 1, 1970, expressed as a decimal number in a 32-bit value. This results in a wraparound in the year 2106, but since PHP doesn't have a fixed 32-bit type to handle timestamps, it's possible for PHP to transparently change the timestamp size to 64-bit in order to remain Y2.106k compliant. Your applications won't notice it.

Another advantage of timestamps is the fact that a large number of PHP functions convert them into human-readable dates and back. It's also easy to do calculations with timestamps—to get a time difference between two events, for example, you just have to subtract one timestamp from the other.

Listing 1.13 **Corrected API.**

```
void calendar_add_event(int timestamp, string description);
void calendar_delete_event(int timestamp, int seconds);
```

As you can see, it can be very important to check for existing formats and methods for handling a special kind of data. The current format not only shortens the argument list by 350%, it's also—by accident—the native format of the underlying architecture to handle date and time. Checking native formats and existing standards is a step never to be underestimated in your research phase; during development, nothing should occur to you simply "by accident." Knowing the territory is mandatory.

Keeping this in mind, let's take a look at the third required function, retrieving a list of upcoming events. We'll run into problems now, since the return value isn't going to be a single value but rather a variable list of associated values:

Timestamp 1 =>   Description 1

Timestamp 2 =>   Description 2

Timestamp 3 =>   Description 3

The data could be returned by having parameters passed by reference (read more about them in Chapter 2, "Advanced Syntax"):

```
//
// List function in pseudocode
//

function calendar_get_event_list($range, &$timestamp, &$description)
{
```

```
while($current_timestamp < $range)
{
    $timestamp[] = $next_event_timestamp;
    $description[] = $next_event_description;
}

}
```

This pseudocode would fill two arrays, $timestamp and $description, with all upcoming events in the requested range. Index 1 would thus contain the timestamp for event 1 in $timestamp[0] and the description for event 1 in $description[0].

This is a sub-optimal solution, however, since having two separated variables handling grouped elements is poor style. To handle grouped elements, a grouping datatype should be used—either a class (the only way to create structured types in PHP) or an associative array.

Associative arrays have the advantage of being searchable both by key (the indexing component—in regular arrays, usually 0, 1, 2, 3, and so on) and by value (the informative component), but have no predefined structure. Moreover, they have a variable structure that can be changed on the fly, resulting in data that's not guaranteed to have a valid structure, and are a bit clumsy to handle.

Classes have the advantage of showing their structure perfectly, but need a predefined datatype. If we defined a datatype for the return value now, for consistency we should also use this datatype to create and delete events. This in turn would require us to modify the existing functions afterward—it's undesirable to add just one function. You can see now that detailed theoretical planning beforehand could have saved us valuable time; defining a structured datatype for appointments before even starting to define the first two functions would have enabled us to use this datatype then, leaving us with a straight-to-the-point solution that we could reimplement now in our list function.

Since a class would introduce a style break into the code, we'll use an associative array. The list function won't be returning an error code, so we'll use the return value of the function to pass the data back to the caller. Remember that if you intend to use error codes, you should make all functions return an error code even if they'll always succeed. Usually, the user of your API won't know whether a function can fail, and will expect every function to return an error code if some of your functions have already returned error codes. You should also create a consistent error code scheme—but more about that in Chapter 3.

Back to the list function. This could be the future prototype:

```
function calendar_get_event_list($range)
{
    // Retrieve event list
}

$event_list = calendar_get_event_list($required_range);
```

continues

```
for($i = 0; $i < count($event_list); $i++)
    print("Event at $event_list[$i]["time"]: $event_list[$i]["text"]<br>");
```

This code might produce something like the following:

```
Event at 95859383: Team meeting
Event at 95867495: Deadline for Telco project
Event at 95888371: XML Seminar
```

Looks okay, but there's another major mistake in the code. In the `for()` loop, the data is returned in the two-dimensional array using the associative keys `time` and `text`. The variables were named differently earlier; they were `$timestamp` for the time and `$description` for the descriptive text. When filling an associative array, use the same name for keys that you've chosen for the appropriate variables; in this case, the `for()` loop should be able to access the array as follows:

```
function calendar_get_event_list($range)
{
    // Retrieve event list
}

$event_list = calendar_get_even_list($required_range);

for($i = 0; $i < count($event_list); $i++)
    print("Event at $event_list[$i]["timestamp"]:
    ⇒$event_list[$i]["description"]<br>");
```

Summary

Application development is more than just scribbling down code, getting the syntax right, and making sure that the software runs. Because software won't be read only by a computer but also by other programmers (or you) in the future, source code should be clear and concise. Well-written code is easy to read, extensively commented, and uses natural-language expressions. APIs should make clear and consistent interfaces available, be structured into logical units, and abstract the back end. And because larger projects aren't self-explanatory even with the clearest code, technical documentation is needed.

The coding conventions presented in this chapter are based on common sense guides from the accumulated experience of many programmers, not on mandated rules. They're not hard to follow—and they'll make your life and those of your fellow programmers a good deal easier.

> *Approach it and there is no beginning;*
> *follow it and there is no end.*
> *You can't know it,*
> *but you can be it,*
> *at ease in your own life.*

2

Advanced Syntax

The world is formed from the void,
like utensils from a block of wood.
The Master knows the utensils,
yet keeps to the block:
thus he can use all things.

AS MENTIONED IN CHAPTER 1, WE BELIEVE that *to truly master a language, it's crucial to understand not just the syntax and semantics of the language, but its philosophy, background, and design characteristics.* In order to master PHP, you have to know about all its specialties as well.

PHP Syntax

PHP is a mixture of different languages. You can see a strong influence from C (some say Java, but Java also inherited from C). While PHP's syntax is strongly influenced by C, its semantics differ from C's semantics. PHP is interpreted and knows no strict variable types. When you refer to a variable, its type is determined "on the fly" and treated just as the current situation requires. This is a somewhat simplified explanation, but you should keep this in mind when developing.

PHP is an interpreted language, in which code is evaluated and executed step by step. Add to that fact PHP's way of handling variables, and you've introduced a lot of possibilities to programming, but also a lot of traps. This chapter deals with the typical do's and don'ts for using advanced syntactic and algorithmic features:

- Defining constants
- Array functions
- Classes
- Linked lists
- Trees
- Associative arrays
- Multidimensional arrays
- Variable arguments and variable argument lists
- Variable variable names
- Variable function names
- Self-modifying high-level code
- Polymorphism

The following sections cover all these issues in more detail.

Defining Constants

While there is no expression or construct to define constants in the form of unmodifiable variables in PHP, you can nevertheless accomplish this objective by using *defined values*. Defined values should be used to replace all fixed values such as error codes, file format constants, special strings, and whatever else will have a special meaning to the program or library and not change during execution.

Defined values have the great advantage that they clarify the meaning of special values, while at the same time providing another level of abstraction:

```
// read file type from input
$file_type = fgets($file, 32);

// decide what kind of file it is
switch($file_type)
{
    case FT_GIF_IMAGE:   /* handle GIFs here */
                         break;

    case FT_PNG_IMAGE:   /* handle PNGs here */
                         break;

    case FT_ZIP_ARCHIVE: /* handle ZIPs here */
                         break;
}
```

Note: By *special values*, we're referring to "magic numbers" or special strings. For example, if you want to access a GIF file from your program, and internally your program recognizes GIF by the "magic number" 6 (just because it's chosen so by the programmer—it could as easily be 1234), then you can create a definition for this value: `define("GIF_FILE", 6);` and further on access your "magic number" by the keyword `GIF_FILE`.

This code snippet reads an identifier from an input file and then decides how to act on this identifier. The identifier indicates whether the following data is a GIF image, a PNG image, or a ZIP archive. The identifiers might look like this:

GIF image	`"GIF_IMG"`
PNG image	`"PNG_IMG"`
ZIP archive	`"ZIP_ARC"`

These identifiers would then be defined in an include file:

```
define("FT_GIF_IMAGE", "GIF_IMG");
define("FT_PNG_IMAGE", "PNG_IMG");
define("FT_ZIP_ARCHIVE", "ZIP_ARC");
```

This setup has the advantage that you can keep all identifiers in a central place. If one of the identifiers needs to be changed, you only need to change its definition—otherwise, you would have to dig through the code, searching and replacing each occurrence of this string. Using defined values, this work will be reduced to changing a single line of code.

The names of defined values should always be written in uppercase to denote them as such, and in most cases they should have prefixes, just like library functions. In the preceding example, the identifiers have been prefixed with `FT_` for *file type*.

Try to use defined values as often as possible. Whenever you encounter a situation in which you might hardcode a value into your program, hardcoding is probably a bad idea. Operating systems or similar low-level–oriented programs usually have the largest list of definitions because, to allow them to be portable, every little bit has to be abstracted. They can't make assumptions about the byte size, the word size, the register size—generally everything you see is abstracted in some way. Since PHP is portable *per se*, meaning that it's not bound to any certain hardware or other environmental configuration (its interpreter won't change the environment regardless of the underlying operating system), it's not really necessary to be as extreme with definitions in PHP. But it's good coding style.

Array Functions

The most important array functions are `list()`, `each()`, and `count()`.

`list()` is sort of an operator, forming an lvalue (a value that can be used on the left side of an expression) out of a set of variables, which represents itself as a new entity similar to an element of a multidimensional array. As arguments, it takes a list of variables. When something is being assigned to it (a list of variables or an array element), the list of variables given as arguments to the `list()` operator is parsed from left to right. These arguments are then assigned a corresponding value from the rvalue (a value that's used on the right side of an expression). This is best explained using a code example:

```
$result = mysql_db_query($mysql_handle, $mysql_db,
                    "SELECT car_type, car_color, car_speed
                    FROM cars WHERE car_id=$car_id");

list($car_type, $car_color, $car_speed) = mysql_fetch_row($result);
```

Note: This code is used here strictly for example. It's not a good idea to implement code like this in real-life programs, as it relies on the fields remaining in the same order. If you change the field ordering, you have to change the variable ordering in the `list()` statement as well. Using associative arrays and manual value extraction imposes an overhead in programming but results in better code stability. Code as shown above should only be implemented for optimization purposes.

The SQL query will select the values `car_type`, `car_color`, and `car_speed` from a table containing car information. The result of the query is then retrieved using `mysql_fetch_row()`, which returns the three values in an array. `car_type` will be at index 0, `car_color` at index 1, and `car_speed` at index 2. Read from left to right, these values will be assigned value by value to the arguments given in the `list()` statement.

Thus, you'll have the following assignments:

List Argument	SQL Field
$car_type	car_type (array index 0)
$car_color	car_color (array index 1)
$car_speed	car_speed (array index 2)

The `list()` statement is very useful when you want to separate a collection of values into single variables—something that happens quite often when doing database programming. Note, however, that `list()` can only act as lvalue, not as rvalue—you can't use `list()` to exchange a set of variables. For example, the following statement won't work:

```
list($var1, $var2) = list($var2, $var1);
```

The statement `each()` is often used in combination with the `list()` statement. `each()` traverses an array and returns each of its elements in a key/value combination. This is done by "walking" the input array. PHP assigns an internal pointer to each array. This pointer initially points to the first element of the array. Each call to `each()` returns the element that's being pointed to by the internal pointer; afterward, this pointer will be incremented.

The return format of the key/value pair is a four-element array with the keys `"0"`, `"1"`, `"key"`, and `"value"`. This means that it can be used as both an indexed array and an associative array. The indexed part of the array (with the keys `"0"` and `"1"`) contains the key of the source element at index `0`; the value can be found at index `1`. The same information can be accessed by using the associative part of the array. (Actually, separating associative and indexed parts of an array is not correct here, since indexed arrays are just a special form of associative arrays—theoretically, they're different things, but in practice they're the same in PHP. See the later discussion for details.) The key of the source element is contained in `"key"` and the value in `"value"`. For example:

```
$my_array = array("Element 1", "Element 2", "Element 3");
```

This will simply create an array with the following contents:

```
Element 1
Element 2
Element 3
```

To better understand the principle behind `each()`, it's useful to create a more detailed listing of this array:

Key	Value
0	Element 1
1	Element 2
3	Element 3

This is the listing of all key/value pairs contained in the array `$my_array`. Now we'll use `each()` on it:

```
list($key, $value) = each($my_array);
```

This first call to `each()` returns the first four-element array containing the first key/value pair from `$my_array`. Note that since we only gave two arguments to the `list()` operator, only the values from the four-element array can be assigned: These are `"0"`, the first key, and `"Element 1"`, the first value element from `$my_array`.

The following code lists the contents of an array:

```
$my_array = array("Element 1", "Element 2", "Element 3");

while(list($key, $value) = each($my_array))
    print("Key: $key, Value: $value<br>");
```

This script produces an output like that shown in Figure 2.1.

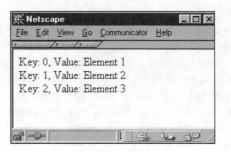

Figure 2.1 Array listing using each().

You can also use each() to show the elements that each() itself returns:

```
$my_array = array("Element 1", "Element 2", "Element 3");

while($four_element_array = each($my_array))
{
    while(list($key, $value) = each($four_element_array))
        print("Key $key, Value $value<br>");
}
```

This would produce the result shown in Figure 2.2.

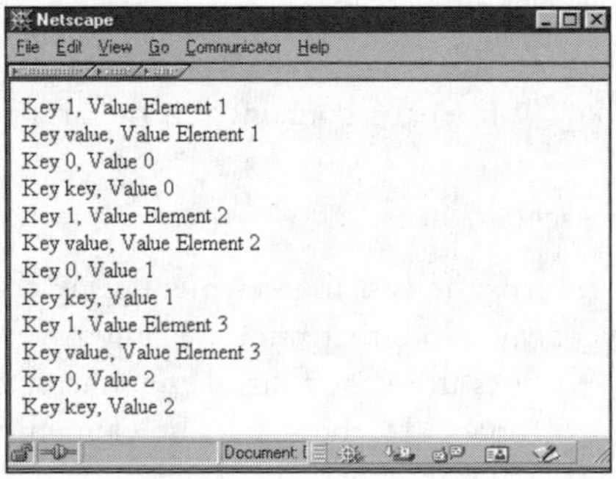

Figure 2.2 Return values of each().

You can clearly see the entries 1, value, 0, and key in the output, and 0 and 1 should be used in conjunction with each other just as "key" and "value". Notice that each pair represents one entry of the source array.

Using each() on an indexed array might not seem to make sense at first, since the elements of an indexed array can be read much more easily by using a for() statement—however, there's a few traps in this. First of all, as indexed arrays are a special form of associative array in PHP, PHP allows nonconsecutive array indices; in other words, you might have an array like this:

Key/Index	Value
0	Landon
3	Graeme
4	Tobias
10	Till

This array only has the indices 0, 3, 4, and 10 in use—the rest are simply not assigned. Using the count() function (which returns the number of assigned elements in an array) on this array will correctly return four assigned elements, but you won't be able to use a for() statement on this array because you don't know the corresponding keys to all values:

```
$my array = array(0 => "Landon", 3 => "Graeme", 4 => "Tobias", 10 => "Till");

for($i = 0; $i < count($my_array); $i++)
    print("Element $i: $my_array[$i]<br>");
```

This will give the output shown in Figure 2.3.

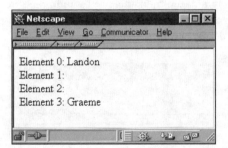

Figure 2.3   Invalidly accessing a nonconsecutive array consecutively.

Error Reporting

If you have set up PHP to report invalid array indices, a few warnings will appear as well. It's a good idea to set the level of error reports as high as possible during development.

Using a simple for() loop is not enough for arrays of this kind; it accesses indices that don't have a value assigned. If PHP provides a stricter environment, this would result in an exception and immediate termination of the script. Therefore, whenever you're unsure about the contents and consistency of arrays, you're doomed to using each().

each() is also a very good tool to ensure that you're not accessing arrays out of their bounds—another reason for exceptions. PHP handles out-of-bound accesses in a quite relaxed manner (it will most likely only send you a warning); however, we have managed to crash PHP repeatedly by using invalid array accesses. The best case was that PHP just quit with an exception; the worst was that the PHP module suddenly used 100% of the CPU time and the server process had to be killed—a situation that should be avoided by all means in a production environment. Even though this was most likely triggered by buggy internal array handling in PHP, you still shouldn't try to force invalid array accesses. It's very bad coding practice, and since PHP provides each(), list(), and associated functions and operators to secure your code, you should use them as well.

The original purpose of each() was to use it with "real" associative arrays, which use non-numeric keys to index data. Whenever this is the case, it's impossible to gain access to the stored data without a function that can list all available keys (assuming that you don't know which keys are in use). These arrays could be organized similarly to the array described earlier, but with keys and values having the opposite order:

```
$my_array = array("Landon" => 1, "Graeme" => 2, "Tobias" => 3, "Till" => 4);

while(list($key, $value) = each($my_array))
    print("Key $key, Value $value<br>");
```

Now you have the array indexed by name, not by number—how are you going to find out which names are contained in the array if you don't use predefined keys? each() allows you to do so, as Figure 2.4 shows.

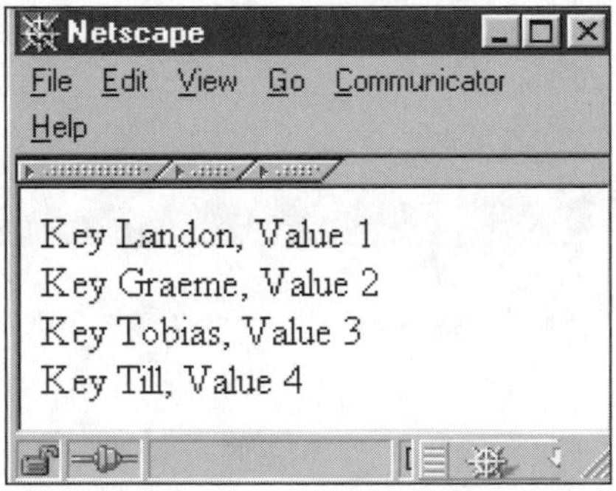

Figure 2.4   Associative array listing using each().

Not a very surprising result; nevertheless, quite useful to know.

One last important note about each(): To enable you to retrieve one key/value pair per iteration, PHP has to remember which pair you last accessed. Consequently, when doing another iteration on the same array, no two of the same key/value pairs will be returned. To reset the internal array counter, you have to use the function reset().

This function makes PHP's internal pointer move back to the first element of the array, whose value is also the return value of reset().

The following script accesses the same array twice, in two different loops, both times using each():

```php
$my_array = array("Landon" => 1, "Graeme" => 2, "Tobias" => 3, "Till" => 4);

print("<h2>Looping without reset()</h2>");

print("<h3>First loop</h3>");

for($i = 0; $i < 2; $i++)
{
    list($key, $value) = each($my_array);
    print("Key $key, Value $value<br>");
}

print("<h3>Second loop</h3>");

for($i = 0; $i < 2; $i++)
{
    list($key, $value) = each($my_array);
    print("Key $key, Value $value<br>");
}
```

As the output in Figure 2.5 shows, the second loop *will not* start from the first element again; instead, it continues where the first loop left off. This is due to PHP's internal array pointer not having been reset. A small modification to the script creates a different result (see Figure 2.6):

```php
$my_array = array("Landon" => 1, "Graeme" => 2, "Tobias" => 3, "Till" => 4);

print("<h2>Looping with reset()</h2>");

print("<h3>First loop</h3>");

for($i = 0; $i < 2; $i++)
{
    list($key, $value) = each($my_array);
    print("Key $key, Value $value<br>");
}

print("<h3>Calling reset()</h3>");

reset($my_array);

print("<h3>Second loop</h3>");

for($i = 0; $i < 2; $i++)
{
    list($key, $value) = each($my_array);
    print("Key $key, Value $value<br>");
}
```

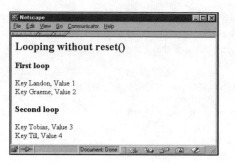

Figure 2.5 Using each() without reset().

Figure 2.6 Using each() in conjunction with reset().

A call to each() has been inserted between the two loops. The second usage of each() restarts retrieving key/value pairs from the first element.

Along with reset(), several functions are available to split up the activities of each(): next(), prev(), and current(). Using these functions, it's possible to manually traverse an array in both directions. next() returns the current element and then advances the internal array pointer; prev() does the same but moves the array pointer in the opposite direction. current() simply returns the array element currently being pointed to. However, these functions return false whenever they encounter an empty, unassigned element, as well as when encountering the end of the array. There's no way to distinguish both cases; thus, these functions should be used only when each() is not a choice and the situation of encountering an unassigned element can be eliminated.

In addition to the functions just described, many other PHP functions deal with arrays. For a complete description, refer to the manual. With PHP 4.0, the number of array functions increased tremendously; covering all of them here wouldn't allow us to focus on more important issues.

PHP and OOP

In the early 1990s, the most popular compilers—for example, the family of Borland compilers—became able to handle the object-oriented programming (OOP) extensions of such "base languages" as Pascal and C. Suddenly, classes, objects, templates, and inheritance were *the* buzzwords, *the* hottest topics in software development. OOP was hip and a lot of companies jumped onto the trend by converting all their software packages from procedural to object-based applications. Today the hype has faded, but a language that can't handle objects is still considered out of date. PHP supports objects, and in this section we discuss the pros and cons of OOP with PHP.

We think that the movement to develop all software OOP-style only is a little bit doubtful. Big software packages have been converted into objects with a lot of financial effort—not even counting the time it took the developers to completely rethink, restructure, and reimplement thousands of lines of code. These software packages were running perfectly using a procedural approach, and some of them didn't even need object support. We have seen advertisements for software security systems that said "now completely reimplemented using OOP." All these systems did was check a dongle (a little hardware device plugged into the parallel port of a PC to serve as a hardware key), maybe ask for password phrases, and in some cases encrypt executables they were being linked to. The applications relying on those packages often didn't even have to call a special procedure to initiate the password check; some of these packages were self-executing when the application was run. In other cases, the environment check was reduced to a call of a single function—but who needs an object for a single function? Internally, the execution of the program code was strictly linear, and hardware access was already abstracted by procedures. (And actually, some of the ads were just lying.)

The most questionable case that we encountered was that of a developer who was working on a graphics library to draw complex mathematical two- and three-dimensional objects. He based his decision to use objects on the fact that he met a Borland representative at a conference, and this person suggested using OOP. Creating valuable software systems based on suggestions? Not the way to go.

What advantages do objects have, how is OOP different from the procedural approach, and why should we think about this anyway?

The last question first. It's important to think about whether to use OOP with PHP because it makes no sense to use a technique that might impose more overhead in development, is not well supported by the underlying architecture, and, finally, won't make any difference to your application. Procedurally oriented projects can be as effective, as maintainable, and as extensible as object-oriented projects. Table 2.1 shows the most important differences between these two approaches.

Table 2.1 **Object–Oriented Programming Versus Procedural Programming**

Objects	Procedures
Complete data encapsulation	No data encapsulation; only works using parameter abstraction
Allows multiple instances easily	No multiple instances; different datasets have to be handled by using copies of all variables
Allows additional functionality while preserving the interface by using inheritance	No inheritance; additional functionality only by API providing another API layer or changing the API completely
Self–centered; the object keeps its dataset by itself and is solely responsible for keeping it valid and for granting access to other parties	Globally oriented; procedures can't keep their own datasets; data is provided by the caller and managed only indirectly by the procedures
Provides very easy means to assure data integrity, initialization, and cleanup (constructors/destructors)	Hard to assure data integrity; initialization and cleanup has to be done explicitly
Isolated namespace	Names have to be introduced into the global namespace

This table lists only the most significant differences; there are more, but you can already see that it doesn't look very good for procedures. Are procedures really as bad as it seems, though? Does it mean that OOP as a new "technology" will replace the old one? It depends on your goals and the platform you're working on. In our case, the platform is PHP. PHP supports objects, of course, but in a very special way. This is related to the variable handling of the interpreter.

Whenever PHP encounters a statement for which write access to a variable is needed, it evaluates and calculates the data that will be written into the variable, copies it, and assigns the result to the target space in memory. (This description is a little bit simplified, but you get the idea.)

```
$some_var = 2;

$my_var = $some_var * 3;

$new_var = $some_var + $my_var;
```

Looking at this script, PHP will

- Create space for $some_var and write 2 into it.
- Create space for $my_var, retrieve the value of $some_var, multiply it by 3, and assign it to the newly allocated memory.
- Create space for $new_var, retrieve the values of $some_var and $my_var, total them, and write them back to the new place in memory.

Well, this sounds nice and logical—but these are simple types and you've worked with them many times already. Things are *very* different (and illogical) when PHP is handling classes:

```
class my_class
{
    var $var1, $var2, $var3;
}

$my_object = new my_class;

$my_object->var1 = 1;
$my_object->var2 = 2;
$my_object->var3 = 3;

$new_object = $my_object;

$new_object->var1 = 3;
$new_object->var2 = 2;
$new_object->var3 = 1;

print("My object goes $my_object->var1, $my_object->var2,
➥$my_object->var3 !<br>");
print("New object goes $new_object->var1, $new_object->var2,
➥$new_object->var3 !<br>");
```

What do you think this will produce as output? The script first declares a class, creates *one* instance of it, and assigns values to its three properties. After having done this, it creates a new reference to this object, reassigns its properties, and then just prints out each property by using both references. Remember, *one* instance. Figure 2.7 shows the result.

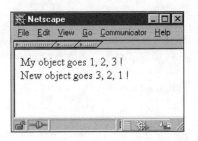

Figure 2.7 PHP creating a copy instead of a reference.

If you're not surprised now, you either know PHP very well already or haven't thought enough about objects yet. PHP has created a copy, a new instance of `my_class` instead of just a new reference! This is not the desired behavior, since the `new` operator is supposed to create an instance of `my_class` in memory, returning a reference to it. Thus, when assigning this reference to another variable, only the reference should be copied, leaving the original data untouched—similar to a file system link, which allows access to the same data through different locations on the file system. This behavior of PHP—creating copies of referenced data rather than just the reference itself—may not sound important enough to focus on; however, you'll see in a moment that it actually does make a difference.

Note: At the time of this writing, both PHP 3.0 and PHP 4.0 are using copy syntax. A chat with someone closely involved in the core development revealed that the plan is to change the default behavior to use a reference syntax, but this change would cause a loss of backward compatibility. A possible change is planned with version 4.1—if this happens, information contained here will be invalid for all future versions.

Warning

PHP 3.0 does not implement proper garbage collection. Whenever you're writing something into a variable, new space is being allocated in memory instead of reusing the old space. `unset()` can work around this a bit—even though it doesn't release the memory, it marks it as being reusable—however, after some time, long-term scripts will eat up your server's memory. If you intend to run long-term scripts, make sure that you free database results with (for example) `mysql_free_result()`, and use `unset()` on all variables that no longer contain valuable information. No memory will be freed until the whole script is terminated!

For example, take a tree structure. The class building a tree node will look like this:

```
class tree_node
{
    var $left_child, $right_child;
    var $value;
}
```

Just a simple tree node, of course, but it has everything we need: a link to the left child and a link to the right child, as well as a variable containing the contents of this node. Now we'll build a simple tree:

```
$root_node = new tree_node;
$left_node = new tree_node;
$right_node = new right_node;
```

```
$root_node->value = 1;
$left_node->value = 2;
$right_node->value = 3;

$root_node->left_child = $left_node;
$root_node->right_child = $right_node;
```

This code simply builds a tree with one root node and two children, assigning a different value to each of them. Traversing the tree could be done with a function like this:

```
function traverse_tree($start_node)
{

    $node = $start_node;
    print("Value is $node->value<br>");

    print("Traversing left tree:<br>");
    traverse_tree($node->left);

    print("Traversing right tree:<br>");
    traverse_tree($node->right);


}
```

Forgetting for the moment that this recursive function will never return because our tree doesn't have a stop-marker set (the function won't know which node actually has a child and which node doesn't), let's take a look at how it works instead and how PHP will handle it.

The critical point is already reached in the first line, where $node is being assigned a value. $start_node as parameter contains the instance of the node from which to start, and the assignment to $node will create a copy of it. The fact that it creates a copy is not that important for a function that simply recurses the tree and prints out the node contents, but it can be very important as soon as you plan to change the tree somewhere.

Now assume that you want to write a function that appends a new node to the leftmost leaf in the tree. No problem—just write a recursive function that counts the jumps to the left and returns the leaf with the highest count. After that, simply change the child links of this object and you're done. Wait a second. Are you really done? Think a moment about what you've changed (see Figure 2.8). You've changed the *copy* of the leftmost leaf, not the leaf itself! As soon as your function returns, your changes are lost, gone for good.

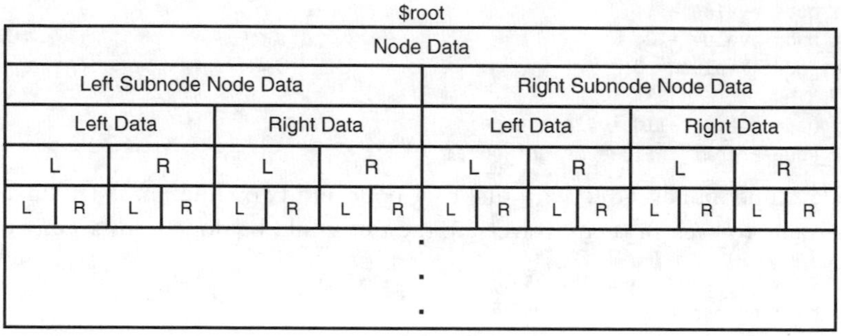

Figure 2.8   Trees that are built using copy syntax.

You could return a reference to the instance and change it using this simple "pointer" mechanism that PHP provides. Then you will have changed the object itself and not its copy. As soon as you're going to traverse the tree again, though, you'll see something strange—nothing seems to have changed. And indeed, nothing has changed. This is because the *parent* of the node you wanted to change keeps its own copy of the same data! Remember, `$node->left` is nothing more than another copy of a node in the tree, and this is the copy that the tree-walker will evaluate. The copy you changed will remain outside the tree and end up in the garbage collector. To change this node as well, you'd need to pass references to the parents as well, to the parents of the parents, and to their parents in turn. You'll end up in another recursive function, which is more than tricky to code and won't work in 99% of all cases.

Classes: PHP 3.0 Versus PHP 4.0

PHP 4.0 has learned from the inability of PHP 3.0 to handle object referencing and now supports "true" references. "True" is in quotes here because they don't really point to the memory the other variable is occupying; PHP only interprets these variables as references and acts differently. Embedded in the preceding example, the code would look like this:

```
// create multiple references to the original object
$new_object = &$my_object;
$another_object = &$new_object;
```

This code creates two references to the same object. Note that `$another_object` is being assigned as a reference to `$new_object`, not as a copy of it. When trying to copy references, PHP won't copy the reference but instead will create a copy of the referred variable. Only when you subsequently use references (to copy a reference, you're required to use the reference operator again), both `$new_object` and `$another_object` can be used to modify data within `$my_object`.

For the different PHP versions, we'd make the recommendations shown in the following sections.

Classes in PHP 3.0

Data: Don't use classes for complex data structures that require true pointers (such as trees). If you have to, try to limit class usage to data collection, not data management. *Code:* Use classes only to structure APIs that are not hurt by the copy syntax. Think about whether your project might be realized with procedures; if so, seriously consider this option. Procedures are reliable and proven to work, while objects bear quite a few traps.

Classes in PHP 4.0

Use classes with care, and make sure that you can differentiate between copies and references of objects. Pay attention to which types you're passing and how to deal with them; as soon as you forget a single magic ampersand (&), PHP will create a copy of your object and most likely break consistencies in your data.

Classes have been improved in PHP 4.0, but we're still skeptical. We have heard opinions on both sides—one group insisting that objects are trash and not to be used in a language like PHP, and the other group favoring objects over any procedural approach, even in PHP 3.0. For those who are working with procedures only, objects seem to be a sleeping beast that's better left untouched; for the OOP gang, the "PP" (procedural people) are idiots. It's almost like a religious war. Wherever we brought up the topic, it quickly resulted in endless and resultless discussions.

We honestly think that both extremes are wrong. It's never a good idea to ignore features, nor it is a good idea to make use of them without considering the drawbacks. We dislike saying that it's a matter of personal preference, as technologies should never be treated as such. Our recommendation: Free yourself of any prejudices you might have—especially the prejudices of others—and then decide objectively what's best for your project.

Implementing Classes

Leaving pros and cons behind, classes are an important language element, and it seems that there's always a demand for explanation of class implementation in PHP.

Classes in PHP are pretty straightforward to implement. You'll know most of the keywords from other languages:

```
class shopping_cart
{
    var $item_list;

    function pick($item, $quantity)
    {

        $this->item_list[$item] += $quantity;
```

continues

```
    }

    function drop($item, $quantity)
    {

        if($this->item_list[$item] > $quantity)
            $this->item_list[$item] -= $quantity;
        else
            $this->item_list[$item] = 0;

    }

}
```

This code defines the class shopping_cart with the members $item_list, pick(), and drop(). Note that there's no way to distinguish between public and private members. In PHP, everything defaults to public—meaning that you can access all properties and member functions of a class from the outside, without restrictions.

This simple example class implements some kind of shopping cart (as the name suggests) with one variable containing the cart's contents in an associative array ($item_list), and two functions (pick() and drop()) to add and remove items. Member functions are declared just like regular functions except that they're implemented within the class definition. Class properties (variables inside classes) are defined using the keyword var.

Note: It's not possible to have separated class declarations and implementations in PHP. You always have to implement all functions directly in the class declaration.

Accessing Objects

Member functions can be called by either using the "old" syntax of instance->member() or the "new" syntax instance::member(). Similarly, properties are accessed using instance->property or instance::property. The latter form is especially useful to call a parent's constructor or for accessing other members not located in the current object (more on that topic in the later section "Inheritance"):

```
class extended_cart extends shopping_cart
{

    function extended_cart()
    {

        shopping_cart::shopping_cart("Mousepad", 1);

    }

    function query($item)
    {
```

```
        return($this->item_list[$item]);

    }

}
```

This extended version of the `extended_cart` object has a constructor that calls the
parent's constructor to correctly initialize the rest of the object tree. Note that without
explicitly calling the parent's constructor from this constructor, the parent would never
be initialized. (Nor would its parent in turn, etc.)

PHP also features an alias pointing to the current instance of an object. This alias is
named `this` and gives access to all members of the actual instantiation. This is needed
for all self-references; PHP doesn't introduce a new local scope within class definitions.

Note: Since PHP doesn't introduce a new local scope within class definitions, make
sure that you're including the keyword `this` everywhere that you're doing references
within your object. Forgetting to use `this` will instruct PHP to refer to the global
scope, which is very prone to bugs!

Constructors

Constructors are defined like regular functions as well, except that their names must
be equal to the class names. *PHP knows no destructors.* Constructors can take arguments
like any other function—even optional arguments (see the later section on variable
argument lists for more details about optional parameters).

Note: Since PHP 4.0, constructors can only take scalar values as parameters (strings,
integers, etc.), but no arrays or objects, which was still possible in PHP 3.0.

To add a constructor to the preceding example, we can add a little piece of code:

```
class shopping_cart
{
    var $item_list;

    function shopping_cart($item = "T-Shirt", $quantity = 1)
    {

        $this->pick($item, $quantity);

    }

    function pick($item, $quantity)
    {

        $this->item_list[$item] += $quantity;

    }

    function drop($item, $quantity)
```

continues

```
        {

            if($this->item_list[$item] > $quantity)
                $this->item_list[$item] -= $quantity;
            else
                $this->item_list[$item] = 0;

        }

    }
```

The constructor, contained in shopping_cart::shopping_cart(), takes two optional arguments—if no arguments are specified, upon instantiation the shopping cart will "prefill" itself with one T-Shirt. Otherwise, it will take the wanted items:

```
$default_cart = new shopping_cart;            // this cart will fill itself with
                                              →one T-Shirt by default
$mug_cart = new shopping_cart("Mug", 2);      // this cart will contain two mugs
```

Inheritance

Adding functions to objects shouldn't be done by rewriting old code but by overloading existing structures instead. New objects can inherit from old objects by using the keyword extends. As the name suggests, this will define a new class that *extends* an existing one:

```
class extended_cart extends shopping_cart
{

    function query($item)
    {

        return($this->item_list[$item]);

    }

}
```

This extended cart extended_cart now contains all properties and member functions from shopping_cart with the addition of another function, query(), which allows us to check the quantity of any given item in the cart.

Note: The class extended_cart doesn't have its own constructor. If a child class doesn't have a constructor, PHP (since version 4.0) automatically calls the parent's constructor. However, by default PHP will never call a parent's constructor. Thus, if you need to set up your parent object, make sure that you call its constructor manually.

Special OOP Functions

PHP features a few handy functions that make dealing with objects easier. The following table describes these functions.

Function	Description
string get_class(*object object*)	Returns the name of the specified object instance as a string.
string get_parent_class (*object object*)	Returns the name of the parent class of the specified object instance as a string.
bool method_exists (*object object*, *string method*)	Tests whether the function named in *method* is actually a member of *object*.
bool class_exists (*string classname*)	Tests whether *classname* is an existing defined class.
bool is_subclass_of (*object object*, *string classname*)	Determines whether *object* is a subclass of *classname*.

Note: These functions do not exist in PHP 3.0.

Shopping Cart Source Code

This section shows the full example of the OOP shopping cart implementation (see Listing 2.1). This shopping cart is extremely simple, of course, but nevertheless useful.

Listing 2.1 **Shopping cart source code.**

```
class shopping_cart
{

    var $item_list;

    function shopping_cart($item = "T-Shirt", $quantity = 1)
    {

        $this->pick($item, $quantity);

    }

    function pick($item, $quantity)
    {

        $this->item_list[$item] += $quantity;

    }

    function drop($item, $quantity)
    {
```

continues

Listing 2.1 **Continued**

```php
        if($this->item_list[$item] > $quantity)
            $this->item_list[$item] -= $quantity;
        else
            $this->item_list[$item] = 0;

    }

}

class extended_cart extends shopping_cart
{

    function query($item)
    {

        return($this->item_list[$item]);

    }

    function get_contents()
    {

        return($this->item_list);

    }

}

// you can instantiate shopping_cart the regular way
$cart = new shopping_cart;

// you can make use of the variable arguments of the constructor
$cart = new shopping_cart("Cap", 2);

// you can also use extended_cart, which in turn calls the
// constructor of shopping_cart implicitly
$cart = new extended_cart;

// or you can use the inherited features of the constructor
$cart = new extended_cart("Cap", 2);

// of course, you can also use the inherited functions
$cart->pick("Mug", 1);

// ...or use any functions in the object itself
while(list($item, $quantity) = each($cart->get_contents()))
    print("We have $quantity of $item");
```

Linked Lists

Linked lists, a special form of trees, are one of the most typical data structures to organize dynamic datasets. We're assuming that you already have an understanding of the structure, concept, and usage of linked lists, so we won't go deeply into their implementation here; we'd rather concentrate on the elemental do's and don'ts.

As described in the previous sections, PHP 3.0 creates copies of object instances rather than referring to them by using a pointer. This only enables a very limited, WORM-like use of linked lists: write once, read multiple. Linked lists can be created, but not modified. When you try to modify an element in the list, you lose the reference to all following elements in the list. Regrouping of elements is impossible for the same reason.

Similarly, double-linked lists can't be realized in PHP 3.0 (at least, we haven't managed it, and we spent quite a few hours in debugging sessions before finally giving up). Because each node would need a new copy of the list tail to which it's linking, you would have to create a multitude of redundant lists with the same content just to enable the "go back one element" feature.

PHP 4.0, supporting true references, doesn't impose these limits. Lists can be created and regrouped randomly—even double-linked lists. Note, however, that it's very tricky to distinguish between references and actual copies of list elements.

Beware of dangling pointers—so say programmers of "conventional" languages. We'd like to modify this for PHP: *Beware of redundant copies.*

> When working with lists, create a bulletproof library that handles all your needs in the most general way. Test it intensively and make sure that it performs correctly. This will prevent you from having to search for erroneous code accessing your lists in incorrect ways and eventually destroying them.

Linked Lists and Trees—A Workaround

As mentioned earlier, it's a good idea to create a bulletproof library for your needs—one that's easily extensible and features everything related to the required task. We'd like to present a real-life example here: a library that we've developed to handle trees, and that also works with PHP 3.0. You can find the complete source code on the CD-ROM.

The library is able to handle double-linked trees with two children per leaf node, each node having one content container for mixed variables. Every action that can be performed with the tree has been incorporated into the API, detaching the tree design from the code that accesses it.

This is exactly the reason why this tree works with PHP 3.0 (seemingly contradicting what we said earlier). The tree is based on arrays and not on pointers; because PHP features dynamic arrays, with a little bit of effort it's very easy to use such arrays to implement a dynamic tree.

The idea is not new. It has its origins many years ago and is not hard to understand. Instead of carrying a pointer with each node that addresses another place in memory to the next node, each node contains indices into the array to each node it's linked to. This also has the advantage that PHP is able to warn you of invalid indices, and you can copy your whole tree by just assigning the variable that contains the tree array to another variable. On top of that, you can serialize the whole tree and save it "as is" to any place you want.

To give another, more theoretical explanation: Think of the memory that's available to your program as one big array. The size of the elements would probably be bytes, in the case of physical RAM, but the size of each element doesn't really matter. The important thing is that a pointer is simply a number indexing one of these elements and thus pointing out the beginning of each structure you're placing into your RAM. Now, abstracting the whole thing into a language construct (a "real" array), you have the same situation at a higher level: The PHP array now contains your "RAM," and each array element will represent one of the tree nodes. Pointers become indices into this array, and referencing is done simply by retrieving the correct element from the array.

Using arrays enables you to create a lot of "RAMs," increasing and decreasing their size, disposing of them as a whole or just a single element; overall, a very comfortable method of memory management. Having all this integrated into a solid library gives you a nice tool.

Figure 2.9 shows how the tree library internally handles the tree nodes in an array.

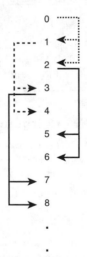

Figure 2.9 A tree contained in an array.

The library consists of the following functions:

Function	Description
`array tree_create()`	Creates a new tree
`int tree_allocate_node` (`array tree`)	Allocates a new node in the tree
`int tree_free_node` (`array tree, int handle`)	Frees a node in the tree
`int tree_link_left` (`array tree, int link_to, int child`)	Links a node as left child to another node
`int tree_link_right` (`array tree, int link_to, int child`)	Links a node as right child to another node
`int tree_get_parent` (`array tree, int handle`)	Returns the parent of the given node
`int tree_get_left` (`array tree, int handle`)	Returns the left child of the given node
`int tree_get_right` (`array tree, int handle`)	Returns the right child of the given node
`int tree_assign_node_contents` (`array tree, int handle, mixed` `contents`)	Assigns data to the content container of a node
`mixed tree_retrieve_node_contents` (`array tree, int handle`)	Retrieves data from the content container of a node

Feel free to add more functions here; for example, the library doesn't have functionality to merge trees, detect dead leaves (leaves that exist in the array but are detached from the main tree and thus cannot be accessed anymore), and so on. This code is an excellent way to experiment and learn.

The library is pretty straightforward. `tree_create()` creates a new array for the tree and initializes the first element as the root element. All references to other nodes are integer indices within the array (see `$idx_up`, `$idx_left`, and `$idx_right` in the source). -1 marks a reference as being used. For example, if one node doesn't have a left child node, `$idx_left` would contain -1. To mark an element itself as being in use or not (meaning that it has data assigned to it), another flag is defined: `$free`. This variable just contains 1 (in use) or 0 (not in use).

`tree_create()` creates one dummy node, marks it as being free with all references unused, and assigns it to slot 0 in the tree array. Then it returns this array to the caller. *Note:* The caller doesn't have to know anything about this array—not even that it actually is an array. The program should simply assume it to be some kind of "handle" for the tree. As PHP doesn't feature explicit types, this works very well.

`tree_allocate_node()` searches for a free node within the tree array by checking the `$free` flag for each existing node. If none of the nodes is marked as being free, it simply allocates a new one and adds it to the tree array. This is where PHP's dynamic structure comes in handy—if we had to use arrays of fixed sizes, we'd run out of nodes sooner or later. The found node is then marked as being in use and returned as a handle to the caller.

`tree_free_node()` does basically the opposite: It marks the specified node as being unused by clearing the `$free` flag. This imposes three problems: First, freed nodes are not really freed; they're just *marked* as being free. Suppose you want to construct a complex tree with lots of nodes and then run an optimizer over it, which generally decreases the total node count by half and leaves lots of "ghost nodes" in the array after the optimization run. Assume that you'd initially allocate 1,000 nodes and free 500 of them during optimization. This would result in an array consisting of 1,000 nodes, but just 500 of them marked as being used. This is quite a waste of memory, so an automatic garbage collector would be a nice idea for these special cases.

Garbage collection leads to the second problem, namely *zombie nodes*. Zombie nodes are nodes that are marked as being in use, but unlinked from the tree, unable to be referenced anymore (see Figure 2.10).

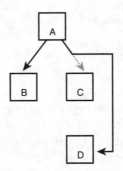

Figure 2.10   Zombie nodes in a tree.

As the library knows about all nodes in the tree and their internal linking between each other, zombie nodes can easily be identified—this is still missing in the code, however.

The third problem is quite similar to zombie nodes: *broken links*. Broken links are links that originate from one node and point to an unused/nonexistent node (see Figure 2.11). Links "break" whenever you detach a node from the tree, marking it as free, before having modified all other nodes that reference this node.

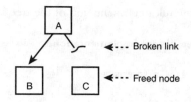

Figure 2.11   Broken links in a tree.

Again, this can be overcome with strict checking in the library functions and the garbage collector.

`tree_link_left()` and `tree_link_right()` link a node as left and right child, respectively, by assigning the associated handle to the `$idx_left` and `$idx_right` properties in the node structure. You can find their counterparts in `tree_get_left()` and `tree_get_right()`, which read the handles of the left and right links, respectively, from the node. Additionally, `tree_get_parent()` determines the parent node of a subnode.

To store contents in the tree and retrieve data from it, you can use `tree_assign_node_contents()` and `tree_retrieve_node_contents()`. Again, PHP's dynamic character is most helpful in this case, as we don't need to fix our nodes to certain datatypes. It became a common practice in C++ to instantiate trees using class templates, which generated, for example, tree classes for integers (only). Even though you could instantiate as many trees for as many datatypes as you liked, it wasn't easy to store dynamically typed content with this method. PHP simply accepts mixed types, which, for example, allows you to suddenly change all nodes' datatypes, and so forth.

Exercise: Implement Proper Garbage Collection into the Tree Library

Hint: You can introduce a new flag into the node structure for reference counting; this makes automatic garbage collection easier and faster.

Don't underestimate exercises. *Knowing how* to do something is substantially different from *being able* to do something. We highly encourage you to at least try to improve the library. It's definitely not a waste of time, even if you don't succeed. Marie Freifrau von Ebner-Eschenbach: "Für das Können gibt es nur einen Beweis: das Tun." (Freely translated: "There's only one way to prove ability: doing it.")

Listing 2.2 shows the full implementation of the tree library:

Listing 2.2 **The tree library implementation.**

```
//
// This structure keeps a tree node
//
class tree_node
{
    // array indices linking to neighboring nodes
    var $idx_up;
    var $idx_left;
    var $idx_right;

    var $free;

    // contents of this node, this is a mixed variable
    var $contents;
}

function tree_create()
{

    // create a new, empty array
    $return_array = array();

    // allocate the root node
    $root_node = new tree_node;

    // all other linking indices are invalid
    $root_node->idx_up = -1;
    $root_node->idx_left = -1;
    $root_node->idx_right = -1;

    // this node is unused
    $root_node->free = 1;

    // create dummy contents
    $root_node->contents = "";

    // assign root element to array
    $return_array[0] = $root_node;

    // return it back to caller
    return($return_array);

}

function tree_allocate_node(&$tree_array)
{
```

```php
    // find a free node
    for($i = 0; $i < count($tree_array); $i++)
    {
        // retrieve node from array
        $node = $tree_array[$i];

        // is it in use?
        if($node->free)
        {
            // no, it is not in use, allocate it
            $node->free = 0;

            // assign node back to array to update the tree
            $tree_array[$i] = $node;

            // now return this node's index as handle
            return($i);
        }
    }

    // we haven't found a free node, so allocate a new one
    $node = new tree_node;

    // invalidate all indices
    $node->idx_up = -1;
    $node->idx_left = -1;
    $node->idx_right = -1;

    // this node is NOT free
    $node->free = 0;

    // assign dummy contents
    $node->contents = "";

    // now add this node to the tree array
    $tree_array[] = $node;

    // return new index as handle
    return(count($tree_array) - 1);

}

function tree_free_node(&$tree_array, $handle)
{

    // retrieve node from tree
    $node = $tree_array[$handle];

    // check if it is really allocated
    if($node->free)
        // this node is free, return an error code
```

continues

Listing 2.2 **Continued**

```
        // note that this only serves diagnostic
        // purposes since it wouldn't hurt the tree
        // if we'd just mark it as free
        return(-1);

    $node->free = 1;

    // assign node back to tree
    $tree_array[$handle] = $node;

    return(1);

}

function tree_link_left(&$tree_array, $link_to, $child)
{

    // retrieve nodes
    $link_node = $tree_array[$link_to];
    $child_node = $tree_array[$child];

    // check if nodes are allocated
    if($link_node->free ¦¦ $child_node->free)
        // return error, we do not allow linkage
        // of free nodes
        return(-1);

    // link nodes together
    $link_node->idx_left = $child;
    $child_node->idx_up = $link_to;

    // write nodes back into the array
    $tree_array[$link_to] = $link_node;
    $tree_array[$child] = $child_node;

    // return success
    return(1);

}

function tree_link_right(&$tree_array, $link_to, $child)
{

    // retrieve nodes
    $link_node = $tree_array[$link_to];
    $child_node = $tree_array[$child];

    // check if nodes are allocated
    if($link_node->free ¦¦ $child_node->free)
```

```
        // return error, we do not allow linkage
        // of free nodes
        return(-1);

    // link nodes together
    $link_node->idx_right = $child;
    $child_node->idx_up = $link_to;

    // write nodes back into the array
    $tree_array[$link_to] = $link_node;
    $tree_array[$child] = $child_node;

    // return success
    return(1);

}

function tree_get_parent(&$tree_array, $handle)
{

    // retrieve node from array
    $node = $tree_array[$handle];

    // check if node is actually allocated
    if($node->free)
        // node is not allocated, return error
        return(-1);

    // node is allocated, return its parent
    return($node->up);

}

function tree_get_left(&$tree_array, $handle)
{

    // retrieve node from array
    $node = $tree_array[$handle];

    // check if node is actually allocated
    if($node->free)
        // node is not allocated, return error
        return(-1);

    // node is allocated, return its left child
    return($node->left);

}

function tree_get_right(&$tree_array, $handle)
{
```

continues

Listing 2.2   **Continued**

```
    // retrieve node from array
    $node = $tree_array[$handle];

    // check if node is actually allocated
    if($node->free)
        // node is not allocated, return error
        return(-1);

    // node is allocated, return its left child
    return($node->right);

}

function tree_assign_node_contents(&$tree_array, $handle, $contents)
{

    // retrieve node from array
    $node = $tree_array[$handle];

    // check if node is actually allocated
    if($node->free)
        // node is not allocated, return error
        return(-1);

    // assign contents to node
    $node->contents = $contents;

    // assign node back into array
    $tree_array[$handle] = $node;

    // return success
    return(1);

}

function tree_retrieve_node_contents(&$tree_array, $handle)
{

    // retrieve node from array
    $node = $tree_array[$handle];

    // check if node is actually allocated
    if($node->free)
        // node is not allocated, return error
        return(-1);

    // return contents of this node
    return($node->contents);

}
```

Associative Arrays

Arrays are another basic structure in programming languages. Arrays provide means for storing a fixed set (or *collection*) of the same datatype in a convenient way, making each element of your set indexable by using a unique key.

In the typical "conventional" programming languages, arrays are handled like this:

```
int my_integer_array[256];          // allocate 256 integers in this array
```

This C code snippet declares an array called `my_integer_array`, containing 256 integers. You can address each of these integers by indexing the array with an ordinal value, for this array in a range from 0 to 255. (C starts counting from 0; the given number in the array definition specifies the number of integers you want to have available.) Indexing looks like this:

```
int my_integer = my_integer_array[4];
```

This retrieves the fifth element (remember, C starts counting from 0) from the array and stores it in `my_integer`.

Due to the nature of compiled languages, you were always bound to the previous definition of your variables. If you suddenly needed more than 256 integers in the array above, this was impossible. Of course, you could have defined this variable as a pointer to an integer array and allocated 257 elements for it—but what if you suddenly needed another element? You'd have to allocate new space, copy the old array contents, and free up the old, unused space.

PHP takes a different approach. Because PHP knows no typical variable declarations (only type definitions), new variables are allocated on the fly. Whenever you create a new variable by introducing its name into the namespace, you simply create storage space bound to this name—nothing more. The kind of data residing in this space is not restricted to a certain variable type. It can be reinterpreted on the fly, and of course resized, reallocated, whatever.

Take a look at this:

```
$my_var = 1;
$my_var = "Used to be an integer";
$my_var = array("Oh well, I like arrays better");
```

The first line creates a new variable `$my_var`. PHP will find that an integer is going to be assigned to it; thus it sets the initial type of `$my_var` to integer. The second line, however, overwrites the contents of `$my_var` with a string. Using one of the conventional programming languages, this would have resulted in an error at compile time, or at least an exception during runtime. But PHP dynamically changes the type of `$my_var` to String and reallocates the variable so that enough storage space for the string is available. The third line then changes the type of `$my_var` once more by creating an array out of it. PHP handles all cases transparently without complaining. (We know that other languages out there exist without strict variable types, but we won't classify these as "conventional" languages here.)

Note: PHP 3.0 doesn't have proper garbage collection. When reallocating a variable, memory that's already allocated is not always being reused. In long-term scripts (or scripts doing heavy processing), this might result in big chunks of "dead memory." When using memory-intensive scripts that run for a long time, monitor their memory usage in a testing environment before releasing them to a production environment, to make sure that your server won't get blown away. PHP 4.0 is not vulnerable to this problem.

Because formal variable declarations are not needed in PHP, variable usage is completely dynamic. A special case in PHP's dynamic variable handling is arrays. You probably know the common array type, the *indexed array*. Indexed arrays are arrays that are indexed by ordinal numbers. These ordinal indices typically range from 0 to *n*, *n* being the highest possible index. Languages such as Pascal allow indexing with different ranges such as from 3 to 18; however, these ranges are transformed back to 0-based indexes at runtime. The key feature of these ordinally indexed arrays is that you can compute another index from any given base index. For example, suppose you want to read out three consecutive array elements, starting from index 2:

```
$base_index = 2;

for($i = $base_index; $i < $base_index + 3; $i++)
    print("Element $i is $my_array[$i]<br>");
```

In every iteration of the `for()` statement, this little snippet computes the next index into the array by incrementing `$i`.

Associative arrays don't have this feature. The special thing about associative arrays is that they can be indexed with non-ordinal keys, such as strings, for example. Every string used as an index has a value *associated* to it, thus the name *associative arrays*. As you can imagine, giving a string as base index doesn't allow guessing the next valid index in the array. Thus, associative arrays can't be used to order data elements in an ordinal way. You have to know the array keys to retrieve their associated values.

Apart from that, the functions `list()` and `each()`, discussed earlier, can be used to traverse associative arrays.

Indexed arrays are just a special form of associative arrays in PHP. Doing an `unset()` on one of the elements in an indexed array will leave all other elements (and their ordering) intact, but produce a nonconsecutive array. See the earlier descriptions of `list()` and `each()` for details.

Multidimensional Arrays

As the name suggests, *multidimensional arrays* are arrays with more than just one dimension. One-dimensional (or single-dimensional) arrays are the form in which arrays are mostly seen:

```
$my_array[0] = 1;
$my_array[1] = 777;
$my_array[2] = 45;
```

To index this type of array, you only need one index, which limits the number of possible values to the range of this index. But it's often very useful to create multidimensional arrays when handling complex datasets. Typical examples include bitmaps and screen buffers. When you look at your monitor, you see (at least these days) a two-dimensional projection of your desktop. The windows, bitmaps, command lines, cursors, pointers—everything is 2D. To represent this data in a convenient way, you could of course serialize everything into arrays with a single dimension—but the more appropriate method is to use arrays with dimensions equal to those of the input data. For example, in order to store a bitmap (a set of pixels) for a mouse pointer, you just add another index to your array:

```
// clear mouse bitmap
for($x = 0; $x < MOUSE_X_SIZE; $x++)
    for($y = 0; $y < MOUSE_Y_SIZE; $y++)
        $mouse_bitmap[$x][$y] = 0;
```

This would clear a mouse bitmap, setting all elements to 0—using two loops, one for each dimension. Figure 2.12 shows a graphical representation of two-dimensional data with the data elements residing in a coordinate system. Internally, in memory, the data elements will of course be stored serialized (RAM only has one dimension in indexing); however, a coordinate system is the proper visualization analogy.

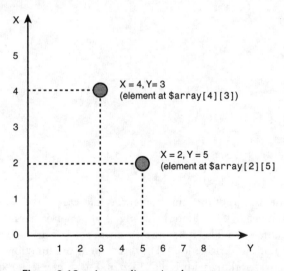

Figure 2.12   A two-dimensional array structure.

Arrays don't have a limit on the number of maximal dimensions (frankly, we haven't tried yet—but there will hardly be any use for arrays with 16 dimensions or more). Dimensions can also have different types (first dimension associative, second dimension indexed by integers, third dimension associative again, and so on). Thus, they're also very useful for representing statistical data, for example.

Variable Arguments

When using functions, it's often necessary to return more than one value or change the given parameters. For example, `fsockopen()` returns the socket handle as a return value, but is also able to return an error code along with descriptive text for eventual errors:

```
// try to open a socket for HTTP with a 30 second timeout
$socket_handle = fsockopen("www.myhost.com", 80, $error_nr, $error_txt, 30);
if(!$socket_handle)
{
    print("Couldn't connect to HTTP host.<br>");
    print("Error code: $error_nr, Reason: $error_txt<br>");
}
```

If a connection to the desired host could not be established, this code prints an error code and an error reason. The variables for these were originally being passed to `fsockopen()` as parameters. However, as these parameters are declared as "passed by reference" in the `fsockopen()` declaration, `fsockopen()` is able to modify them and make these changes globally available after it returns.

Usually functions don't access their parameters by reference. When they modify their values during execution, they work with a local copy of the original value:

```
function calculate($a, $b, $c)
{

    $a = $b + $c;

}

$i = 1;
$j = 2;
$k = 3;

print("I $i, J $j, K $k<br>");
calculate($i, $j, $k);
print("I $i, J $j, K $k<br>");
```

Both print statements output the same content. While `calculate()` modifies $a during execution, the contents of $i will not be changed, although it has been passed as an argument for parameter $a. This is because `calculate()` is working with a *copy* of the original variable, not the variable itself. Thus, as soon as the function returns, the copy of the variable it was working with is discarded and its contents are lost.

As is the case with `fsockopen()`, it might sometimes be desirable to keep changes to a parameter and make them visible in the global scope. In order to do this, a variable must not be passed as a copy, but *by reference*. Passing variables by reference results in the function only getting a pointer to the memory block where the original variable resides. Using this pointer, the function can access the global instance of the variable and change it directly:

```
function calculate(&$a, $b, $c)
{

    $a = $b + $c;

}

$i = 1;
$j = 2;
$k = 3;

print("I $i, J $j, K $k<br>");
calculate($i, $j, $k);
print("I $i, J $j, K $k<br>");
```

As you can see here, only one character is different—the ampersand (&) was missing in the previous snippet. This character, when put in front of a function parameter, denotes it to be passed by reference.

Note: You don't have to change the line that calls the function to include an ampersand (&). PHP automatically converts your parameters to references when it finds a function that wants them passed this way.

So, as `calculate()` changes $a, it's not changing its local copy of $i, but accessing $i's global storage space, modifying it directly. Moreover, as it's not working with local memory, the changes to $i are not lost when the function returns.

Passing parameters by reference is often a very useful method to return more than one value from a function or to "magically" change your variables when using multiple function calls to do complex calculations in a row. However, you should avoid splitting structures and pressing them into parameter lists when you could also return the data in a structure directly. Try not to overuse these kinds of parameters. Never make this your daily tool—it's actually a very dirty practice (functions are not supposed to modify their parameters in the global scope—sometimes evil bugs occur due to this), but often helps to ease things and just allow you to do clever tricks.

A possible example is the "automatic" update of so-called "run variables." *Run variables* are variables that change their values during an algorithmic loop. (Counter variables in `for()` statements are a special case of these.) A concrete example that benefits from this is the Run Length Encoding (RLE) algorithm, which is widely known because it has been used (and still is used) in such formats as ZSoft's PCX picture format.

The RLE algorithm is a simple compression algorithm that benefits from the fact that a lot of low-color images store the same data bytes repetitively (especially bitmaps that have only two colors, black and white). Take a look at this representation of a simple cube:

```
11111111111111111111
10000000000000000001
10000000000000000001
10000000000000000001
10000000000000000001
10000000000000000001
10000000000000000001
10000000000000000001
10000000000000000001
11111111111111111111
```

With a bit of imagination, you can see a cube of 0s with a border of 1s. If you would write this to a file "as is," you would need $20 \times 10 = 200$ elements (20 columns by 10 rows). We're assuming here that one element equals at least one byte, disregarding the fact that a simple compression could already be done by packing the information into bits.

You can see, however, that storing the data as is doesn't make sense. If you would dictate the data to someone else to write it down, you wouldn't read it "one one one one one one one [...] one zero zero zero zero zero [...] zero one one one [...]," but would tell the writer "twenty ones, another one, eighteen zeros, [...]."

The same approach is taken by the RLE algorithm, which counts the number of consecutive elements not changing their value and then stores them using a "count/value" pair. After compression, the data above might look like this:

```
21, 1, 18, 0, 2, 1, 18, 0, [...], 18, 0, 21, 1
```

The first element is always the counter, the second element the data element. To decompress this, you simply need to read the counter and then output the following data element as often as the counter indicates. As you can see, this "trick" reduced the number of required elements from 200 to 34.

The problem with this algorithm is that when it encounters a lot of different elements in a row, it creates a bigger output data than the original input data, because storing a lot of elements with a data count of 1 quickly renders the algorithm ineffective.

To overcome this, a little quirk can be added, namely a "counter threshold." Each type of data has a typical range of counters; in the data above, for example, the counter never exceeded 21. In fact, the values used most often were 18 and 2. Thus, by restricting the counter to a range of 1–31, we're able to place "literal data" that doesn't need compression into the input stream—the compressor simply spits out all input data elements greater than 31 without a count in front of them. The result is that the algorithm is now 100% optimal for all input values larger than 31. All values less than or equal to 31 will still be compressed non-optimally, but this can be ignored.

To decode the data, it's now crucial to distinguish between literal data elements and compressed data elements, as shown in Listings 2.3, 2.4, and 2.5. This is where variable arguments are most handy.

Listing 2.3   **The RLE compressor.**

```
function encode_data()
{

    // do initial setup on our variables
    $current_count = 0;
    $status = read_from_input($current_byte);
    $old_byte = $current_byte;
    $output = array();

    // as long as there's input data, loop
    while($status)
    {
     // check if the current byte matches the last one
     if($old_byte == $current_byte)
     {
         // there's a match, increase counter
         $current_count++;

         // does the counter exceed the threshold?
         if($current_count == COUNTER_THRESHOLD)
         {
          // it does, flush cache and restart
          $output[] = chr($current_count);
          $output[] = $current_byte;

          $current_counter = 0;
         }
     }
     else
     {
             // bytes don't match

             // do we have a cached pair?
             if($current_count > 1)
             {
              // yes we do, write it
              $output[] = chr($current_count);
              $output[] = $old_byte;

              $current_count = 1;
             }
             else
             {
              // we don't have a cached pair,
              // write literal
```

continues

Listing 2.3 **Continued**

```
                if(ord($old_byte) < COUNTER_THRESHOLD)
                {
                    // this byte could be mistaken as a counter
                    // value, so write a dummy pair
                    $output[] = chr(1);
                    $output[] = $old_byte;
                }
                else
                {
                    // can't be mistaken as counter value, just
                    // write the value directly
                    $output[] = $old_byte;
                }
            }
        }

        // set current byte as old byte
        $old_byte = $current_byte;

        // get new byte and loop
        $status = read_from_input($current_byte);
    }

    return($output);

}
```

Listing 2.4 **The RLE decompressor.**

```
function get_encoded_pair(&$count, &$value)
{

    // check input stream
    if(!read_from_input($data_element))
    {
        // no input data available, return
        // zero count and dummy data
        $count = 0;

        // indicate failure
        return(0);
    }

    // test if this is literal data
    if(ord($data_element) >= COUNTER_THRESHOLD)
    {
        // this is literal data, return
        // count of one and data element
```

```
            $count = 1;
            $value = $data_element;
    }
    else
    {
        // this has been a count, assign it
        $count = ord($data_element);

        // try to retrieve the data element
        // itself
        if(!read_from_input($value))
        {
            // input data is corrupted,
            // return zero count
            $count = 0;

            // indicate failure
            return(0);
        }

    }

    // return success
    return(1);

}

function decode_data()
{

    // initialize output array
    $output = array();

    // decompress all data into the array
    while(get_encoded_pair(&$count, &$value))
    {
        for($i = 0; $i < $count; $i++)
            $output[] = $value;
    }

    return($output);

}
```

Listing 2.5 **Usage example for the RLE engine.**

```php
//
// this declaration must exist and be equal
// both for the compressor and decompressor
//
define("COUNTER_THRESHOLD", 32);


//
// this tool function is needed for both the
// compressor and decompressor to read data
//
function read_from_input(&$data_element)
{
    // This is a dummy function to retrieve a data element
    // from the input data. It could contain code to read
    // from an array, from the standard input, or something
    // completely different.
    // As an example, this function reads from a global
    // file. (Not a good idea to have global files but
    // just for the example's sake.)
    global $file_handle;

    // check if we have reached the end of the file
    if(feof($file_handle))
    {
        // we did, return error
        return(0);
    }

    // we did not encounter the end of the file,
    // so read next element
    $data_element = fgetc($file_handle);

    // return success
    return(1);
}

// include compressor and decompressor
include("compressor.php3");
include("decompressor.php3");

// define filenames
$original_file = "data.original";
$compressed_file = "data.compressed";
$decompressed_file = "data.decompressed";

// -> all procedures need the global variable $file_handle
// (bad practice but best for a simple example)

// open input file
```

```
$file_handle = fopen($original_file, "r");
if(!$file_handle)
    die("Error opening file.");

// encode it
$output = encode_data();

// close input file
fclose($file_handle);

// open output file
$file_handle = fopen($compressed_file, "w");
if(!$file_handle)
    die("Error creating file.");

// write decoded data
for($i = 0; $i < count($output); $i++)
    fputs($file_handle, $output[$i]);

// close output file
fclose($file_handle);

// open input file
$file_handle = fopen($compressed_file, "r");
if(!$file_handle)
    die("Error opening file.");

// decode it
$output = decode_data();

// close input file
fclose($file_handle);

// open output file
$file_handle = fopen($decompressed_file, "w");
if(!$file_handle)
    die("Error creating file.");

// write decoded data
for($i = 0; $i < count($output); $i++)
    fputs($file_handle, $output[$i]);

// close file
fclose($file_handle);
```

This example shows very nicely how the decoder and reader logic can be split into smaller, separate functions. The actual decoder is now only a few lines long. The function that supplies input data can be detached from the rest of the code and the "decision maker" that differentiates between literal and compressed data is again in a separate, small, easy-to-understand function.

A clever trick is to return literal data with a count of 1, so that the decompression loop doesn't have to worry about this again—it can simply write the data it's being supplied with to the output array.

The error checking could be improved some, but we're leaving this up to the reader. It's not hard to do.

Variable Argument Lists

Variable argument lists, also often called *optional parameters*, allow you to pre-assign function parameters with a default value. If the caller doesn't specify a value for the argument, the default value is assumed. This makes it possible to supply the caller with a list of optional parameters that *can* be used but don't *have* to be used.

Optional parameters are defined as follows:

```
function open_http_connection($hostname, $port = 80, $timeout = 10)
{

    $socket = fsockopen($hostname, $port, $timeout);
    /* rest of the code goes here */

    return($socket);

}

$regular_socket = open_http_connection("www.myhost.com");
$slow_socket = open_http_connection("www.myhost.com", 80, 20);
$test_socket = open_http_connection("testserver.myhost.com", 8080);
$slow_test_socket = open_http_connection("testserver.myhost.com", 8080, 20);
```

The function `open_http_connection()` accepts one regular argument named `$hostname` that specifies the name of the host to which the function is supposed to connect. Additionally, it has two optional arguments, `$port` and `$timeout`, containing the port number to connect to and the connection timeout in seconds, respectively.

These two have pre-assigned, default values, indicated by the equal sign (=) followed by the wanted default value. Thus, whenever these arguments are not given by the caller, PHP just replaces the missing fields with their default values.

As you can see in the call examples, the very first call only uses `$hostname`. `$port` and `$timeout` are missing, so PHP just fills in the default values, which makes the call equal to this:

```
$regular_socket = open_http_connection("www.myhost.com", 80, 10);
```

In turn, you can still specify the optional parameters and overwrite their defaults, as seen in the second call. The value for `$port` is still 80, but `$timeout` is now set at 20 seconds.

You need to supply the default arguments whose value you'd like to change, as demonstrated by the third example. Here, only `$port` is given as `8080`. `$timeout` is not given and thus remains at its default value of 10 seconds.

The fact that PHP can't guess which value belongs to which parameter requires you to put all optional parameters at the end of the argument lists. If you'd put $hostname as the only required parameter at the end of the list (and $port and $timeout in front of it), the first call that only specified $hostname would make PHP think that the string for the hostname would actually be the value for $port, and thus create a lot of confusion.

Also, you can't just pick a random set of optional parameters for which you'd like to supply values—if you have a function that accepts three optional parameters and you only want to change the last one in the argument list, you still have to supply the default values for the other two parameters. (Shown in the second call above as well, where only $timeout is changed.)

In PHP 4.0, real variable arguments are possible. A function can take more arguments than the function definition lists, and you can access any number of arguments with the functions func_get_args(), func_num_args(), and func_get_arg().

The return value of func_get_args() is an indexed array that's filled with all argument values passed to the function, from left to right:

```
function show_arguments()
{

    $argument_array = func_get_args();

    for($i=0; $i<count($argument_array); $i++)
    {
        print("$i => $argument_array[$i]<br>");
    }

}

show_arguments("Leftmost", "Middle", "Rightmost");
```

The func_num_args() function returns the number of passed arguments; func_get_arg() returns a specific argument. For example, func_get_arg(0) would return the first argument.

Variable Variable Names

Variable variable names. For those who don't know about it (and for us, when we heard it the first time)—weird! *Variable variable names* are about accessing variables whose names you don't know beforehand and construct during runtime. This feature is possible in PHP because of its interpreted nature. PHP just walks through the code and translates whatever it finds to something useful. The following code constitutes the simplest example for variable variable names:

```
<?

$my_var = "hello";
```

continues

```
$$my_var = 1;

?>
```

In the second line, $my_var is prefixed with $$. Basically, this is how variable variable names work. Of course, you could nest variable variable names to get variable variable variable names (and so on), but with variable variable names you can already do pretty neat tricks.

A real-life example: phpPolls, the voting booth software described in Chapter 1, "Development Concepts," makes use of variable variable names. To protect itself from users voting twice in the same poll, one of the protection mechanisms is based on cookies. Whenever a user votes, a cookie is set, named with a configurable prefix and a unique ID identifying the poll. As cookies are reintroduced into the global namespace, whenever a user tries to submit a vote, phpPolls checks for the existence of a global variable named like the cookie name it constructed before. If a variable with this name exists, phpPolls rejects the vote.

To perform this task, variable variable names are extremely handy. Following is an excerpt from the phpPolls source code:

```
$poll_object = mysql_fetch_object($poll_result);
$poll_timeStamp = $poll_object->timeStamp;

$poll_cookieName = $poll_cookiePrefix.$poll_timeStamp;

// check if cookie exists
if(isset($$poll_cookieName))
{
    // cookie exists, invalidate this vote
    $poll_voteValid = 0;
}
else
{
    // cookie does not exist yet, set one now
    setCookie("$poll_cookieName", "1", $poll_cookieExpiration);
}
```

The code first retrieves the unique ID for the cookie, which consists of the poll's timestamp, and then assembles this with the cookie prefix $poll_cookiePrefix to form the name of the wanted variable, $poll_cookieName. Using isset(), the existence of the variable (and thus the cookie) is determined and acted on accordingly.

Variable Function Names

Of course, what we said about variable variable names in the preceding section is also valid for function names. Function names can be constructed using variables, providing a dynamic way of processing data, installing modifiable callbacks, and the like. Instead of hardcoding function names, you can use string variables to specify the functions you want to call:

```
function my_func($a, $b)
{

    print("$a, $b");

}

$function = "my_func";

$function(1, 2);
```

After the declaration of my_func(), the variable $function is assigned a string "my_func". Since this string is the same as the name of the function you want to call, you can use it when calling my_func().

Of course, this is a very simple example of variable function names. They're very useful when you have to switch between a set of different functions, depending on a number of variable flags.

Suppose you want to decode email attachments. These can have different formats—to name just two, base64 and uuencoded. Creating a "closed" parser that only understands one or two encoding formats and can hardly be extended is not a good idea; as soon as new formats are demanded, you'll be stuck. This case is almost ideal for variable function names:

```
function decode_base64($encoded_data)
{

    // do something with the encoded data

    return($decoded_data);

}

function decode_uuencoded($encoded_data)
{

    // do something with the encoded data

    return($decoded_data);

}
```

continues

```
$mail_text = fetch_mail();
$encoder_type = determine_encoding($mail_text); // returns: "base64" for Base64
                                                // returns: "uuencoded" for
                                                ➥UUEncoded

$decoder = "decode_".$encoder_type;

$decoded_data = $decoder($mail_text);
```

This code automatically determines the correct handler for the input data.
determine_encoding() returns a string indicating the type of data to be decoded, for
each of which a corresponding function must exist. The name of the function to be
called is then written into $decoder and called right away.

The drawback of this method is that it's dirty. You can hardly see a "default"
behavior in it—the decoding mechanism is completely dynamic and might crash if
determine_encoding() produces a meaningless result. However, it's a very comfortable
way to deal with the input data. As soon as new encoding types appear, you only have
to create an appropriately named function and adjust determine_encoding() to return
the corresponding string.

As long as you make determine_encoding() bulletproof, meaning that it will always
return a meaningful string (even if it's only a dummy), we would say that this
technique is totally legal to use. As long as you can make sure that your script will
remain in a defined state throughout runtime, this way of dynamic data handling is fit
for production environments.

A real-life example of a script that makes extensive use of variable function names
is phpIRC (discussed in the following chapter). phpIRC is an IRC layer for PHP,
providing access to IRC (Internet Relay Chat) networks through a comfortable API.
As the handling of input data is nonlinear and completely user-dependable, phpIRC
knows a set of events classifying each incoming packet. The user can install handlers
into phpIRC for each event, to be able to react on each type of incoming traffic.
phpIRC stores the names of the callback functions in an internal array; as soon as data
arrives, it scans its callback array for functions matching the detected type of data,
calling all matching functions in a row. This allows for dynamic data processing similar
to the email example described earlier, and is very handy when you can (or want to)
decide how to deal with upcoming events only at runtime.

Taking this further, you can use variable function names to change the behavior of
your scripts at runtime and also install user-defined "plug-ins" that attach themselves
to the code at runtime, making additional functionality available to the script without
having to change a single line of code.

Polymorphism and Self-Modifying Code

The drawbacks of variable function names (and partially variable variable names) is
that you always have to have a "fixed" part of the program (in the case of variable
function names, a list of previously declared functions that you can use) and then a
"variable" part (the part that constructs the function names into a variable and then

calls the function whose name has been constructed). This implies that for every possible constructed name, you have to create a function beforehand in order to let the program operate correctly—kind of restricting.

This can be overcome by completely dynamic programs—programs that generate themselves on the fly. Originally, this was an idea from the "early" days of programming, partially invented by game programmers and virus writers.

It all started with self-modifying code. In the inner loops of games—for example, the procedures that were responsible for drawing a buffer to the screen—speed was (still is) very crucial. However, as processing time was not an infinite resource, people had to think of new ways of getting the most out of their equipment.

Often it was the case that, in this innermost loop, quite a few decisions had to take place. For example, if a buffer copy routine only had to copy every second line to the screen on some occasions, you would have a few if()/then constructs embedded into the part of the code that needed them the least. These constructs took away precious processing time, and since this innermost routine was taking something like 80% of the total processing time of the overall program, speeding it up by 50% by removing these constructs would result in 40% additional available computing power.

Creating a set of routines to handle each case wouldn't have helped much, however; you would have wasted code space and just moved the decisions elsewhere. Of course, eventually you could have gotten a better overall performance, but not the *optimal* performance.

Thus, the technique of self-modifying code was invented. Whenever a part of the program would modify one of the conditions of the innermost if()/then constructs, instead of adjusting the responsible flags accordingly, it just reprogrammed the inner loop in such a way that it would act as desired; that is, exactly as it would if it would evaluate the flags. The necessary modifications were often only a matter of changing one or two bytes, and no more expensive than setting a set of flags. This would only work on the machine code level, of course, and was extremely system-dependent—but it was also extremely powerful.

Virus programmers finally took this technique to the extreme by creating *polymorphic programs*. Polymorphic programs are called polymorphic because they change their own code while still performing the same task. The simplest method to create polymorphic code was to compress the viruses and choose a different compression algorithm or different compression parameters every time. This resulted in different bytecode after every compression, but after decompression the original program was restored. (Try looking at ZIP archives containing the same data with different compression levels—they look substantially different, but always expand back to the same data.) The more complicated method was to dynamically regroup instruction blocks while keeping the algorithmic structure intact—a method that sometimes required extremely sophisticated code, but that was also very effective. As every method resulted in a change of the bytecode, different signatures for each infection of the virus were created, making it almost impossible for antivirus software to detect them—while the viruses were able to happily infect every program they found.

How does this relate to PHP? Of course, you can't create polymorphic programs like this—PHP's architecture prevents runtime modifications of code that has already been parsed—but nevertheless there's useful stuff in it. One possibility: dynamic function parsers, as described in the next section.

Dynamic Function Generator

While we were writing this book, someone in the German PHP mailing list was asking for a way to handle the processing of mathematical functions that were entered by a user. He wanted to know how he could display a function graphically that was entered by a user using a Web formula with PHP, but he didn't know how to deal with the textual input: How could you turn something looking like f(x) = m * x + b into a graph?

The discussion quickly moved into one of the traditional paths; everyone started thinking big, really big, instead of seeing the simple, obvious things. *Uni sono* (Latin, "with one voice"), the common method to approach the problem seemed to be the following:

1. Analyze input data.

2. Create a parsed representation (something related to compiler techniques).

3. Let a processor run over the parsed representation and generate step-by-step numerical output data.

Our concrete example, f(x) = m * x + b, would look like this:

1. See that this is a function depending on x, where m and b are variables.

2. Create a structure to internally represent the function text for easier handling; for example, make a tree of variable bindings to the multiplication sign (*) and plus sign (+).

3. Let a function vary x (which we found to be the variable this function depends on) and store output data for y, then interpolate.

This is the *de facto* approach taught in universities, seen in complex example sources, and so on. Nobody seemed to be able to make himself free of this pre-thought solution and create a more innovative solution. Ever thought about what PHP does when it interprets your scripts?

1. Analyze input source.

2. Generate a parsed representation.

3. Let a processor run over the parsed representation.

Alright, this is very simplified, but basically what we need. So why not transform the input function into valid PHP code and let PHP do the work for us? PHP supports dynamic coding, as you've seen elsewhere in this chapter, so the whole task could turn into something very trivial.

Indeed, the regular expressions required to transform a simple math function into PHP code are extremely easy. Assuming that all variables consist of a single character and that only legal PHP math operators are used (+, -, *, etc.), the following line can do the job:

```
$php_code = ereg_replace("([a-zA-Z])", "$\\1", $input_function);
```

This line transforms m * x + b into $m * $x + $b. Building a little bit of code around this regular expression and making a few simplifying assumptions, we can construct a dynamic function plotter very quickly, as shown in Listing 2.6.

Listing 2.6   **Dynamic function parser and plotter.**

```
//
// define global constants
//
define("PLOT_MIN", 0.1);
define("PLOT_MAX", 100);
define("PLOT_STEP", 0.5);
define("DIAGRAM_HEIGHT", 300);
define("DIAGRAM_HORIZON", 150);

function parse_function($in_string)
{

    // define a custom function header
    $header = "";
    $header = $header."function calculate(\$req_code, \$x)\n";
    $header = $header."{\n";
    $header = $header."eval(\$req_code);\n";

    // define a custom function footer
    $footer = "\n}\n";

    // convert all characters to PHP variables
    $out_string = ereg_replace("([a-zA-Z])", "$\\1", $in_string);

    // prepend header, create equation, and append footer
    $out_string = $header."return(".$out_string.");\n".$footer;

    // return result
    return($out_string);

}

function create_image()
{
    // export this variable
    global $color_plot;

    // we calculate the X scale based on the plot parameters
```

continues

Listing 2.6 **Continued**

```php
    // the diagram height is fixed as we do not check for the
    // function's extreme points
    $width = PLOT_MAX / PLOT_STEP;
    $height = DIAGRAM_HEIGHT;

    $image = imagecreate($width, $height);

    // allocate colors
    $color_backgr = imagecolorallocate($image, 255, 255, 255);
    $color_grid = imagecolorallocate($image, 0, 0, 0);
    $color_plot = imagecolorallocate($image, 255, 0, 0);

    // clear image
    imagefilledrectangle($image, 0, 0, $width - 1, $height - 1, $color_backgr);

    // draw axes
    imageline($image, 0, 0, 0, $height - 1, $color_grid);
    imageline($image, 0, DIAGRAM_HORIZON, $width - 1, DIAGRAM_HORIZON,
    ➥$color_grid);

    // print some text
    imagestring($image, 3, 10, DIAGRAM_HORIZON + 10, PLOT_MIN, $color_grid);
    imagestring($image, 3, $width - 30, DIAGRAM_HORIZON + 10, PLOT_MAX,
    ➥$color_grid);

    // return image
    return($image);

}

function plot($image, $x, $y)
{
    // import the color handle
    global $color_plot;
    // set these as static to "remember" the last coordinates
    static $old_x = PLOT_MIN;
    static $old_y = 0;

    // only plot from the second time on
    if($old_x != PLOT_MIN)
        imageline($image, $old_x / PLOT_STEP, DIAGRAM_HEIGHT -
        ➥($old_y + DIAGRAM_HORIZON), $x / PLOT_STEP, DIAGRAM_HEIGHT -
        ➥($y + DIAGRAM_HORIZON), $color_plot);

    $old_x = $x;
    $old_y = $y;

}
```

```php
// see if we've been invoked with a function string set
if(!isset($function_string))
{
    // no, there's no function string present,
    // generate an input form
    print("<html><body>");
    print("<form action=\"".basename($PHP_SELF)."\" method=\"post\">");
    print("Function definition: <input type=\"text\"
        ⇥name=\"function_string\" value=\"(m*x+b)/(x/3)\"><br>");
    print("Required PHP code: <input type=\"text\" name=\"req_code\"
        ⇥value=\"\$m = 10; \$b = 20;\"><br>");
    print("<input type=\"submit\" value=\"Parse\">");
    print("</form>");
    print("</body></html>");
}
else
{
    // translate input function to PHP code
    $parsed_function = parse_function($function_string);

    // *** NOTE: security holes! (see book contents) ***
    eval($parsed_function);

    // create image
    $image = create_image();

    // plot the function
    for($x = PLOT_MIN; $x < PLOT_MAX; $x += PLOT_STEP)
    {
        $y = calculate($req_code, $x);
        plot($image, $x, $y);
    }

    // set content type
//  header("Content-type: image/gif");
    header("Content-type: image/png");

    // send image
//  imagegif($image);
    imagepng($image);

}
```

The script is executable; you can use it directly in your browser. On first invocation, it will notice that you haven't supplied a function to plot yet and display a little input form, as shown in Figure 2.13.

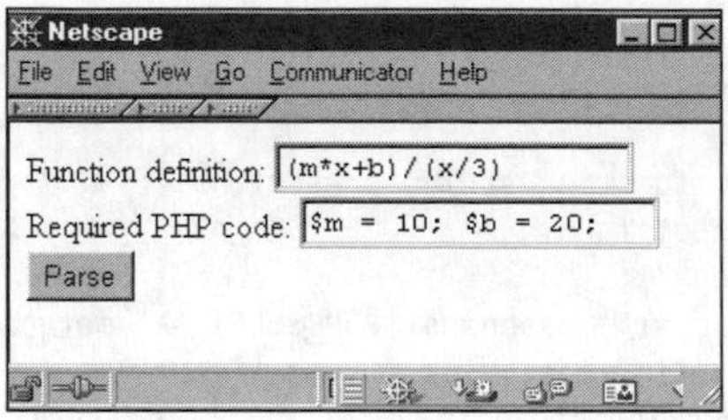

Figure 2.13   Input form of the dynamic function plotter.

The first field takes the function that is to be plotted. This example makes the assumption that *x* is always the only variable this function depends on. In the second field, you can enter a bit of PHP code that will be executed prior to evaluating the function statement in order to allow assignments to constants (in our case, *m* and *b*).

Warning

The technique used here to directly execute PHP code with `eval()` supplied by the user should *never* (we repeat: *never ever*) be used like this in production scripts. Executing user code introduces a huge security hole into your programs, as everyone could send something like `system("rm -r /*");` and delete all data your Web server has access to. It has been done this way here as we want to concentrate on dynamic code generation and execution; for an elaborate discussion about how to secure your scripts (and avoid execution of malicious code), see Chapter 4, "Web Application Concepts," and Chapter 5, "Basic Web Application Strategies."

For now, you can simply click Parse. Figure 2.14 shows what will appear next.

So how did the script get from the input form to this graphical output? Let's discuss the inner workings step by step.

After you have submitted the input form, the script starts executing the `else()` clause of the main `if()` statement. The first function called is as follows:

```
// translate input function to PHP code
$parsed_function = parse_function($function_string);
```

`parse_function()` creates the PHP code from the supplied user input by applying a regular expression to it. To make comfortable use of the math function, it's embedded into a small function, which just assigns the appropriate values to the constants (by referring to user input again) and then executing the math statement, returning the resulting value to the caller.

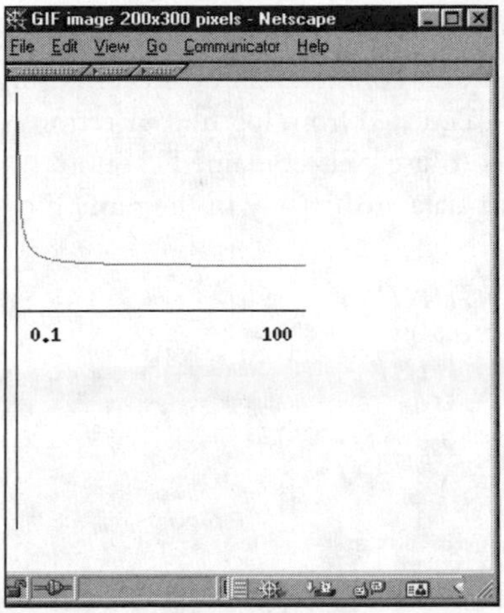

Figure 2.14   Sample output of the function plotter.

The function generated by `parse_function()` would be as follows for the example `(m * x + b) / (x / 3)`:

```
function calculate($req_code, $x)
{
    eval($req_code);
    return(($m * $x + $b) / ($x / 3));
}
```

`$req_code` contains the input from the second form field, in this example `$m = 10; $b = 20;`. Executing that using `eval()` results in correct variable assignment for the next line, which already does all the calculation—and that's it!

Note: For important information about the `eval()` statement, see the earlier warning!

The rest is straightforward function plotting; the `for()` loop iterates through a predefined range and uses `calculate()` to determine the curve's Y value in each iteration.

Self-Modifying Counter

To name just a simple example, hit counters can be created using self-modifying code. Usually, hit counts would be calculated from log files or retrieved from a database— but a much simpler method is to use "self-contained" counters. *Self-contained* means that counter code and counter data are actually in the same file:

```
$counter = 0;
/////////////////////////////////////
// Do not modify above this point
/////////////////////////////////////

// increase counter
$counter++;

// write counter back to ourselves
$file = fopen(basename($PHP_SELF), "r+");
fputs($file, "<?\n\$counter = $counter;");

// print counter (or do something else with it)
print("$counter hits so far");
```

In the first line, the counter is reset to 0. The next line then increases it, and now comes the interesting part: The code opens its own file and replaces its first line. This results in a different interpretation of the file when it's being processed by PHP the next time—the source would look like this:

```
$counter = 1;
/////////////////////////////////////
// Do not modify above this point
/////////////////////////////////////

// increase counter
$counter++;

// write counter back to ourselves
$file = fopen(basename($PHP_SELF), "r+");
fputs($file, "<?\n\$counter = $counter;");

// print counter (or do something else with it)
print("$counter hits so far");
```

The first line now sets $counter to 1 and not to 0. Every time the file is processed, the first line will change and reflect the number of hits this file has had so far.

Note: This code will have trouble handling concurrent accesses. Two PHP processes might read the file at the same time (and write to it at the same time as well), which would result in an incorrect hit count. You definitely will run into trouble using this technique without process locking in a high-traffic environment.

Summary

In this chapter, you've learned a lot about PHP's advanced syntax and good coding practices. You've seen how to create constants using `define()`. Then the more tricky aspects of arrays were outlined, and you learned that you should use `list()/each()` to traverse hashes. We've explained PHP's OOP features, and shown you how and when to use them—and when to stick to procedural programming instead. Because PHP is an interpreted language, it allows many features that would be very hard to implement with traditional compiled programming languages: variable variables and functions, self-modifying code, and runtime evaluation of source code. With this knowledge, you're well prepared for advanced PHP programming, and a big step further on your way to becoming a PHP wizard.

3

Application Design: A Real-Life Example

Prevent trouble before it arises.
Put things in order before they exist.
The giant pine tree
grows from a tiny sprout.
The journey of a thousand miles
starts from beneath your feet.

APPLICATION DESIGN IS A TOPIC SO BROAD that a whole book couldn't fully cover it. The term *application design* contains merely every single part of development, from data structure layout, flow charts, and entity-relationship diagrams to code layout, documentation, and anything in between. Because it is so important, however, we decided not to exclude it from this book, but instead to tackle a discussion of application design by restricting the topics covered to a "hands-on" example, namely phpChat. This chapter will give you an in-depth view of this real-time chat server application implemented in PHP, similar to an extended software case study. We hope that you can extract useful information and methods to use when designing your next application.

Many of the boxed notes in this chapter contain remarks about techniques common to application design that you should memorize and try to use directly on the suggested example (or phpChat in general), and indirectly on your next project. *Note:* Another, more theoretical but shorter discussion about application design can be found in Chapter 7, "Cutting-Edge Applications."

Project Overview

When designing an application, you start with the idea of what the application is supposed to do. In the case of phpChat, the application is supposed to provide a browser-based chat service.

The chat should have the following features:

- **Real-time chat.** No deferred relaying of messages and no refreshes.
- **No client-side programming.** The browser should be confronted only with pure HTML (and eventually some JavaScript).
- **Networkable.** It should be possible to link chat boxes.
- **Generic.** Make as few assumptions about the target systems as possible and introduce as few requirements as possible.
- **No design enforcements.** Separation of code and page layout.
- **Easy to use and administer.**
- **Unlimited number of clients and chat rooms.**

Once you've gotten this far and know what your application is supposed to do, you have to evaluate the concept and create a more detailed overview of how the application should be laid out.

Take the time to write down all the requirements. It helps a lot, especially as a reminder later on.

When designing an application with a customer, this step is called *creating the specifications* (or just *specs*). At this point, the customer can still influence the layout of the application. This is very important because the application must meet the requirements listed in this step, or it won't be approved by the customer.

The Customer Is Always Right, Even When He's Wrong

Customers who contract you for an application often do not have enough expertise to design such an application by themselves, which is why they hire you. When discussing requirements with customers, guide them when they're suggesting bad solutions. For example, if the customer says, "I want a chat that displays full-screen images of every chatter, refreshed at least every second," you might make this counter-suggestion: "Wouldn't it be better to try to stick to thumbnail views next to each line? Most of your chatters won't have enough bandwidth to display full-screen pictures at all."

But be careful; never insist on your point of view (except when customers want you to implement unrealistic features). After all, customers pay you to implement *their* vision. To avoid losing a contract, you may have to accept temporarily implementing a bad solution (when you see that you can't talk the customer into doing it the right way), and then later on change it when the customer sees that it won't work out using their strategy.

For this project, you will take the role of the project manager and the authors will be your customers. Since we're nice customers, we won't keep insisting on nailing down further details of this application; we'll leave the rest of the design to you. Whenever this chapter hits a point where a choice or decision can be made, sit back and try to make your own choices. Closely evaluate all facts and then compare your results with the conclusions discussed in the book.

Comparing Technologies

Before even starting to think about code layout, there's a phase we don't know what else to call but "getting things together." This is the intermediate step between the idea and the specs/code layout stage—figuring out the inner workings and on what to base them.

To make it clearer, let's go back to the very beginning:

- What do we want to create?
- How are we going to create it?
- Are there any existing implementations of our idea already?

- Do similar systems exist that perform almost the same task?
- If so, can we reuse anything from that design?
- Can we reuse foreign techniques, maybe add up to our system with them?

Questions over questions.

The first is easy to answer. We want to create a chat system. How? Well, with PHP, and somehow server-side—we don't know much more about it at this time.

Are there already any chat systems or something similar out there? Indeed there are. It starts right at your shell—the "talk" command allows you to chat with other people that you can reach via a valid network link (or local link), as shown in Figure 3.1.

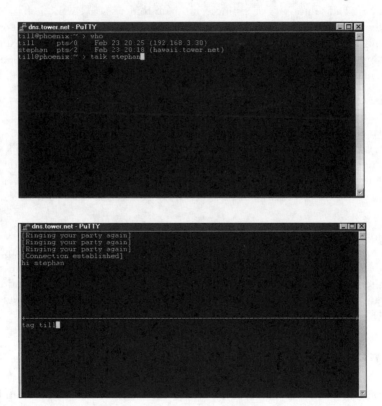

Figure 3.1   The traditional "talk" command.

Of course, this isn't as powerful as we'd want it to be, but it's a start. Next, we could surf the Web to look for pages that have one of the (nowadays almost obligatory) chat links. Although they differ widely in look and feel/implementation, most of them can be boiled down to the following:

- Java for fancy interfaces, although some use plain HTML.
- A proprietary protocol with a single server (or simply database-backed).
- Few predefined rooms.
- Few predefined commands.

Apart from these chat setups, there are chat applications and networks such as Mirabilis' ICQ or the diverse Instant Messaging Systems—systems that don't always provide real-time services and generally require additional proprietary client software to be installed on every participating system.

However, one system stands out from the list. *IRC* (*Internet Relay Chat*) is a widely-known and long-used chat protocol used by many networks, some of which carry hundreds of thousands of users simultaneously. The IRC protocol is text-based—a drawback when operating under high load (long string commands generate much more traffic than single binary characters), but this also makes it significantly easier to process. Most current IRC servers support compressed backbone links, which greatly reduce traffic.

Although IRC requires special client software on every participating system, we can "tweak" this requirement to our advantage: Why not provide the client software ourselves server-side, and abstract it by using an HTML interface and allowing each user access to the network through an HTML client? This would give us control over what the user can do (each user is required to use our HTML client). Additionally, we have all the advantages of an existing network system: reliable client software, proven concept, hundreds of tools, etc. We could even allow users to use their own client software—an option to be avoided in most cases, however, as we want to create a "closed" chat network. On a closed network, you know every way that each client can access your network. By limiting the access points to specific setups, you greatly reduce the risk of being attacked.

This directly leads to the question, do we need a real protocol such as IRC? Or would it be sufficient to simply use a database-driven protocol, with a remote synchronization feature to provide the requested networking abilities?

Questions such as this will arise every time you plan an application, and they'll arise *often*. Make sure that you've got all of them covered, and make sure that no questions will arise at a later stage during development. *This* is the point where you can still address these questions; *later on* you might be unable to resolve them (and eventually get your project kicked into the trash). A good project is a project without doubts, without uncertainties, without inconsistencies, and without unforeseen eventualities. Make sure that after your planning phase you can assure a stable, fully evaluated situation!

So let's get back to answering the question: Do we need an open (and perhaps too complex) protocol such as IRC, or should we stick with a conventional database approach? The simplest method to find an answer is also the most logical one—compare pros and cons and choose the option with the best results.

Implementing IRC as a protocol into the chat system will introduce a significant amount of complication because of protocol processing—processing network protocols requires nonlinear coding, something that isn't really supported by PHP. (To react to network messages, we need an event-based system.) On top of that problem, we'd need a way to handle message exchange efficiently; that is, dealing with messages *from* a user and *for* a user (which, unfortunately, may not always be handled in the same way). This problem exists in the database-backed solution, too, of course, but the database-backed solution doesn't require protocol handling. A lot of databases are supported natively by PHP, and those that aren't are most likely supported indirectly by ODBC. To gain the ability of networkable chat boxes, we'd only need to create a tool that can synchronize between chat boxes. (Unless you only want to run one central database server that's accessed by all boxes simultaneously.)

What would you choose?

Spoiler: phpChat is based on IRC, and this is why:

- Using a database, we'd introduce some kind of "proprietary," private protocol that wouldn't be able to interface to other standard systems. In times of interoperability and interconnectivity, this is a bad thing.

- An IRC library that functions well (namely phpIRC, see `www.phpwizard.net/phpIRC`) abstracts access to IRC networks into a set of easy-to-use API functions—and makes IRC handling equal to database handling in terms of code complexity.

- Existing IRC server software handles all the itsy-bitsy teenie-weenie problems of user management, reliable traffic forwarding, routing, etc., across networks. The software has been around for a long time and is proven to work, plus it's available for all types of systems.

- IRC is extremely scalable. If you run into load problems on server A at peak times or due to unforeseen events, simply fire up server B and dynamically establish a server connection into the existing chat (IRC allows you to do so, and is fully automated)—and you now have another server with enough free capacity for additional users.

IRC Network Basics

Having chosen a communication standard for the chat, we should take a look at how exactly IRC networks are built.

> Ideally, you should have evaluated the IRC network basics discussed in this section prior to choosing IRC—since it's a bad thing to find out that IRC introduces a complicated structure after already having made the decision to use it. To this point, however, we've been working with "common knowledge" about using IRC networks, just for the sake of application planning. Now that we've led you to the "right" method to use for the application (IRC), this section provides the details you need to execute that plan.

IRC networks distinguish between clients and servers. Users can participate on the network only by using a special client software that establishes a client link to a server. All servers on the network are interconnected using special server links. Current implementations of IRC servers only support hierarchical structures, meaning that there must not be redundant ways to reach a server. This forms the net into a tree-like structure prone to network splits, but also greatly simplifies routing: All servers simply have to send all incoming data to all other links, without fearing to send redundant information to a server.

Each server can have a number of clients; the maximum number depends on the number of connections the server is willing to accept (of course, limits also exist in terms of network capacity and server load). As shown in Figure 3.2, each server can reach every other server across more or fewer server hops, so each server simply sends all incoming data to all outgoing links. For example, Server C and Server F might carry clients participating in the same channel (*channels* are IRC's chat rooms—places where people can "meet" and "talk"). In this example, Server C would send the data via the only link it has: Server B. Server B then distributes the data to its other links, namely Server A and Server D. Server A doesn't have any other links, so it won't do anything, but Server D would pass on the data to Server E, and Server E in turn to Server F. Pretty easy to implement, but with one drawback: If Server A doesn't have any clients connected to it participating in the channels to which Server C sends data, all data for Server A targeted at this channel would simply waste bandwidth.

RFC for IRC

Similar to all open standards on the Internet, the basics of the IRC protocol have been specified in an RFC (Request For Comments). The RFC for IRC is RFC 1459, which can be retrieved, for example, at www.irchelp.org, a site that carries a lot of information on IRC.

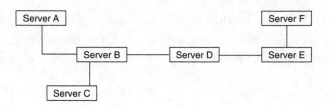

Figure 3.2   A sample IRC network structure.

This is one of the main problems of this "limited by design" network: All public traffic has to go to all servers. But will this problem really arise under the conditions in which we intend to implement our IRC network? Surely not, as the number of clients we intend to handle will never be so large as to be harmful, given a standard server-hosting situation. In internal networks, this problem shouldn't arise at all.

To reduce the total number of critical links, the network can be laid out to follow its physical topology. If one server is connected with higher capacity than the rest, for example, it can take more leaf nodes than others (connecting lots of leaf nodes to a server with a small backbone wouldn't even make sense). Another option is to set up the routing to fit the network. For example, U.S. servers are homed in the States, German servers are homed in Germany, and so on. Frankfurt has an overseas link to New York; thus, the IRC server in Frankfurt should link to New York's server (following the network's physical layout). It could also be done in another way: Frankfurt could link to, say, Poland. But if Poland doesn't have its own overseas link, the traffic routed from Frankfurt to Poland would need to find some other way to cross the ocean—it would be routed to some other country (or even two or three countries) until it finds a free overseas link. This additional routing wastes a lot of bandwidth; thus, attempts are being made to adapt the IRC network structure to best fit the underlying physical network structure.

These design problems are present only in the biggest networks, carrying tens of thousands of users. These networks really need to find reliable links for their backbones. Typical Web-based chat rooms or networks are unlikely to carry more than 1,000 clients at once, so you shouldn't run into serious problems at first. To avoid complications, however, it's a good idea to plan around these sorts of problems that may arise eventually.

From a server's point of view, the network looks like Figure 3.3.

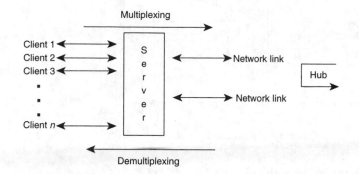

Figure 3.3   Network structure from a server's point of view.

The structure implemented here is similar to a mixture of a multiplexor, demultiplexor, and a hub. In the direction client to network, the server compresses all data from the clients and sends it to the network links. In the other direction, it determines which information from the network is important for which client and sends it to the appropriate link. All incoming data from the network that has to be passed on to the other network links is sent on directly.

Basically, this is the setup we'd need for our own chat system. Now take a minute and try to imagine how we can achieve our goal. We need a working server environment that fits the following description:

- Accepts IRC network links
- Accepts IRC client links
- Provides a Web-based user interface
- Is as easy to implement as possible

Fitting the Application into the Network

If you came up with a plan to develop your own server in PHP (or something similar), rethink a bit. You might have gotten a bit confused with the idea that implementing a chat server means implementing a network server. This is indeed something we wanted to lead you to, but don't want you to *do*, as this is simply unnecessary—there's already a well-written server software available for all systems. So how about using one of the existing servers and representing our server to the network as a client? The only thing we'd have to do is to add another layer of abstraction to the network, as shown in Figure 3.4.

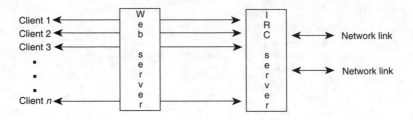

Figure 3.4 phpChat as an abstraction layer to the server.

The Web server will run the PHP chat server. For each client connection it accepts, it will create a client connection to the IRC server. This way, we can make sure that all data we get for this client is meant only for this client—and nobody else. Each chat process will carry a single user, and doesn't have to worry about other users. User coordination, traffic control, and so on can be done by the IRC server, for which we'll simply take one of the freely available servers.

This technique also has the advantage that this chat server application can be used as a safe gateway to IRC networks (see Figure 3.5). A lot of corporate and private networks are behind firewalls that filter IRC ports. Since this chat is only communicating via HTTP to its clients (which is not filtered), only the chat server itself needs an open connection to an IRC server.

Therefore, the only thing we're going to do is to implement the client software that would otherwise be required on the user's side on our Web server. IRC knows all the commands that are required to set up a powerful chat, and the networking issues can all be solved by using standard "off the shelf" server software that's already available. Thus, if our interface supports all features of IRC in a convenient way, we're done with our work.

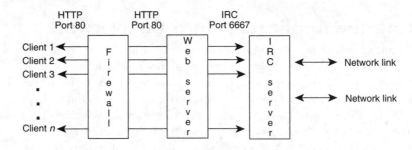

Figure 3.5 phpChat as a safe IRC gateway.

Interfacing the Network

As we mentioned earlier, IRC requires some processing overhead. Hacking a complete protocol handler for interfacing with IRC is a bit of a complex task, but we favored IRC instead of the database-backed solution because an API already exists that does this work for us.

Know the market! It's essential for every programming project to know which parts have already been done by other people and which still need to be done. Never reinvent the wheel! Especially for commercial projects, it can pay off tremendously to buy foreign bulletproof solutions for specific tasks, rather than design and develop one yourself. The latter is sometimes more expensive and much more time-consuming. On top of that, external solutions are usually constantly being improved—a process that's totally independent of the progress of your own project. By receiving an upgrade from an external company, you simply replace a part of your application with a newer version. This way, you can upgrade certain parts of your application without having to put your own work into the changes. Plus, when using existing libraries, you automatically agree to build your project on common, standardized APIs, which is always a great benefit.

On the other hand, binding yourself to foreign products can prove to be a negative decision if the producer fails to improve the product or keep it up to date, as well as if bugs in it aren't corrected.

In our experience, Open Source products have been the most successful external parts to be integrated. Open Source products are being improved and extended extremely rapidly and are usually oriented at common and open high-potential standards.

Exercise for the Reader

Search for applications/libraries written in PHP that make use of IRC and compare them in terms of design, flexibility, and ease of use. Of course, the implementation is also interesting (but shouldn't be your main focus). The design is always the most crucial part of development; after the design is finished, the actual implementation is usually straightforward and easy to do (even though a lot of programmers think differently).

The library we've chosen for this project is phpIRC (`www.phpwizard.net/phpIRC`), for these reasons:

- It's easy to use.
- It's a powerful, complete API.
- It uses event-based processing.

The use of event-based processing is particularly interesting here. This is a technique usually implemented in traditional applications; for example, all Windows programs are event-based. *Event-based programs* run in an endless loop, waiting for something (an event) to happen. Events can include user input, mouse movements, network events (incoming packets), etc. As soon as an event is signaled, the program breaks out of its main loop and searches for a procedure that handles this event. All procedures that want to handle the event that just occurred are called with the specific parameters of the event (for example, packet data of incoming network traffic).

Concretely, using "traditional" programming, an incoming ping would be handled as shown in Listing 3.1:

Listing 3.1   **Pseudocode for handling a ping.**

```
again:

wait_for_network_data();

if(incoming_data == ping)
{
    send_pong();
    update_traffic_counter();
}

goto again;
```

This code waits until it receives data from the network, then tries to find out whether the data was a ping. If so, the code sends a pong back and updates a traffic counter for statistical reasons. After that, it just jumps back to where it began. Imagine this with hundreds of events, some of which might depend on others, some not, some only under certain circumstances…A pain!

However, event-based programming makes it significantly easier, as shown in Listing 3.2:

Listing 3.2   **Event-based pseudocode for handling a ping.**

```
event_handler ping()
{

    send_pong();
```

```
}

event_handler incoming_data()
{

    update_traffic_counter();

    case of ping: handle_event(ping);
}

while(not_done())
{

    wait_for_event();

    case of network_data: handle_event(incoming_data);

}
```

The code looks bigger, but also much clearer. The main loop waits for an event to happen. If it finds that an event happened and that it was triggered due to incoming network data, it dispatches this event using the central procedure handle_event(). This function then determines a handler for the event and calls it. The handler in turn updates the traffic counter and launches another event if the first event was a ping. After dispatching the event using handle_event() again, a pong is sent.

> Alternatively, both ping() and incoming_data() could register themselves to the event "incoming_data". However, creating two different events gives a greater variety of events and thus allows for much more detailed, target-oriented processing.

It's a bit strange at first getting used to event-based processing of information (it works similarly to a finite-state machine), but it has many advantages:

- A modular structure is forced on the application. Each module works independently of the other modules and can easily be changed, exchanged, or extended.

- Any part of the program can trigger any kind of event and thus enforce any type of reaction in the application (in other words, you can control any part of your code from any other part of your code).

- From one central point of the program, all data can be dispatched to all recipients transparently. You don't have to worry about manually copying and transforming structures; each event handler takes care of receiving its data on its own.

- New code can be plugged into the application extremely easily, just by creating a procedure that registers itself to the appropriate event.

Thus, once the main event-dispatcher framework is created, the whole application can be created by writing handlers, handlers, and more handlers.

Get familiar with the techniques used to implement finite-state machines. These are elemental in programming and information processing in general.

Luckily, the event-dispatcher framework is already contained in phpIRC, so we won't need to do that programming for this project.

Interface Structure

phpIRC forms the IRC client part of the application and is responsible for all network communication. This means that it also needs to be in control all the time to be able to react to network messages in a timely manner. If phpIRC's message-processing functions were activated only occasionally, safe, secure, and speedy communication couldn't be guaranteed. For this reason, phpIRC forces a special program layout, as shown in Figure 3.6.

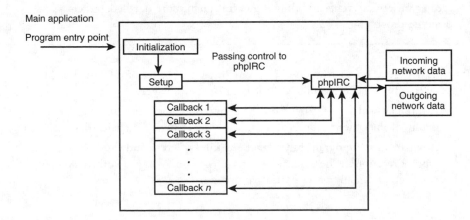

Figure 3.6   phpIRC's forced application layout.

After doing initialization and setup, the application has to surrender control to phpIRC. phpIRC then enters its main event loop and waits for something to happen. During setup, the application has to register callbacks for each event it wants to process (for example, incoming private messages, incoming server messages, and so on). These callbacks are the only possibility for the application to regain control. phpIRC then dispatches all events to all functions that have registered themselves with the library. These functions can in turn enter another idle loop in phpIRC to wait for another event to happen, or they can use phpIRC's API to perform certain actions on the network (send private messages, join/leave channels, and so on).

This very basic layout already allows for downstream communication, which means that phpIRC is able to receive messages from other users. People could actually "talk" to your script.

Note: Downstream means from the network to the user. *Upstream* is the opposite, from the user to the network.

Exercise for the Reader
Structure a downstream interface that makes use of phpIRC's features. Implement it on paper to become familiar with phpIRC's API. Then build a simple downstream interface that logs onto IRC and displays all messages from a specified channel.

Downstream Communication

Since chatting is a real-time task, meaning that it happens as you do it and causes instant replies, we don't want to introduce latency into the interface. *Latency* describes the reaction time of the interface; for example, the time from the point when the reader presses the Enter key to submit a message until it shows up in the chat window. Even though a latency of less than a second might objectively be a very short wait, it *seems* extremely long and annoying to the user. Ergo, incoming messages must be displayed at once (or at least as soon as possible). HTTP is a stateless protocol, however, and doesn't allow instant updates of pages without reloading a complete document. Of course, there are multipart documents and automatic refreshes, but these options introduce a very nasty flicker each time the page loads again, require database buffering for output, and introduce lag because of constant reconnects and data transfer from the Web server.

One solution is "streaming HTML," something that's not officially supported anywhere, but works nevertheless: The script that does the interface output simply idles in an endless loop and doesn't terminate the HTML page the browser is receiving. When something has to be sent to the user, it's printed and immediately flushed from the server's buffers. This way, the browser is constantly rendering and always displays the most up-to-date data. One problem persists in this approach, however; no complex HTML entities can be rendered on the fly. For example, you can't output the rows of a table one by one, because the browser requires all rows and columns of the table to be present completely to determine the final size of the table. As long as you restrict yourself to outputting text lines one after another, and only use tables when you can print them all at once, everything works fine.

Quirks such as streaming HTML are common tricks that you should know. Always keep yourself informed about such things.

Streaming HTML also has one implication that some see as drawback and some as advantage: Since the client connection stays open, there must always be one server process handling it. This means that every client requires at least one Web server process to be running only for that client. The advantage is that no overhead "per hit" occurs. Usually, when the client requests a document, a new process has to be spawned; the script generating that document has to be loaded, parsed, and executed; and finally, the data has to be sent. Since the server process now remains in memory, however, spawning, script loading, and interpretation only have to be done once per client. On sites that would otherwise have hundreds of hits per second, this might be a definite advantage. However, each process now stays resident in memory and demands RAM for itself—on Intel x86 systems equipped with Linux, Apache, and PHP 4.0, such processes tend to be as big as 2MB each. Consequently, a small server with minimal RAM on board would soon start to run from swap—and that means death.

   Note: Swap memory is virtual memory that's meant to extend the RAM—the physical amount of memory on a computer. Swap memory is stored on a hard disk, which is extremely slow. When physical memory is all used up, modern operating systems start allocating new memory in the slow swap memory. If a chat server gets hit by a lot of clients at once, which eat up all physical memory and start running in swap memory, the operating system will constantly have to exchange parts of the RAM with parts of the swap memory (since programs can't be executed from swap memory), and this starts a "cycle of death": The operating system notices that a process in swap needs to be run and loads it into RAM, but has to put another running process from RAM into swap. It executes the process in RAM but finds the old process (now residing in swap) has to be run, so it swaps it back into RAM, and so on and so on. You can quickly kill a server this way, forcing it to be reset or taken off the net. By the way, this is also a common "denial of service" attack, a bit similar to the ones that Yahoo! and others were exposed to earlier this year.

Would you have thought about the implications of resident processes? If not, make sure you do next time! Keep evaluating every situation fully.

Upstream Communication

Upstream communication—that is, accepting user input and sending it to the network—is the next stage to consider.

Here's the hard part: We can't send data to the IRC network from just any process. Why not? Because IRC is a state-sensitive protocol, communication is bound to a specific client connection. PHP doesn't allow taking over foreign sockets from other processes; thus, the main process that also handles downstream communication (the process that acts as IRC client) runs isolated from all other processes. The question now is how we can open a door to pass data into the main client.

> How would you implement upstream communication? Make at least a theoretical approach. Draw the dataflow on paper. If you haven't done so already, write down at least three possibilities for runtime data exchange.

The downstream process must keep running and may not be terminated. We can't simply reinvoke it using a POST or a GET for passing data, since that would mean launching another process, with the need to re-login, re-setup, etc. Using such an approach would result in constant login/quit sequences that would be extremely disturbing in a chat. And it would result in data loss, since during the time between a logout and a login, lots of messages could be transmitted (which would be invisible to the newly logging-in client).

> The chat could be based on a single bot that stayed online all the time and recorded all messages for all users into a database. The user interface would then only need to extract all meaningful data from the database. However, two problems stand against this possibility: a) The chat would be mainly database-backed (something we wanted to avoid); and b) It wouldn't make the clients visible to other IRC clients, as the bot would be the only "real" client on the network. This would make usage of the IRC network ridiculous.

Thus, we need at least two independent processes: one that handles the IRC communication and can't be interrupted, and another to accept incoming messages from the user. Some sort of "container" must then be used to interface between the two processes. Figure 3.7 illustrates this problem.

Figure 3.7 Upstream communication.

The situation can be compared to a car race. The driver racing on the track is the "main client" and the racing team in the pit is the user input field. The driver is bound to the race he's in; he can't just leave the track and stop to see what's going on. Whenever the racing team flags him in for a pit stop, they "interface" to him—giving him a signal to make a break after the next lap.

What's being done is (leaving radio communication aside) to signal every time the driver passes the finish line. This signal works as the "interface" to the driver. Basically this is what we need to do, too—signal to our main process. Since the main process is event-based, we frequently get the chance to take control over the application and do what we want to do. This means that we can install a handler that "looks" frequently for a signal from the outside. The method to periodically stop and check for incoming data is called *polling* and will be the preferred method for phpChat. phpIRC features idle callbacks, which get invoked every time phpIRC has nothing to do and simply waits for something to happen on the network. Tagging a handler to this event enables us to watch out for a signal. Now, how are we going to signal something? This is actually pretty easy, using one of the following methods:

- Set a flag in a database.
- Create a lockfile in the file system.
- Use semaphores.
- Set a flag in shared memory.

These are basically the methods that we have with PHP to "leave a message." The following sections describe each method.

> Pipes can't be used for interprocess communication here, because a pipe requires two processes to be running at the same time. Our situation requires interfacing one constantly running process from other, short-term processes.

Note: Of course, more exotic methods are available, such as sending emails between processes. We've seen people doing this, but we won't go into that option here, as the disadvantages should be clear to the reader.

Setting a Flag in a Database

Setting a flag in a database is probably the *de facto* standard method for PHP users: Connect to a database, leave some data in it, let it be processed further by other processes. This method is extremely easy to implement and is available on all systems, but has a disadvantage. Can you tell what the disadvantage is?

The disadvantage doesn't come from the database *stuffer* (the process that inserts user messages) but rather from the database *reader* (the main process that retrieves all user messages from the database). To achieve a good "chat feeling," we need as little latency as possible—and thus a very good response time. The response time is crucial for Web-based chat, as this is how the user will actually feel "integrated" into the action. When the messages come slower and slower, users quickly become frustrated and quit. Our testing showed that a latency of more than a second is too much. To stay below this value, the poll frequency in which the main process has to read messages from the database must be very short; the default value in phpChat is 0.5 seconds (two checks within a second). Now, as soon as a lot of clients have to be handled by the chat system, the database gets quite busy and takes up more and more resources. At about 40-50 queries per second, our test server spent about one third of its processing time simply executing database queries. Even if this was a disqualifying benchmark for the database system (it should have been able to process many more queries), some optimization is obviously necessary, and this isn't the ideal setup.

Creating Lockfiles

Our next idea was that, if the database took up too many resources when handling interprocess communication, a file system might be more efficient.

But the file system clearly lost the race. Again, the stuffer wasn't the problem—creation of the lockfiles worked smoothly. To detect whether a lock was set, however, lots of calls to `clearstatcache()` had to be done in order to correctly determine whether a lockfile had been deleted or was still present. `clearstatcache()` had such a hard impact on the system performance that we didn't try to look further into this option; the chat only worked at a quarter of the performance it reached using the database-backed approach.

> Create your own benchmarks. Make test scripts accessing the database and the file system at high frequency. Write down your results and compare them. This is always a good idea when evaluating data-exchange methods—never trust theoretical descriptions of what the systems *can* be capable of! In practice, most things will look different.

Using Semaphores

Of course, the reasons for the poor performance of the former approaches are easily recognized.

> What are the reasons? Try to find and write them down. Try to find the critical points—this is crucial when having to optimize later on. "A chain is only as strong as its weakest link," and software is only as fast as its slowest inner loop. The process of finding these bottlenecks is called *profiling* and is extremely important.

When using a database, the bottleneck is the database: the time required to invoke the database, let it execute the (relatively small) query, retrieve the result, and determine what to do next (called the *overhead*) is pretty long compared to the result we're getting. In other words, we're using a huge software system designed for complex data storage to exchange simple, Boolean values—if there's something a database was *not* designed for, it's this. No wonder it didn't perform optimally; the bottleneck is the overhead, the time required for setup and deinitialization.

The file system performed badly because it was not designed for this usage, and because of other limitations: PHP doesn't include optimal file-system access methods. Determining the existence of a file requires constant cache invalidations and recaching—again, large overhead for a trivial task.

So why not use something completely different? We're surely not the first people having to deal with interprocess communication; others must have come up with good solutions for this already. And so we reach the next possibility: semaphores.

Semaphores do exactly what we want to do: They work as signals. Semaphores are counters stored in shared memory. You can "acquire" a semaphore and thus increase its counter, and you can "release" a semaphore, decreasing its counter. Additionally, there's the possibility of waiting for a semaphore to become free, meaning that its counter falls back to zero. This option has one drawback, however: Semaphores were meant to lock resources, to create some kind of scheduling mechanism allowing many processes to wait for available time on a device, or something similar. Whenever you're waiting for a semaphore to become free, the process that's waiting is put to sleep and cannot perform other tasks. If the main process was waiting for the user-input field to signal a new message, it would sleep and couldn't process the incoming network traffic.

No reason to give up yet; people have come up with still other solutions.

Setting Flags in Shared Memory

Shared memory is similar to semaphores, but a bit more versatile; shared memory is memory that's available to every process in a system. Multitasking systems are usually designed in such a way that each process is running completely isolated from other processes for security reasons. Different processes can share data by setting up and connecting to special memory blocks, namely *shared memory blocks*. These blocks can then contain variables (or any other kind of data, but PHP only supports storage of concrete variables).

This is exactly what we want: the ability to store a Boolean value in a place in memory where every process can look at it. Since shared memory works (as the name suggests) only in RAM, it's extremely fast and requires almost no overhead. With this option, every chat process looks for its own variable in shared memory and only issues a query to the database whenever it finds that variable set by the user-input field.

> Why is the data exchange still based on a database at the very end? Try to find some answers.

The database is still being used for one main reason. Shared memory is not supported by default in PHP; you need to specifically compile support for it into PHP. However, many people with access to a PHP-enabled server don't have the option of recompiling PHP because they only rented space on the server, because they don't have sufficient rights, or maybe because others depend on a certain setup of PHP. Leaving the database in as the final data-exchange path makes use of shared memory as an optional optimization. People who can't use it can simply disable it and still have a fully working version of the chat server—operating at suboptimal performance, but operating.

> When creating an application designed for widespread distribution, keep in mind that not everyone will have the same setup as you—and probably not the possibility of re-creating your very special setup. Even though PHP is 99% system-independent, some things do depend on the system. Carefully calculate whether enforcing certain circumstances is worth a potentially huge loss of customers.

Interface to the User

Now that we moved all the tricky parts with the data exchange out of the way, the actual HTML interface to the user is trivial. We know how to accept input from the user and how to deal with network communication. The last "problem" is packaging the generated output for the user in a convenient way. HTML offers only one way to have different windows act independently in one browser view: framesets. The interface typically consists of the user-input field; the chat output field; a *nickname list* (or just *nick list*), which shows other participating clients in the same room; and an action panel to allow one-click control over the chat for actions such as nickname changes, joins, parts, quits, and so on. These activities can all be handled by single processes whose output will be integrated into a frameset.

The main process, also responsible for the chat-output streaming, will keep state information updated in a database that all other interface components can access, retrieve, and display in a suitable fashion (see Figure 3.8).

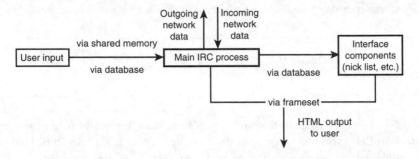

Figure 3.8 The final application layout.

Interface to the Developer

An interface for developers? What does this have to do with chat? And how is it supposed to work? Typically, most applications suffer from the disability of being "solid," meaning being either completely unmodifiable or difficult to modify by foreign developers. In terms of end-user-oriented software (for example, desktop environments such as Windows, KDE, MacOS, etc.), hardly anyone will ever find the ideal solution. Similar to a chat system, most people who download it say, "Hey, great, but it lacks this and that," or "Cool, but I don't like the way it does *xyz*."

Without an easy, clearly exposed path for modification by anyone using it, most applications end up in the trash. Most people won't even try to work on a program they didn't develop themselves if the ease of doing so doesn't hit them right in the face.

This means that for the chat application to consistently enforce independence of code and interface layout (allowing an interface to HTML developers) and to consistently enforce independence of data-processing steps, we need to create a solid *application core* (the part of the application that nobody should ever need to change) which interfaces to a distributed set of *plug-ins* (the part of the application that most people will want to change somehow).

Think again about the importance of these enforcements. Would you like an application to be designed like this? Would you even need it? Think about how this could be realized.

Interface to HTML Developers

In terms of the HTML interface, abstraction of code and layout is done using templates. This is the easiest possibility for tweaking an application to your needs, yet it's also the most powerful. Within seconds, you can change the look and feel—without having to modify a single line of code. Everyone with basic HTML knowledge could completely restructure the way the application would show itself to a user. As this method is discussed elsewhere in this book, we won't go deeper into it here. To find more details about using templates, please read Chapter 5, "Basic Web Application Strategies."

Interface to Code Developers

Providing an interface to other developers is usually associated with the term *API* (*Application Programming Interface*). APIs are normally provided by libraries (such as phpIRC), but not by complete applications. But applications that have the capacity to be extended by a programmer are much more successful than applications that must be used "as is." Of course, in terms of PHP applications, anyone can modify the source code, but many people refrain from analyzing a complex system and applying modifications to it. Thus, the application itself needs to expose certain ways of being extended.

Note: We're differentiating here between *applications* and *libraries*. Libraries are meant to be used by applications, cannot be run stand-alone, and are generally much easier to extend than applications. Applications consist of a full, closed system.

Try to find out how common applications can be extended. For example, for your favorite text-processing tool, see whether the developers provided the capacity to extend the tool's functionality.

Two primary possibilities of extending applications have evolved: Either the application provides scripting capabilities (similar to macros), or the application is able to use plug-ins. As for PHP, implementing a script language in a time-critical part of a system…we don't need to think any further. On top of that, the complexity of creating a full-fledged parser is way too much to ask. But plug-ins are much easier to implement and have many advantages. A *plug-in* is a little piece of code that can register itself with the application and catch certain events from it, get access to internal data, and so forth. While integrating seamlessly with the main system, plug-ins still remain isolated files that can be detached and spread separately. They can be attached to the system without having to modify a line of code, which allows a system administrator without any knowledge of PHP to extend the application by using foreign code. Concretely, this is realized as shown in Figure 3.9.

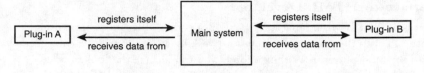

Figure 3.9   Chat system with plug-ins.

Design your own plug-in-system, at least theoretically. Create a minimal
application that's able to register plug-ins with itself and execute them.

When starting up, phpChat includes an include file, which in turn includes all wanted
plug-ins. Listing 3.3 shows how this include file works:

Listing 3.3   **The plug-in includer.**

```
/////////////////////////////////////////////////////////////////////////////
//
// Plug-in Integrator
//
/////////////////////////////////////////////////////////////////////////////

include("chat_plugin_out_htmlspecialchars.php3");

include("chat_plugin_out_link_transform.php3");

include("chat_plugin_out_colorcodes.php3");

include("chat_plugin_clock.php3");

include("chat_plugin_cmd_basic.php3");
include("chat_plugin_out_basic.php3");


/////////////////////////////////////////////////////////////////////////////
```

Each of the plug-ins is built up in the same way, consisting of a main part and an
event part. The main part calls two functions in phpChat, with the following names:
`chat_register_plugin_init()` and `chat_register_plugin_deinit()`. Each function
takes as a parameter the name of another function, which should be called for plug-in
initialization and plug-in deinitialization, respectively.

phpChat adds these function names to an internal table. Upon initialization of the
chat, as soon as phpChat is fully set up, it makes a run through the initialization table
and calls the initialization function of every plug-in that registered itself. Similarly,
upon shutdown, it runs through the deinitialization table. This method allows signaling
the plug-ins to activate and deactivate themselves.

To be useful in the application, phpChat offers a set of events to which each plug-in can attach itself. During plug-in initialization, each plug-in tells phpChat to send a set of desired events. Events might include the chat being idle, the user submitting a new message, the user clicking on a nickname in the nick list, an incoming message from the network, and so on.

At runtime, the plug-ins can intercept these events and perform certain tasks. The clock plug-in, for example, registers itself to the "idle" event and checks the current system time frequently. After a predefined number of minutes, it announces the time to the user.

For most events, phpChat also sends parameters (such as the message texts for incoming messages), which the plug-ins are allowed to change. For example, the list of plug-ins in Listing 3.3 includes plug-ins named `htmlspecialchars` and `link_transform`. These plug-ins change the output of messages; `htmlspecialchars` applies a call to `htmlspecialchars()` to all printed text (for security reasons, so that no one can insert malicious HTML code into the chat), and the link transformer detects all URLs and email addresses and prefixes them with `<a href=""></a>` or `mailto:`, respectively, so that users can click links right in the chat window (see Figure 3.10).

Figure 3.10   The plug-ins at work.

As you can see, plug-ins offer an extremely powerful way of extending a complex system. Consequently, phpChat has abstracted most of its own internals into plug-ins as well. The complete command interpreter has been moved into a plug-in, as well as the complete set of text formatting/printing procedures. This means that there is only a solid kernel that doesn't have to be changed because there's simply nothing in there that would require changing—the rest can be freely modified, extended, even removed, without any impact on system performance or operability. Have you ever seen an application that doesn't complain about someone deleting its files? Using this technique, an application won't complain—and will even dynamically adapt to it.

Plug-ins can be used in many ways, not just for chat programs. For example, you could also build a portal site consisting of the traditional news page, an email interface, etc. Using plug-ins, you can design a "site kernel" that handles all basic issues such as providing page layout, database back end, sessioning, and so on. Based on the site kernel, you can then create plug-ins for displaying news, sending and receiving email, even for providing different methods of logging in. Even if it's quite an effort, we encourage you to create a plug-in-based application as an exercise. It will be worth the work.

Listing 3.4 shows a plug-in template implementing a "dummy" plug-in as code base for new plug-ins.

Listing 3.4 **A plug-in template.**

```
<?

//
// Use these variables to tell the plug-in installer how you named your
// initialization and deinitialization functions. This is done to eliminate
// the need for changing the installer code, which would ask for errors.
//
$plugin_init_function = "myplugin_init";
$plugin_deinit_function = "myplugin_deinit";
//
//
//


//////////////////////////////////////////////////////////////////////////////
//
// myplugin_idle_callback(int code, mixed parameter) - example callback
//
//////////////////////////////////////////////////////////////////////////////
//
```

```
// This is an example for a callback function. See below on how to register
// and remove it from the call chain.
//
// $code specifies the reason for invocation, $parameter contains all callback
// information.
//
// The return value should always consist of a modified or unmodified version
// of the input parameter $parameter. The return value is used as input
// parameter for the next callback. This allows for multi-stage message
// processing and such.
//
/////////////////////////////////////////////////////////////////////////////

function myplugin_idle_callback($code, $parameter)
{

    return($parameter);

}


/////////////////////////////////////////////////////////////////////////////
//
// myplugin_init() - initializes this plug-in
//
/////////////////////////////////////////////////////////////////////////////
//
// Put all your initialization code in here. This code will be called as soon
// as the main bot is all set up with connecting and callback installation;
// thus, you can rely on a safe environment.
//
// Although the return value is currently not used, "0" should indicate
// initialization failure and "1" initialization success. This might be used
// later on to enable plug-ins to stop the current chat session right after
// login.
//
/////////////////////////////////////////////////////////////////////////////
//
// Return value:
//    0 - error
//    1 - success
//
/////////////////////////////////////////////////////////////////////////////

function myplugin_init()
{

    // register callbacks here
    chat_register_callback(CHATCB_IDLE, "myplugin_idle_callback");

    return(1);
```

continues

Listing 3.4 **Continued**

```
}

//////////////////////////////////////////////////////////////////////
//
// myplugin_deinit() - deinitializes this plug-in
//
//////////////////////////////////////////////////////////////////////
//
// All deinitialization code should go here. This function is called before
// the bot goes down; thus, all network connections are still active.
//
// Although the return value is currently not used, "0" should indicate
// deinitialization failure and "1" deinitialization success. This might be
// used later on to force delayed shutdowns.
//
//////////////////////////////////////////////////////////////////////

function myplugin_deinit()
{

    // remove callbacks here
    chat_remove_callback(CHATCB_IDLE, "myplugin_idle_callback");

    return(1);

}

//////////////////////////////////////////////////////////////////////
//
// NOTE: DO NOT CHANGE ANYTHING BELOW THIS POINT!
//
//////////////////////////////////////////////////////////////////////

// installer code starts here

// register initialization function
chat_register_plugin_init($plugin_init_function);

// register deinitialization function
chat_register_plugin_deinit($plugin_deinit_function);

// installer code done

//////////////////////////////////////////////////////////////////////

?>
```

The main code registers the initialization and deinitialization routines for this plug-in. The plug-in initializer then installs the callbacks this plug-in wants to intercept, and the deinitializer removes them.

Administration and Security

No system is a good system if it can't be administered. The days when "Netiquette" made it a point of honor to be polite and integrate oneself into the community are long gone. Nowadays it's common to be exposed to hacks, harassment, and other forms of attacks—and unfortunately, most of them don't stay at the verbal level. There's hardly anything to say against digging for security leaks and other holes in an application or network system. Constantly exploiting them, however, is worthy of condemnation, yet a lot of people consider it "fun." This demands an external interface, running independently of the main system, which allows full control over all of the application's data and users. In terms of a chat system, this means that we need to be able to kick users, moderate their messages, and secure chat rooms.

Note: Not all features listed here are implemented into the code on the CD-ROM. The basic administration system is complete and fully functional, but we'd like you to exercise and extend the code base with the features you feel appropriate. If you haven't made significant extensions to larger applications, we honestly urge you to gain the experience now.

The question for our chat program is this: Where do we fit in the administration? We have a few possibilities:

- **At network level:** We could filter users connecting to the server.
- **At PHP level:** We could prevent users from logging into the chat.
- **At database level:** We could discard messages from users from the database.
- **At IRC level:** We could use IRC's native network administration features.

Network Level

Securing at network level only allows two possibilities: letting a connection through or not. This could be realized using a firewall or other possibilities of IP masking. This method is limited, complicated, insecure, and in general not what we want.

PHP/Web Server Level

Securing at the Web server level basically allows connection to the server but restricts clients from logging in using password protection (or different methods of authentication). Basically it again boils down to letting a connection through or not, which is not really satisfying.

However, this method can be used to emulate user bans. The common bans for IRC, namely K-lines and G-lines (local and global bans of users), cannot be used with a Web-based chat system, as all connections originate from the Web server. The only ban-able address would be the address of the Web server, which would completely ban the whole interface from the network. To still be able to filter out special users, connections should be evaluated at the PHP level.

Database Level

The database level is a totally different approach. Clients are allowed to log in and chat, but their messages and session information are filtered in the database. Either an external tool or the chat code itself would check for the user to be allowed to say or do something and, based on this info, allow his/her messages to be inserted into the database—or not. But this strategy requires a very tight integration into the main chat code, is not very flexible (and kind of clumsy), and is inelegant to implement.

IRC Level

IRC provides native administration features built into the server code and network protocol (we hope you read the RFC and are familiar with these possibilities). Administration can even be done by regular users. Three levels are available:

- **Channel operators.** These operators have administrative control over channels. They can kick users, "mute" them, ban them, make other users into operators, and such (this level is available to all users).
- **IRC operators.** These operators have administrative control over the network (but not channels). They can kill users from the net, ban them, establish network links, and so on (this level is only available to special users).
- **Services.** Services have administrative control over channels but no control over the network, and are not able to perform like regular users. They also require a special login procedure (this level is only available to special users and is meant for automated clients).

As you can see, administration at IRC level can be done using a client running separately from the main chat system. A separate client with IRC operator and channel operator status would give the ideal combination of features that we need an administration system to have. Basically, only IRC operator status is needed initially, since as soon as the administration client has gained IRC operator status, it can gain channel operator status everywhere by killing all users from a channel. This is not a very nice method, but more effective and versatile than patching the IRC server code to give IRC operators equal rights to channel operators.

Implementation

The implementation of the chat administration is designed to be quite similar to the main chat script. A bot is launched, which, with the help of phpIRC, logs into IRC and tries to register itself as IRC operator. Then it waits for further commands from a Web interface. These commands are issued like those in a database-backed RPC (remote procedure call). The bot will frequently query a table in the database that contains input commands for it. The commands are put into the database by the Web interface and consist of a function name, a session ID, and a parameter array. Whenever the bot finds a new command in the database, it executes it and writes the command results in an output table along with the session ID. Thus, the Web interface just has to write a command with a self-generated session ID and then only needs to wait until a result dataset with the same session ID pops up in the output table (see Figure 3.11).

This method allows flexible remote control over the bot.

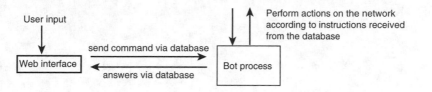

Figure 3.11 Database-backed RPC control over the administration bot.

Summary

In this chapter, you've learned from a real-life example how to plan a development project. We've outlined the typical stages of development:

- Analyzing the requirements.
- Choosing an appropriate technology.
- Defining interfaces and APIs.
- Implementation.

You've followed us through the whole development phase, and we've drawn conclusions from our example that are applicable in most software projects. With this background, you're ready for the next part of this book, and we'll introduce you to some important concepts of Web applications in the next chapter.

II

Web Applications

4

Web Application Concepts

We join spokes together in a wheel,
but it is the center hole that makes the wagon move.
We shape clay into a pot,
but it is the emptiness inside that holds whatever we want.
We hammer wood for a house,
but it is the inner space that makes it livable.

To understand the implications of WEB APPLICATION concepts, you need to differentiate between applications and single scripts. A *script* is a utility, and as such doesn't have any context. It doesn't know about other scripts in your system. An *application*, however, is designed to perform more advanced tasks. An application needs to maintain state and execute transactions, because it's interactive. Because it generally requires more user interaction than a single script, you also need to worry about security and usability. Of course, the return for all this toil is that you can create the next Yahoo! yourself. It's applications that make the Web interesting.

HTTP and Sessions

Imagine a KDE application, Kedit for example. (KDE is a windows manager for Linux and compatible X systems.) A typical operation might include opening a file, modifying its contents, and saving it under another name. Kedit knows what you're doing in every step of this process. It knows that you're editing the file, where the cursor is, where you move the mouse, and so on. Even if you open a second instance of Kedit, it won't get confused; selecting Save in instance 1 won't save the file from instance 2. This is possible because Kedit (or the operating system, to be exact) knows how to associate your actions with a specific instance of the application—it receives an event like "In the instance with the PID 4711 (a PID is a unique process identifier on UNIX systems), the mouse has moved to the coordinates 10, 4."

Maintaining State

When Tim Berners-Lee designed the Hypertext Transfer Protocol in 1991, he decided to make HTTP as fast as possible and therefore leave out any state information.[1]

HTTP has no mechanism to maintain state; thus HTTP is a *context-free* or *stateless* protocol. Individual requests aren't related to each other. The Web server (and thus PHP) can't easily distinguish between single users and doesn't know about user sessions. Therefore, we need to find our own way to identify a user and associate session data (that is, all the data you want to store for a user) with that user. We use the term *session* for an instance of a user visiting a site where one or more pages are viewed. For example, a typical online shopping session might include putting an item into the shopping cart, going to the checkout page, entering address and credit card data, submitting the order, and closing the browser window.

The good news is that there's more than one way to manage sessions. The bad news is that no way is perfect. Let's first sort out the ways that *don't* work, even if they might seem to be good choices.

At first, the typical PHP programmer tries to ignore the problem and find a workaround for it. The obvious workaround is to store all data on the client instead of on the server. This leads to forms with a lot of hidden fields or very long URLs. It becomes impractical with more than two files and more than one variable to save. An only slightly more intelligent method is to use cookies to store all information on the client side.

Data shouldn't be stored on the client side for several reasons:

- You lose control over the data—as long as the user doesn't return to your site, you can't access the data. And worse, that data may be manipulated when you get it back. Ninety percent of all Web site defacing and breakings come from applications accepting tampered data from the client side and trusting that data. Do not keep data on the client. Do not trust data from the client.

- If you use GET/POST, the storage isn't persistent across sessions.

- If you rely exclusively on cookies, you have a problem because some users won't accept cookies—they simply disable cookies in their browsers.

- The data is hard to maintain because you need to save all data on every page. Each variable needs to be URL-encoded, added to a form as a hidden field or added to the URL, or saved as a cookie. This is difficult for a single variable such as the session ID, let alone dozens of variables!

Thus, the data needs to be stored on the server. Where exactly you store it isn't all that important; it can be in a relational database management system (RDBMS), plaintext file, dBASE file, etc. Because a Web application generally already uses a relational database such as MySQL, this should be the preferred storage medium.

To associate the data with a user, you need a *session identity number*—a key that ties the user to his data. But, as mentioned earlier, HTTP lacks a mechanism to identify users. What should you use, then, to brand the user?

One idea that may come to mind immediately is to use the user's IP address. While this approach sounds logical at first glance, the associated problems disqualify it from being used:

- Many ISPs force dial-up users to use proxy servers; of course, $REMOTE_ADDR will show the IP of the proxy. If two AOL users try to use your Web application at the same time, things would get messed up.

- Some ISPs (for example, cable access providers) change their users' IP addresses once in a while to prevent them from running Web servers.

- Last but not least, the user could decide to close his Internet connection, go for coffee, and return 15 minutes later to your online shop (with a different IP, of course).

After you accept the fact that there's no generic way to identify the user with some predefined magic number, the only solution left is to create a session ID of your own and pass it from page to page. ("How?" you ask. Read on, we provide details a bit later.) This ID must be very random, or your users will try to predict it and take over other sessions. If the ID is linear, for example a normal number (page.php3?ID=5), you can bet that one user will try to open page.php3?ID=6. It may only be embarrassing if normal users can see each other's shopping carts, but it becomes a very dangerous security threat when hackers take over other sessions to steal credit card numbers or produce fraudulent orders.

PHP has a built-in uniqid() function, but because it's based on the system time, it's not secure enough to be used for a session ID. However, you can combine it with a hash function and rand() to construct a truly random string with 2^{128} possible elements:

```
srand((double)microtime()*1000000); // Seed the random number generator
$session_id = md5(uniqid(rand())); // Construct the session ID
```

Accessing the User's IP Address

You can access the user's IP address from the environment variable $REMOTE_ADDR. Use phpinfo() to get a list of all available environment variables.

Anyone who tried to crack this would have to perform a brute force attack over all possible elements; the attacker would have to find a valid session ID from 340,282,366,920,938,463,463,374,607,431,768,211,456 possible values. Cryptoanalysts Van Oorschot and Wiener developed a theoretical search machine for MD5 and estimated in 1994 that such a machine (estimated cost: $10 million) would take 24 days on average to crack an MD5-encrypted message.[2]

If this worries you, you should consider disconnecting your server from the Internet.

By the way, md5(uniqid())—the same construct from above without a rand() call—would not be sufficiently random; because uniqid() is based on the system time, it can be guessed if the hacker learns the local system time of the server. The space to be searched is then considerably less than 2^{128}.

Session ID Propagation with Cookies

Now the only remaining issue is making the session ID available to all pages of your application. One way to do it is by setting a cookie containing the ID. If you want to be able to identify a user over multiple visits, using cookies is the only possibility. Unfortunately, a percentage of your users may have turned off cookies in their browsers (some estimates show figures of up to 20%). Depending on your target audience, it may be acceptable to redirect these users to a help page explaining how to enable cookies.

Passing the session ID with cookies is by far the easiest method for the developer. Except for setting the cookie, nothing needs to be done by your application.

Manual URL Rewriting

You can also use manual URL rewriting for session ID propagation. This means that you pass the session ID via GET/POST or you "hide" it in the URL. You need to alter all frame, form, and a HTML tags to include a reference to your ID:

```
// A frame source definition
printf('<frame src="page.php3?session_id=%s">', $session_id);

// A hidden form field
printf('<input type="hidden" name="session_id" value="%s">', $session_id);

// A normal link
printf('<a href="page.php3?session_id=%s">Link</a>', $session_id);
```

If you have image maps, inline frames, or JavaScript redirects in your application, you'll also need to alter those.

URL rewriting has several drawbacks:

- It introduces a considerable amount of additional work for you as developer. You have to manually add the session ID to all links. If you forget a single link, the user's session will be lost.

- It reveals that your pages are generated dynamically, and some search engines will refuse to index the pages at all. Other search engines will cut everything after the question mark from the URL.

- The session ID will be added to users' bookmarks and printouts. We even know of articles in technical journals that have the session ID of a Web site included as part of a reference. From a usability point of view, it's harder for users to manually alter the URL to find specific resources on a site.

- The session ID is logged in proxy servers and shows up in the HTTP_REFERER CGI environment variable for other sites.

Dynamic Paths

Let's see if we can avoid some drawbacks of URL rewriting. For a start, you can add the ID to your URL in the Amazon.com way (see Figure 4.1) to make it look like `http://server.com/page.php3/<session-id>`. With this method, the session ID is part of the path to the script, and the URL looks like a static page to search engines and spiders. This works because the Web server knows that `page.php3` is a script, and stops looking further in the URL for files. But this way the session ID is not automatically available in your PHP script. You need to parse the path yourself to get access to it:

```
function session_start_from_path()
{
    global $HTTP_HOST, $REQUEST_URI;

    ereg("/([0-9a-z]{32})", $REQUEST_URI, $regs);
    $session_id = $regs[1];

    if(!isset($session_id) || empty($session_id))
    {
        srand((double)microtime()*1000000);
        $session_id = md5(uniqid(rand()));

        $destination = "http://$HTTP_HOST$REQUEST_URI/$session_id";
        header("Location: $destination");
    }

    session_id($session_id);
    session_start();
}
```

All other drawbacks of URL rewriting still apply to dynamic paths, though.

Figure 4.1 Amazon.com hides the session ID in the URL.

Dynamic Paths with *mod_rewrite*

You can avoid at least the hassle of manually encoding the session ID with a clever trick. What if the URL looked like this?

```
http://server.com/<session-id>/page.php3
```

The browser would automatically send the session ID on every request, treating it as part of the directory. Of course, if you try to use this format as is, you'll only get a File Not Found error, because there's no directory that looks like the session ID. We need a way to remove the session ID from the path before the Web server actually sees the URL.

This is where `mod_rewrite` comes into play. This is an Apache module that applies complex regular-expression transformations to a URL before passing it to the Apache server. Using `mod_rewrite`, we can simply strip out the session ID from the URL; this is an internal change to the URL, and only Apache will see it—the client won't. Apache will see a normal request without session ID, while it's still available in the usual variables for PHP.

Getting mod_rewrite

The `mod_rewrite` module is not compiled into Apache by default. Please see Apache's `INSTALL` file for instructions on how to compile Apache with this module.

An URL like this:

```
http://www.server.com/b6ac8ca8e453cdc43e6078abf044cdb5/script.php3
```

can be rewritten with this rewriting rule:

```
RewriteEngine On
RewriteBase /
RewriteRule ^[0-9a-z]{32}/(.+) /$1
```

The first line tells mod_rewrite to start up. The second line explicitly sets a base directory, which is only needed when using mod_rewrite in a local context, for example in an .htaccess file. The third line finally defines the regular expression used for the URL rewriting. Our expression simply strips out the session ID from the URL.

To start the session, we use a function very similar to the one we wrote earlier. Only the initial redirect is different:

```
function session_start_from_rewrite()
{
    global $HTTP_HOST, $REQUEST_URI;

    ereg("/([0-9a-z]{32})", $REQUEST_URI, $regs);
    $session_id = $regs[1];

    if(!isset($session_id) || empty($session_id))
    {
        srand((double)microtime()*1000000);
        $session_id = md5(uniqid(rand()));

        $destination = "http://$HTTP_HOST/$session_id$REQUEST_URI";
        header("Location: $destination");
    }

    session_id($session_id);
    session_start();
}
```

During all requests, the browser will assume the URL with the session ID included, and therefore send the session ID automatically with every request. This frees you from the hassle of rewriting all links yourself. That is, as long as you use only relative links in your application; if you use absolute URLs (for example, /directory/script.php3), you still need to rewrite those manually.

Dynamic Paths with PHP 4.0

Automatic URL rewriting is one of the *very* cool new features of PHP 4.0. To enable it, you need to configure PHP with --enable-trans-id and recompile it. Then the session ID in the form *<session-name>=<session-id>* will be added automatically to all relative links within your PHP-parsed pages.

> **Not for High-Performance Sites**
>
> While this is a handy feature, it should be used with caution on high-performance sites. PHP has to look at each individual page, analyze it to see whether it contains relative links, and eventually add the ID to the links. This obviously introduces a performance penalty. We recommend using mod_rewrite or DNS tricks instead.

Details on session ID propagation in real life will follow a bit later. First, we'd like to show you another way of session ID propagation, arguably the most geeky method.

DNS Tricks

The need to tag all links in an application with the session ID can be really annoying. PHP 4.0 has a way to do it automatically, but it may be a severe performance hit on larger sites, and it doesn't work with PHP 3.0.

We may have a solution for you.

Up front, the caveats: You need to be able to change the DNS record for your server, and the server you want to use for this kind of session ID propagation needs its own, static IP. Name-based virtual hosting won't work here.

You meet these requirements? Great. If you're proficient with name servers, you may know that wildcard entries can be used in DNS configuration. These entries usually map any arbitrary hostname to a specific IP; for example, we've got this entry to direct requests for everything below phpwebdev.com to the IP 194.242.199.228:

```
*.phpwebdev.com    IN    A    194.242.199.228
```

A request for http://this.is.one.cool.domain.phpwebdev.com will be redirected to the specified IP. Since the hostname is arbitrary, Apache must be configured to handle the IP—as opposed to name-based virtual hosting, where the hostname must be fixed and known. Our Apache configuration looks like this:

```
<VirtualHost 194.242.199.228>
    ServerAdmin tobias@dev.phpwebdev.com
    DocumentRoot /home/www/htdocs
    ServerName phpwebdev.com
</VirtualHost>
```

Our trick will also work fine if Apache's main server is bound to this address.

The scope of this is of course to encode the session ID in the hostname itself. On the first request to the application, the session ID is created, and the client is redirected to the new URL containing the tagged hostname, which will look like this:

```
355e1bce8828d4fb5c83c1e35ad02caa.phpwebdev.com
```

The advantage is clear: As long as you use relative links in your application, it's no longer necessary to bother with any manual URL rewriting!

We have modified the earlier session start function to extract the session ID from the hostname:

```
function session_start_from_host($host)
{
    global $HTTP_HOST, $PHP_SELF;

    ereg("([0-9a-z]{32})\.", $HTTP_HOST, $regs);
    $session_id = $regs[1];
```

```
if(!isset($session_id) || empty($session_id))
{
    srand((double)microtime()*1000000);
    $session_id = md5(uniqid(rand()));

    $destination = "http://$session_id.$host$PHP_SELF";
    header("Location: $destination");
}

session_id($session_id);
session_start();
}
```

A Compromise for Real Life

You've learned several ways of session ID propagation, which all work for real-life scenarios more or less efficiently. There may be some other methods—for example, embedding all your pages within a single frame and using JavaScript in the embedded pages to access the main frame's session ID—but as they rely on JavaScript, special layout setups, or other kludges, they usually aren't applicable in professional Web applications.

In real-life applications, we generally recommend using a combination of cookies and either dynamic paths or DNS tricks. If available, encoding the session ID in the hostname saves some work for the developer.

In the current session, the user's session ID is encoded into the URL or the hostname. Using the PHP 4.0 automatic URL rewriting is also an option, if the site won't get too much traffic. This works with all browsers, with cookies or without—ensuring that you reach the broadest user base possible. If the user has cookies enabled, the ID is also stored as a cookie. The next time the user visits, he or she will be identified automatically through the cookie, and you can welcome him or her with a personalized index page, as Amazon.com does. If the browser lacks cookie support, the user has to log in with a username/password—but afterward, he or she can use the site as any other visitor.

Summing up, proper session management does the following:

- Stores session data on the server.
- Uses a random session ID to identify a user.
- Saves the session ID (and only the session ID) on the client side using cookies, GET/POST, the script path, or DNS tricks.
- Ideally, automatically uses other means for session ID propagation if the user has disabled cookies.

PHP's Built-in Session Library

Luckily, PHP 4.0 has basic session management built in, as shown in Listing 4.1. While it's very easy and straightforward to use and may suffice for your needs, it lacks some of the advanced features that the PHPLib provides. Because the PHPLib also provides modules for user authentication, permission management, and a database abstraction layer, it's still a very important library, and is covered in Chapter 6, "Database Access with PHP."

Listing 4.1 **A basic example of using PHP's built-in sessions.**

```
// Start the session
session_start();

// Init the counter
if(!isset($counter))
{
    $counter = 0;
}

// Output session ID and counter
printf("Our session ID is: %s<br>", session_id());
print("The counter value is: $counter");

// Increment the counter
$counter++;

// Register our session variable
session_register("counter");
```

This example displays the session ID and a counter that increments each time you access the page. Of course, this example is different from a normal page counter—the session (and thus the counter) is tied to one specific user. With PHP's default configuration, the session cookie has a lifetime of 0; if you close the browser and reopen it, the counter restarts from zero, as the cookie has been deleted.

Let's take a closer look at the PHP 4.0 session functions. PHP's session management library offers the characteristics described earlier:

- It stores session data on the server. Because the library uses different storage modules, you can keep the data in plaintext files, shared memory, or databases. This reflects exactly what we've explained about storage media: Where exactly data is being kept isn't really important (well, as long the performance of the medium is sufficient).

- It uses a random session ID to identify a user.

- It saves the session ID (and only the session ID) on the client side using cookies, GET/POST, or the script path. (The PHP library provides all of these methods; we show how to use them a little later.)

- If the user has disabled cookies, the application can use other means of session propagation.

A Session's Life

A PHP 4.0 session is started by calling `session_start()` or implicitly as soon as you register a session variable with `session_register()`. On startup of the library, PHP checks whether a valid session ID exists by performing the following actions:

1. If `track_vars` is set to `false`, the library checks the global namespace for a session ID. If one is found, the library won't send a cookie with the session ID anymore, but it will also define the `SID` constant.

2. If `track_vars` is enabled and no session ID has been found in the global namespace, the `$HTTP_COOKIE_VARS` array is checked for a session ID. If one is found, no cookie will be sent, and the `SID` constant won't be defined.

3. If no session ID has been found yet, the `$HTTP_GET_VARS` and `$HTTP_POST_VARS` arrays are checked for a session ID. If one is found, the `SID` constant will be defined.

4. If no session ID has been found yet, the path (`$REQUEST_URI`) is parsed for a string in the form `<session-name>=<session-id>`. If found, the `SID` constant will be defined.

5. If the client request specified an external HTTP referrer (from a non-local site) and `extern_referer_check` (note the single "r") is enabled in the PHP configuration, the session ID is refused and marked as invalid. This introduces some additional security, as it prevents users coming from other PHP sites taking over a session (which is still highly improbable, however, due to the algorithm used for the generation of the session ID).

Generally, the `SID` constant will be defined unless the session library knows for sure that the client supports cookies; in other words, unless the session ID is found in the `$HTTP_COOKIE_VARS` array.

If no session ID has been found with all these checks, or if it has been rejected, it means that a new session should be started and a new session ID is created.

If a valid session ID exists, the frozen variables of that session are reactivated and reintroduced to the global namespace. It's as easy to handle session variables as it is to handle `GET`/`POST` variables: If you register a variable named `foo`, `$foo` is made accessible as a global variable automatically after calling `session_start()`. It's also added to the global `$HTTP_SESSION_VARS` array when `track_vars` is enabled. Because the `serialize()` function was improved in PHP 4.0, it's also feasible to treat objects (classes) as session variables.

Enable track_vars and register_globals

You need to have `track_vars` and `register_globals` enabled in your PHP configuration to use all functionality of the session-management library.

All variables you want to preserve across page requests need to be registered to the session library with the `session_register()` function. Note that this function takes the *name* of a variable as argument, not the variable *itself*. To register the variable `$foo`, you'd use this:

```
session_register("foo");
```

This code:

```
session_register($foo);
```

would produce something meaningful only if `$foo` was the name of another variable:

```
$bar = "This is a string";
$foo = "bar";
session_register($foo);
```

You can use `session_unregister()` to remove variables from the session library.

As with real life, it's not always easy to tell when a session's life ends—unless it's a violent death, forced by `session_destroy()`. If the session is to die of old age, different configurations need to be taken into consideration. If you propagate the session ID via cookies, the default cookie lifetime is `0`, meaning that it will be deleted as soon as the user closes the browser. You can influence the cookie's lifetime with the configuration value `lifetime`. Because the server doesn't know whether the cookie still exists on the client side, PHP has another lifetime variable that determines how long *after the last access* to this session the data should be destroyed: `gc_maxlifetime`. But performing such a cleanup of old sessions (called *garbage collection*) on every page request would cause considerable overhead. Therefore, you can specify with what probability the garbage collection routine should be invoked. If `gc_probability` is `100`, the cleanup will be performed on every request (that is, with a probability of 100%); if it's `1` as by default, old sessions will be removed with a probability of 1% per request.

If you don't use cookies but pass the session ID via `GET` or `POST` instead, you need to pay special attention to the garbage-collection routines. People might bookmark URLs containing the session ID, so you need to make sure that sessions are cleaned up often—if the session data still exists when the user accesses the page with the session ID at a later time, he'll simply resume the previous session instead of starting with a new session, which may not be your intention. On the other hand, don't set the `gc_probability` too high, especially if you're using file-based session storage. Running a garbage collection in this case involves `stat()`ing all session files, checking for the last modified time of these sessions. That's a very expensive operation and should not be started too often. Usually a `gc_probability` of `5` to `10` should be appropriate, especially if you destroy sessions when you're finished with a transaction (for example, when the user checks out of your shop).

Storage Modules

To read and save session data, PHP uses storage modules, thus abstracting the back end of the library. Currently, three storage modules are available: `files`, `mm`, and `user`. By default, PHP uses the `files` module to save the session data to disk. It creates a text file named after the session ID in `/tmp`. In the previous example, the content of this file would look like this, which is a serialized representation of the variable:

```
counter¦i:4;
```

You probably won't ever need to access this file directly.

If you need higher performance, the `mm` module is a viable alternative; it stores the data in shared memory and therefore isn't limited by the hardware I/O system. The last module, `user`, is used internally to realize user-level callback functions that you define with `session_set_save_handler()`.

The real power lies in the capacity to specify user callbacks as storage modules. Because you can write your functions to handle sessions while still being able to rely on the standardized PHP API, you can store sessions wherever and however you want—in a database like MySQL, XML files, on a remote FTP server (okay, the latter wouldn't make much sense, but you get the idea).

The function `session_set_save_handler()` takes six strings as arguments, which must be your callback functions. The syntax of the function is as follows:

```
void session_set_save_handler(string open, string close, string read,
►string write, string destroy, string gc)
```

Serializing Data

Serializing means the transformation of variables to a byte-code representation that can be stored anywhere as a normal string. Without this feature, it wouldn't be possible, for example, to store PHP arrays into a database. Serializing data is very useful for preserving data across requests—an important facet of a session library. You can use `serialize()` and `deserialize()`, but note that in PHP 3.0 these functions don't work correctly on objects (classes); class functions will be discarded.

Excluding Arguments

To leave out one argument, pass an empty string (`""`) to `session_set_save_handler()`.

The functions are defined as follows:

- `bool open(string save_path, string sess_name)`

  This function is executed on the initialization of a session; you should use it to prepare your functions, to initialize variables, or the like. It takes two strings as arguments. The first is the path where sessions should be saved. This variable can be specified in `php.ini` or by the `session_save_path()` function—you can use this variable as a wild card and use it for module-specific configuration. The second argument is the session's name, by default `PHPSESSID`. The `open()` function should return `true` on success and `false` on error.

- `bool close()`

  This function is executed on shutdown of a session. Use it to free memory or to destroy your variables. It takes no arguments and should return `true` on success and `false` on error.

- `mixed read(string sess_id)`

  This important function is called whenever a session is started. It must read out the data of the session identified with `sess_id` and return it as a serialized string. If there's no session with this ID, an empty string `""` should be returned. In case of an error, `false` should be returned.

- `bool write(string sess_id, string value)`

  When the session needs to be saved, this function is invoked. The first argument is a string containing the session's ID; the second argument is the serialized representation of the session variables. This function should return `true` on success and `false` on error.

- `bool destroy(string sess_id)`

  When the developer calls `session_destroy()`, this function is executed. It should destroy all data associated with the session `sess_id` and return `true` on success and `false` on error.

- `bool gc(int max_lifetime)`

  This function is called on a session's startup with the probability specified in `gc_probability`. It's used for garbage collection; that is, to remove sessions that weren't updated for more than `gc_maxlifetime` seconds. This function should return `true` on success and `false` on error.

The example in Listing 4.2 puts the user callback functions into action, defining a storage module to save session data to a MySQL database. (The full example, including the necessary MySQL table schema, is included on the CD-ROM accompanying this book.) Because `session_set_save_handler()` currently accepts only simple functions and no class functions, we've used good old structural programming instead of a class. Because inheritance or multiple instances wouldn't make sense for this type of code anyway, it's not a big loss.

Listing 4.2   **A MySQL storage module for the PHP 4.0 session library.**

```
$sess_mysql = array();
$sess_mysql["open_connection"] = true;
↪// Establish a MySQL connection on session startup?
$sess_mysql["hostname"]        = "localhost";  // MySQL hostname
$sess_mysql["user"]            = "root";       // MySQL username
$sess_mysql["password"]        = "";           // MySQL password
$sess_mysql["db"]              = "book";       // Database where to store the
                                               ↪sessions
$sess_mysql["table"]           = "sessions";   // Table where to store the
                                               ↪sessions

function sess_mysql_open($save_path, $sess_name)
{
    global $sess_mysql;

    // Establish a MySQL connection, if $sess_mysql["open_connection"] is true
    if ($sess_mysql["open_connection"])
    {
        $link = mysql_pconnect($sess_mysql["hostname"], $sess_mysql["user"],
        ↪$sess_mysql["password"]) or die(mysql_error());
    }

    return(true);
}

function sess_mysql_read($sess_id)
{
    global $sess_mysql;
    // Select the data belonging to session $sess_id from MySQL session table
    $result = mysql_db_query($sess_mysql["db"], "SELECT data FROM
    ↪".$sess_mysql["table"]." WHERE id = '$sess_id'") or die(mysql_error());

    // Return an empty string if no data was found for this session
    if(mysql_num_rows($result) == 0)
    {
        return("");
    }
    // Session data was found, so fetch and return it
    $row = mysql_fetch_array($result);
    mysql_free_result($result);

    return($row["data"]);
}

function sess_mysql_write($sess_id, $val)
{
    global $sess_mysql;

    // Write the serialized session data ($val) to the MySQL session table
```

continues

Listing 4.2   **Continued**

```php
    $result = mysql_db_query($sess_mysql["db"], "REPLACE INTO
    ➥".$sess_mysql["table"]."VALUES ('$sess_id','$val', null)")
    ➥or die(mysql_error());

    return(true);
}

function sess_mysql_destroy($sess_id)
{
    global $sess_mysql;

    // Delete from the MySQL table all data for the session $sess_id
    $result = mysql_db_query($sess_mysql["db"], "DELETE FROM
    ➥".$sess_mysql["table"]." WHERE id = '$sess_id'") or die(mysql_error());

    return(true);
}

function sess_mysql_gc($max_lifetime)
{
    global $sess_mysql;
    // Old values are values with a Unix less than now - $max_lifetime
    $old = time() - $max_lifetime;
    // Delete old values from the MySQL session table
    $result = mysql_db_query($sess_mysql["db"], "DELETE FROM
    ➥".$sess_mysql["table"]." WHERE UNIX_TIMESTAMP(t_stamp) < $old") or
    ➥die(mysql_error());

    return(true);
}

/*
 * Basic Example: Registering above functions with session_set_save_handler()
 *
$foo = 10;
session_set_save_handler("sess_mysql_open", "", "sess_mysql_read",
➥"sess_mysql_write", "sess_mysql_destroy", "sess_mysql_gc");
session_start();
session_register("foo");
echo "foo: $foo";
$foo++;
 *
 */
```

Page Caching

The session library also allows you to control how pages are cached. This is done via the HTTP `Cache-Control` directives. In the PHP configuration, the `cache_limiter` directive can be set to `nocache`, `private`, or `public`. As discussed in Chapter 6, this is very similar to the behavior of the PHPLib (but note that the PHPLib uses just `no` instead of `nocache`).

Page caching is set to `nocache` by default. This prevents caching at all, and is also the standard behavior of all PHP pages, as you may know. For dynamically generated pages, this is usually the preferred method, since these pages will often differ from request to request. However, you may want to rethink this strategy for certain parts of your application that don't change often—your server hardware will thank you for it. The output header will look like this:

```
Expires: Thu, 19 Nov 1981 08:52:00 GMT
Cache-Control: no-cache
Pragma: no-cache
```

Setting `cache_limiter` to `private` will allow browsers to cache the pages, but not proxies or other gateway applications. Note that this differs from the `proxy-revalidate` directive; in the latter case, the proxy is allowed to keep the content of the page to issue a revalidation instead of a full retrieval. The generated HTTP headers will look similar to these:

```
Expires: Thu, 19 Nov 1981 08:52:00 GMT
Cache-Control: private, max-age=10800
Last-Modified: Thu, 03 Feb 2000 15:56:11 GMT
```

The last possible value, `public`, allows full caching by both the client and proxies. Be careful when using the `public` cache option: Pages generated with this setting may be available to third-party users who have access to proxies.

When using public caching, the `cache_expire` PHP configuration directive will be taken into account. This directive specifies the number of seconds after which the cache will expire. The generated headers could look like this:

```
Expires: Thu, 03 Feb 2000 18:56:11 GMT
Cache-Control: public, max-age=10800
Last-Modified: Thu, 03 Feb 2000 15:56:11 GMT
```

PHP 3.0 Sessions

Because the PHP 4.0 sessions API is nice and intuitive to use, we wanted to have that for PHP 3.0, too. Having a consistent session interface for both versions would be great, we thought—and for some small projects you just don't want to use the PHPLib. So we had a closer look at `sessions.c` and ported it over to native PHP 3.0. While we didn't preserve some internals, such as the algorithm used for the generation of the session ID, we tried to make the API 100% compatible to PHP 4.0. Some limitations obviously do exist: Automatic URL rewriting isn't available, for example. But if you keep the documented differences in mind, it should be possible to use our library as a drop-in replacement of the PHP 4.0 session functions. The full source code can be found on the CD-ROM.

Our port can also help you to understand in detail how the PHP internal session library works. The `session_start()` function, for example, mirrors the original C function very closely.

Security Considerations

Example 1. In early 1999, we performed a Web site audit for a leading online job database. During the analysis, we discovered a security issue that left us speechless. The Web site had an associated online shop where visitors could buy books related to the topic of job hunting. The shop had been developed by an independent contractor who had already built several other online stores based on his Perl scripts and had made available on his Web site a demo including significant parts of the source code. Each time a visitor ordered an item, a plaintext file was generated, containing all order information, even credit card data—all unencrypted. And not only that, the files were stored on a publicly visible directory on the Web server—"for the convenience of the Web site maintainers," as he told us. This directory was "protected" only by the fact that it was declared as not browseable in Apache's configuration. Because the filenames followed a standard naming convention in the form "yyyy-dd-mm-hh-mm-ss.txt," it would have been a no-brainer for a hacker to write a script to search for files.

Example 2. Network Solutions, for a long time the only domain registrar, had the idea in September 1999 to give a free Web mail account to their premium customers. They created a username and a password for each account and mailed it to the respective customer. The username consisted of the customer's last name ("doe")—and the password was the same as the username except that a trailing "nsi" ("doensi") was added! For over 24 hours you could log into the system by entering other customers' "passwords." You could change the password, read mail sent to that account, and even send mail in the name of that customer.

Both security problems were caused not by flaws inherent in the programming language used, but by improper programming. PHP itself is very secure—we have never heard of holes like ASP's `::$DATA` bug. This issue, discovered in June 1998, allowed any user to view the source code of ASP scripts over the Web, simply by appending the string `::$DATA` to the file's URL (for example, `www.server.com/script.asp::$DATA`)—a software developer's nightmare. An earlier Windows-only security issue allowed you to access the source by specifying a URL like `www.server.com/script.asp.` (note the trailing dot), and after the `::$DATA` bug, on some versions of Personal Web Server for Windows you could use `www.server.com/......./` to get access to the entire hard disk, not just the Web server's document root tree.

Security has to be taken into consideration in the very first step of using a scripting language—its installation. As you know, PHP can be installed as a server module (Apache module, ISAPI/NSAPI plug-in) or as stand-alone CGI program.

If you install it as a server module, it's part of the underlying Web server and inherits its security. There are no known PHP-specific attacks for this kind of setup. Of course, you still need to have a secure server, but that's too broad a topic to cover here.

CGI programs, on the other hand, have been famous for a wide variety of possible attacks—both intrusion and denial-of-service attacks. Traditionally, the most serious problems arise when putting a script interpreter into the `cgi-bin` directory of a Web server. With some script interpreters, users would be able to execute any command through it. PHP tries to prevent some of these attacks. If invoked from the Web, it discards command-line parameters passed by the CGI interface—requests such as `http://server.com/cgi-bin/php?etc/passwd` will fail.

Unfortunately, another attack directly related to flaws in the CGI specification is still possible: You can access any file below the Web server's document root, even if the directory is protected by `HTTP-AUTH` (an `.htaccess` file), just by calling through via the PHP interpreter: `www.server.com/cgi-bin/php/secret-directory/file.html` would allow you to view `file.html` even if `secret-directory` is protected by an `.htaccess` file. If you're using Apache, enable `--enable-force-cgi-redirect` when compiling PHP to avoid this problem. Please refer to the installation section in the PHP manual for more detailed information on this topic.

Of course, choosing a secure installation is only the first step. A good programmer will keep an eye on security throughout the development process. There are so many possible risks that we can't possibly cover them all within this chapter. Instead, we'll try to give you some generally applicable advice.

Don't Trust the Web

All data coming from the Web is insecure and should be validated by your application. For example, there's no guarantee that your script is invoked from its associated form interface—users could bypass the HTML form and call the script directly, possibly specifying parameters via their own `GET` or `POST`.

Validating form data is one of the most tedious tasks a Web application developer has to do in his or her daily work. Basic checks can be automated with the routines of the library featured in Chapter 5, "Basic Web Application Strategies." For more complicated validation, we haven't found a generic way yet—so we do it manually. Such scripts follow the typical logic outlined in Chapter 5, which we call the *PHP Normal Form.*

Executing System Commands

Pay special attention to security when working with files or executing system commands. Imagine a typical source-viewer script that takes a filename as argument and displays the file in colored mode:

```
show_source($file);
```

You intend the script to be called with script.php3?file=script.php3, but what if somebody calls it with script.php3?file=/etc/passwd? Right—you have a problem because you trusted variables coming from the Web to be in a certain range (for example, the current directory). It's absolutely necessary to enforce such assumptions on the server, for example by using this code snippet instead:

```
show_source(basename($file));
```

Let's look at another example, a directory viewer that we found on the Web. (Listing 4.3 shows a slightly modified and shortened version.) The author, Marcus Xenakis, kindly gave us permission to include it here.

Listing 4.3 **Directory browsing with security risks.**

```
print("<pre>");
exec("ls -la $dir", $lines, $rc);
$count = count($lines) - 1;
for ($i = 1; $i <= $count; $i++)
{
    $type = substr($lines[$i], 0, 1);
    $name = strrchr($lines[$i], " ");
    $name = substr($name, 1);
    $dire = substr($lines[$i], 0, strpos($lines[$i], $name));
    printf('<font color="%s">', ($type == d) ? "blue" : "black");
    print("$dire</font>");
    if ($type == "d")
    {
        if ($name == "." or $name == "..")
        {
            print("$name<br>");
        }
        else
        {
            printf("<a href=\"".basename($PHP_SELF)."?dir=%s\">$name</a><br>",
            ⮡empty($dir) ? $name : "$dir/$name");
        }
    }
    else
    {
        printf("<a href=\"%s\">$name</a><br>",
        ⮡empty($dir) ? $name : "$dir/$name");
    }

}

print("</pre>");
```

While he confirmed our assumption that the script should be placed in a trusted environment, it shows some techniques that would make it a dangerous security leak if naïve users placed it into a publicly accessible directory. For a start, invoke it with `Directory_Viewer.php3?dir=/etc`. Nice, isn't it? You can browse *any* directory on the system from which PHP is allowed. But that's not enough: You can execute any command using that little script and easily gain root access to the server hosting it.

The key section is this line:

```
exec("ls -la $dir", $lines, $rc);
```

The variable `$dir`, provided the user, is passed directly to `exec()`. As you may know, you can concatenate shell commands with ;—so what do you think will happen when `$dir` is equal to `"/etc; cat /etc/passwd"`? If you want to pass this as an argument, you'd need to URL-encode the string, of course, so the script would be called like this:

```
Directory_Viewer.php3??dir=/etc%3B+cat+%2Fetc%2Fpasswd
```

And yes, it would display the contents of `/etc/passwd`. Instead of the `cat` command, you could execute any other command, for example `fetch`, to get and install a Trojan horse from your own server.

The remedy for this specific problem is to pass the `$dir` variable through `EscapeShellCmd()`, thus masking all critical characters that could be used to trick the shell to execute concatenated commands. Also, it may be a good idea to restrict it to list only subdirectories:

```
$secure_dir = str_replace(".", "", $dir);
$secure_dir = $DOCUMENT_ROOT.dirname($PHP_SELF)."/$secure_dir";
$secure_dir = EscapeShellCmd($secure_dir);
```

The principle remains: Never trust variables provided by users. Of course, this is valid for all scripting languages, not just PHP. The same hole is present in ASP using the `FileSystem` object, or in Perl when executing user-defined commands.

Tainted Variables

We must stress this: All data coming from the user space is to be treated as tainted, untrustworthy, contaminated, potentially evil. The Internet is outside the application space in this case; in trust management, this is called a *trust boundary*. The application space is a trusted environment; the Internet is not. Passing data from your program to the client doesn't need much special attention (given that it gets its data from trusted systems—for example, the database system must be on an equal trust level with the application itself). The only instance in which you have to take special precautions is when you want to guarantee that data is received only by one specific client, or that the client can be sure to retrieve the data from a specific instance (your server). With a normal HTTP transfer, these guarantees can't be enforced; you're advised to use SSL or an equivalent encryption layer in such a case.

Bringing data from a lower security level to a higher level (as when importing user variables) requires more care. You can't assume that the supplied data meets any requirements—not even if you supplied the data to the client in the first place. For example, you could check data in an HTML form with JavaScript on the client side, but you can't assume on the server that the data is in the format you expect because the user could have turned off JavaScript, or could have submitted the form from a Telnet prompt. Another common error is supplying data to the user and taking it for granted that it doesn't get changed. For example, a page might display account information for a user, called after the user has logged in with a query string like `script.php3?user_id=1`. Of course, nothing prevents the user from changing the variable `user_id` to something other than 1 and editing anyone's data.

Many Web applications today check contents provided by one user for another user. For example, it will be hard to find a message board allowing you to enter `<script>` tags or similar HTML code. For a developer, an easy mistake is limiting checks to only this kind of data—and neglecting data that's intended to be used only by the client itself. After all, why would a user enter malicious code that only the user will see?

The point is that "injecting" script or HTML code into the application is a severe trust violation. The malicious code is executed with the application's security level: It appears to be coming from the application itself.

Often, users can be tricked into seeing content that originally was only for another user's eyes. Let's construct a search engine, phpVista. A user submits a keyword, and the engine searches the Web for it. As you plan it, you imagine that only the user who wants to actually search will see the results, so you don't bother encoding special characters into the keywords. A user could enter `<script>alert("Hello World")</script>` as a keyword, and would actually get a JavaScript pop-up message in the browser (if JavaScript is enabled). As long as users enter the search terms themselves, this isn't much of a problem; the worst case would be that they crash their own browsers with malicious JavaScript.

But wait. Why shouldn't users point others to the results for a certain search they find useful? For example, on `phpWizard.net` you can find a form that automatically searches Amazon for all PHP-related books.

Now the issue gets hairy. An attacker can have a link to search results for the term `<script>alert("Hello World")</script>` on his or her public Web site. All users who follow this link (or submit the search form) will get the infamous "Hello World" message as a pop-up message in their browsers. You can do a lot more dangerous things than displaying messages, though. If we extend the example a little bit, we can use phpVista as a search engine in an e-commerce Web site, which uses proper session management and stores the session ID in cookies. If we also increase our attacker's IQ, he or she drops the Hello World pop-up and uses another JavaScript instead to read the cookie information and send it to the attacker's Web site, where he or she waits for incoming session IDs, takes over the other users' sessions, and buys some nice gifts for the folks at `phpWizard.net`.

While we're good at making up stories, this could have really happened: Amazon's product search engine didn't properly encode tags—until two days after a related security advisory from the CERT was released, which can be found at `www.cert.org/advisories/CA-2000-02.html`.

Even if you keep all this advice in mind and check all user-supplied variables, it's very easy to make the *wrong* checks. For some applications, for example, it's desirable to allow certain HTML tags in data. One of these tags is the `<p>` tag, which allows formatting text in paragraphs. It can take an `align` attribute, which specifies the paragraph's alignment. To match this opening tag, on a first try you could use the regular expression `<p[/>]>`. But many browsers support general scripting behavior on a wide series of tags; a user could submit any JavaScript embedded in the `onClick` or `onMouseOver` event of the `<p>` tag—and execute malicious code again.

The first step is to understand that all these threats taken together result in a very ugly picture. You have to be really careful if you want to avoid all traps. This is also the main reason we recommend having dedicated security consultants in an application-development team.

Some very general hints and guidelines to minimize these risks:

- Use sessions instead of passing data from page to page on the client.
- Validate all data from user space; this may include encoding or replacing the less-than sign (<), the greater-than sign (>), and the ampersand (&), and paying special attention to double quotes ("), single quotes ('), and whitespace, at least in tag attributes and attribute values.
- Make sure that your application operates in a trusted environment.
- Pay special attention to PHP's variable order (see the next section).

PHP's Variable Order

You know that PHP automatically makes available all `GET` and `POST` variables in the global namespace. Did you know that you can turn off this feature in PHP 4.0?

Although the automatic introduction of all variables is one of the features that make PHP so easy for novice users, it can be problematic in larger and more complex applications. If you access user-passed variables from the global namespace, you can't be sure where they really come from: Is it `GET`, `POST`, or cookies?

If you don't care about variable order, you accept that any user can call your script using *either* `GET` or `POST`. If not a security issue, this is at least bad style—*you* should be able to choose how the data is delivered to your application. Of course, PHP provides a method to access variables from a specific namespace: If `track_vars` is enabled in the HPP configuration, you can access an associative array for each namespace. The following table shows the available arrays:

Array Name	Contents
$HTTP_GET_VARS	Variables from a GET request
$HTTP_POST_VARS	Variables from a POST request
$HTTP_COOKIE_VARS	Variables from cookies
$HTTP_ENV_VARS	Environment variables, for example $SHELL
$HTTP_SESSION_VARS	Session variables
$HTTP_SERVER_VARS	Server variables, on our box $argc and $argv

Note that PHP 3.0 knows only the first three arrays.

Some clever project managers are known to set the PHP configuration directive register_globals (available only in PHP 4.0) to false, to force their programmers to use the $HTTP_*_VARS arrays.

You can also influence the order in which variables are added to the global namespace. By default, the variables_order configuration directive is set to "EGPCB". This tells PHP to introduce variables in this order:

1. Environment variables
2. GET
3. POST
4. Cookies
5. Built-in variables (server variables)

This means that if the user passes a PATH variable in the GET request, he or she would overwrite the environment variable—newer values override previous values. By using getenv() or by changing the variables_order directive, you can make sure that you actually access environment variables and not user-supplied variables.

Session variables always overwrite variables coming from any other space; because they're coming from an already secured trust zone, this avoids a lot of security problems.

Don't Reinvent Cryptography

Cryptography is the science of using mathematics to encrypt and decrypt data. It enables you to store sensitive information or transmit it across insecure communication channels so that it can't be read by anyone except the intended recipient. *Data encryption* is a science of its own—don't even try to invent your own encryption algorithms. Use established algorithms such as RC5 or Blowfish.

Encrypting with MCrypt Functions

If you compiled PHP with the mcrypt module, a wide variety of powerful encryption and decryption algorithms are at your disposal. The later section "The MCrypt Functions" shows how to use this module and how to find out which algorithms are supported on your system.

There are two types of encryption: symmetric encryption and public-key encryption.

Symmetric Encryption

Symmetric encryption, also referred to as *secret-key encryption*, uses the same key for encryption and decryption of data. *Data Encryption Standard (DES)* is a common example of this method. DES is a complex algorithm developed by IBM in the 1970s and approved by the U.S. Bureau of Standards in 1976. While it's relatively easy to crack this 56-bit algorithm (the DES Challenge III, a cracking effort sponsored by RSA Data Security, lasted for only 22 hours until the encrypted message was deciphered), it can still be used to encrypt non-critical data. Some data just needs to be "hidden" from normal system users and not be encrypted in a cryptographically secure way—it's a matter of cost versus benefit.

Using symmetric encryption, both sender and receiver of an encrypted message have to know the secret key phrase (the password). If only two people are involved in the exchange of messages, this is no problem. But consider a system with 100 subscribers, any of whom should be able to communicate in secret with the others. If the system used a single key phrase, user Joe couldn't verify in a secure manner that a message had been sent by user Jane. To allow this, every user would need to have a distinct key phrase—and every user would need to know all the other users' key phrases. Ninety-nine key phrases from others to manage, let alone remember—that doesn't sound like fun at all.

The main problems of secret-key cryptography are that the number of key phrases increases with the number of users in the system, and that each user must keep as many keys as there are users.

Public-Key Encryption

Consider the 100-user system just discussed in the preceding section. Instead of requiring 99 other users to know his secret key, Joe makes a key publicly available and maintains one private, secret key. Any of the 99 other users could now use the public key to encrypt a message and send it to Joe—and only Joe could decrypt it with his private key. There is an obvious flaw in this system: We've lost authentication. Joe won't know who sent him the message because any user could have encrypted it. The sender of a message therefore needs to *sign* it with his private key so that the recipient can check it against the sender's public key to guarantee authenticity and integrity of the data. This system is called *public-key cryptography*, and the two most well-known algorithms for it are Diffie-Hellman and RSA (RSA stands for Rivest, Shamir, and Adleman, the inventors of the RSA cryptosystem).

The main advantage of public-key over secret-key cryptography is the increased level of security and convenience. Private keys need never be transmitted to another party—by contrast, secret-key cryptography requires the exchange of the secret key over a communications channel, raising the possibility for an attacker to discover the key by eavesdropping during transmission.

Another advantage is that public-key systems can provide digital signatures, in which a user signs his message with his private key. Secret-key cryptography, on the other hand, would require a central database with copies of all secret keys of a system to allow digital signatures—Kerberos uses this method, for example. Of course, a central point with critical data is always a source of risk.

A potential disadvantage is performance; many secret-key algorithms are significantly faster than public-key systems.

Public-key cryptography isn't meant to replace secret-key cryptography; in some situations, public-key cryptography is unnecessary and secret-key cryptography alone is sufficient. When storing data on the server, for example, you'll probably use single-key cryptography. Because there are no distinct users in this scenario and the system knows the key for encrypting and decrypting, there's not much advantage to having a public and a private key. To transfer data to a remote system, on the other hand (for example, when sending orders from an online shop via email), public-key cryptography is preferred, as sender and recipient are two different users, communicating over an insecure channel.

The Standard in Encryption: Pretty Good Privacy (PGP)

Unfortunately, PHP doesn't yet include support for Pretty Good Privacy (PGP). As there are some Open Source alternatives readily available (for example, Gnu Privacy Guard (www.gnupg.org), we're sure that this is only a matter of time. Meanwhile, we've developed the basic class shown in Listing 4.4 to interface a command-line version of PGP. This class allows you to encrypt, decrypt, and sign files or strings with PGP 6.5.1.

Listing 4.4   **PHP interface to PGP 6.5.1.**

```php
class pgp
{
    var $pgp_bin    = "/usr/bin/pgp";  // Path to PGP binary
    var $tmp_path   = "/tmp";          // Path where temporary files are stored
    var $error;                        // Used to store the last error message

    function pgp()
    {
        // Check if the PGP binary exists
        if(!file_exists($this->pgp_bin))
        {
            $this->error = "PGP binary file ".$this->pgp_bin." does not exist.\n";
            return(false);
        }

        // Check if the PGP binary is actually executable
        if(!is_executable($this->pgp_bin))
        {
```

```
            $this->error = "PGP binary file ".$this->pgp_bin." is not
            ↦executable.\n";
            return(false);
        }

        return(true);
    }

    function _check_file($file)
    {
        if(!file_exists($file))
        {
            // Create a temporary filename in the path specified as class variable
            $temp_file = tempnam($this->tmp_path, "PGP").".asc";

            // Gently touch the file
            touch($temp_file);

            // Open the newly created file, write the string passed as argument
              ↦$file to it
            $fp = fopen($temp_file, "w");
            if (!$fp)
            {
                $this->error = "Could not open temporary file $temp_file for
                ↦writing in _check_file().\n";
                return(false);
            }
            fputs($fp, $file);
            fclose($fp);

            // Assign the temporary filename to $file
            $file = $temp_file;
        }

    return($file);
    }

    function _exec_pgp_command($args)
    {
        // Create a temporary filename in the path specified as class variable
        $temp_file = tempnam($this->tmp_path, "PGP").".asc";

        // Execute the PGP command
        $command = $this->pgp_bin." -o $temp_file $args ";
        exec($command);

        // Open the temporary file created by PGP and read it into $contents
        $fp = fopen($temp_file, "r");
        if (!$fp)
        {
            $this->error = "Could not open temporary file $temp_file for
            ↦reading in _exeo_pgp_command().\n";
```

continues

Listing 4.4. **Continued**

```php
            return(false);
        }
        $contents = fread($fp, filesize($temp_file));
        fclose($fp);

        // Delete the temporary file
        unlink($temp_file);

        // Return the encrypted contents
        return($contents);
    }

    function encrypt($file, $my_user_id, $to_user_id)
    {
        $file = $this->_check_file($file);
        $ret =  $this->_exec_pgp_command("-e -u \"$my_user_id\" -a \"$file\"
        ➥\"$to_user_id\"");

        return($ret);
    }

    function sign($file, $my_user_id)
    {
        $file = $this->_check_file($file);
        $ret =  $this->_exec_pgp_command("-s -a -u \"$my_user_id\" $file");

        return($ret);
    }

    function encrypt_sign($file, $my_user_id, $to_user_id)
    {
        $file = $this->_check_file($file);
        $ret =  $this->_exec_pgp_command("-es -a -u $my_user_id $file
        ➥$to_user_id");

        return($ret);
    }

    function encrypt_conventional($file, $passphrase)
    {
        $file = $this->_check_file($file);
        $ret =  $this->_exec_pgp_command("-c -a -z \"$passphrase\" $file");

        return($ret);
    }

    function decrypt($file, $my_user_id)
    {
        $file = $this->_check_file($file);
        $ret =  $this->_exec_pgp_command("-c $file -u \"$my_user_id\"");
```

```
            return($ret);
    }

    function decrypt_conventional($file, $passphrase)
    {
        $file = $this->_check_file($file);
        $ret =  $this->_exec_pgp_command("-z \"$passphrase\" $file");

            return($ret);
    }
}
```

Because the pgp class is only calling your system's PGP binary with the appropriate arguments, you need a correctly configured PGP system. Specifically, your private key must be set up correctly and all public keys for which you want to encrypt need to be in your local key ring. The public key must be a trusted key, or PGP will ask if it's okay to encrypt for that user, and the class will fail.

All functions work with either a file or a string. If you pass a string, it will be saved to $tmp_path as a temporary file because PGP works only with files.

Warning: On a multiuser system, anyone may be able to read this file! The use of this class on a non-trusted system (meaning that untrusted users are allowed to access it) should be carefully evaluated.

The class has six "public" functions, and two others are used internally. These functions return false if an error occurs—in that case, you can access a verbose error message from $pgp->error.

- void pgp()

  The constructor of the class checks whether the PGP binary is accessible. Returns true on success or false on error.

- mixed encrypt(*string what*, *string my_user_id*, *string to_user_id*)

  PGP-encrypts the argument what, which may be a filename or a string, with the private key of *my_user_id* for the public key *to_user_id*. Returns the encrypted text or false on error.

- mixed sign(*string what*, *string my_user_id*)

  Signs the argument *what* with *my_user_id*'s private key. Returns the signed text or false on error.

- mixed encrypt_sign(*string what*, *string my_user_id*, *string to_user_id*)

  Signs *what* with *my_user_id*'s private key, then encrypts it for *to_user_id*'s public key. Returns the signed and encrypted text or false on error.

- mixed encrypt_conventional(*string what*, *string passphrase*)

  Encrypts *what* with conventional encryption only, using *passphrase* as the secret key. Returns the encrypted text or false on error.

- mixed decrypt(*string what*, *string my_user_id*)

  Decrypts *what* with *my_user_id* as private key. Returns the decrypted text or
  `false` on error.

- mixed decrypt_conventional(*string what*, *string passphrase*)

  Decrypts *what* with traditional decryption, using *passphrase* as the secret key.
  Returns the decrypted text or `false` on error.

The MCrypt Functions

With the MCrypt library, many block algorithms are available, including DES,
TripleDES, Blowfish, and IDEA. Space doesn't allow for explaining all these algorithms here, or giving recommendations on how to choose one for a specific scenario;
this is covered in detail by many in-depth books and online articles, some of which
you can find listed in the Resources section of the CD-ROM.

Unfortunately, another library means another API style, and as indicated in Chapter
1, "Development Concepts," we think this is bad style. Why does `mcrypt_cbc()` take an
argument defining whether to *encrypt* or *decrypt* data? Wouldn't it be more logical and
consistent to have two functions, `mcrypt_encrypt_cbc()` and `mcrypt_decrypt_cbc()`?
There's no `session_var()` taking `REGISTER` or `UNREGISTER` as argument, is there?

Well, let's stop complaining. After all, we could simply edit the source for the
MCrypt interface and define these additional functions—that's the advantage of Open
Source software. So back to the topic. The example in Listing 4.5 shows the MCrypt
functions in use. The example loops through an array containing all possible MCrypt
algorithms and encrypts a message with each algorithm.

Listing 4.5 **MCrypt routines.**

```
// Set up an array of algorithms generally supported by MCrypt
$algorithms = array(
        MCRYPT_BLOWFISH,
        MCRYPT_DES,
        MCRYPT_TripleDES,
        MCRYPT_ThreeWAY,
        MCRYPT_GOST,
        MCRYPT_CRYPT,
        MCRYPT_DES_COMPAT,
        MCRYPT_SAFER64,
        MCRYPT_SAFER128,
        MCRYPT_CAST128,
        MCRYPT_TEAN,
        MCRYPT_RC2,
        MCRYPT_TWOFISH,
        MCRYPT_TWOFISH128,
        MCRYPT_TWOFISH192,
        MCRYPT_TWOFISH256,
        MCRYPT_RC6,
        MCRYPT_IDEA
        );
```

```
$message = "Hello PHP world.";  // Message to be encrypted
$secret = "Secret password";    // Secret key

for($i=0; $i<count($algorithms); $i++)
{
    // If this algorithm is available, $algorithms[$i] is an integer constant
    if (is_integer($algorithms[$i]))
    {
        print("<b>$algorithms[$i]:
        ".mcrypt_get_cipher_name($algorithms[$i]).":</b><br>");
    }
    else
    {
        print("<b>$algorithms[$i] is not supported</b><br>");
        continue;
    }
    // Get the block size of the current algorithm
    $block_size = mcrypt_get_block_size($algorithms[$i]);

    // Create an initialization vector from device /dev/random
    $iv = mcrypt_create_iv($block_size, MCRYPT_DEV_RANDOM);

    // Encrypt the plaintext with $algorithms[$i]
    $encrypted = mcrypt_cbc($algorithms[$i], $secret, $message,
    MCRYPT_ENCRYPT, $iv);

    // Decrypt it again
    $unencrypted = mcrypt_cbc($algorithms[$i], $secret, $encrypted,
    MCRYPT_DECRYPT, $iv);

    // Output plaintext and ciphertext
    print("Ciphertext: $encrypted<br>");
    print("Plaintext: $unencrypted<p>");
}
```

MCrypt uses block cipher algorithms to encrypt and decrypt data. *Block ciphers* are an application of the symmetric encryption method mentioned earlier, as opposed to public-key encryption. When encrypting a message with a block cipher, different modes of operations can be used to apply the cipher to the plaintext. ISO92b defines four generic modes that can operate on cipher blocks of any size: Electronic Code Book, Cipher Block Chaining, Cipher Feedback, and Output Feedback.

- *Electronic Code Book* (*ECB*) mode should be used with care. Each 64-bit block of plaintext is encrypted independently, one after another, with the specified algorithms. Plaintext patterns are not concealed—they show up as iterations in the encrypted text. ECB is therefore suitable only for encrypting random data, for example an MD5-hash.

- *Cipher Block Chaining* (*CBC*) prevents this problem by XORing each block with the previous block before encrypting it. Thus, the encryption of each block depends on previous blocks, and the same 64-bit plaintext block can encrypt to different encrypted blocks, depending on its position in the message. As it can also take an initialization vector as random seed for the XOR, it's much more secure than ECB.

- *Cipher Feedback* (*CFB*) mode does it the other way around: Plaintext is encrypted, then XORed with the previous plaintext block. CFB's advantage is that it works with blocks of less than 64 bits and can therefore be used to encrypt byte streams.

- *Output Feedback* (*OFB*) mode is similar to CFB, but has an advantage: Bit errors that might occur during transmission don't affect the decryption of neighboring blocks. However, by changing the encrypted text, the plaintext can be manipulated easily, just as with ECB mode.

In practice, CBC is the most widely used mode. TripleDES with CBC mode provides all the security you'll ever need in your Web applications.

Have Qualified Staff on Your Team

At the point when security becomes an important issue in a project, it helps to have qualified people for quality assurance and security auditing. Even if you're a very experienced programmer, you're human—and you may err. Having another professional look over your shoulder on crucial parts of a project provides for the necessary double-checking.

Unfortunately, it's difficult to find qualified and affordable personnel with expertise in software security. The topic is increasingly being taught at universities, but not even the best education can compensate for missing real-life experience—this is true for all jobs in the new media industry, but especially for the computer and software security field. These difficulties can be solved, though; by releasing your software under an Open Source license, it's quite possible that the industry's experts themselves will examine your system. Open Source, with its open development process, enforces *real* security—not security through obscurity, but security against all possible attacks by an attacker with full knowledge of the system and its source code.

Even if Open Source is not an option, you can apply many of the software development principles used in the Open Source community to your own product. Continuous peer review, for example, helps to avoid the most common security bugs introduced by insufficient testing.

Peer review can be formalized as regular code inspections, which help not only to avoid security-related flaws, but also other, more general software bugs. In weekly meetings, a team of up to five persons goes through new source code and inspects it for common errors such as missing boundary checks, unused variables, or security issues. A moderator keeps track of defects found and ensures that they're corrected later by the original developer. A typical testing scenario could be constructed like this:

1. A team of two to five developers is formed.

2. For about 60 minutes, the source code (about 200–300 lines of code) is inspected. Each team member goes through the code line by line, with the aim of fully understanding what each line does. All found defects are noted.

3. The moderator collects the notes and passes them to the original software developer, who should not be a member of the inspecting team. Rework can consist of changing code, adding or deleting comments, restructuring or relocating functions, etc.

We'd call this *discount software inspection*. In traditional software engineering, inspection is much more imposing; Fagan Inspection, as originally introduced by Michael Fagan of IBM in 1976,[3] requires more preparation, detailed checklists, and more frequent meetings. Web application development resembles rapid application prototyping, as a quick time to market is especially important. Inspection methods that are too time-consuming and resource-intensive are just unrealistic.

Authentication

You'll soon see that you need another technique again and again: authentication. For example, if your users should be able to access some parts of your Web site only after having registered themselves with the system, you need authentication.

The Login Process

Let's first look at the theoretical concepts of authentication. The login process happens in three stages: identification, authentication, and authorization.

Identification Stage

To be able to authenticate a user, you need to know his or her identity—you ask the user for an identification. Identification is a statement of who the user is: This can be a username, a customer number, or anything else, as long as it's unique among your user base. The term *user* in this context may mean a person, a process, or a system (for example, a node in a network).

Identification *is not* authentication! The fact that a user reported an identity doesn't mean that this identity is guaranteed to be authentic. Without authentication, the identity is suspect.

Authentication Stage

After getting the user's claimed identification, you need to verify this claim. This is the job of an authentication system. Users' identities are verified using one of three authentication types: something they know, something they have, or something they are.

On the Web, the "something they know" method, also called *authentication by knowledge*, is the most commonly used method. Users can choose or are assigned a password, which they have to remember and keep secret. Authentication is performed by checking whether the user's identity is confirmed by the password. Other variants are Personal Identification Numbers (PINs), pass phrases, or asking for data about the user that only the user can know. The principal weakness of this kind of authentication is the fact that it's often very easy to learn something that somebody else knows. It may even be possible to *guess* the magical "something they know" without having to access it—think of brute force attacks of shell logins. With Web applications, the advantages of authentication by knowledge usually outweigh this security imperfection; the user can take the password anywhere and has access to it all the time. Another advantage is the simplicity of this method and the ease of implementation.

Examples of *authentication by ownership* ("something they have") include keys, magnetic-strip cards, and badges. Unlike the first method, authentication by ownership is more difficult to duplicate, as the authentication elements are physical objects. For the Web, this kind of authentication hasn't yet been established as a valid technique, despite some efforts to introduce magnetic-strip cards for public-key encryption systems.

The third type of authentication is even more common. *Authentication by characteristics* ("something they are") is, for example, used in firewall systems to grant access to an object only to systems with a certain IP address or range. Outside the Web, you can increasingly see authentication by characteristics in systems using retina scans or fingerprints as authentication elements. While this method is the most secure of all three (after all, the goal of authentication is to verify who you are, and this type is very closely tied to this goal), it's also the most cost-intensive to set up. As we've already outlined, IP addresses can't be taken into consideration when identifying individuals, so you'd still need a personal identification system using a peripheral product.

Of course, the different authentication methods can be combined to eventually produce more secure results; for now, however, let's continue in our login procedure with authentication by knowledge.

The user specifies an authentication element, commonly a password, along with his or her claimed identity. But how is this information transferred from the client to the authentication system? Identification data is commonly subject to interception by an intruder sitting between the user and the authentication system (a man-in-the-middle attack). As a consequence, you need to protect against eavesdropping; a trusted path—a secure communications channel—is necessary to transmit the password. Always keep in mind that an authentication chain is only as secure at the least secure element—having 128-bit pass phrases won't help if you transmit them over a normal HTTP connection to the authentication system.

All Communication Should Be Secure

Even when the identification data is transmitted over a secure communication channel like SSL, there's room for man-in-the-middle attacks if the other communication after the authentication is not encrypted. An attacker may get the session ID by eavesdropping, and can so effectively hijack the user's session and take over the user's identity (for example, to buy articles in an online shop). To avoid this, all communication would need to be handled over a secure channel.

The authentication element is checked against an authentication database. The system holding the database and the way the authentication elements are stored need to be secure and trusted. The authentication database needs protection from general access, and authentication elements should be stored encrypted.

Backup systems need to be secure and trusted, too. Proper trust management also involves setting up roles that define who can access specific parts of a trusted system in which way(s). But trust management is too vast a topic to be covered here.

Authorization Stage

If the authentication indicates that the user's identification is correct, the system completes the login process and associates the user's identity and access-control information with the user session. In trivial applications, the access-control information may merely consist of a flag that the current user is successfully authenticated. In more complex situations, the system may also associate a security level or permission level, defining what the current user is allowed to do in the application (for example, there may a superuser or a read-only user group). Depending on the level of needed security, the system needs to log successful or failed login attempts; for example, the C2 Security Standard requires systems to audit all login events.

HTTP-Authentication

HTTP provides a method for user authentication: HTTP Basic Authentication. On pages that require authentication, the Web server replies with a special header to the client:

```
HTTP/1.1 401 Authorization Required
WWW-Authenticate: Basic realm="Protected Area"
```

The browser will then pop up a modal dialog box asking for username and password. Unfortunately, this type of authentication really merits the "basic" prefix—there are a number of drawbacks:

- To log users out, you have to apply tricks.
- To log users out after a defined idle time, you have to apply more tricks.
- If you need groups of user (what we called "permission levels" earlier), you need your own application logic to filter individual users to groups.
- It's impossible to brand the login process; the pop-up dialog will always be the same, regardless of the Web site.
- Novice users are generally scared of these dialogs. And you can't provide any help, as you can't modify the dialog.
- HTTP Basic Authentication over PHP is only possible with the module version.
- It's restricted to directories. What if you want to protect only one page? With Apache directives, that's impossible; you'd have to use HTTP Basic Authentication over PHP.

All this leads to the conclusion that it might be wiser to use something else except in the most basic scenarios, where you know that your audience is used to these dialogs and you don't need permission levels or idle timeouts.

PHP Authentication

PHP native authentication, on the other hand, makes it possible to use arbitrary login screens and authentication procedures, as it's form-based. For authentication to work, you also need session-management functions. Once the user is logged in, you need to remember this state across multiple requests.

You can write your own authentication library using the PHP session-management functions introduced earlier, or you can use the PHPLib. With its `Auth` class you can manage authentication, and using the `Perm` class lets you set up complete authorization levels. For details on how this works, see Chapter 6.

Why Usability Matters

You might wonder why a section about usability is included in a book about software development. We feel it's a necessity for any serious developer to know about basic principles for information architecture, user interface engineering, and usability.

As Web applications get larger and more complex, Web developers are challenged more than ever to create effective and functional Web sites, and usability becomes a key feature of these sites.

What is usability? The characteristic of how easy it is to learn and use an information system is referred to as the system's *usability*. As the developer of an application, it's probably easy for you to use it—but you may be surprised at how difficult other users find your system. Initially, they're completely unfamiliar with it and might try to use it for different things than you intended!

While usability engineers have tried to integrate usability issues into an early stage of software development, this effort hasn't been very successful. But usability needs to play an important role from the beginning of each project—starting to think about usability in the beta test phase is insufficient. We think usability should be placed on the same level as other traditional characteristics for software quality—such as correctness, maintainability, and reliability. As soon as you, as a software developer, understand the importance of usability in determining the quality of an application, you'll strive to enhance the user experience. How you can achieve better usability in your applications may vary from project to project, but some key principles form the heart of all user-centered development:

- Early focus on users, directly involving them in the design process
- Early and continuing evaluation of the application
- Empirical measurement of usability, even in early stages of the development
- Iterative design and development

Usability in Web Applications

Web applications have different characteristics than desktop applications.

With HTML, you can't control layout in a 100% reliable way, and you have to accept compromises in the display. Your site may be viewed on a broad variety of display devices, ranging from Palm Pilots to Web TV to a standard browser on an 800 × 600 screen.

User interaction is slowed due to the low bandwidth available today, and you can run only the most basic scripts with JavaScript on the client side.

In traditional software development, you can control where the user can go; you can gray out menu items or display a modal dialog box that blocks the application until the user answers questions. But you can't control the user's way through your Web site—he or she may be coming via direct links, from bookmarks, or from search engines.

And you can't expect users to read a manual to become familiar with your Web application—as is commonplace with traditional software—because users move between different sites at a rapid pace. The hypertext structure often leads the user to use the Web as a whole and not as a single application or Web site.

But basic usability engineering principles from "Usability 101" still apply, and we need to discuss some of these generic rules. The following guidelines depend on each other; you'll need to figure out what importance to give to individual rules on a specific application.

A user-friendly Web application has these characteristics:

- It's suitable for the task it should perform.
- It's controllable by the user.
- It conforms to user expectations.
- It's personalized.
- It's self-explanatory.

Is It Suitable?

The application should help the user to achieve his goal in an effective and efficient way. Users generally don't care about fancy graphics; they simply want to reach their objective—whether that objective is information retrieval or something more specific, such as ordering a product. In an online shop, for example, the system should assist the user to go through the ordering process as painlessly as possible. Amazon.com has set the standard on this: Once a user is registered into the system, it takes a single click to order a product. But task suitability may begin with single dialogs:

- Show only information the user actually needs to reach his or her goal.
- Make default values available. For example, prepopulate a date field in a form with the current date.

- Don't require the user to perform unnecessary steps. Instead of displaying error information on a new page, thus requiring the user to remember which fields were filled out incorrectly and go back to the previous page, provide the error messages directly in the form (use the PHP Normal Form). Figure 4.2 shows a comparative example of these two approaches.

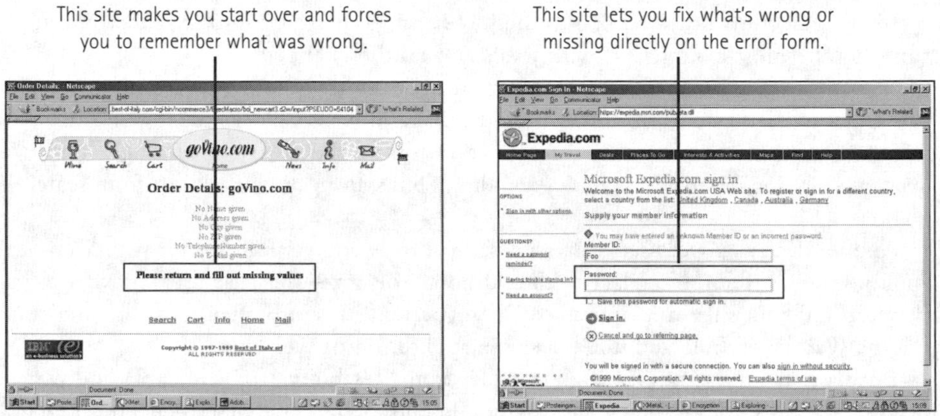

This site makes you start over and forces you to remember what was wrong.

This site lets you fix what's wrong or missing directly on the error form.

Figure 4.2   Steps in form validation: good and bad examples.

Can the User Control It?

A Web application is user controllable if the user can influence the speed and direction of the application until he reaches his goal.

The speed of a dialog box should always be under the user's control and not dictated by the application. This sounds obvious, but we've seen a great example of how you can break even this basic rule. After you had filled out a form incorrectly, the application showed an error message and took you back automatically to the form after five seconds. Of course, the data you had entered correctly wasn't saved, and you had to start over again (if you cared—we simply left that site). Users who switched to another software or browser instance after having submitted the form would never even see the error message.

You should also give the user control of the amount of data displayed. If a form extends over multiple steps, allow the user to switch between the different steps without losing data. Users often choose functions by mistake and need a way to leave the unwanted state. If the application is suspended by the user, make it possible to resume it at a later time.

Being controllable also means that the application should adapt to the user's needs and characteristics. In an intranet, for example, you can expect more experienced users, as they'll get used to the system in their daily work. Thus, the navigational structure and the application should provide shortcuts or accelerators to reach common goals—for example, providing pull-down menus to quick-jump to a specific page. These users also need more advanced help pages to satisfy their different knowledge level.

Does It Conform to User Expectations?

Consistency is one of the strongest contributors to usability. As Jakob Nielsen, the world's most famous usability specialist, puts it in his Law of the Web User Experience: *Users spend most of their time on other sites.* Conventions established on most other Web sites should therefore not be handled differently on your site. Dr. Nielsen's biweekly Alertbox columns show so much of his experience and know-how that they're a must-read for anyone working with product development in the information technology business. In his Alertbox for August 22, 1999, Dr. Nielsen provides a good example of what happens when an application fails to conform to user expectations:[4]

> *Eric Davis, an Information Architect with Resource Marketing, recently reported on a usability test of shopping cart terminology. The draft design featured the term "Shopping Sled" since the site (selling winter sports products) had a desire to stand out and avoid standard terminology. Result: "50% of users did not understand The Sled concept. The other 50% said that they figured out what it meant because it was in the same location as a cart would be. They knew that you had to add to something, and the only something that made any kind of sense was the Sled." Lesson: Do not try to be smart and use new terms when we have good words available that users already know.*

Consistency also means that the behavior of and data display in dialog boxes should be uniform:

- Always display system messages (status feedback, error or success messages) in the same place on a page and in the same layout.
- Label buttons and links with a consistent naming scheme.
- Use a consistent means to change the state of a dialog. For example, always place the submit button of a form in the lower-right corner.
- Don't invent your own GUI elements if you can avoid it. For example, a Web site we audited used images instead of plain HTML check boxes. Clicking on the image reloaded the page with a new variation of the check box image (depending on the previous state, either checked or unchecked). It would be hard to find a more annoying method.

Is It Personalized?

"Personalized content" is one of the top buzzwords on the Internet today. We don't really mean the same thing as the marketing people deliberately promoting *personalized* advertising, *personalized* spam mail, or *personalized* news. For us, personalized Web applications simply means applications that are tailored to the needs and cultural characteristics of individual users.

As European Internet users, we often see the saying confirmed that U.S. citizens tend to have an America-centric view of the world. Usernames that choke on German umlaut, scheduling applications where you can't enter timezone information, information systems relying on U.S. ZIP codes—the list could go on *ad infinitum* (see Figure 4.3). While it may cost time and resources to develop an application that can be used by an international audience, it certainly pays off; as of September, 1999, about 50% of the Web's users were not from the U.S.

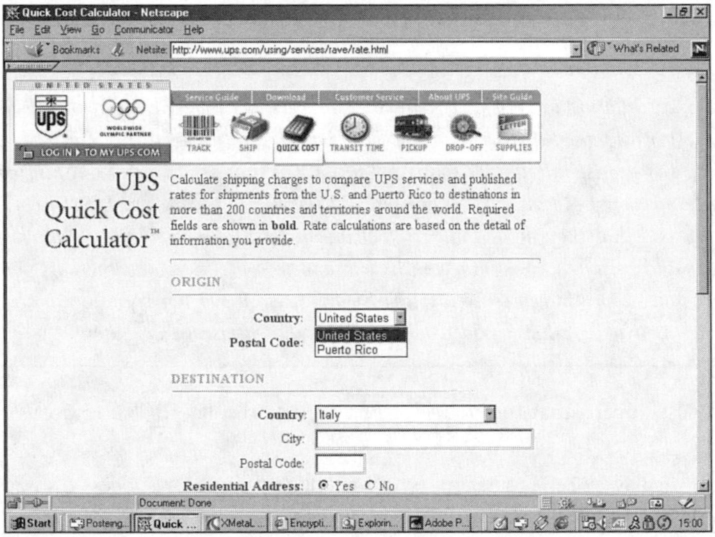

Figure 4.3   The UPS shipping cost calculator accepts only the U.S. and Puerto Rico as origin for a package, even though UPS ships from 50 countries.

Is It Self-Explanatory?

An application is self-explanatory if it helps the user to learn and understand the system. This is especially important on the Web; most users are novices with respect to your site. Users move from Web site to Web site, and usually they won't remember the conventions and rules from your site the next time they visit it. So it's better to spend time simplifying a dialog box than to spend time making available a help system for each form field. (For non-trivial forms, though, a context-sensitive help system is appropriate.)

For many applications, we've found that it helps the user to make a demo available where the user can experiment or is led through step by step.

Bringing consistency to an application also helps to make it self-explanatory. If a warning message always appears in the same layout at the same place, the user will recognize it as a system warning more easily.

Discount Usability Engineering

In real life, people rarely use the recommended usability-engineering methods on software development projects. One important reason for this failure is the cost of using traditional usability-engineering techniques. In the highly respected magazine *Communications of the ACM*, authors Mantei and Teorey[5] estimated in 1988 that the "costs required to add human factors elements to the development of software" were over \$120,000—regardless of the size of the software development project—as the estimation consisted largely in evaluating fixed costs like testing and evaluation, lab construction, product analysis, and so on, which don't change with the size of the project and code under development. This figure is more than the *entire budget* of many Web site development projects. It's no surprise that a project manager reading about such sums dumps usability methods altogether.

Jakob Nielsen's "discount usability engineering" approach (`www.useit.com/papers/guerrilla_hci.html`) is intended to make usability engineering easier, cheaper, and less time-consuming. When he researched this method in 1989, he found that for most projects it wasn't necessary to apply all traditional usability engineering methods. Indeed, with a basic set of techniques, he was able to improve usability considerably.

Based on the principle of early focus on users, he uses these techniques, discussed in the following sections:

- Scenarios
- Simplified thinking aloud
- Heuristic evaluation

Scenarios

A *scenario* is a very reduced set of features or functionality that's subject to usability testing. Traditional usability engineering uses more complex test cases, which are difficult to set up and difficult to test. Since the "discount scenario" is small, you can afford to change it frequently and use it for testing different versions of a prototype.

Such a scenario is constructed on the basis of a task analysis of the real users and their work in order to be as representative as possible of the actual use of the system. Typical scenarios might be the tasks "Print the document" or "Book a flight to Honolulu for January 1st, 2001," which can then be user-tested with the simplified thinking aloud method (described in the following section).

Simplified Thinking Aloud

In a *thinking aloud* study, a user is monitored while performing a previously defined task in a scenario. Traditionally, these studies were conducted by psychologists or usability experts who videotaped the testers and then conducted detailed analysis. Again, this sophisticated methodology is cost-intensive and may be intimidating to developers. However, it's possible to run a test without a sophisticated lab, simply by bringing in some real users, giving them some typical test tasks, and asking them to think out loud while performing the tasks.

Simplified thinking aloud tests ideally involve three to five users, while the traditional method requires ten or more users to get valid data. But the focus of discount usability engineering isn't gaining statistically valid data; it's finding most of the usability problems as fast as possible. Indeed, studies show that most usability problems can be found with the first tests performed.

Instead of videotaping the participants, the experimenters take notes on paper about the users' behavior. Recording, watching, and analyzing videotapes is expensive and involves at least one additional person to handle the camera. Analyzing paper notes is quick and nonetheless efficient. The time gained is better spent on running additional tests and testing different iterations of an interface.

Heuristic Evaluation

Heuristic evaluation is a method to find usability problems in an interface. A small set of evaluators tests the interface and judges its compliance with established user interface design principles (the *heuristics*). These principles may be those described earlier, Nielsen's 10 Recommended Heuristics for user interface design (see sidebar), or a custom set of principles tailored for a specific environment.

Evaluators don't need to be usability experts—even non-experts can find many usability problems by heuristic evaluation, and many of the remaining problems would be revealed by the simplified thinking aloud test. As different people locate different usability problems, it also helps to let three to five people perform a heuristic evaluation. One project lead should then organize the results from each evaluator and create a detailed test report that should be presented at an interdisciplinary brainstorm meeting.

With heuristic evaluation, only the interface is tested for problems. The evaluators don't actually use the system; they simply take the heuristics as a checklist and try to find as many offenses against them as possible. Therefore, this approach must be used as a complement to the other discount usability engineering methods.

Jakob Nielsen's Ten Usability Heuristics

(www.useit.com/papers/heuristic/heuristic_list.html)

Visibility of system status

The system should always keep users informed about what is going on, through appropriate feedback within reasonable time.

Match between system and the real world

The system should speak the users' language, with words, phrases, and concepts familiar to the user, rather than system-oriented terms. Follow real-world conventions, making information appear in a natural and logical order.

User control and freedom

Users often choose system functions by mistake and will need a clearly marked "emergency exit" to leave the unwanted state without having to go through an extended dialogue. Support undo and redo.

Consistency and standards

Users should not have to wonder whether different words, situations, or actions mean the same thing. Follow platform conventions.

Error prevention

Even better than good error messages is a careful design that prevents a problem from occurring in the first place.

Recognition rather than recall

Make objects, actions, and options visible. The user should not have to remember information from one part of the dialog to another. Instructions for use of the system should be visible or easily retrievable whenever appropriate.

Flexibility and efficiency of use

Accelerators—unseen by the novice user—may often speed up the interaction for the expert user such that the system can cater to both inexperienced and experienced users. Allow users to tailor frequent actions.

Aesthetic and minimalist design

Dialogs should not contain information that is irrelevant or rarely needed. Every extra unit of information in a dialog competes with the relevant units of information and diminishes their relative visibility.

Help users recognize, diagnose, and recover from errors

Error messages should be expressed in plain language (no codes), precisely indicate the problem, and constructively suggest a solution.

Help and documentation

Even though it is better if the system can be used without documentation, it may be necessary to provide help and documentation. Any such information should be easy to search, focus on the user's task, list concrete steps to be carried out, and not be too large.

Usability: Just Do It

Nielsen says, "Two of the fundamental slogans of discount usability engineering are that 'any data is data' and 'anything is better than nothing' when it comes to usability." We encourage you to try discount usability engineering—and to apply it in your development as often and regularly as possible. It doesn't cost much and will significantly enhance the user experience.

Summary

In this chapter, you have learned the basics of session management, how to pass data from page to page, and how to recognize your users. You can create sessions with PHP 3.0 and 4.0 using different storage methods, and know which ones to choose under which circumstances. On top of that, you have learned to pay attention to securing the data your users will entrust to you, as well as to securing your site against misuse. You know the basics of different encryption technologies and their application fields.

Usability is not a foreign word for you anymore, and we hope that you've learned about the importance of making your site simply suitable for its purpose. You know most of the common *faux pas* and can identify interface design weaknesses without rocketing your development costs sky-high.

After all, it's your users who finally decide about success or failure of your projects—and this chapter has shown you how to satisfy them.

References

[1]See the historical protocol definition at www.w3.org/Protocols/HTTP/AsImplemented.html.

[2]Wiener, M.J. "Efficient DES Key Search." *Technical Report TR244*, School of Computer Science, Carleton University, Ottawa, Canada (May 1994).

[3]Fagan, M. E. "Design and Code Inspections to Reduce Errors in Program Development," *IBM Systems Journal*, Vol. 15, No. 3 (1976): 182–211.

[4]Nielsen, Jakob. "Alertbox" (August 22, 1999). See www.useit.com/alertbox/990822.html.

[5]Mantei, M. M., and Teorey, T.J. "Cost/benefit analysis for incorporating human factors in the software lifecycle," *Communications of the ACM* 31, 4 (April 1988): 428–439.

5

Basic Web Application Strategies

When people see some things as beautiful,
other things become ugly.
When people see some things as good,
other things become bad.

Cʜᴀᴘᴛᴇʀ 4, "Wᴇʙ Aᴘᴘʟɪᴄᴀᴛɪᴏɴ Cᴏɴᴄᴇᴘᴛs," ᴅᴇsᴄʀɪʙᴇs ᴛʜᴇ fundamental differences between Web applications and stand-alone scripts, and shows methods to solve the most basic problem—session management. This chapter explores strategies to deal with other common issues that arise when working on larger projects. While we will present solutions that we've found to be time-saving, effective, and easy to implement, we encourage you to evaluate whether they really fit your needs—the chapter is titled "Web Application Strategies" and not "Web Application Solutions" for a purpose. It's better to spend more time on evaluation than on having to reorganize a project; as stated in Chapter 1, "PHP Concepts," *time is the most valuable resource that you will never have enough of.*

In the beginning, there was the HTML form. Almost every Web application solicits information from the user. Therefore, it's important to pay special attention to form validation routines—you need to find a generic handling routine if you don't want to reinvent the wheel over and over. The first part of this chapter describes the PHP Normal Form and how to use the `EasyTemplate` class to separate code from design.

Using a template mechanism allows for better collaboration in multiple-discipline development teams. But it's only a small facet in team management; we also show how to organize your projects and how to use version-management software.

Then, on the way to the next chapter, we'll stop by in the marketing department and discuss the real benefits of multi-tier applications.

The PHP Normal Form

How do you validate your form data? Using JavaScript? A second action-handler script? Maybe not at all, or only partially?

As explained in Chapter 4, data supplied by a user in a form submission or query should be treated as "contaminated" until it has been validated by your application. So you'd better check that input. But how to validate it?

JavaScript is one commonly used method. But JavaScript should never be the only validation method used—the user may have turned it off due to the security risks related to client-side scripting, or the browser may not even support it. In a worst-case scenario for your Web site users, you'll have to deal with disabled JavaScript capabilities. Because of the different implementations of JavaScript among browsers, more complicated validation—for example, pattern matching with regular expressions—is either completely impossible to realize or a development nightmare. And while *security through obscurity* is never a good principle, sometimes you don't want the user to see all your validation rules using the View Source feature of his browser.

Of course, if it was reliable to use, JavaScript (or better client-side validation in general) would be our preferred method. The primary advantage of client-side validation is speed: Syntactical validation could be done instantly, eliminating the need to send the form data to the Web server, parse it there, and send an entire page as response back to the browser—a tedious and slow procedure. In the current situation, however, JavaScript can only be used as an add-on for server-side validation.

So PHP comes into play again. Even with PHP, there are many ways to provide form validation. Most new users will choose the straightforward technique of having two separate files—one containing the HTML of the form and one containing the PHP action-handler script. This is most common with traditional Perl/CGI scripting. In most situations, we dislike this scenario for its several drawbacks:

- You need two separate files. As innocent as this may sound, it becomes quite a problem when dealing with large projects containing hundreds of PHP files.
- It leads to those "Your form has an error, please use your Back button to return to the form" pages that we bashed in Chapter 4.
- It's easier to pre-populate form fields when validation and form are in one file—it doesn't matter then where the "pre-populating" data comes from, whether from the user in case of an error, or from a database for an editing page.

From our experience, the PHP Normal Form (shown in Figure 5.1) is the most versatile option to process forms. Of course, other strategies may fit better to your specific needs, but the logic we outline in the Normal Form is so generic that it can be applied to most forms. Basically, the PHP Normal Form combines the user interface (the form) and application logic in one page, while still separating HTML layout from code. On the first request of the page, the form is shown. When the user submits it, the application validates the data.

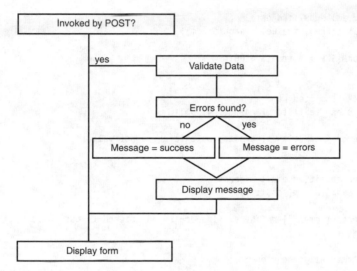

Figure 5.1 The PHP Normal Form.

Let's construct a simple form as an example (Listing 5.1 shows the source). We want the user to enter his or her name and email address. At the top of the script, the application logic checks whether the script has been invoked by submitting the form. If this is the case, the CGI environment variable `$REQUEST_METHOD` is set to `POST` and the application knows it should begin to validate the form data.

Listing 5.1 **Sample PHP Normal Form.**

```
/*
 *      mixed sprint_error(string string)
 *      Return a formatted error message or nothing if the passed argument is
        ↪empty
 */
function sprint_error($string)
{
    if(!empty($string))
    {
        return("<br><font color=\"red\"><b> ! </b></font>$string\n");
    }
}
```

continues

Listing 5.1 **Continued**

```php
// Initialize $message
$message = "Please fill out this form:";

// Has the form been posted?
if($REQUEST_METHOD == "POST")
{
    // Initialize the errors array
    $errors = array();

    // Trim all submitted data
    while(list($key, $value) = each($form))
    {
        $form[$key] = trim($value);
    }

    // Check submitted name
    if(!is_clean_text($form["name"], 4, 30))
    {
        $errors["name"] = "The name you entered is not valid.";
    }

    // Check submitted email address
    if(!is_email($form["email"]))
    {
        $errors["email"] = "The email address you entered is not valid.";
    }

    print('<div align="center">');

    // Can the form be processed or are there any errors?
    if(count($errors) == 0)
    {
        print("The form has been processed.<p>");
        printf("Name: %s<br>", $form["name"]);
        printf("Email: %s<br>", $form["email"]);
        phpBook_footer("../");
        exit;
    }
    else
    {
        $message = "There were some errors. Please see below for details.";
    }

    print('</div>');
}

// Create a new EasyTemplate class
$template = new EasyTemplate("PHP_Normal_Form.inc.html");

// Assign template values
$template->assign("HEADER", $message);
$template->assign("ACTION", basename($PHP_SELF));
$template->assign("NAME_VALUE", isset($form["name"]) ? $form["name"] : "");
```

```
$template->assign("EMAIL_VALUE",  isset($form["email"]) ? $form["email"] : "");
$template->assign("NAME_ERROR", sprint_error($errors["name"]));
$template->assign("EMAIL_ERROR",  sprint_error($errors["email"]));

// Print the template
$template->easy_print() or die($template->error);
```

Tip: $REQUEST_METHOD is obviously a variable of global scope and thus not available inside functions. You can access it there using the $GLOBALS array with $GLOBALS["REQUEST_METHOD"] or by doing a global $REQUEST_METHOD;.

The submitted data is validated for syntactical correctness using two functions from the file String_Validation.inc.php3, which provides some commonly used string validation functions (see Table 5.1). When an error in the submitted data is found, an appropriate error message is inserted into the associative array $errors. This helps later to determine whether an error had been found—if count($errors) is greater than 0, the application reacts accordingly and doesn't process the form.

Table 5.1 **String Validation Functions from** *String_Validation.inc.php3*

Function	Purpose
is_alpha()	Checks whether a string contains only alphabetic characters; optionally checks for minimum and maximum length.
is_numeric()	Checks whether a string contains only numeric characters; optionally checks for minimum and maximum length.
is_alphanumeric()	Checks whether a string contains only alphanumeric characters; optionally checks for minimum and maximum length.
is_clean_text()	Checks whether a string contains an extended set of characters that may occur in Western alphabet names (includes all alphabetic characters, umlaut characters, all kinds of quotes); optionally checks for minimum and maximum length.
is_email()	Checks whether the string is a syntactically valid email address (see the later discussion on the limits of this function).
contains_bad_words()	Checks whether the string contains words defined in the array $bad_words inside the function. This is helpful for bulletin boards, discussion rooms, and so forth, where you want to avoid insulting language.
contains_phone_number()	Checks whether a string contains phone numbers—any 10+ digit sequence, optionally separated by parentheses, spaces, hyphens, or slashes.

Validating an Email Address

Validating an email address is a common problem. Our approach only verifies the syntactical correctness using the following regular expression:

```
$ret = ereg(
        '^([a-z0-9_]¦\\-¦\\.)+'.
        '@'.
        '(([a-z0-9_]¦\\-)+\\.)+'.
        '[a-z]{2,4}$',
        $string);
```

- Must contain a defined set of characters before the at (@) sign
- An @ sign
- A hostname with a minimum length of two characters
- A top-level domain with a minimum length of two characters

In most cases, such validation is sufficient—but it's by no means a complete check against the official syntax defined in RFC 822. The RFC allows for email addresses in the form *"Name" <mail@host.com>*, which our check would reject. But our check also doesn't test whether the email address actually exists.

Occasionally, you'll see another approach that seems to be more stringent at first glance, but fails too often in real life to be useful. It's based on the fact that SMTP, the Simple Mail Transfer Protocol, provides feedback as to whether a local user exists. By sending the SMTP header indicating the recipient's address or username on the local system, the SMTP server responds with a status code of 250 if the user exists and a status code of 550 if the user is unknown to the system. So far, so good—in theory. Unfortunately, many mail servers are configured to accept all users; they'll answer all requests with "250—Recipient OK." We tried it with one of the mail servers we use; because our mail server was configured that way, we got the expected response of accepting all users. Because SMTP is a clear-text protocol, you can easily verify this behavior by "simulating" an SMTP session over Telnet:

```
bash-2.01$ telnet smtp.dnet.it 25
Trying 194.242.192.2...
Connected to ns.dnet.it.
Escape character is '^]'.
220 ns.dnet.it ESMTP Sendmail 8.9.3/8.9.3; Tue, 26 Oct 1999 14:02:43 +0200 (MET)
HELO www.profi.it
250 ns.dnet.it Hello www.profi.it [194.242.192.194], pleased to meet you
MAIL FROM: tobias@dnet.it
250 tobias@dnet.it... Sender ok
RCPT TO: this.user.doesnt.exist.for.sure
250 this.user.doesnt.exist.for.sure... Recipient ok
QUIT
221 ns.dnet.it closing connection
Connection closed by foreign host.
```

> A better idea would be to check whether the MX (Mail eXchange) host exists, for example by using the
> getmxrr() function. But this can still slow down the validation considerably if the remote host's DNS
> server is slow to access or lookups are not in the local cache, so use it with care. Keep in mind that there
> can be more than one MX host, and it's sufficient if any one of them is reachable.
>
> Yet another method is brought up sometimes: The PHP script could finger the user on the remote host to
> verify an email address. Of course, this only works if a) a finger server is set up, and b) the username
> matches the email address. That doesn't happen very often.

Figure 5.2 shows the application's reaction on erroneous input: An error message is
displayed just below the offending input field, providing instant feedback to the user.
All form fields are pre-populated with the user's inputs, so no data is ever lost. If no
error was discovered in the validation phase, count($errors) equals zero and the
application can process the data: store it in a database, send it via email, whatever.

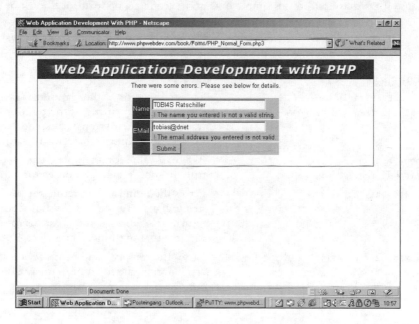

Figure 5.2   The PHP Normal Form in action.

Another little trick we find useful is to have all form data combined in one array,
named $form in the example. If you want to apply a validation rule to each single
element submitted by the user, this proves to be very handy—it's simply a matter of
looping through the array. The example uses this to remove leading and trailing
whitespace from form data by using trim().

Tip: Unlike PHP 3.0, PHP 4.0 supports multidimensional arrays in forms. This actually makes it realistic to have all form variables, including `select multiple` fields, contained within one array.

Using HTML Templates

You may have noticed that there's no HTML code in the form example. Indeed, we have "outsourced" the HTML to a separate file called `PHP_Normal_Form.inc.html`. This is a template file, containing all HTML layout and some template tags such as `{HEADER}`.

Maybe this sounds familiar to you because you've already used the class `FastTemplate`. `EasyTemplate` leaves out the advanced features of `FastTemplate`—all it does is provide a fast interface to replace scalar tags in templates with a string value. Because it restricts itself to this simple operation, it offers a performance boost of over 120% compared to `FastTemplate` when parsing our form template.

The template class we developed has just three functions: `assign()`, `easy_parse()`, and `easy_print()`, described in the following table:

Function	Description
void `EasyTemplate` (*string template_filename*)	The constructor of the class. Takes as argument the filename of the template you want to use. If an error occurs, the `$error` variable will contain the error message.
bool `assign` (*string tag, string value*)	Assigns a value for a template tag. Returns true on success and false on error.
mixed `easy_parse()`	Parses the template and returns it as a string. If an error occurs, the function returns false and sets the class's `$error` variable to a meaningful message.
mixed `easy_print()`	Parses the template and prints it out. If an error occurs, the function returns false and sets the class's `$error` variable to a meaningful message.

Tip: A constructor in PHP always returns `void`—no matter what you're trying to do with `return()`.

What's the advantage of using templates? The main advantage is separation of layout and code. Any designer can open the template file in his favorite HTML authoring software without having to worry about breaking the script code. And the developer doesn't need to deal with HTML at all.

The alternative would be embedding PHP code directly in the HTML. If you were to redesign your application, you'd have a hard time changing the HTML code manually.

But why didn't we use `FastTemplate`? First of all, it would be overkill for this situation—and if overkill means a 120% performance loss, we're not thinking twice about creating a more specific solution.

Just because the PHP Normal Form is our favorite way of validating form data, that doesn't mean that it's the only method or even the best method for handling your specific problem. You may object that the PHP Normal Form as we presented it here doesn't provide a high-level interface for forms—for each form you write, you have to develop the script to validate the data. Well, you're a clever person and you're certainly right; other people seem to have the same idea. The standard PHP library `PHPLib` includes an object-oriented approach to form handling: `OOH Forms` and `tpl_form`.

These classes provide an object-oriented interface to HTML forms. They can validate user input client-side using JavaScript and server-side using PHP regex. Instead of writing HTML code directly, `OOH Forms` lets you use its functions to create form elements. This object-oriented notation appeals to some people, and we encourage you to evaluate the package. The API is quite complex but it's documented well on the Web site at `http://phplib.netuse.de`. Our feeling is that automation of form validation doesn't work well in real life because there's often too much complexity involved: Some form input depends on previously submitted data, uses complex string-validation rules not expressible with regex, or involves other external sources such as databases. This can't be abstracted well enough to provide completely generic validation routines.

Note: At the time of this writing, first efforts were started to integrate a template API into PHP 4.0. This is certainly to be welcomed, because it will offer standardized, open template handling.

Project Layout

The time arrives when even 12-hour days, weekend toil, and gallons of coffee and Jolt cola won't be enough for a single developer to complete a project on time. For the average programmer, this is a significant break in life: No more lonely hacking on his own code, using that cool style only he can read, being his own boss, only turning up from coders' underground from time to time to get a pizza.

No—now he has to worry about standards, style, and project management. But maybe, as a reward, he can get back to normal working hours again, freeing some time for non–work-related things. Who knows, maybe he can even start socializing again?

Team Collaboration

The Internet introduced the capacity to communicate and work together over long distances, regardless of the geographical location of individual team members. This opens great new possibilities for distributed teams. Large companies are not limited by geographic boundaries today. Indeed, many corporations develop software applications by blending experts' skills from many different geographic regions.

Project management is a critical component in effective management of distributed software development. When a new project is started, people know nothing. They don't know what to do and they don't know when to do it. They need someone who coordinates activities, allocates responsibilities, and monitors progress and results. They need a project manager.

Software development project management is so vast a topic that we can't cover it in this book, unfortunately. Many good methods and resources are available, and we encourage you to review them if you have no formal training on the subject. This includes literature from The Mythical Man Month to methods like the Personal Software Process.

We'll focus on the stages of a project in which technical development is involved. You have already seen in Chapter 3, "Application Design," how to plan and lay out an application programming interface (API). Indeed, this was a mini-project of its own. We made some silent assumptions in that discussion: how to organize the code in directories, who's on the development team, how different versions of the API are maintained.

In real (larger) projects, however, you'll have to make these decisions yourself. And since they form the basis of your project, you'd better think twice before you commit to something that could prove inadequate later.

Directory Structure

The most basic—but nevertheless often neglected—technical decision to make when beginning the source code development of a new project is what directory layout to use. Generally, we use the following structure:

```
/home/www/phpwebdev.com/live/cgi-bin
                        htdocs
                        htpasswd
                        include
                        logs
/home/www/phpwebdev.com/staging/cgi-bin
                        htdocs
                        htpasswd
                        include
                        logs
/home/www/phpwebdev.com/dev/cgi-bin
                        htdocs
                        htpasswd
                        include
                        logs
```

Looking at the first directory unit, notice that there are separate directories for included files (libraries, configuration files, templates) and password files (for use with .htaccess files). Password files should never be accessible over the Web, as the passwords contained therein are encrypted with weak standard algorithms and thus attackable with a cracking program. Include files may not need to be protected from outside access for security reasons, but it's always a good idea to store them outside the document root. Even if the Web server should fail to parse a document because of a misconfiguration, important libraries that might contain trade secrets, system information, or innovative algorithms won't be visible to Web surfers.

Tip: On all projects, we use a file named configuration.inc.php3 that defines configuration data in the scope of the project. This file also defines the base path of the project—this makes it easier to include additional files located in subdirectories later in the script.

There are three different directory groups: live, dev, and staging.

- The subdirectory live contains the production environment (the actual Web site).
- dev is used for the development server.
- staging is the transition from dev to live and is used for quality assurance and final testing before a rollout.

Separation of development and live server becomes indispensable on larger sites—you simply can't afford to edit live Web applications. A script error would immediately affect hundreds or thousands of users. Think about what could happen if this script error produced data inconsistencies on a production database...

So the solution is to differentiate between a development server and a production server. In our example, these two servers are on the same physical machine. The development server could be made accessible under dev.phpwebdev.com with appropriate access restrictions; for example, IP-based filtering. On larger and more critical systems, it's usually better to move the development server to a second, identically configured server. This makes it easier to test software updates, operating system reconfigurations, hardware changes, etc.

But why the staging server, a third server? Does this sound exaggerated? Not if your team is large enough to contain dedicated staff for quality assurance (QA) or security auditing. For a complex site, you'll often need to spend considerable time on testing before launching a revision. Developers can't be required to wait idling while the QA staff is banging on the development server. Another reason to include a staging server in your setup is that developers feel it's safer this way to introduce more significant changes to the development server—they don't need to worry that much about breaking other developers' code. If a problem occurs, they can solve it before the project manager commits the development version to the staging server. Of course, if someone breaks the staging server, he'll still need to do the traditional thirty push-ups.

How does a typical development life cycle work using such a setup?

1. The new project is started by creating the directory structure and setting up CVS (more on CVS shortly).

2. Developers check out a copy of the development branch.

3. Developers commit their changes to the development branch.

4. After a significant milestone has been reached and the system is ready for testing, the project manager transfers the development code to the staging server.

5. QA and security perform their tests on the staging server. Issues that are found are reported to the developers.

6. The developers fix bugs and return the project to QA unless no more bugs are found.

7. To launch, the staging server is copied over to the production server. Don't forget the launch party at this point!

Note that we talk here only about the code development stage of the project. Of course, the project as a whole still follows the cycles of software engineering:

1. Project initialization.

2. Analysis.

3. Design.

4. Technical specification and database design.

5. Implementation (that's what we're talking about).

6. Quality assurance.

7. Release.

CVS: Concurrent Versions System

When multiple developers work on one project, the potential for version conflicts arises; this is even more likely when the developers are working not in the same cubicle but distributed across national boundaries. What happens if two developers edit one file at the same time? The changes of one developer will inevitably be overwritten. What happens if a script authored by John doesn't work anymore after having been changed by Jane? John will have a hard time figuring out what Jane had changed.

This is where *version control systems* come into play. This software "remembers" previous versions of a file, allowing you to revert to an older version quickly (a sort of extended undo). The version software will notify you when other developers have edited files you're working on and allow you to react to conflicts. And finally, it will remember *who* made certain changes.

CVS is a software that does all of the above—and is even free (Open Source). The development of PHP itself is managed with CVS, and such successful projects as everyone's favorite Web server (Apache), the Mozilla project, and KDE trust CVS to manage the work of dozens of individual developers. Even the XML source code of this book is maintained with CVS. The authors are in Germany (Till) and Italy (Tobias), the publisher (New Riders) and the editors are located in the U.S., the tech reviewer is in Australia, and we all work on one central repository called `phpBook` on a CVS server in northern Italy. The repository contains all the text, some PHP utilities to create unified versions of the individual chapter files, some resource files for XMetaL (described shortly), the code examples, and the figures. On our local systems, we use WinCVS or command-line CVS to administer the files and work on the text with XMetaL, SoftQuad's XML editor, in a very comfortable way.

Many software projects have a similar scenario: The developers are spread across the globe. CVS is ideal for Internet-based software development: It's a client/server application utilizing the Net as transport layer, and maintains a central repository of the source code. Within the repository, single projects are organized in modules. Each developer checks out a module from this repository and works on the local version—this is a great way to reduce the online time, especially when you have to use dial-up Internet access. When the developer is done with his changes, he commits the updated file to the repository. The CVS software handles all the rest and does the following:

- Associates a version number to each revision of a file.
- Stores a log entry for each revision.
- Keeps track of who has checked out a file to work on it.
- Warns you when others have edited a file you want to check in.

Let's walk through a typical CVS session at the beginning of a project. There are two developers, John and Jane, who are working on the implementation of an API. We assume that their project manager has set up a complete CVS server, created a repository module named `f-api` (as in fictitious API), and set the CVS environment variables in their shell accounts accordingly. (For more information about the installation of the CVS server or client, please refer to the CVS reference manual.)

The first step for both developers is logging into the CVS server and checking out a copy of the module. This is done using the `cvs checkout` command, which will create a directory named after the module (in our example, `./f-api`):

```
john@dev:/mnt/daten/home/john > cvs login
(Logging in to john@www.phpwebdev.com)
CVS password: <password>
john@dev:/home/john > cvs checkout f-api
cvs server: Updating f-api
U f-api/config.inc.php3
U f-api/f-api_read.php3
U f-api/f-api_write.php3
```

Now that each developer has a local copy of the whole project, they both can start editing the files. They have agreed that John will work on `f-api_read.php3` and Jane on `f-api_write.php3`. This is an important concept to note: *CVS cannot replace team communication!*

After John has finished his initial pass of development, he's going to transfer the file back to the central repository. Because no one else has edited the file in the meantime, all it takes for this action is a single CVS command:

```
john@dev:/home/john/f-api > cvs commit f-api_read.php3
```

CVS will now launch the system's standard text editor—on UNIX systems often `vi`; on Windows, Notepad—and ask for a log message that will be associated with this revision. This message can be viewed by the other developers, so it should accurately describe the work that has been performed. Messages like "changed file" or "new feature" don't make any sense and should be avoided. Try to write a concise and clear summary of the work that has been performed; keep in mind the guidelines raised in Chapter 1, "Development Concepts," for inline source code comments. Some development teams even use the log messages to automatically provide the customer with a detailed account of work that has been performed to date. For example, following is an example of a well-written log message:

```
Fixed bug #42; implemented additional checks on user-data (int, date),
see spec p25
```

Unlike other version-control systems, such as RCS or Microsoft's Visual Source Safe, CVS doesn't lock files as soon as you check them out. This means that multiple developers can edit files simultaneously, and is a great advantage in our eyes. In our scenario, both Jane and John could simultaneously edit the `config.inc.php3` file. As soon as John checks in a file that has been modified and checked in by Jane, he'll get a warning and will need to update his local copy before he can commit the file. In simple cases—for example, if John has edited a function at the top and Jane has edited a function at the bottom of the file—CVS will merge the two versions together automatically and John can commit the combined version right away. In other circumstances, an automatic merge may not be possible. Imagine the following original line in the configuration file:

```
define("FT_ZIP_ARCHIVE", "ZIP_ARC"); // GZip Archive
```

John modifies the constant and commits into the repository:

```
define("FT_ZIP", "ZIP_ARC"); // GZip Archive
```

Jane clarifies the comment in the discussed line:

```
define("FT_ZIP_ARCHIVE", "ZIP_ARC"); // GZip Archive (not PkZip compatible!)
```

Obviously, she's working on a non-current version of the file and the need for a merge becomes apparent. When Jane tries to commit her version, CVS shows a warning:

```
jane@dev:/home/jane/f-api > cvs commit config.inc.php3
cvs server: Up-to-date check failed for `config.inc.php3'
cvs [server aborted]: correct above errors first!
cvs commit: saving log message in /tmp/cvs07789baa
```

This means that she needs to bring her local version up-to-date before a commit is possible again:

```
jane@dev:/home/jane/f-api > cvs update config.inc.php3
RCS file: /usr/local/cvsroot/config.inc.php3/config.inc.php3,v
retrieving revision 1.3
retrieving revision 1.5
Merging differences between 1.3 and 1.5 into config.inc.php3
rcsmerge: warning: conflicts during merge cvs
server: conflicts found in config.inc.php3
C config.inc.php3
```

This is a case where an automatic merge is not possible. Instead, CVS creates a special version of the file in conflict, containing special markers to denote conflicting sections. Within this marker, CVS shows the local version of the section in question and the version from the remote repository:

```
<<<<<<< config.inc.php3
    define("FT_ZIP_ARCHIVE", "ZIP_ARC"); // GZip Archive (not PkZip compatible!)
    =======
    define("FT_ZIP", "ZIP_ARC"); // GZip Archive
>>>>>>> 1.3
```

The first group contains Jane's version, the second the version from the repository. It's now Jane's responsibility to go through the code and correct the conflicts. This may be a simple matter of adding the other developer's changes to the local version, or a complex issue that must be resolved with other project members in a phone call or meeting. Even in our simple example, Jane would probably have to talk with John about the reasons he shortened the constant from FT_ZIP_ARCHIVE to FT_ZIP.

As soon as Jane has resolved all conflicts, she can commit the file to the repository and CVS will happily accept it:

```
jane@dev:/home/jane/f-api > cvs commit config.inc.php3
```

In turn, John can now update his local version with the unified copy to complete this round of editing.

Manual merges are rare, and we've found that you can often avoid them by maintaining proper communication between team members. The few conflicts that cause headaches are nearly all due to poor communication between developers—a problem no source-control system can avoid.

Now that Jane has had to deal with conflicts, she's getting cautious and wants to check the status of the file f-api_write.php3. She issues a CVS status command:

```
jane@dev:/home/jane/f-api > cvs status f-api_write.php3
```

The command shows that her local copy is the most current available. These are the status codes in CVS:

Code	Description
Up-to-date	The local copy is identical to the copy in the CVS server.
Locally Modified	The local copy has been modified and not yet committed.
Locally Added	The file has just been added in the local directory.
Locally Removed	The file has just been removed in the local directory.
Needs Checkout or Needs Patch	The version in the remote repository is newer than the local copy, which needs to be updated.
Needs Merge	The version in the remote repository is newer than the local copy, which has also been modified. This will result in a merge after the update.
File had conflicts on merge	There was a manual merge and its conflicts have not yet been resolved.
Unknown	The file is not under CVS control.

Each revision committed by a developer is automatically tagged with a version number. As we've already said, this allows the retrieval of any version of a file. Using the cvs diff command, a developer can even view differences between arbitrary versions without actually retrieving the file. The default action for cvs diff is to compare the local revision with the remote version:

```
jane@dev:/home/jane/f-api > cvs diff f-api_write.php3
```

By using the -r option, which allows her to specify the revision with most CVS commands, Jane can compare the local copy with remote revision 1.1 (the original version):

```
jane@dev:/home/jane/f-api > cvs diff -r 1.1 f-api_write.php3
Index: config.inc.php3
===================================================================
RCS file:
/usr/local/cvsroot/config.inc.php3/config.inc.php3,v
retrieving revision 1.1
retrieving revision 1.3
```

```
diff -r1.1 -r1.5 3c3
< define("FT_ZIP_ARCHIVE", "ZIP_ARC"); // GZip Archive
...
> define("FT_ZIP", "ZIP_ARC"); // GZip Archive (not PkZip compatible!)
```

While CVS is usually very good at merging different revisions of a file, under certain circumstances it's easier to avoid merges. For example, if the diff shows extensive changes on the remote server, and Jane has made only a few changes in her version, she may want to abandon her version in favor of the revision in the CVS repository. To do so, she'd simply delete the local file and do a new checkout from the server.

CVS Timesavers: GUIs and CVSweb

If you know the basic CVS commands described in the preceding section, you hold the full power of a command-line tool in your hands: You can use CVS in remote shells, automate processes with shell scripts, and show your colleagues that you really know the ins and outs of your job. For everyday work, however, we prefer a GUI.

For Windows workstations, WinCVS, available from www.wincvs.org, is a nice utility to help in getting the job done (see Figure 5.3). This software doesn't hide the complexity of CVS by any means, but it gives you convenient access to the most-often-needed features through a graphical front end.

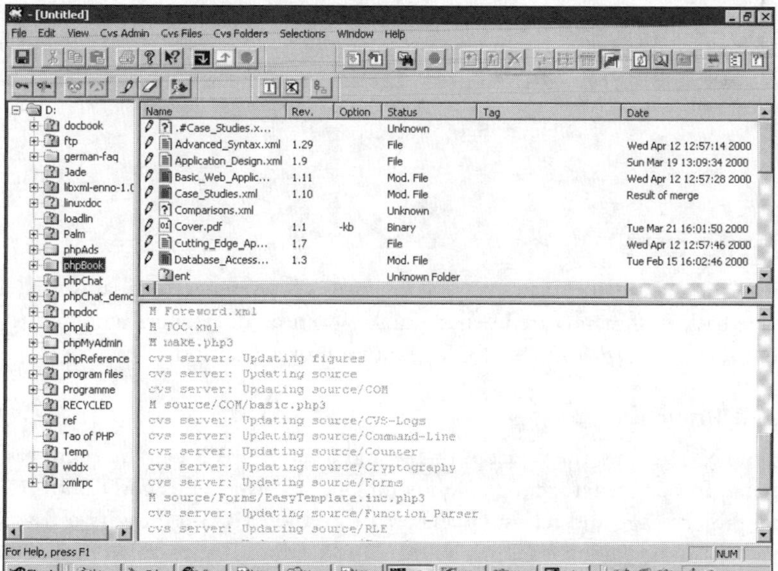

Figure 5.3   WinCVS.

Another very useful tool is CVSweb, a Perl CGI script that gives you an overview of your CVS repositories. It helps to manage larger projects by displaying each file in a list with its last log message, date of modification, and author (see Figure 5.4). You can request any revision of a file and view nicely colored diffs between arbitrary versions.

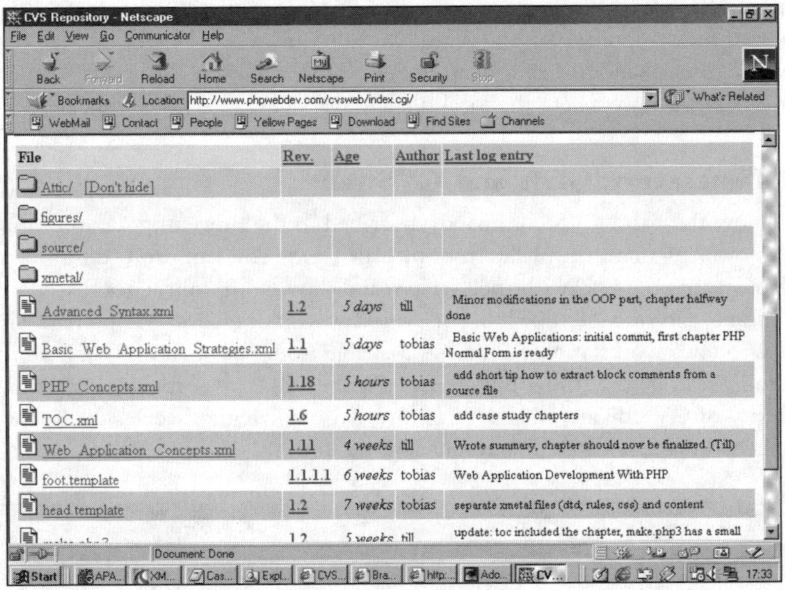

Figure 5.4   The CVSweb interface.

Advanced CVS

Of course there's a reason that Per Cederqvist's CVS reference manual is such a long beast. The basic commands are learned quickly even by developers who are new to CVS, but the advanced features of CVS require more attention.

Tags and Branches

For example, CVS uses the concept of *tags* and *branches*. CVS tags are quite easy to understand. In our earlier example, John and Jane had worked eagerly until reaching the final project stage and releasing version 1.0 of their F-API. Now, two days later, an important customer discovers a bug in the API. A quite-easy-to-solve bug, actually— but our developers have already moved on with development and can't release the current source code as a stable version. If they wanted to apply the bug fix, they'd have to find out which version of each file was in the release, check that revision out from CVS, and create a new release. That may be possible with the three files from our example, but they'd be stuck back to their weekend toil if the project involved a considerable number of files.

The solution CVS offers is to associate a verbose tag with a specific revision when a milestone has been reached. Before the release, Jane tags the files with the name of the release:

```
jane@dev:/home/jane/f-api > cvs tag rel-1_0
```

If she needs to retrieve the release version at a later time, she can simply issue a `cvs checkout` command on this tag:

```
jane@dev:/home/jane/f-api > cvs checkout -r rel-1_0 f-api
```

And voilà, there's release 1.0 again. It will be created in the `./f-api` directory.

Branches are a bit more complex, but you can think of them as stricter tags. Indeed, when you want to have a more rigorous separation of two code bases (which are still related to a single project), you'd create two branches. To get back to our example, John and Jane want to separate a development version of their API and a stable version—just as in the Linux kernel development.

A new branch is created using the `cvs tag -b` command. To start a development branch with the current code base, Jane executes this command:

```
jane@dev:/home/jane/f-api > cvs tag -b dev .
```

The name of the newly created branch is `dev`. To create a local copy of this branch, Jane checks it out from CVS as she would normally, with a tagged version:

```
jane@dev:/home/jane/f-api > cvs checkout -r dev f-api
```

The difference between normal tagged files and branched files becomes apparent now: All Jane's further commands will act on this branch and not affect the main, stable branch. All commits, updates, and so on will use the `dev` branch, enabling her to work on the development branch without altering the main branch. But be careful: Maintaining different branches can be an administration nightmare. We suggest that you use a maximum of three branches per project.

Tip: To see to which branch a file belongs, use `cvs status`. The *Sticky Tag* output will contain the branch name and revision number.

A common task is merging a branch back into the main branch. From time to time, Jane wants to add the new features from the development branch to the main branch. This is done by first checking out the main branch and then applying the diffs from the development branch:

```
jane@dev:/home/jane/ > cvs checkout f-api
jane@dev:/home/jane/f-api/ > cvs update -j dev .
```

The `-j` (join) option in the `cvs update` command tells CVS to merge the differences from the development tree to the local copy.

Tip: The main tree's branch name is always `HEAD`. Knowing this, Jane could merge the main tree to the local development branch by executing `cvs update -j HEAD`.

After having resolved potential conflicts, Jane can now commit her copy to the main tree, and the backport is complete.

Automated Notifications

At this point, Jane will have to inform her colleague again of the merge. As we've said, CVS cannot replace effective communication within the team. But it can help.

The CVS server can be set up to perform a certain action on each commit. Sending email to a mailing list server could be such an action. By setting up a mailing list or alias group for each project, it's easy to broadcast all commit messages, including logs, to all project members.

To accomplish this, one of the CVS administrative files, namely the `loginfo` file, needs to be edited. This file controls how commit information is handled—you can send it by mail, but also log it to a file, store it in a database, etc.

You can alter the administrative files directly in the system's `CVSROOT` directory. The recommended way to change them is via CVS, though—this way you'll have all the regular features and the safety net of CVS. To start a session, check out the `CVSROOT` directory:

```
jane@dev:/home/jane/ > cvs checkout CVSROOT
```

Then edit the `loginfo` file. The first part of a line is a regular expression that's tested against the directory or file being committed. If a match is found, the remainder of the line is the program to be invoked. The program should expect the commit information on standard input. You may also have one line in the file starting with `DEFAULT` instead of a regular expression: This directive will be considered if no directory is matched. Another special directive is `ALL`, which will be invoked in all cases. Two examples for such lines:

```
^phpBook$ /cvs/loginfo_process_phpBook.sh
ALL /cvs/loginfo_process_all.sh
```

The first shell script, `loginfo_process_phpBook.sh`, is only invoked for the `phpBook` repository. The second script, `loginfo_process_all.sh`, will be invoked on every commit, regardless of the repository, because it's marked with the `ALL` keyword.

As part of the program to be invoked, a set of special variables can be used to give extended information about the commit. These variables are identified by a preceding percent sign (`%`), similar to the format declaration in `printf()`. If more than one variable is used, they must be grouped inside curly braces. The available variables are shown in the following table.

Variable	Meaning
s	Filename
V	Version number before the commit
v	Version number after the commit

As soon as you use one of these variables, another string containing the name of the CVS module is automatically added before the variable.

To send mail to John and Jane, the following line could be used:

```
^f-api /bin/mail -s "CVS update: %s" -c john jane
```

But what if the commit message should also be logged to a file? CVS matches only the first entry for a directory, so specifying another line for `^f-api` wouldn't help. Without doubt, a shell script could handle it, but what if the routine should be extended to log the message to a database later? Listing 5.2 shows how to solve this problem with PHP. In the `loginfo` file, it's called like this:

```
phpBook /usr/local/cvsroot/CVSROOT/Commit_Info.php3
➥"/usr/local/cvsroot/CVSROOT/logs/default.log" "CVS update %s" till tobias
```

This line tells CVS to invoke the script `Commit_Info.php3` when a commit happens for the `phpBook` repository. The script gets invoked with at least three arguments (four in our example):

- A filename where a log summary for this commit should be stored.

- The subject line of the email message.

- The recipient(s). One recipient email address is required; simply provide a list of addresses as shown in the preceding example if you want to send the message to more recipients.

Listing 5.2 **Mail and log a commit info message.**

```
// Check for correct number of arguments
if(count($argv) < 4)
{
    print("Usage: Commit_Info.php3 logfile subject to-address [to-address
...]\n");
    print("\n");
    print("A script to log and mail CVS commit messages.\n");
    print("  From Web Application Development with PHP\n");
    print("  Tobias Ratschiller and Till Gerken.
    ➥Copyright (c) 2000, New Riders Publishing\n");
    exit;
}

// First argument is the logfilename
$logfile = $argv[1];

// Second argument is the mail's subject
$subject = $argv[2];

// Initialize the body variable
$body = "";

// Get the commit message passed via stdin
$fp = fopen("php://stdin", "r") or die("Fatal Error: could not read from stdin.");
while(!feof($fp))
```

continues

Listing 5.2   **Continued**

```
{
    $body .=  fgets($fp, 64);
}
fclose($fp);

// Mail the message to all specified recipients
for($i=2; $i<count($argv); $i++)
{
    mail($argv[$i], $subject, $body);
}

// Log the message
$fp = fopen($logfile, "a") or die("Fatal Error: could not write logfile
↪($logfile) for writing");
fputs($fp, "$subject\n");
fputs($fp, "$body\n");
fputs($fp, "--------------------------------------------------------------\n");
fclose($fp);
```

Why use PHP for such command-line scripting? Even if it was originally intended as a Web scripting language, PHP has evolved in a way that allows it to be used for tasks like this. By simply compiling PHP as a stand-alone binary, you can invoke it as a script interpreter just like Perl. On UNIX systems, you can set the first line of the file to the script interpreter:

```
"#!/usr/bin/php
```

By setting the executable bit for it, you can invoke it as any other regular executable file on UNIX systems:

```
tobias@dev:/home/tobias/ > chmod +x script.php
tobias@dev:/home/tobias/ > ./script.php
```

On Windows, you can associate the file extension `.php` with the interpreter to achieve the same result.

The script shows two important concepts often needed in command-line scripts: accessing arguments passed to the script and reading from standard input. PHP automatically sets up an array named `$argv` that contains the script's filename as first entry and as subsequent entries all arguments to the script. This is actually the same behavior as in C. Just as in C, there's another variable, `$argc`, containing the number of arguments. Of course, you can also use `count($argv)`. For example, if you call a PHP script with `php script.php3 foo`, `$argv[1]` would contain the first argument, `foo`.

The other noteworthy part of the code is reading from standard input. PHP 4.0 allows you to use so-called *PHP streams* with `fopen()`. To accept user input on the command line or read in data passed from another program, `php://stdin` is used. The script uses it to read the log message provided by CVS; you could also prompt for user input with a similar function. Listing 5.3 shows it in action.

Listing 5.3 **Prompt for user input using PHP input/output streams.**

```
function readln()
{
    // Initialize return value
    $ret = "";

    // Read from stdin until the user presses enter
    $fp = fopen("php://stdin", "r") or die("Fatal Error: could not read from
    ↪stdin");
    do
    {
        $char = fread($fp, 1);
        $ret .= $char;
    }
    while($char != "\n");

    return($ret);
}

print("Please enter your firstname:\n");
$firstname = readln();

print("You entered: $firstname\n");
```

The other available streams are php://stdout and php://sterr. This provides an effective and platform-independent way of accessing standard input, standard output, and the standard error-handling device. Indeed, this works even on Windows 98/NT.

The concept of PHP streams was introduced with PHP 4.0 and is not available in the 3.x tree. On UNIX systems, you can work around this limitation by directly accessing the UNIX devices /dev/stdin, /dev/stdout, or /dev/stderr. Of course, this works only on systems with valid devices. Most current UNIX systems have it— Windows is left out again.

If you use CVS to manage all your files on a Web site project—not only source code but also images, archives, Flash, etc.—you'll soon notice that there are some limits with binary files. Text diffs don't make sense on binary data—it's usually not of much interest to you which bits in an image file have changed.

CVS can indeed create problems when treating all files as ASCII. CVS treats certain character sequences as keywords; for example

```
$Id: Basic_Web_Application_Strategies.xml,v 1.5 1999/12/15 15:49:55 tobias Exp $
```

and substitutes them on commit with the expanded counterpart, which may create a mess with binary data.

You can manually specify the -b option if you cvs add a file, but that soon becomes a kludge to remember and use consistently. It would be easier if CVS could enforce the binary type on some file extensions. Luckily, this is easy using the administrative file cvswrappers. This file allows you to set up actions that will transform files on each commit or checkout. It's similar to the loginfo file in that it will be invoked on a commit, but, unlike directives in the loginfo file, it can execute actions that will alter the file in question. To treat images and archive files as binary, the cvswrappers file could look like this:

```
*.gif -kb *.jp[e]g -kb *.png -kb *.gz -kb *.ta -kb *.zip -kb
```

This will automatically append the -kb to all CVS commands involving files matched by the specified filter. The -k option prevents CVS from trying to use keyword expansion; the -b switch indicates a binary file and disables the ability to produce text diffs for this file.

Sometimes you need to interface external command-line tools with the Web. Many UNIX programs expect input on standard input and output the results of the computation to standard output—for example, sort. The easiest way to pass input and read output of the program is by using popen() and PHP streams. popen() opens a unidirectional pipe to a program and allows you to pass data to its standard input. And as you already know, you can use fopen() to read the standard input, to which the external program will write. A simple example could look like this:

```php
// Open a writing pipe to the sort command
$fpout = popen("sort", "w");

// Open stdin with PHP-Streams
$fpin = fopen("php://stdin", "r");

// Output some characters to sort
fputs($fpout, "a\n");
fputs($fpout, "c\n");
fputs($fpout, "b\n");

// Close the pipe to sort - sort will now process the input
// and write it to stdout
pclose($fpout);

// Sort's stdout is stdin for us - so read it until feof().
while($c = fread($fpin, 1))
{
    print($c);
}
```

CVS Quick Reference

While CVS features about 25 main commands, a multitude of options, and even more possible combinations, in real life you usually need only a small set of commands. The following table provides a quick overview that can serve as a reminder for the basic commands.

Command	Example	Description
cvs login	cvs login	Logs into the CVS server; this will ask for your password.
cvs checkout	cvs checkout phpBook	Gets a module from the CVS repository. Usually used to check out a module (entire directory under the top level).
cvs update	cvs update TOC.xml	Updates your local copy of a file or directory.
cvs commit	cvs commit TOC.xml	Sends your local version of files or directories to the CVS server.
cvs add	cvs add TOC.xml	Adds a new file or directory to the CVS server. The addition will be completed the next time you commit.
cvs remove	cvs remove TOC.xml	Deletes a file or directory from the CVS server. The deletion will be completed the next time you commit. Note that this command doesn't actually delete a file; you can still access older versions.
cvs status	cvs status TOC.xml	Shows the modification status of your local version.
cvs diff	cvs diff TOC.xml	Shows the differences between two versions of a file. The default is to show the differences between the local copy and the remote version.
cvs log	cvs log TOC.xml	Shows the CVS log messages for all revisions of a file.

Three-Tier Applications

With larger development teams, effective means for organizing a project become vital. By now, you've seen methods of handling the separation between layout and code, organizing directory structures, and using a version-control system for managing the source code. As soon as you talk about distributed development, phase separation, and business processes, marketing people will jump on you and yell about multi-tier applications. What's all the fuss about?

Traditional Client/Server

In the past, a traditional, non–Web application was responsible for handling everything from user input to application logic to data storage. These three entities were interwoven with each other, making it difficult or impossible to change one of them without affecting the others. If you wanted to provide such an application to multiple users, you'd have a problem: What if the data format changes? What happens if you're required to change the application logic? You'd have to provide all users with a new local copy of the application, an unfeasible approach for larger systems.

With the advent of object-oriented analysis, design, and programming principles, business applications became component-based. User interfaces were commonly deployed on workstations, and data and application logic was hosted on a mainframe server. The term *client/server* has been used to describe this separation of layers or tiers. A two-tier client/server architecture provides a basic separation of tasks. The *client*, or first tier, is responsible for the presentation of data to the user (user interface), and the *server*, or second tier, is responsible for supplying data services to the client and handling the application logic. So far, so good, but you see that the two-tier model still combines two distinct concepts in the second tier (the server): data services and application logic. The application logic is the heart of the program, responsible for data validation, processing rules, etc.

The data services manage the application's raw data and consist often of a relational database management system (RDBMS) or a mainframe legacy system, in which a company has already invested considerable time and money. The interweaving of these two concepts in a two-tier application introduces problems of scalability, reuse, and maintenance. Take the recent introduction of the Euro as the official currency throughout the European Community: If an application hadn't cleanly separated application logic from data, both tiers would need to be changed. Hard-coded currency values in the data validation were to be altered as well as the data-storage format of currency amounts.

Using a multi-tier approach, all three concepts can be cleanly separated.

PHP and Multi-Tier Applications

The concept of multi-tier systems became popular in the early 1990s and is now establishing itself as the enterprise application software architecture for the late 90s and early 21st century. A *multi-tier* (often referred to as *three-tier*) architecture provides greater application scalability, lower maintenance, and increased reuse of components. Three-tier architecture offers a technology-neutral method of building client/server applications with vendors who employ standard interfaces, providing services for each logical layer. Look at the three-tier model in Figure 5.5—doesn't it look familiar to you as a Web application developer? In the first tier is a thin client—translated to the world of Web applications, this would be the browser. The middle tier (application server) is obviously PHP (and the Web server as host application), while the third tier consists of an RDBMS.

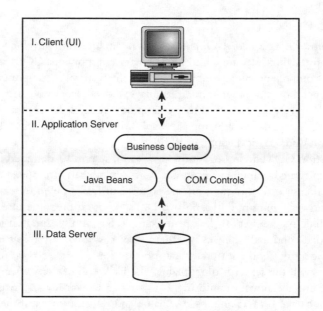

I. Client (UI)

II. Application Server

Business Objects

Java Beans

COM Controls

III. Data Server

Figure 5.5   Multi-tier application layers.

Working with PHP leads to a basic three-tier model in such a coherent way that you don't even notice it. But there is (or was) a catch to using PHP as an application server. Until version 4.0, PHP was not fully prepared to access third-party software objects and was therefore not the best tool to use in business scenarios with similar requirements. This has changed, and we feel this is one of the most dramatic points in the evolution of PHP. The current version allows you not only to access COM controls on Win32 systems, but also to execute Java methods on any system with a Java Virtual Machine (JVM).

There are three standard architectures for such enterprise-wide object reuse: (D)COM from Microsoft, JavaBeans/RMI from Sun Microsystems, and CORBA from the Object Management Group. The most widely used at this time is COM, because of the broad use of Windows systems (see the next section for details on using PHP and COM). However, enterprises with heterogeneous environments will prefer Java or CORBA for their wider platform support.

For example, JavaBeans (and alternatively COM objects) are available to access SAP R/3 systems through their Business API (BAPI) interface, enabling you to integrate the SAP business framework into your application server layer. Think about the possibilities this would introduce to an e-commerce system: You could effectively combine a front-end online shop with the enterprise warehousing application in the back end.

PHP and COM

The *Component Object Model* (*COM*) is a software architecture developed by Microsoft that allows abstracting software chunks into binary components. COM defines a standard for component interoperability and specific features a component must have. It doesn't depend on any programming language; indeed, Microsoft shows efforts to establish COM as an open IETF (Internet Engineering Task Force) standard. COM objects can be accessed by any compliant application and programming language; for example, from Visual Basic, Delphi, or PHP.

The question COM addresses is this: How can a system be designed in such a way that binary software components from different vendors can interoperate? Microsoft's first proposed answer to this question, the concept of DLLs, failed miserably. Because of the missing versioning in DLLs, no two DLLs exposing the same interface could be used on a single system. Let's make up an example. Say you've got a server-monitoring application that continually checks whether a server is down and logs the collected data. You have a front end with pretty statistics and some logic to react in an appropriate way if the server is unreachable. The back end of the software could be a DLL performing the actual monitoring: Let's say that `ServerSpy.dll` exposes a function `is_reachable()`, taking a server name and returning `true` if the server is reachable or `false` if it's not.

We haven't defined what kind of server to monitor yet—indeed, it could be a Web server, mail server, name server, or any other system, and the function declaration itself as well as the back end wouldn't need to be changed. The only part needing a change would be the implementation of the function `is_reachable()`.

With DLLs, you could have exactly one monitoring service on the system—*either* Web server spy *or* mail server spy, etc. If you install another DLL, it would overwrite the previous one.

Your application couldn't let the user choose between available monitoring services. Nor would it be possible to have a different version of one service available on the system. If another software vendor created a better implementation of `ServerSpy.dll` and sold that to your customer, it would again overwrite your version of the DLL. If the function worked exactly the same, all would be great—otherwise, your application would stop working.

A proper component model tries to solve these problems. COM provides a way to identify components through a globally unique ID (GUID), allowing you to use many services concurrently—the operating system knows all installed components and your application could query it for components in the category "Server Spy monitoring services." COM provides versioning, allowing you to have different versions of a component on the system without affecting each other.

And finally, it provides component introspection, allowing you to see which methods and properties a component exposes.

You probably have heard of ActiveX controls. ActiveX controls, also known as *OLE controls* or *OCX* because of Microsoft's creative marketing department, are simply an application of COM components. They provide a reduced set of COM interfaces so that they're smaller and better suited for use on high-latency networks. You can use ActiveX controls almost the same way as full-fledged COM controls.

Then there's *DCOM*, the *Distributed Component Object Model* protocol, which introduces COM components to the world of distributed network applications. Basically, it's a protocol for object-oriented remote procedure calls useful for distributed, component-based systems. PHP 4.0 works with both COM and DCOM on Win32 systems. At this time, it doesn't work on other platforms where COM would be available (such as Apple or Solaris).

Invoking (D)COM controls with PHP 4.0 is very easy. COM is a reserved class name that you can instantiate by passing the control's name to the constructor. You then have a complete instance of the COM object where you can execute functions or set and read properties as if it were a PHP class. For properties that can't be expressed using PHP syntax (for example, because they contain a dot or other characters invalid for PHP), you can use the following helper functions:

- bool com_set(*class com_object, string property_name, string property_value*)

  Assigns a value for a property on the COM object instantiated in *com_object*. Aliases for this function are com_propset() and com_propput(). Returns true on success and false on error.

- mixed com_get(*class com_object, string property_name*)

  Returns the value of a property on the COM object instantiated in *com_object*. Alias for this function is com_propget(). Returns the property's value on success and false on error.

The source code in Listing 5.4 shows the basic use of the COM feature. It creates an instance of the COM class using the Softwing.EDConverter component, a freely available currency-conversion utility. Then the member method Triangulate() is invoked and the returned result displayed. It can't get much easier...

Listing 5.4 **A basic COM example.**

```
$amount = 1000;          // Amount to be converted
$curr_from = "DEM";      // ISO currency symbol of original currency
$curr_to = "ITL";        // Symbol of the target currency

// Instantiate new COM object
$conv = new COM("Softwing.EDConverter") or die("Unable to instantiate
➥Euro-Converter");

// Execute a component method on the COM object's instance
$ret = $conv->Triangulate(10000, "ITL", "DEM") or die("Exception triggered by
➥Triangulate() on line ".__LINE__);

// Print the result
print($ret);
```

> To create an instance of a DCOM component on a remote system, pass the
> hostname as second argument to the constructor. For example:
>
> ```
> $comp = new COM("My.Component", "remote.server.com");
> ```

In PHP 3.0, you can't use the COM class; instead, you need to use the com_load(),
com_invoke(), com_set(), and com_get() functions. Our example would look like
Listing 5.5.

Listing 5.5 **A basic COM example with PHP version 3.0.**

```
$amount = 1000;          // Amount to be converted
$curr_from = "DEM";      // ISO currency symbol of original currency
$curr_to = "ITL";        // Symbol of the target currency

// Instantiate new COM object
$conv = com_load("Softwing.EDConverter") or die("Unable to instantiate
➡Euro-Converter");

// Execute a component method on the COM object's instance
$ret = com_invoke($conv, "Triangulate", "10000", "ITL", "DEM") or
➡die("Exception triggered by Triangulate() on line ".__LINE__);

// Print the result
print($ret);
```

The syntax of these functions (that are not available in PHP 4.0) is as follows:

- int com_load(*string component_name*)

  Instantiates a COM component and creates a reference to it. The returned integer
  value must be used in the following com_*() calls. Returns false and throws a
  warning if an error occurs.

- mixed com_invoke(*int com_identifier*, *string function_name*[, *mixed
  argument1*[,...]])

  Invokes a COM component's method and returns the method's return value. The
  first argument of the function is a valid COM identifier as created with
  com_load(). The second argument must be the name of a component method.
  As optional third and following arguments, you can specify arguments for the
  invoked method. This function returns false on error.

- bool com_set(*int com_identifier*, *string property_name*, *string property_value*)

  Assigns a value for a property on the COM object instantiated in *com_object*. Aliases for this function are com_propset() and com_propput(). Returns true on success and false on error.

- mixed com_get(*int com_identifier*, *string property_name*)

  Returns the value of a property on the COM object instantiated in *com_object*. Alias for this function is com_propget(). Returns the property's value on success and false on error.

PHP and Java

Java, the "language du jour" for many corporate software developers, is increasingly being used in all areas of development. Since version 4.0, PHP can be compiled to support the calling of native Java functions, effectively enabling you to use enterprise Java components in a multi-tier environment.

Installation of the Java support is not difficult. You have to keep the following things in mind:

- You need to install a Java Virtual Machine (JVM) on your system first; we have used the freely available Open Source Kaffe 1.0.5 implementation.
- PHP needs to be compiled as DSO with APXS, meaning that it will be loaded as a shared module into Apache. You can find instructions for this in the INSTALL.DSO file of the PHP distribution.

Please look at the README file in the ext/java directory for additional instructions.

Once you have the Java support in PHP, the syntax is similar to the one invoking COM components. Indeed, both make use of an advanced Zend internal feature called *object overloading*. The term *overloading* in software engineering means that a construct can react differently depending on the context. Function overloading consequently means that a function can be different depending on the order or type of the arguments.

For example, in C++ you can have two function declarations similar to these:

```
void add(int Left, int Right);
void add(double Left, double Right);
```

Depending on whether you pass an int or double value to add(), the respective function will be called. Developers usually try to avoid such ambiguity, though, as it can be a nightmare to debug.

The Zend engine allows similar function overloading internally and uses it to realize object overloading. Depending on the context (the class name, for example), an object can mean quite different things: It can be a normal user-defined class, but it can also be something much more sophisticated like a COM or Java interface.

Much like with COM, creating a new Java object is done by instantiating the overloaded Java class. The constructor argument is the Java class to be used:

```
$system = new Java("java.lang.System");
```

On the returned object, functions can be used in the same way as with COM objects.

To read and write properties, you have to use helper functions (remember, with the COM module, properties can be accessed directly), getProperty() and setProperty():

```
$system = new Java("java.lang.System");
printf("Java version = %s\n", $system->getProperty("java.version"));
```

Summary

In this chapter, you've learned about the basic strategies common to all Web applications. You know how to deal correctly with user input, and how to validate forms and verify their contents. You can make use of templates to separate code from layout; moving on from there, you know how to coordinate your team efforts and deal with more than one person working on a single file. The benefits of version-control systems have been discussed, and you can structure your projects on disk in a clear manner. You can make advanced use of the flexible CVS system. Finally, multi-tier applications have been discussed that also implement interfaces to foreign languages.

Equipped with this knowledge, you are now able to face the design and implementation of cutting-edge applications in later chapters.

6

Database Access with PHP

When you handle the master carpenter's tools,
chances are that you'll cut your hand.

A DATABASE IS A WEB DEVELOPER'S DAILY TOOL, and he or she should know SQL at least as well as PHP. Most data models of Web applications involve a relational database. While novice users may try to avoid the perceived overhead of SQL and a relational database management system (RDBMS), the advanced developer appreciates the features it provides. Anything nontrivial—for example, concurrent accesses, searching and sorting, or allowing relations between different datasets—quickly becomes a pain when using storage methods like flat files or arrays. Databases are built for efficient organization and retrieval of data, and in most cases there's no need to mimic this feature set in pseudo database systems.

This chapter introduces you to accessing databases with PHPLib, and shows two of the many features of this library: user authentication and permission management.

PHPLib: The PHP Base Library

As we've already mentioned earlier in this book, the PHPLib can save you a considerable amount of hassle in your daily programming routine. Some concepts will show up again and again when developing Web applications: session management, authentication, separation of layout from code. The PHPLib is a solid set of objects that provide solutions for these necessary tasks.

For many programmers, the PHPLib is intimidating when looking at the documentation and the examples. Indeed, it is a complex set of classes, and the different objects are dependent on each other in a nontrivial way. However, once you have mastered the installation and the writing of your own base classes, it's not at all difficult to use, and you'll see examples that are straightforward and easily understandable.

The PHPLib can currently be found at `http://phplib.netuse.de/`. Its documentation provides detailed installation instructions, so we won't rephrase that here; we'll assume that you have a properly set up PHPLib environment, with `prepend.php3` prepended to every script automatically (this is the setup recommended in the documentation). Also, we won't include a description of each function and property in this chapter, as the documentation does—instead, we'll try to show you the big picture and explain the PHPLib with our own words.

History

The first development of PHPLib was performed by Boris Erdmann and Kristian Koehntopp in 1998. Working on a large project at an ISP in Kiel, Germany, they realized that they were programming the same procedures again and again. The way in which they solved these problems was not very satisfying.

For example, they needed a login procedure that wasn't based on HTTP Basic Authentication, because this authentication method is neither secure nor user-friendly. For proper authentication, they needed working session management (as we've outlined in Chapter 4, "Web Application Concepts"). So they began to develop an object-oriented library for session management and authentication, building on an idea for session management by Karl-Heinz Wild. As with many Open Source projects, more and more people joined this project over time, and it grew very quickly. Today, the PHPLib contains modules for many aspects of authentication and session management, but also methods to create HTML input forms, tables, and trees.

Advantages and Disadvantages

As we said in Chapter 1, "Development Concepts," you should choose your weapons carefully. The PHPLib is best suited for projects taking more than two days to develop. The first use of the library will cause you more work than usual: It takes time to read the documentation, it takes time to understand the concepts, and it takes time to resolve your mistakes.

The PHPLib seems to be ideal for projects with more than one software developer. It forces the programmers to use similar interfaces, and it encourages object orientation, which can at least bring a better structure to an application. Also, as the PHPLib requires some understanding of more advanced aspects of PHP and Web applications in general, it takes developers in a team to a comparable knowledge level.

Because the PHPLib is written in native PHP, it isn't as fast in operation as a C extension of PHP. On the other hand, this makes it more flexible. Because the libraries are written as classes, you can easily make changes to fit it for your needs. Indeed, you *will* need to make some changes: The PHPLib is not a packaged product ready for use. You should be aware that you need to provide some functions yourself.

The dependencies between the different PHPLib classes are complex; for example, you can't use the session-management functions without using the database abstraction layer part of the library. If you just need session management, you may be better off using PHP 4.0's session functions or our PHP 3.0 backport. Nevertheless, please read on—the PHPLib has some features that can definitely make your life easier.

Important Files

In the PHPLib distribution, there are two files that you'll probably need to change: `local.inc` and `prepend.php3`.

The file `prepend.php3` loads the files that should be available on all pages using the PHPLib. By default, it loads the database back end for MySQL and uses the SQL storage container for session management. To switch from MySQL to Postgres, for example, you would need to change the line

```
require($_PHPLIB["libdir"] . "db_mysql.inc");  /* Change this to match your
➥database. */
```

to include `db_pgsql.inc` instead of `db_mysql.inc`.

If you use other classes from the PHPLib (the `Template` class, for example), it's recommended that you include them in `prepend.php3`.

The `local.inc` file is where the customization of PHPLib is done.

Customizing the PHPLib

The base classes of the PHPLib aren't used directly in most cases; you define your own derived classes instead, which are customized to fit your environment. There are already default implementations shipping with the PHPLib, which we will use later in our code examples. These implementations make certain assumptions about your system; for example, that you use MySQL. If these assumptions don't fit for your application, the file `local.inc` is the place to make changes; the recommended technique is to create a new object as extension to `DB_Sql`. By doing so, you avoid the need to set these configuration variables in every application—instead, you define them once in the class.

You're advised to adjust `local.inc` for your own needs, and you should at least change the name of the `Example_Session` class; its name is used as the name of the session cookies and passed in the URL in GET mode—it doesn't look very professional if `Example_Session` shows up in your URL.

Database Abstraction

A *database abstraction layer* is an API to provide a set of functions to deal with a multitude of databases in an implementation-independent way. By changing the back end of the database abstraction layer, you can easily switch from MySQL to Oracle, for example. Perl's *DBI* (*DataBase Interface*) is such a layer, and one of the most well-known features of the PHPLib is its database abstraction layer organized in the `DB_Sql` class.

Portability

For a professional Web application programmer, database abstraction can be useful and important. The base of every application is its data-model, a set of data structures for general-purpose usage, often contained within a database. While PHP supports a great number of databases, every database has a different application programming interface (API). Using these native APIs, operating system and database-independent development is impossible—if you want to port an application from MySQL to Oracle you have to be prepared for some heavy work, unless you use an abstraction layer like the PHPLib. Table 6.1 shows how database interfaces can differ from system to system.

Table 6.1 **APIs to Access MySQL and Oracle**

Description	MySQL	Oracle 7
Connect	`mysql_connect()`	`ora_logon()`
Query	`mysql_query()` or `mysql_db_query()`	`ora_parse()`, then `ora_exec()`
Get next row of result	or `mysql_fetch_array()`	Works with offsets: `ora_columnname()`, `ora_getcolumn()`
Number of rows in a result set	`mysql_num_rows()`	Not possible, as Oracle starts to return rows prior to knowing the total number of rows in the result set.
Last inserted primary key ID	`mysql_insert_id()`	No equivalent in PHP functions.

Of course, you usually don't change your database in a weekly rhythm, so this may not be of much importance to you. Also, portability between databases is only a dream even if you use the PHPLib, if you haven't planned it in your project from the beginning. Real life shows that the problem is not porting the API, but the database-specific functions. You can create truly portable database code only by accepting that you can't use specific features of an RDBMS—but then you end up re-creating that feature in your code, which may lead to applications that are harder to maintain and slower.

If your aim is to program portable code, you have to work around the specialties of the underlying database. The PHPLib can make this task a bit easier; for example, it has built-in sequence handling and a simple table-locking mechanism, which work in a database-independent way. Lately, the PHPLib developers have added the class Query, which is intended to abstract simple queries (inserts, updates, WHERE statements, and some others, which cover about 80% of the normal database usage), to make them database-independent. Currently this class works for MySQL and Oracle 7 (and up) only.

Two other features of PHPLib's database abstraction layer are at least as important as portability, and those are real time-savers in your daily applications. The following sections describe these features.

Debugging Mode

The class DB_Sql has a debug mode that allows you to see what queries are sent to the database. To switch debugging on, just insert $db->Debug = true; in your program after having instantiated the class. In our programs, we typically have a global DEBUG constant, which we assign to the DB_Sql class in a similar way:

```
define("DEBUG", true);
$db->Debug = DEBUG;
```

When debugging is switched on, the DB_Sql class will print out some values from function calls and much additional information. This can be a great help if you're searching for an error, or if you want to verify that the SQL queries your script is generating are correct.

Error Handling

The PHPLib takes care of handling all errors that could result from database-related functions. As a positive side effect, the code you write using DB_Sql is more compact, because you don't have to bother with error handling yourself.

With the default settings, a script stops at every error it encounters. This can be controlled by changing the class variable $Halt_On_Error, which is set to yes by default. Setting it to report causes the library to print the error without exiting the script. Setting this variable to no instructs the library to ignore all errors. This may result in unwanted side effects, for example in inconsistent data, when a failing database query is ignored—so be careful with this option. In production applications, error messages should be informative and appear in a common layout, adjusted to the site's corporate identity. To apply your own formatting to error messages, you can create a new class extending DB_Sql and override the function haltmsg() there. Because this function controls the output of all error messages, it's easy to customize messages this way:

```
class test_db extends DB_Sql
{
    function haltmsg($msg)
    {
        print("Database Error: $msg<br>");
        printf("MySQL said: %s<br>", $this->Error);
    }
}
```

The haltmsg() function is solely responsible for outputting the error message; actually stopping the script or cleaning up after an error is left to the PHPLib. The function is invoked only if $Halt_On_Error is set to either yes or report. The variable $msg, passed as argument to haltmsg(), contains a verbose description of the error encountered. You can also access $this->Error and $this->Errno to retrieve the messages produced by the database engine.

DB_Sql Example

A short example will show you best how the Db_Sql class is used. The source code in Listing 6.1 connects to a database and displays the whole contents of a single table. It uses the Example_Db class defined in local.inc, which extends Db_Sql and forms a reference implementation of how you can create your own customized classes. For simplicity's sake, we use the sample implementations from the PHPLib distribution in the following code snippets.

Listing 6.1 **First simple example of how to use *DB_Sql*.**

```
// Instantiate Example_DB class
$db = new Example_DB;

// Connect to RDBMS
$db->connect("test", "localhost", "root", "");

// Create SQL statement
$sql = "SELECT * FROM test";

// Execute query
$db->query($sql);

// Loop through result set
while($db->next_record())
{
    // Loop through the $db->Records hash
    while(list($key, $value) = each($db->Record))
    {
        // Print only non-numeric indexes
```

```
        print(is_string($key) ? "<b>$key</b>: $value<br>": "");
    }

    print("<p>");
}
```

The first line creates a new instance of the DB_Sql class. By default, this class is defined in the file db_mysql.inc (loaded in prepend.php3) and uses MySQL as database engine.

The next step is connecting to the database. Of course, you have to change the values to your settings; in this example, we connect to the database test on localhost, with the username root and no password.

You can also set these properties explicitly using their respective class variables:

```
$db = new Example_Db;
$db->Database = 'test';
$db->Host     = 'localhost';
$db->User     = 'root';
$db->Password = '';
```

At the call of $db->query() PHPLib will notice that no connection has been established yet and will open one automatically, using the values defined earlier in these class variables.

Our example continues with $db->query(), which handles everything you need to send a query to the database. It connects to the selected database (if not already done), and it handles errors that could happen. If we had set $db->Debug to true, this function would output the SQL query before sending it to the database.

Then $db->next_record() is called in a while loop. This function gets the next row from a set of results and stores the retrieved row in the array $db->Record. If there are no more rows in the result set, the function returns false, terminating the loop.

The second loop traverses the $db->Record array and outputs the field names along with their respective contents. Because this array contains the contents with both a numeric index (similar to arrays returned by the default usage of mysql_fetch_array()) and the field name as key, we make sure to output only the array entry where the index is a field name.

Compare the PHPLib example in Listing 6.1 with the example of traditional programming in Listing 6.2. They're approximately the same length, but the PHPLib example inherits all the advantages we explained earlier. By changing one file, you can change the underlying database layer. You have more powerful error handling than in the other example; by changing one class variable, you can instruct the PHPLib to halt on errors, report them, or ignore them, while the traditional example simply exits on error. And last, but not least, you have complete debugging support built in.

Listing 6.2 **Example of traditional programming.**

```
// Connect to RDBMS
$link = mysql_connect('localhost', 'root', '') or die(mysql_error());

// Select database
$db = mysql_select_db('test') or die(mysql_error());

// Create SQL statement
$sql = "SELECT * FROM test";

// Execute query
$res = mysql_query($sql) or die(mysql_error());

// Loop through result set
while($row = mysql_fetch_array($res))
{
    // Loop through the $db->Records hash
    while(list($key, $value) = each($row))
    {
        // Print only non-numeric indexes
        print(is_string($key) ? "<b>$key</b>: $value<br>": "");
    }

    print("<p>");
}
```

Be aware of one possible trap: You should restrict yourself to using one database per application. PHP has problems handling access to different databases in one script—especially with MySQL. PHP assumes that it can silently reuse connections that have been established using the same username and password. Look at the following example:

```
$res_one = mysql_connect("localhost", "root", "") or die(mysql_error());
$res_two = mysql_connect("localhost", "root", "") or die(mysql_error());
```

You would expect that you had two different connection identifiers here, right? You haven't, though, as PHP reuses the open connection in the second mysql_connect() call. Printing the connection identifiers, $res_one and $res_two, will output the same resource identifier for both variables. The implication of this behavior is that using mysql_select_db() on one link will also change the context on the other connection. This also applies to the objects in the PHPLib: Using one database for DB_Sql and a different database for the session data will result in problems. Unfortunately, at this time there's no workaround for this problem.

Sessions

The PHPLib provides at least equivalent functionality to PHP's built-in session management library; even the names of the functions are often the same. While it is similar in many ways to PHP's internal session management, it's not identical. One nice additional feature is the automatic fallback mode (described in the following section).

Automatic Fallback

By default, the session management works with cookies. As outlined in the "HTTP and Sessions" section of Chapter 4, this should be the preferred technique (when supported by the client), and it's the easiest method of session ID propagation. But you can change it to the GET/POST method by changing one variable, $mode. The $mode variable defines which method should be used as the primary method of session ID propagation. It can be either cookie or get; the default value is cookie.

The PHPLib provides an automatic fallback mode at runtime. If the variable $fallback_mode is set to get, the GET/POST mode will be used when the preferred mode specified in the variable $mode (usually cookie) is not supported by the client. Setting $mode to cookie and $fallback_mode to get makes the most sense. The PHPLib will try to use cookies; if they're not supported, it will fall back to the GET/POST mode. In detail, the PHPLib checks for cookie support in this way:

1. On the first request to a PHPLib-powered page, the PHPLib tries to set the session cookie named after the Session class instance.

2. Next, it redirects the user to the same page with the session ID appended as query string, using the following code:

```
header("Location: ". $PROTOCOL. "://".$HTTP_HOST.$this->self_url());
```

3. The PHPLib checks whether the session ID can be found in the $HTTP_COOKIE_VARS array. If so, the session remains in cookie mode. If the session ID can't be found, the client doesn't accept cookies and the session switches to get mode.

Page Caching

The Session class also allows you to control how pages are cached. Its class variable $allow_cache can be set to no, private, or public. Its default value depends on the version of the PHPLib; for example, with release 7.2 it's set to private, with subsequent versions it's set to no. The page-caching mechanism is very similar to the one provided in the native session functions of PHP 4.0.

Serializer

In PHP 3.0, you couldn't serialize objects easily. The `serialize()` function didn't preserve class methods properly, and there was no way to do it manually. The PHP 3.0 support for objects was missing one important thing: introspection. There was no way to get the name of a class or the name of its parent class. Therefore, the PHPLib needed to use a workaround: It simply required classes to have two additional values, `$classname` and `$persistent_slots`, which contained the name of the class and the class variables to be serialized, respectively. Knowing the class name, the PHPLib could create PHP code instantiating the class (`$class = new class;`) and store it in the session data repository. When the session data was reactivated, this code was executed with `eval()`. Do you remember the self-modifying counter example from Chapter 2, "Advanced Syntax"? The PHPLib uses the same concepts.

Note: With PHP 4.0, these workarounds are no longer necessary. PHP 4.0 has functions like `get_class()` and `get_parent_class()` to allow better class introspection. And `serialize()` now works transparently on objects.

Session Example

In your daily work, using the PHPLib session object is just as easy as using the PHP 4.0 session library. The example in Listing 6.3 reflects this; it does the same work as the example in Chapter 4:

Listing 6.3 **A basic example of using PHPLib's *Session* class.**

```
// Create a new instance manually
$sess = new Example_Session;

// Start the session
$sess->start();

// Register our session variable
$sess->register("counter");

// Init the counter
if(!isset($counter))
{
    $counter = 0;
}

// Output session ID and counter
printf("Our session ID is: %s<br>", $sess->id);
print("The counter value is: $counter");

// Increment the counter
$counter++;

// Save the session state
$sess->freeze();
```

The only significant difference between this example and the PHP 4.0 example is that the PHPLib uses an object–oriented approach.

Like the PHP 4.0 session library, the PHPLib uses storage modules (called *containers* in PHPLib terminology) to store session data. The container classes all start with a CT_ prefix. An SQL database is the most common way to store session data, but the PHPLib also knows other container classes.

The available container classes in PHPLib 7.2 are as follows:

- CT_Sql is the default container and stores the session data in a database. It has the following class variables:

Name	Description
$database_class	The name of the DB_Sql class, which should be used to connect to the database.
$database_table	The name of the table that will be used to store the session data.
$encoding_mode	This variable controls how the session data is stored. It can take two values: base64 or slashes. Normally you shouldn't change the default value (base64); this way, session data will be encoded with Base64 prior to being stored in the database. For debugging purposes, you may want to use the alternative method, slashes, to store session data as plain text in the table.

- In terms of features, CT_Split_Sql is identical to CT_Sql. It must be used if the underlying database is unable to store enough data in one field for the session data, especially if the database has problems with binary large objects (BLOBs). CT_Split_Sql is not compatible with the tables of CT_Sql.

  To change the length at which the class splits up the session data, you can use the variable $split_length, whose default value is 4096 (4KB).

- CT_Shm stores session data in shared memory. You need to have compiled PHP with shared memory support in order to use this. This container is faster because it stores session data directly accessible in memory. The drawbacks are that if you have to restart your server for any reason, all session data is lost. Also, the number of concurrent sessions is limited due to the memory consumption. Each session takes up a certain amount of memory (the amount depends on the quantity and size of the session variables), and after all available memory has been consumed, no more new sessions can be created.

These class variables are different from those of `CT_Sql`:

Parameter	Description
`$max_sessions`	Maximum number of simultaneous active sessions. The current default is 500.
`$shm_key`	Unique key for the shared memory segment that should be used. It's important to make this key unique for each application.
`$shm_size`	The size of the shared memory segment in bytes. This size could be calculated approximately with the formula `shm_size = max_sessions * session_size`, where the session size could be an average size of about 600 bytes. The default value is 64000 (64KB).

- `CT_Dbm` uses a UNIX DBM file to store session data. This type of database stores data as key/value pairs in regular files on a system. The only variable you should set is `$dbm_file`, which is the filename of your DBM file. The file has to exist with the proper rights; the server needs write access to it.

- `CT_Ldap` stores session data in an LDAP (Lightweight Directory Access Protocol) server. PHP has to be compiled with LDAP support to use this container. The `CT_Ldap` class has the following properties:

Item	Description
`$ldap_host`, `$ldap_port`	Hostname and port number of the LDAP server.
`$rootdn`, `$rootpw`	Root distinguished name and password of the LDAP server, used to connect to it.
`$basedn`	Below this distinguished name, the session data should be stored.
`$objclass`	Name of the object class (can be compared with an SQL table name).

If you look at `local.inc`, you'll see a series of class definitions; three of them actually concern our example:

```
class DB_Example extends DB_Sql {
  var $Host     = "localhost";
  var $Database = "phplib";
  var $User     = "tobias";
  var $Password = "justdoit";
}

class Example_CT_Sql extends CT_Sql {
  var $database_class = "DB_Example";       ## Which database to connect...
  var $database_table = "active_sessions"; ## and find our session data in this
}
```

```
class Example_Session extends Session {
  var $classname = "Example_Session";

  var $cookiename     = "";                ## defaults to classname
  var $magic          = "Hocuspocus";      ## ID seed
  var $mode           = "cookie";          ## We propagate session IDs with cookies
  var $fallback_mode  = "get";
  var $lifetime       = 0;                 ## 0 = do session cookies, else minutes
                                           ↪until the session expires
  var $that_class     = "Example_CT_Sql"; ## name of data storage container
  var $gc_probability = 5;
}
```

As you can see, the classes form a relation; in the Example_Session class, the variable
$that_class is set to the name of the Example_CT_Sql class, and in Example_CT_Sql,
the $database_class variable points to the class DB_Sql. Figure 6.1 shows this
relationship in detail.

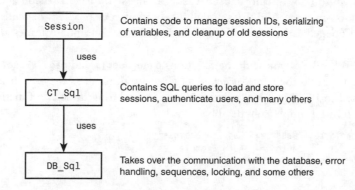

Figure 6.1   Relationship model of the classes DB_Sql, CT_Sql, and Session.

Our example didn't use the base classes, but extensions of them as defined in
local.inc. Figure 6.2 shows these dependencies.

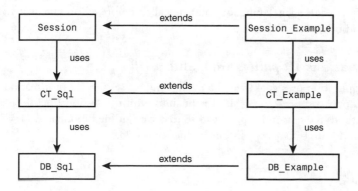

Figure 6.2   Dependencies and relationships in the example.

Abbreviations I: *page_open()*

Let's assume that you want to develop a larger application, using session management, database abstraction, and PHPLib's authentication and permission-management features. So you need to instantiate the session, authentication, and permission objects. Your `local.inc` file will look something like this:

```
$sess = new Session_Example;
$sess->start();

$auth = new Auth_Example;
$auth->start();

$perm = new Perm_Example;
$user = new User_Example;
$user->start();
```

Because the classes depend on each other, you have to initialize them in the correct order, and you cannot instantiate `User_Example` unless you have a session and an authentication instance. And that's not all. The end of your program depends on what classes you opened earlier; the order in which the classes' cleanup routines are called is important.

The PHPLib helps you with the functions `page_open()` and `page_close()`. The documentation calls them *page-management functions*, and indeed they can handle all work related to PHPLib initialization and shutdown. Using these two functions, we can shorten our example considerably:

```
page_open(array("sess" => "Session_Example",
                "auth" => "Auth_Example",
                "perm" => "Perm_Example"));

[...]

page_close();
```

The `page_open()` function in the example creates instances of `Session_Example`, `Auth_Example`, and `Perm_Example`, named $sess, $auth, and $perm, respectively. You can now use these instances directly, for example with `$sess->register()`.

Note: The `page_open()` function must be called before all output, as it will set a cookie and other HTTP headers.

Abbreviations II: *purl(), url(),* and *pself()*

If your application uses `cookie` as the main mode of session ID propagation, and `get` as fallback mode, you need to tag all of your links with the session ID. To use any of the other methods for session ID propagation that we outlined in Chapter 4, you'd have to extend the PHPLib to accept another value for $mode.

But the PHPLib makes even manual URL rewriting a lot easier. It provides the url() function, which appends the session ID to links when in get mode:

```
$link = $sess->url("script.php3");
```

If your session is currently in get mode, the resulting $link variable would look something like this:

```
script.php3?Example_Session=2e4c3670ce9a143fee398aec282f960c
```

The function handles even query strings correctly; it wouldn't get confused if you called it with an URL containing a parameter, for example script.php3?foo=bar.

As a shorthand for printing the resulting link, you can use PHPLib's purl() function, which works the same way as url() but also outputs the generated URL. Similarly, self_url() and pself_url() generate and output (with the latter function) a tagged link to the current file.

Authentication

The "Authentication" section of Chapter 4 mentioned that HTTP Basic authentication has a number of drawbacks, and that you can avoid those with PHP-based authentication. The following sections provide details.

Advantages of PHP Authentication

This section continues where we left off in the "Authentication" section of Chapter 4. We discussed there that HTTP Basic Authentication has a number of drawbacks, and that you can avoid those with PHP-based authentication. The PHPLib features sophisticated classes for handling user authentication and permission management.

The PHPLib authenticates sessions; thus it depends on the Session class. On those pages in which you need authentication, the following page_open() call should be made to instantiate a session and authentication object:

```
page_open(array("sess" => "Session_Example", "auth" => "Auth_Example"));
```

Being based on sessions introduces a number of advantages for the authentication:

- The username and the authentication element are sent only once, at the login. Once authenticated, the server stores the authentication data inside the session, and doesn't transmit username or authentication element again. This is different than in HTTP Basic Authentication, where the username and password are transmitted in the HTTP headers of each request. But it also means that, if you lose the session, you lose the authentication.

- The authentication procedure on the server can be complex. It can use any database or any other mechanism you can think of. The authentication is handled by an undefined function of the Auth class (auth_validatelogin()) and you have to implement it.

- It's not limited to a whole directory, but can be different for individual files of the application, and can even implement authentication levels inside a script. It's possible to hide parts of the script from users who are not allowed to access them.

- Users who aren't known to the system can register themselves before logging in. A registration form is offered and the PHPLib will automatically create a standard entry in the user database.

- Authentication via PHPLib works even with the CGI version of PHP.

- You can log users out cleanly. This means that you can give your users the chance to terminate the current sessions (a logout button).

- Users can be logged out automatically after a certain idle time. Doing so provides additional security for your application, because you can prevent session hijacking after a longer idle time.

Auth Example

Let's go ahead with a basic example. The example in Listing 6.4 shows the default PHPLib login screen when you call it for the first time. Log in with the PHPLib default username/password pair of kris/test. After you have been authenticated, you'll see your session ID, your username, and your permissions.

Listing 6.4   **A basic example of how to use *Auth*.**

```
page_open(array("sess" => "Example_Session", "auth" => "Example_Auth"));

printf("Your session id: %s<p>\n", $sess->id);
printf("Your user ID: %s<br>\n", $auth->auth["uid"]);
printf("Your user name: %s<br>\n", $auth->auth["uname"]);
printf("You permissions: %s<br>\n", $auth->auth["perm"]);

page_close()
```

All pages using PHPLib's authentication follow this general structure. First, a page_open() is called; the rest of the script will be executed only after the user is logged in and authenticated. You can safely assume that no user will ever see anything from below the page_open() without being logged in. With a one-line page_open() call, you have added complete user authentication to your script. After you have established the classes you want to use in the application, the PHPLib is indeed that easy to use. Our examples so far have used the example classes provided in the PHPLib distribution. In your work, however, you'll want to create your own classes (derived from the base classes) to better fit your needs. For this, it's necessary to understand a bit more about how the PHPLib works internally.

Auth Internals

Assuming that you use MySQL as your database engine, the following schema will be used for your user table:

```
CREATE TABLE auth_user (
    user_id varchar(32) NOT NULL,
    username varchar(32) NOT NULL,
    password varchar(32) NOT NULL,
    perms varchar(255),
    PRIMARY KEY (user_id),
    UNIQUE k_username (username)
);
```

The primary key is user_id, because internally PHPLib works with this ID, not with a user's username/password pair. This ID (called uid by PHPLib) is a unique string, similar to a session ID, that's created with a combination of uniqid() and md5():

```
$uid = md5(uniqid($hash_secret));
```

Why doesn't the PHPLib simply use a composite primary key involving the fields username and password? This way, it could save the additional user_id field. The reason is that PHPLib's goal is to work with any authentication process and to make interfacing as easy as possible. Having a separate, fixed-length unique identifier for each user makes it easy to have additional tables that are tied in a relational model to the auth_user table.

The trick in our last example was that we simply used the default implementation of the Auth class, as provided by the PHPLib distribution in Example_Default_Auth. You'll almost always need to write your own class, extending the Auth base class. In its core form, the Auth is unusable because it doesn't provide two functions necessary for the authentication. Auth knows neither how you want your login screen to look, nor how you want to handle the authentication. It therefore makes no attempt to do this for you, and you have to define these functions yourself in your derived classes. Listing 6.5 shows an example of such a derived class, which is similar to those found in local.inc as example implementation.

Listing 6.5 **Extending the base *Auth* class.**

```
require("EasyTemplate.inc.php3");
class My_Auth extends Auth
{
    var $classname = "My_Auth";
    var $database_class = "DB_Example";
    var $database_table = "auth_user";

    function auth_loginform()
    {
        // Create template instance
        $tpl = new EasyTemplate("loginform.inc.html");
```

continues

Listing 6.5   **Continued**

```
            // Is the username already set? If yes, it means that the
            // first authentication try failed.
            if(isset($this->auth["uname"]))
            {
                $tpl->assign("USERNAME", $this->auth["uname"]);
                $tpl->assign("MESSAGE", "Either your username or your password are
                ➥invalid.<br> Please try again!");
            }
            else
            {
                $tpl->assign("USERNAME", "");
                $tpl->assign("MESSAGE", "Please identify yourself with a username and
                ➥a password:");
            }

            // Assign action to form, which points to ourselves
            $tpl->assign("ACTION", $this->url());

            // Output the parsed template
            $tpl->easy_print();
        }

        function auth_validatelogin()
        {
            // Global form variables
            global $username, $password;

            // If $username is set, remember it
            if(isset($username))
            {
                $this->auth["uname"] = $username;
            }

            // Set the $uid to false by default
            $uid = false;

            // Select rows corresponding to the submitted username/password
            $query = "
                    SELECT
                        *
                    FROM
                        $this->database_table
                    WHERE
                        username = '$username'
                        AND password = '$password'
                    ";

            // Execute query
            $this->db->query($query);

            // If one row was returned, the user is authenticated
```

```
        if($this->db->num_rows() == 1)
        {
            $this->db->next_record();

            // Set up $uid and $this->auth array.
            $uid = $this->db->Record["user_id"];
            $this->auth["uid"] = $uid;
            $this->auth["uname"] = $this->db->Record["username"];
        }

        return($uid);
    }
}
```

The two class variables $database_class and $database_table are used internally by Auth to save session and authentication information. They don't influence authentication; the login procedure is handled by the two class methods that you need to define: auth_loginform() and auth_validatelogin().

When a user requests a protected page and is not yet logged in, the Auth class invokes the auth_loginform() function. This function should draw a login screen; as this function will be called again if the authentication fails, it should provide the necessary mechanisms to handle failed tries. In our example, we display an error message accordingly, and prepopulate the username form field with the submitted value.

The second function, auth_validatelogin(), is the heart of the class—it performs the authentication. It will be called after the user has submitted the authentication information from the form provided by the auth_loginform() function. The form variables are then global variables, of course, and need to be made global in the function before they can be accessed. How you perform the authentication is completely up to you; in the example, we authenticate against the standard auth_user table from the PHPLib distribution, but you could also use .htaccess-style files, an LDAP server, etc.

If the authentication is successful, the function must return a valid user ID and set up the $this->auth array. This associative array must contain at least two elements: uid is the unique user ID, uname is the username as entered by the user.

If you want to use permission levels with the Perm class (more on this a bit later), you need to set up an additional element: $this->auth["perm"]. This element should contain the permissions the user has, as a comma-separated list of names with no spaces; for example, admin or author,editor. Usually this list will be retrieved from the same storage medium from which you get the user information—in our example, the MySQL database.

If the authentication fails, the function must return `false`; then the `auth_loginform()` function will be called again. Did you notice that we set up `$this->auth["uname"]` regardless of whether the authentication succeeded? The `$this->auth` array is a session variable, and thus persistent across multiple login tries. In the `auth_loginform()` function, we check whether the username has already been specified once, and eventually prepopulate the login form with it.

Now that the user is properly logged into your application, you know exactly who you're dealing with. To manage different permission levels associated with users, you can use another PHPLib class, `Perm`.

Managing Permission Levels

In a typical application, you'll generally have two permission levels: users and administrators. However, some applications require more sophisticated access control. A content-management system, for example, needs many permission levels:

- A superuser, able to change anything in the system, to modify the user system, etc.
- Editors, who can edit articles and content, and approve content submitted by authors.
- Authors, who can create content, submit it for approval to editors, but not approve content.
- Users with read-only access.

Since you know the currently logged-in user and can identify him or her with a unique string (`$uid`), it wouldn't be very hard to write functions to associate the user with a group and present content according to this group. The PHPLib has built-in functionality for handling this.

To use the `Perm` class, you have to add another element to the `page_open()` call. The PHPLib provides a default implementation of the `Perm` class, named `Example_Perm`, but here the same principle applies that we mentioned earlier: To make use of all available functionality and fit your specific requirements, you should derive your own class in `local.inc`.

Listing 6.6 shows an example using `Perm`. It has a bit more functionality than absolutely necessary, because it allows you to log out and log back in with a different username—this makes it easier to see the different permissions levels in use. The sample user provided by the PHPLib (username `kris`, password `test`) has `admin` privileges; the script will show you a "Welcome Admin" message when you log in with this user. As there is only this one user provided in the PHPLib distribution, you need to create a new user if you want to see what the page looks like for users with privileges below `admin`.

Listing 6.6 **Using the *Perm* class.**

```
page_open(array("sess" => "Example_Session", "auth" => "Example_Auth",
➥"perm" => "Example_Perm"));

if(isset($mode) && $mode == "reload")
{
    $auth->unauth();
    print("You have been logged out.<br>");
    printf('If you want, you can <a href="%s"> login again.',
    ➥$sess->url(basename($PHP_SELF)));
}
else
{
    if($perm->have_perm("admin"))
    {
        print("<b>Welcome Admin.</b><br>");
        print('You are logged in with "admin" permissions.<br>');
    }
    else
    {
        printf('You are logged in with "%s" permissions.<br>',
        ➥$auth->auth["perm"]);
    }

    printf("Your user name: %s<br>", $auth->auth["uname"]);
    printf('<a href="%s">Log out</a>',
    ➥$sess->url(basename($PHP_SELF)."?mode=reload"));
}

page_close();
```

Bit Bashing

Bitwise calculations often cause a great deal of confusion among novice programmers, and even advanced developers have occasional difficulties dealing with them. Representing flag values as bit patterns can be very useful, though; the PHPLib uses this for permission levels. It's also used often to store flag values in a single INT field of a database. Consider an application that needs to keep track of a number of different states, for example users' hobbies. Instead of having one field in a database for each hobby and setting that to true or false, you can have a single flag field. Depending on whether the user has a specific hobby, this hobby's bit is switched on or off.

Simply put, bitwise operations are operations that manipulate one or more bits at a time. You know that in the binary system, you have octets of bits— a series of 0 and 1. The decimal number 42 in the binary system is represented as 00101010:

```
Bit position: 7 6 5 4 3 2 1 0
Bit value:    0 0 1 0 1 0 1 0
```

The bit farthest to the right, Bit 0, is known as the Least Significant Bit. Bit 7 is called the Most Significant Bit. To convert from binary system to decimal system and vice versa, you can use `BinDec()` and `DecBin()` in PHP.

Binary operators toggle bits in these octets off or on.

Setting a Bit

To set a bit in a value, you use inclusive OR (`value ¦ value`). For example, if the flag's current value is 3 (meaning that the first and second bits are set), and you want to set the second bit (remember, bit counting starts from 0), you OR the current value with 4 (2 to the second power):

```
$value = 3;
$value ¦= 4;
```

The value is now 7. In the binary system, the operation looks like this:

```
  0 0 0 0 0 1 1
¦ 0 0 0 0 1 0 0
= 0 0 0 0 1 1 1
```

Toggling a Bit

Toggling a bit—switching it to 1 if it's 0 and vice versa—is done using the exclusive OR (XOR) operator (`value ^ value`). If our value is 3 and we want to toggle the first bit (which is currently 1: `0000010`), the following line would be used:

```
$value = 3;
$value ^= 2;
```

The result of this would be 1. In binary:

```
  0 0 0 0 0 1 0
^ 0 0 0 0 0 1 0
= 0 0 0 0 0 0 1
```

Clearing a Bit

Clearing a bit is done most easily by making sure that the bit is switched on, and then inversing it. This requires two bitwise operators, INVERSE and AND (`value & ~value`). To clear the first bit in the value 3, this line can be used:

```
$value = 3;
$value &= ~2;
```

Testing for a Bit

To test whether a bit is set in a value, you use the logical AND operator. It compares two values; if both bits are 1, it returns 1. For example, to test whether the first bit is set in the value 3, you would use this:

```
if(2 & 3)
   // more code
```

Bitwise Shifts

To shift bits left or right, you use the shift operators << and >>. For example, shifting binary 1 left with binary 1 will result in binary 10:

```
    0 0 0 0 0 1
<<  0 0 0 0 1 0
=   0 0 0 0 1 0
```

This can be useful to set bits, as you'll see later in the example.

Operator Precedence

This is a good point to talk about precedence with bitwise operations. Keep in mind that bitwise operators have lower precedence than arithmetic operators. The statement 1 + 2 ¦ 3 will be evaluated as (1+2) ¦ 3. It's also important to remember that bitwise operators have lower precedence than comparison operators. Be careful not to write statements like if(2 & 3 != 0). Instead of testing whether the second bit is set in the value 3 (it is), this statement will test 3 !=0 first, returning true, which will result in 2 & 1—returning 0, which definitely isn't what you wanted.

Example

Let's get back to the hobbies example we mentioned earlier. Assume that the user can choose from four available hobbies: reading, programming, writing, and hiking. We first assign a bit to each hobby:

- reading: 1
- programming: 2
- writing: 4
- hiking: 8

In binary, this represents the following values:

```
reading:     0 0 0 0 0 1
programming: 0 0 0 0 1 0
writing:     0 0 0 1 0 0
hiking:      0 0 1 0 0 0
```

In code, you can define the hobbies with a simple bit shift:

```
define("HOBBY_READING", 1 << 0);
define("HOBBY_PROGRAMMING", 1 << 1);
define("HOBBY_WRITING", 1 << 2);
define("HOBBY_HIKING", 1 << 3);
```

If the user chooses writing and programming as hobbies, you can create a bit pattern by ORing these values:

```
$pattern = HOBBY_WRITING ¦ HOBBY_PROGRAMMING;
```

Later, you can test whether the user has chosen writing as his or her hobby by checking the associated bit in the pattern:

```
printf("Writing %s chosen.", (HOBBY_WRITING & $pattern) ? "is": "is not");
```

To unset the writing bit, you can use this line:

```
$pattern &= ~HOBBY_WRITING;
```

The actual check for the needed permission level is done using the `$auth->have_perm()` function. You pass the permission level you want to check for as argument; our example uses `$auth->have_perm("admin")` to see whether the user has the privilege `admin`. If the user has the needed permissions, the function returns `true`; otherwise it returns `false`.

Each user has associated privileges. Using the `Example_Auth` implementation, the privileges are stored in the `auth_user` MySQL table. You've seen the field earlier:

```
perms varchar(255)
```

A list of valid permissions is defined in the class derived from `Perm`, namely in the `$permissions` class variable. The `Example_Perm` class has the following permissions:

```
var $permissions = array(
        "user"       => 1,
        "author"     => 2,
        "editor"     => 4,
        "supervisor" => 8,
        "admin"      => 16
        );
```

Permissions are translated to bitmaps internally, and calculated with logical OR and AND. The values in this associative array define a bit pattern for each permission level. While this may sound a bit complicated, using bit patterns has some advantages for scenarios like permission levels. For example, it provides for levels that inherit the permissions from lower levels—an `admin` level automatically has `user` privileges, if you design the bit patterns appropriately.

The default setup doesn't have this inclusive behavior: The `admin` level is different from the `user` level, and a user belonging to the `admin` group won't be able to access functionality secured with `$auth->have_perm("user")`. To make this clearer, it helps to visualize how the PHPLib calculates the bit patterns:

- Functionality accessible only to `user` levels. This level has the bit pattern 1.

- The user is in the `admin` level, which has the bit pattern 16.

- These two operands are combined with a logical AND, which results in 0 (verify yourself: `print(16 & 1);`). The result `0` is not the same as the requested level (1), so access is denied.

The essence of this calculation is that the PHPLib tests whether the bit pattern provided as argument to `$perm->have_perms()` has the user's permission bit set. This allows complex combinations.

Let's have a look at another example: Suppose you have four permission levels—`admin`, `editor_in_chief`, `editor`, and `author`. You want the editors not to be able to submit content (`author` level), but the other groups should inherit the permissions below them. The final authorization system looks like this:

- `admin`: inherits `editor_in_chief`, `editor`, `author`

- `editor_in_chief`: inherits `editor`, `author`

- `editor`

- `author`

To calculate the bit patterns for each group, you start at the lowest level, `author`, with a bit pattern of 1 (meaning that the rightmost bit is set). If we wanted the editor to inherit the author level, we'd go on with the author bit pattern and set the next higher bit (1 ¦ 2). For this example, however, we want the author and editor groups to be separate, so we set the `editor` level to the next higher free bit pattern, decimal 2 (binary 10).

If an editor now requests a page protected with `author` permissions, access will be denied:

- required level (`author`): 1

- current level (`editor`): 2

- logical AND of 1 and 2 (1 & 2) is 0, which is not the required level.

The next higher level (third bit by now) is `editor_in_chief`, inheriting `editor` and `author`. This means that bits 1 and 2 must be set in the editor-in-chief's bit pattern, and we also set the second bit (2 to the second power, or 4): 1 ¦ 2 ¦ 4— this results in 7.

To verify the correctness of this:

- required level (`editor`): 2
- current level (`editor_in_chief`): 7
- logical AND of 7 and 2 (`7 & 2`) is 2, which is the required level.

The only level left is the administrator's, which again inherits all levels below it: `7 | 8` (8 is used to set the third bit). This results in 15. To test it:

- required level (`editor_in_chief`): 7
- current level (`admin`): 15
- logical AND of 15 and 7 (`15 & 7`) is 7, which is the required level.

Our permissions therefore are defined as follows:

```
define("PHPLIB_PERM_AUTHOR",            1 | 0);
define("PHPLIB_PERM_EDITOR",            1 | 1);
define("PHPLIB_PERM_EDITOR_IN_CHIEF", 1 | 2 | 4);
define("PHPLIB_PERM_ADMIN",             1 | 2 | 4 | 8);

var $permissions = array(
        "author"          => PHPLIB_PERM_AUTHOR,
        "editor"          => PHPLIB_PERM_EDITOR,
        "editor_in_chief" => PHPLIB_PERM_EDITOR_IN_CHIEF,
        "admin"           => PHPLIB_PERM_ADMIN
        );
```

Summary

You've learned about the basic classes and uses of the PHPLib in this chapter. You've seen that it's a powerful solution for many problems you'll inevitably face when creating Web applications—yet it's easy to use once the necessary framework has been established. It provides a complete infrastructure for session management and user authentication in all aspects.

In the next chapter, you'll see the PHPLib in use with a real-life application. That chapter also shows another class of the PHPLib that we haven't mentioned yet: the `Template` class for separating code from layout.

7

Cutting-Edge Applications

If you realize that all things change,
there is nothing you will try to hold on to.
If you aren't afraid of dying,
there is nothing you can't achieve.

IN THIS CHAPTER, WE'RE GOING TO DELVE FURTHER into modern Web application topics.

In the first section, "Knowledge Repositories," we create a tip repository featuring user ratings, hit counter, and unlimited nested categories. You'll learn about tree structures and put into practice the knowledge gained in Chapter 2, "Advanced Syntax."

XML (Extensible Markup Language) is rapidly becoming the most widely used standard for data exchange. Nonetheless, often generalized explanations ("XML is HTML allowing you to create your own tags") make it hard to understand the real concepts behind it. We try to explain it in detail and give you thorough introduction into XML parsing with Expat, the Document Object Model interface (DOM), and LibXML.

WDDX (Web Distributed Data eXchange) provides a means to exchange programming language structures (objects, classes, arrays, and so on) across the Internet. We'll show why this is useful and how to use it in your own applications.

Knowledge Repositories

In the corporate environment, a clear trend emerged during the last few years: away from product-based planning and toward customer-focused strategy. With this trend, a new technology gained widespread publicity and success: *knowledge management*.

For a company that wants to have a strategic advantage over its competitors, it's necessary to organize corporate knowledge in a way that makes it easily accessible by anyone, all the time. With the dawn of enterprise intranets, this topic was made more current than ever.

In traditional intranets, information is often hard to find because it's spread to many different pages and coming from many different sources. The information that's actually there is often quite useless because it's not indexed and not broken down into smaller logical units, making it hard to search.

What can a company do to solve these problems efficiently? The key lies in proper knowledge management. A lot of companies offer sophisticated solutions, but you may also consider developing your own tools—simpler and therefore easier to use than commercial solutions, or better fitting your company's strategy.

We have a starting point for you. On the CD-ROM to this book, you'll find the full source code for a knowledge database, which could easily be transformed into a support repository or a corporate link directory. The system was originally developed for Zend Technologies, but they have been kind enough to let us distribute it with our book.

The application has a wide range of features: full-text search, an unlimited number of categories and subcategories, a report showing all tips by a specific author and authors with the most submissions, user rating of entries, user submission entries, and more.

The system was realized using the PHPLib for database abstraction and HTML templates. Therefore, the following walkthrough will also give you a thorough overview of application development with the PHPLib. Figure 7.1 shows the application's start screen.

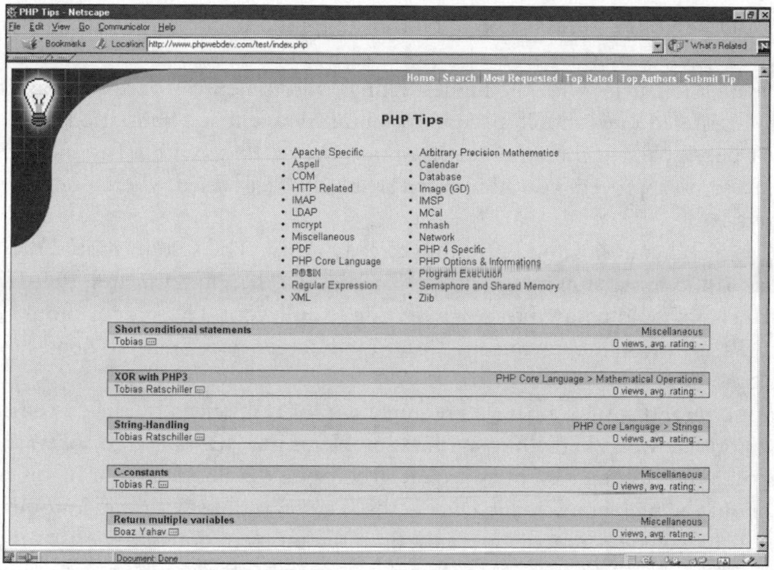

Figure 7.1 The knowledge repository's start screen.

Requirement List

As discussed in Chapter 3, "Application Design: A Real-Life Example," a project starts with compiling the requirements. Usually this is an iterative process in close collaboration with the customer, and is often handled by a systems analyst, project manager, or consultant, often also by programmers. Analyzing the problem domain and writing a requirement list is one of the most important phases in software development, which will in substantial part determine the success of the project. This project was started with a requirement list provided by Zend Technologies.

A software system should be developed to organize PHP facts, tips, and hints, in an easily browseable and searchable manner. The first page of the application should show the available categories below the root category and a list of newly added entries to the database. By clicking on one of the categories, the user can browse the entries below this category. By clicking on an entry, the user gets to a page showing the details of an entry: the title of the entry, the full text, the author's name, the date the entry was added, and the current rating. This page should also make it possible to rate the entry, in a classification from one to five, one being the highest rate.

The software should have a full-text search feature, using AND as default concatenation operator: If the user enters "imap connect" the system should return all entries in the database having "imap" *and* "connect" in their title or body. Search should not be case sensitive.

It should be possible to retrieve all entries submitted by a certain author. Three additional reports should be available, showing the authors with the most entries in the database, the entries with the highest ratings, and the entries accessed most often.

Only registered users should be able to submit new entries. Submitted entries shouldn't be visible, but should be inserted into the database with a flag indicating that they need to be approved. The administrator should be notified when a new entry is submitted.

On the Zend.com site, the PHPLib is already in use. The system should therefore use the PHPLib for session management, database access, and templates. PHPLib's `Template` class should be used to separate code from layout. The system should expose a clean API, as it would be maintained later by different developers at Zend Technologies.

It's not typical that such a detailed requirement list is provided by the customer. Often, customers won't know how business problems may translate into software applications. The customer is not an expert in software development, but he or she knows about the problem domain. During the first discussions with the customer, the analyst usually compiles a requirement list from the problem domain—"What is the application for?" and "What should the application do for the user?" are typical questions in this stage. It's then the analyst's task to help the customer to express the problem in terms appropriate to software solutions. During the analysis phase, the analyst learns more about the problem and can put it into concrete and documentable terms.

Specification

The requirement list gives you a general understanding of the problem. Once you have that, it's time to create guidelines for the actual implementation: Write a specification. The first step for this is to explore the data structures needed.

Try to break up the complex problem into smaller structures. By analyzing the requirement list and the problem domain, it becomes clear that there are three important data structures—the rest of the application is built on them. The most important structure is an entry in the knowledge repository. What forms an entry? From the requirement list, we know that an entry has associated properties: a title, the body, author, category, ratings, and logs. Because we have solved similar problems before, we see a design pattern in this data structure: It's a simple container. But we know that we'll need a way to reference this container. (Drawing from past experience is very important and can distinguish a really good from a mediocre programmer. The toughest problem is easy to solve if you have already solved it earlier.)

Creating the data structure for the category follows a similar procedure, but initially all we know about it is that the structure should have an associated "name" property. The requirement list says that we need nested categories, so this structure needs a unique identifier as well (two categories in different branches could have the same name). Unlimited nesting of categories is also a requirement, but we'll skip this for the moment because it's a separate problem.

The third data structure is already predefined, as we use the PHPLib. It simply maps to PHPLib's Auth class.

This approach is different from traditional top-down engineering and functional decomposition. *Functional decomposition* identifies the functions of a system being built (in our example, "organize facts in categories," "provide reports for most accessed entries," etc.) and breaks them into smaller subfunctions until the functions are atomic and can be mapped directly to program functions. At this time, we make no attempt at doing this, as we have no idea how to define subfunctions as yet. Functional decomposition sounds great—until you try it. It can lead you in a totally wrong direction, and once you're on the way it's practically impossible to correct decisions because you can only divide the function again and again—you'd have to start over completely.

Instead, we try to break the whole problem into design patterns: We try to recognize problems that we have already solved once. Already knowing the solution to a similar problem is the best method for problem solving. For example, we don't need to do any sort of functional decomposition on the authentication problem—we know that we can simply use parts of the PHPLib for this.

The entry and category structures can already be mapped to code. Our application keeps the entry and category structures in classes:

```
class category
{
    var $cat_id, $cat_name, $parent_id;
}

class entry extends category
{
    var $entry_id, $title, $body, $t_stamp, $author, $views, $votes, $rating;
}
```

To use classes was a design decision, and not implied by the requirement list—our previous experience shows that using classes leads to cleaner code because you can have multiple separate instances.

You can see these data structures as different "domains" of the software. They form logical units but interact with each other. The goal of the specification document is to cover all domains in an application. How the domains are represented in code is not important at this point and serves purely for illustrating the structures.

Translating these data structures to a relational model is rather simple. The application uses database tables to store entries in the knowledge repository: available categories, entry ratings, and access logs. The two main tables are entries and categories, with links to the sub-tables ratings and logs. Of course, because MySQL doesn't know foreign keys, these ties need to be handled in application space—for example, if the administrator wants to delete an entry, he also needs to delete the corresponding entries (referenced by the same entry_id) in the tables ratings and logs. Figure 7.2 shows an entity relationship diagram for the table structure.

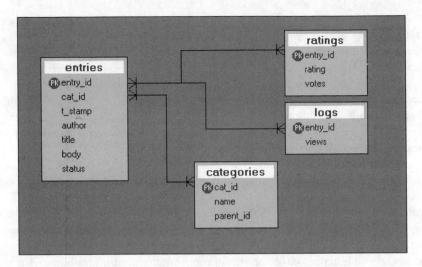

Figure 7.2   Entity relationship diagram (ERD) for the knowledge repository application.

Now that you know the application's basic data structures, the next question is what happens with them. From the requirement list, we know a series of actions that the application should allow. It's now our task to cleanly separate these tasks.

Usually, actions are grouped around the data structures defined earlier. Let's first focus on actions dealing with entries in the database:

- Retrieve a specific entry. This action needs to know the identifier of the entry to be retrieved. The action can fail if there's no entry matching the identifier in the database. It can also fail if system failures occur; for example, if the database system is inaccessible. In case of success, the action returns a structure for an entry.

- Retrieve entries in a specific category. This actions needs to know the name of the category for which entries should be retrieved. It can fail in case of an error, or return a list of valid entries. A list of entries? Wait, we have no such data structure defined yet. Time to return to the specification and add a new structure for lists.

- Retrieve the ten most-recently-added entries.

- Retrieve top-rated entries.

- Retrieve the most-accessed entries.

- Retrieve all entries submitted from a certain author.

And so forth, for all outlined actions and domains. This will result in a comprehensive list of needed structures and actions, documenting the whole project.

To summarize: We've created a requirement list, describing the problem domain and the features the application should have. Putting the requirement list into more concrete terms resulted in a specification. The specification describes data structures and behavior of the application.

After that, it's time to look at details of the application's implementation. We pick two interesting points here, namely the use of templates and the implementation of nested categories in SQL.

The *Template* Class

As shown in Chapter 6, "Database Access with PHP," the PHPLib offers a solution for many problems common to Web application. In our case, the Zend developers already used the PHPLib for parts of their site, so we standardized on it for session management, database abstractions, and HTML templates.

PHPLib's `Template` class allows separation of code and layout, similar to the `EasyTemplate` class we developed in Chapter 5, "Basic Web Application Strategies." This class has a richer feature set than our class; for example, it can contain blocks, which mark sections to be replaced more than one time (useful for rows in tables, for example), and it can open multiple files in one instance and combine them easily. The drawback is that it's less intuitive to use than `EasyTemplate`.

The Template class is completely separate from the rest of the PHPLib, and you can use it without using any other PHPLib features. In case you're interested in looking at the source code for it, you can find it in the file `template.inc` in the PHPLib distribution.

Just like `EasyTemplate`, PHPLib's template class keeps HTML in separate files, using placeholders for data that should be substituted dynamically by PHP. "Scalar" placeholders, which will get replaced by ordinary strings, have the same format as the ones in `EasyTemplate`.

The code in Listing 7.1 processes this simple template.

Listing 7.1 **Basic example of the *Template* class.**

```
// Create a template instance
$tpl = new Template();

// Load file, assign an identifier to it
$tpl->set_file("page" => "basic_template.inc.html");

// Assign contents to the placeholders
$tpl->set_var(array("TITLE" => "This is a Template test",
                     "CONTENTS" => "Hello World!"));

// Parse into a temporary variable (identifier)
$tpl->parse("out", "page");

// Output the parsed template
    $tpl->p("out");
```

continues

Listing 7.1 **Continued**

```
<html>
 <title>{TITLE}</title>
 <body>
  {CONTENTS}
 </body>
</html>
```

The first line creates an instance of the `Template` class. The constructor of the class takes two optional arguments. The first optional argument specifies a base directory where your template files reside (the default is the current directory, `./`); the second argument defines how to handle placeholders that aren't used in your script. This can be one of `keep`, `comment`, or `remove`, the default value being `remove`. If set to `keep`, placeholders are retained—if our example wouldn't assign a value to the `{TITLE}` placeholder, the placeholder would show up as is in the parsed template. Setting the variable to `comment` would produce the following output in our example, if the `{TITLE}` placeholder weren't assigned a value:

```
<html>
 <title><!-- Template : Variable TITLE undefined --></title>
 <body>
  Hello World!
 </body>
</html>
```

Setting the variable to `remove` (the default) would silently delete unassigned placeholders from the template.

The next line in the example uses `set_file()` to assign a template file to the class. This function takes as first argument a handle under which the template file will be referenced in later functions. The second argument is the filename; the file will be searched in the path specified in the constructor (in our example, the current directory). Alternatively, you can pass an associative array to the `set_file()` function, assigning multiple files at once. In that case, the keys of the array are the handles, and the elements define the actual filenames.

After this, strings are assigned to the template's placeholders using `set_var()`. Again, you can pass a single key/value pair to this function, or an associative array for batch processing. The remaining part of the example invokes the parsing function `parse()`) and prints the result (`p()`).

The example shows the most basic usage of the `Template` class; it works with only one template file and replaces each placeholder with one string variable. You could have used `EasyTemplate` for this as well, and it would probably have been faster and more intuitive than the PHPLib approach. However, the `Template` class shows its full strength when used in more complex scenarios.

One of the more advanced features is that the `Template` class can handle multiple template files and combine them into one output file. The knowledge repository application uses this extensively: One page template defines the general look and feel, the Cascading Style Sheets, and the page header and footer, and many smaller templates form the contents within the "parent" template. Look at these excerpts from the application's main page, `index.php`:

```
$tpl->set_file(array(
    "page" => "page.inc.html",
    "table" => "table.inc.html",
    "entry_summary" => "entry_summary.inc.html"
    ));

// [rest of code, assignments, etc]

$tpl->parse("CONTENTS", "table", true);
$tpl->parse("CONTENTS", "entries", true);
$tpl->parse("CONTENTS", "page");
$tpl->p("CONTENTS");
```

The main template is referenced with the identifier `page`. This is basically an HTML framework, containing one important placeholder, `{CONTENTS}`, for the actual contents of the page. This placeholder will be replaced by another, separate template file, referenced as `table`. This works because the `Template` class allows you to append the results of a round of parsing to a placeholder. The script first parses the template file referenced by `table` and then appends it to the main template.

Looking at another template file of the application, `entry_summary.inc.html`, you'll see another advanced feature of the `Template` class: *blocks*. Dynamic blocks are used for parts of a template that will be replaced iteratively with itself. In our case, this is used to display the last five entries in the knowledge base. The `entry_summary.inc.html` template contains a block, which gets repeated to produce five entry summaries. A block is defined in the template using a comment syntax:

```
<!-- BEGIN blockname -->
    block
<!-- END blockname -->
```

In code, the block is accessed using the `set_block()` function. The first argument to this function is the parent reference, usually a reference to the template file. The second argument is the block's name. The optional third argument is the name of a new reference; if omitted, it's assumed to be same as the block's name. For our example, the `set_block()` call would look like this:

```
set_block("table", "blockname");
```

The resulting reference (`blockname`) can then be handled like references produced with `set_file()`, and parsed regularly. Admittedly, this is confusing when you first hear it. Let's see how the `Template` class works conceptually. An important logical unit of the `Template` class is *handles*. Handles are similar to link identifiers (resource IDs): they point to a certain dataset and can be used in various functions as reference to this dataset. You can create handles using one of three methods:

- `set_file()` creates a handle for a template file
- `set_var()` creates a handle for a placeholder inside a template
- `set_block()` creates a handle for a block inside a template

With each of these functions, you can specify the handle that should be created. In `set_file()` and `set_var()`, the handle to create is the first argument (or the keys of the array, if an associative array is passed as argument). In `set_block()`, the handle is the second argument. In functions like `parse()`, `subst()`, or `get_undefined()`, you use the previously created handles to reference the dataset the functions should process. For the functions, it doesn't matter how the handle was created—they work on whole template files as well as on placeholders or dynamic blocks. Let's look at a simpler example again. Say you've got one template file with one placeholder and one dynamic block:

```
<b>{PLACEHOLDER}</b>
<ul>
<!-- BEGIN block -->
   <li> {BLOCK_PLACEHOLDER}
<!-- END block -->
</ul>
```

To parse this, you first define a handle for the whole file using `set_file()`. The normal placeholder can be treated normally, just as we've shown earlier. Then you define a block handle. This block can now be treated the same way as you would treat the file handle itself—it's an equally important, independent division inside the file. Therefore, you can also combine the two handles as we've done earlier with the two separate files. In code, this would look like the following:

```
$tpl->set_file("page", "page.inc.html");

// Assign value to scalar placeholder
$tpl->set_var("PLACEHOLDER", "This is just a test.");

// Create block handle, named "block"
$tpl->set_block("page", "block");

// Create three block instances
for($i=0; $i<3; $i++)
{
    // Replace placeholder for this loop iteration
    $tpl->set_var("BLOCK_PLACEHOLDER", "Loop #$i");
```

```
    // Parse block, append the result to itself
    $tpl->parse("block_handle", "block", true);
}

// Parse and output page
$tpl->parse("page", "page");
$tpl->p("page");
```

This gives the designer the possibility to define row templates without having to deal
with any PHP code. While this adds flexibility to the designer's task, there are still
certain scenarios in which you have no other way than to mix code and layout again.
An example for this is our application's search results page. In the code for this page,
you'll find this section:

```
$entries = kb_get_entries_by_keyword($keywords);
// Any entries found?
if($entries)
{
    $tpl->set_block("tip_summary", "tip", "entries");
    kb_entries_to_template($entries, $tpl);

    $tpl->set_var(array(
            "RESULTS_TITLE" => sprintf(count($entries).
            ➥" %s found:", count($entries) > 1 ? "entries" : "entry"),
            "KEYWORDS" => $keywords
            ));
}
else
{
    $tpl->set_var("MESSAGE",  '<div align="center"><i>No entries
    ➥found.</i></div>');
    $tpl->parse("entries", "tip", true);
}
```

The code checks whether entries matching the search term have been found in the
database, and displays either a message stating that no entries have been found, or the
listing of found entries. In the listing, the code also formats the message according to
whether more than one entry is shown ("1 entry found" versus "x entries found").
This is clearly a layout issue, though—the number of found entries doesn't influence
the application logic at all. Therefore, in an ideal world, the designer would be able to
provide these messages. Maybe the designer would want to format the "No entries
found" message as bold red, and the number of found entries as large and bold. In our
case, the designer would have to kindly ask the programmer to implement it—after
the third change, this becomes pretty frustrating for both designer and programmer.

One approach to solving this problem is to give the template some control back, and let the designer decide on template logic. Templates would then contain a simple meta scripting language, looking like this:

```
{{if ENTRIES_FOUND > 1}}
    {{ENTRIES_FOUND}} entries found:
{{/if}}
{{if ENTRIES_FOUND=1}}
    One entry found:
{{/if}}
{{if ENTRIES_FOUND=0}}
    No entries found for your search!
{{/if}}
```

Of course, it's a fine line between separation of code and layout and mixing them again. Do you prefer layout in the code or code in the layout? It's a chicken-and-egg problem. At the time of this writing, first efforts were underway to create a template API for the standard PHP distribution. The meta script example above is taken from Andrei Zmievski's draft for a template language. Andrei (proponent of the template API and PHP core developer) plans to implement a number of other features; for example, standard predefined variables #ODD or #EVEN inside dynamic blocks. This would make it possible to implement the popular color changes in repeated table rows—which otherwise would need to be handled by the programmer again. Andrei plans to integrate the template API directly into PHP, which would offer a number of advantages over current template solutions, like PHPLib's. First, it would be standard, and software developers could depend on it. Second, as it would be tightly integrated into PHP's core engine, it could be a major performance boost. Parsed templates could be cached in memory, for example.

Recursion with SQL

Our application allows unlimited nesting of categories. We have chosen the most basic and most easy-to-implement solution for nesting categories. The categories table is defined as follows:

```
CREATE TABLE categories (
    cat_id bigint(21) DEFAULT '0' NOT NULL auto_increment,
    name varchar(32) NOT NULL,
    parent_id bigint(21) DEFAULT '0' NOT NULL,
    PRIMARY KEY (cat_id),
    KEY parent_id (parent_id)
);
```

The field responsible for the nesting is of course parent_id; it contains the cat_id value of the category one level above. Actually, this is the most basic tree implementation possible: Each node has exactly one property referencing the parent node. There are a number of drawbacks with this approach, though, the most important being that it's impossible to get all parent nodes for a node with one SQL query. Instead, to get the parent, you need to issue multiple SQL queries; to be exact, you need n-1 single queries for a depth of n levels.

We have chosen a recursive implementation to get the parent nodes in the function `kb_cat_get_parents()`. It retrieves category nodes from the database as long as `cat_id` matches the root category. This can best be visualized with an example. Let's assume there are three nested categories:

```
INSERT INTO categories VALUES (1, 'Main Category', 0);
INSERT INTO categories VALUES (2, 'Sub Category I', 1);
INSERT INTO categories VALUES (3, 'Sub Category II', 2);
```

When called with an initial `cat_id` value of 3, the `kb_cat_get_parents()` function first retrieves the parent ID for this node (which is 2 in our example). Then it calls itself with this ID, forming a recursive function. The terminator of the recursive function is the condition `parent_id == 0`—this is the root category, and no nodes can be above the root category. The function will call itself recursively as long as this condition is not met.

Authentication

The requirements for the application include that only registered users should be allowed to submit new entries. Thanks to the PHPLib, adding authentication to the system is a matter of adding a `page_open()` call to the script you want to protect—in our case, `submit.php`. This way, the user is only able to access the page contents after having been authenticated.

In the `entries` table, we store the unique user ID provided by the PHPLib. As we've shown earlier in this chapter, you can access this ID using the `$auth` array: It's stored in `$auth->auth["uid"]`, and `$auth->auth["uname"]` contains the username.

Our application doesn't deal with user management. Somewhere else on your Web site, you have to provide means to register as user, edit registrations, send forgotten passwords, etc. Because it's up to you to implement this, we also have no chance to get the full name of a user—all we have is a unique user ID and the username. Therefore, there's a function called `real_user_name()`, which takes a user ID as parameter and should return a full name for this user. By default, the function simply returns the user ID again; you should extend the function to look up the user's full name in your database and return it.

The Finished Product

The `real_user_name()` function and all other API functions are held in one central file, `lib.inc.php3`. As all functions have a basic syntax documentation in the source, it's easy to compile an API overview automatically. All we need is a simple `grep` command:

```
grep '^[\\\/ ]*\*' lib.inc.php
```

This is no replacement for complete technical documentation, however, and should serve only as a quick reference. After having defined the API, the rest of the application deals mostly with invoking the API functions and printing the results.

PHP and XML

Note: If you're already familiar with the basic concepts of XML, you can safely skip the next sections giving a short introduction to XML, and continue directly with PHP and Expat.

What Is XML?

XML (Extensible Markup Language) is a meta markup language for documents containing structured information. Let's try to explain it word by word in plain English:

- *XML is extensible.* Take HTML: the tag `<h1>` always denotes a first-level heading. In XML, by contrast, the tag means nothing until you give it a meaning with an accompanying *rule*, the *Document Type Definition (DTD)*.

- *XML is a markup language.* Just as HTML should, theoretically, XML does not provide layout information to the processing application.

- *XML is a meta language.* XML doesn't have a fixed tag set—it provides a facility to define tags.

- *XML works with documents.* Documents. As in *not limited to files*! Documents can come from a database, over the network, or indeed from files.

- *XML defines structured information.* It arranges single parts of data in a larger body and gives it a contextual meaning and a structural relationship.

Structured Information

There's one key concept you'll need to understand when talking about XML: structured documents or—more eloquently—*structured information markup*. Structured markup explicitly defines the structure and semantic content (the contextual meaning) of a document. It doesn't influence the way in which the document will appear to the reader—the interpretation of the data (parsing, layout, etc.) is completely left to the processing application. Take the HTML `<p>` (paragraph) tag: It denotes multiple sentences belonging together to form a logical unit. The tag *per se* doesn't imply how the paragraph should be rendered in the browser; the browser could insert a blank line before or after, indent the first line in the paragraph, or add ornamental borders around it. This is logical markup—the style information is hardcoded into the browser. XML documents are compounded of such logical markup. As in HTML, tags are used to identify the markup information. But in XML, there are no visual elements as in

HTML (think of `<font>`)—it's restricted to logical markup. There's no way to specify a word as italic in XML. You can only mark it for its semantic meaning, for example with `<emphasis>`.

So much for the markup—where's the structure? XML tags can be nested and have a contextual state—that is, it's important where they appear in a document. A tag combination `<chapter><title>` is treated differently than `<book><title>`. There's no limitation on the number of nested elements in the XML specification—the only requirement is that all elements must originate in one root element.

XML's Relatives

The ancestor of XML is SGML. Since it became an ISO standard in 1986, SGML (Standard Generalized Markup Language) has been used to maintain structured documents by large corporations in all industries. However, SGML is a complex standard that's difficult to support in applications. Most SGML applications—editors, storage servers, transformation tools—are therefore quite expensive, often costing well above $10,000.

HTML, on the other hand, has wide industry support and is used on millions of Web sites. It defines a simple type of document for a common class of short articles, with headings, paragraphs, lists, illustrations, and some provision for hypertext and multimedia. But it's very limited regarding flexibility and extensibility. The tags and semantics are fixed—you can't define your own tag for an entry in a Table of Contents. Neither is it suited for media other than computer interfaces—if you ever tried to print articles distributed to multiple files, you know what this means. The very open specification led to a fragmentation with multiple different implementations. As you know, it's an art *per se* to write browser-neutral HTML.

So there was a need to create a new format allowing structured documents to be used over the Web. XML was designed to overcome the limitations in the only viable alternatives, SGML and HTML.

The design goals of XML had some clearly defined points:

- It must be easy to use—both for users and for developers implementing XML parsers. The complexity of SGML is a constraint that needs to be removed.

- XML must be open to support a wide variety of applications and subprotocols. The dependence on a single, inflexible document type as with HTML needed to be eliminated.

- It requires a strict syntax. Optional features lead to compatibility problems when users want to share documents. There was the constant fear that the same could happen as happened with HTML—multiple competing and incompatible implementations.

- It must be compatible with SGML. Members of the development committee were also involved in SGML efforts and had legacy data contained in SGML systems.

The development resulted in a clear specification approved by the World Wide Web Consortium (W3C) as the recommendation *Extensible Markup Language (XML) 1.0* from February 10, 1998.

XML is different from SGML: XML strips out a large number of SGML's more complex and less-used features and creates a new reduced SGML-based application. Because it's a subset of SGML, you can read an XML document with any SGML-compliant system. Every valid XML document is a valid SGML element.

XML is different from HTML: Apart from removing HTML misconceptions, it has important syntactical differences. Plus, XML is fully Unicode-ready; tags, attributes and contents can be in any string encoding defined by Unicode.

Let's look at a short excerpt from the source code of this book:

```
<title>Cutting-Edge Applications</title>
<abstract>
    <para>
        If you realize that all things change,
         there is nothing you will try to hold on to.
    </para>
</abstract>
```

Here you see the tags in use, providing for structured and logical markup. In contrast to HTML,

- Tags are case sensitive.
- Whitespace is significant.
- Opening tags must always have a matching closing tag or be self-closing (for example, `<xref/>`).
- Documents can have an arbitrary valid Document Type Definition.

Thus we can happily summarize: XML removes the enormous complexity of SGML, while still providing all necessary features for structural markup, including the definition of custom document types.

XML's Advantages

But why XML? With all those formal definitions and fact sheets, developers sometimes don't see the usefulness for their daily activities at first. Indeed, why use XML and not Word or Notes? Or your own proprietary storage format? Or a relational database?

The main argument against proprietary formats is just that: They're proprietary. Data that's designed to be used on a heterogeneous network such as the Internet has to be usable on all types of computers connected to it. XML is built out of plain text (as opposed to the binary format of most proprietary applications), making it supportable by all current computing platforms. Besides, proprietary data formats are often (for example in public bodies) just not an option: You don't want to rely on the mercy of a single vendor who could change the format at will, or even abandon it altogether. XML is license-free, vendor-neutral, and platform-independent.

While XML provides means for structured content, it presents a different (but not necessarily opposing) view on content than relational database systems. XML doesn't provide a relational model. It allows unlimited nested levels, which could not be handled by a database system. On the other hand, it misses features found in an RDBMS, such as stringent field types, constraints, keys, and so on. Of course, there are similarities in the two concepts and there is indeed development going on to create a SQL-like query language for XML documents. Anyway, the success of XML shouldn't make you forget the usefulness of the traditional RDBMS; they provide many important processing features that could hardly be modeled in XML, and they're optimized for speed from the ground up.

The overall and *killer* advantage of XML is the separation of logical structure from layout. By having your documents in XML, you can transform them into any representation you want: HTML, PostScript, PDF, RTF, plain text, audio, Braille—from one single source. And as XML (plain text) documents can be parsed with your favorite scripting language, it's easy to change hyperlinks dynamically, change element contents, or associate structures with a database.

And if you're still not convinced, review all those Document Type Definitions that are being developed or are already in use. XML itself is mostly an "under the hood" technology—the meat is the applications that use XML.

What Is XML Used For?

As a structured information markup language, XML is of course used in content management systems, archiving solutions, and corporate document repositories. But plenty of other XML applications and subprotocols exist. Due to the open nature of the standard, DTDs have been developed at a fast pace.

DocBook

The DocBookX DTD is a very popular set of tags for describing books, articles, and other prose documents, particularly technical documentation. It was originally developed in 1991 by the publisher O'Reilly as an SGML DTD for in-house use. It soon became popular with authors and spread to other publishing houses, a change embraced by O'Reilly, which handed over further development to the Davenport Group. In mid-1998, OASIS (Organization for the Advance of Structured Information Standards) officially took over the maintenance of DocBook. When XML became increasingly popular, an unofficial XML version (3.1) was created by Norman Walsh; work is currently underway to transform this to an official release—DocBook 5 will most probably come in SGML and XML flavors.

When we started writing this book, it was clear that we wanted to use an open format such as XML. The DocBook DTD was consequently chosen because it offered all the features we would ever need. All the elements typically used in technical writing are present and, to tell you the truth, even very esoteric ones are included—or have you ever seen a `MouseButton` element (from the quick reference: *The conventional name of a mouse button*) in your word processor?

XML and DocBook offer some clear advantages to us. We can use CVS as a version control tool for both the PHP examples and the book files. Transformation to HTML is easy, either with PHP or using a style sheet processor like James Clark's XT. And editing is very comfortable, thanks to SoftQuad's XMetaL, which allows intuitive visual editing by using Cascading Style Sheets (CSS) for the display in the authoring environment, as shown in Figure 7.3.

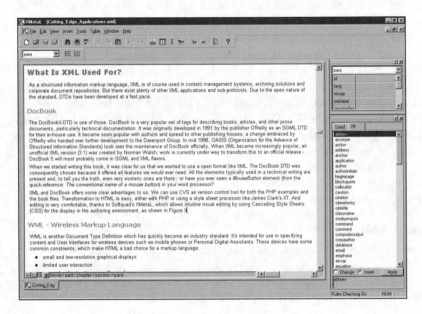

Figure 7.3   SoftQuad's XMetaL XML authoring environment, used for writing this book.

WML—Wireless Markup Language

WML is another Document Type Definition that has quickly become an industry standard. It's intended for use in specifying content and user interfaces for wireless devices such as mobile phones or Personal Digital Assistants. These devices have some common constraints, which make HTML a bad choice for a markup language:

- Small and low-resolution graphical displays
- Limited user interaction
- Narrow-band network access (for now)
- Limited computational resources

WML addresses these issues. It divides content into small pieces ("cards") and organizes them in larger information units ("decks"). To avoid continuous network access, WML defines a set of client-side scripting procedures in XML, for example the ability to set and access variables on the client computer. Because of limited screen real estate, creating meaningful navigation paths is especially difficult on portable devices. WML explicitly requires the user agent—the WAP browser—to have a navigation history and enables WML documents to make use of it, thus freeing the author from some of the responsibility and delegating it to the user agent.

RDF—Resource Description Framework

The RDF specification defines a language to store meta information about Web resources in an XML format. The Web as it is, with its millions of HTML pages, is very difficult to process by automated machines like spiders or robots. Search engines are hitting their limit every day, and even the most clever algorithms don't guarantee meaningful search results, as anyone using the Web for professional research knows. Web pages can only be full-text searched—which is a very limited searching method.

Current HTML allows primitive storing of meta data about a document. As you may know, meta tags can be used to denote keywords for a document, a short summary, and author information. But what if you want to store the publication history of the document? Information about the editors? Any bibliographer will laugh at HTML's meta tags.

In 1998, the W3C formed a committee to research a format for defining meta data and released the *Resource Description Framework* (*RDF*) as a recommendation on February 22, 1999.

RDF extends the format originally used for PICS, a content rating system, and is more and more replacing the Dublin Core Metadata for Resource Discovery standard, another methodology for classifying meta data. RDF has quickly become accepted as a standard mechanism for the global exchange of meta data on the Internet.

XML Documents

XML documents consist of markup and content (called *character data* in XML terms) in the Unicode character set. There are different types of markup, which we'll introduce in the following overview.

Elements

Elements will look familiar to anyone who has worked with HTML. They denote the meaning of a content section. XML cannot contain elements with no closing tag (HTML's `<img>`, for example), but has a distinct notation to identify empty tags:

```
<xref  linkend="end"/>
```

Keep in mind that the nesting of tags is significant—improperly nested tags will lead to badly formed documents.

Attributes

Elements can have *attributes*. Attributes are name/value pairs that occur within the tags after the element name and specify a property of an element. Attribute values must be contained in quotes. No attribute name may appear more than once in the same tag.

Any XML document can optionally (and regardless of the Document Type Definition) have two standard attributes: `xml:lang` and `xml:space`. The `xml:lang` attribute was defined because language independence is one of XML's most important goals.

Without knowing what language a text is written in, it's impossible for an application to display, spell-check, or index it. XML's great Unicode support wouldn't be of any help if the author couldn't assign a language tag to a particular part of a document. Thus the `xml:lang` attribute was introduced:

```
<p>Worldwide declarations of love</p>
<p xml:lang="It">Ti amo.</p>
<p xml:lang="De">Ich liebe Dich.</p>
<p xml:lang="X-Klingon">qabang</p>
```

The language identifier is one of the following:

- A two-letter ISO 639 language code
- A language code registered with the Internet Assigned Numbers Authority (IANA); these begin with the prefix "i-" (or "I-")
- A user-defined code, prefixed with "x-" (or "X-")

The other standard attribute, `xml:space`, isn't as straightforward to understand and use. As mentioned earlier, whitespace is significant in XML—it will be passed to the processing application. But after having read our Coding Style guidelines, you know that whitespace is important to structure and indent code to improve readability. This way it's used for laying out the markup, but it's of no importance for the markup itself or for the character data. On the other hand, an author may well intend whitespace to be preserved.

Because there are these two conflicting views on the subject, the XML committee introduced the `xml:space` attribute that controls the behavior of whitespace. It can only take two values: `preserve` or `default`. On any element that includes the attribute `xml:space="preserve"`, whitespace is treated as "significant" and passed to the processing application as is. The `default` value tells the application that the application's default processing should be applied. Both standard attributes are inherited to sub-elements until they are explicitly reset in an element.

Note: An *XML processor* is the program used to read XML documents. The XML processor makes it possible for an application to access the structure and content of an XML document. Throughout this book, the terms *XML processor* and *XML parser* refer to the same kind of software.

Processing Instructions

Another "element" type you'll find in XML documents is the *processing instruction*, or *PI*. PIs are used to define parts in a document that should not be interpreted by the regular parser engine but instead by a specialized processing handler. They consist of <? and a target name used to identify the application to which the instruction is directed. The long PHP tag (<?php) is of course such a PI and can be used in XML documents to mark PHP code.

Note: In order to be XML-compliant, you have to set the short_tags directive in your PHP configuration to Off and use the long opening tag <?php consistently. The short opening tag would confuse XML, as it wouldn't be a valid processing instruction. On the other hand, tags like <xml would interfere with PHP, as PHP would think of the xml as code, and produce a parse error accordingly.

Entities

Any text that's not markup constitutes the character data of the document. Within this content, an author needs a way to include special characters like < or > that normally would introduce start or end markup sections. Similarly to HTML, XML knows the notation of *entities*. Five entities are predefined:

Entity	Character	Symbol
<	<	less than
>	>	greater than
&	&	ampersand
"	"	double quote
'	'	single quote (apostrophe)

Note: If you use a Document Type Definition, these entities need to be declared if you want to use them.

Using character references, you can insert any arbitrary Unicode character into your document. They consist of the normal notation of references, but with a pound sign (#) following the ampersand. After that, either a decimal or a hexadecimal reference to the Unicode position is inserted. For example, both ℞ and &#x221E refer to the infinity sign (∞). Entities are not limited to a single character, though; they can be of any length. For example, a DTD could define an entity &footer; to contain "Copyright (c) 2000 New Riders."

Comments

XML uses the same notation for *comments* as HTML: <!--comment-->. Comments can contain any data except the literal string -- and can be placed between markup entries anywhere in your document. The XML specification explicitly states that comments are not part of a document's contents—a parser is not required to pass them to the processing application. This means you can't use comments for hidden instructions or the like, as you might be used to doing from HTML (think of using comment tags for hiding JavaScript from older browsers).

CDATA Sections

One special type of content is *CDATA sections*. As soon as you try to embed larger sections of code (containing many occurrences of < or &) into an XML document, you'll find the standard method of referencing special characters through entities awkward. HTML has the `<pre>` tag to turn off markup interpretation for a section—but as XML doesn't know any built-in tags, that's out of our reach. To overcome this, you can mark sections in XML as CDATA, using this construct:

```
<![CDATA[
    print("<a href="script.php3?foo=bar&baz=foobar");
]]>
```

Within a CDATA section, all characters can occur, except for the `]]>` sequence.

Document Prologue

Note: Although *prolog* is the spelling in the official specs, our editor prefers the Americanized (and possibly arcane) spelling *prologue*. XML documents should (but don't have to) begin with an XML declaration that specifies the version of XML being used. This version information is part of the document prologue:

```
<?xml version="1.0"?>
    <greeting>Hello, world!
</greeting>
```

By having this information at the top of a document, a processor can decide whether it can handle the document's version of XML. It's also useful as a method to identify the document's type; just as `#!/bin/sh` in the head of a file declares it to be a shell script, the XML declaration identifies an XML document.

The second important part of the document prologue is the *document type declaration*. Don't confuse this with Document Type *Definition* (DTD)—the document type declaration contains or points to a DTD! The DTD consists of markup declarations that provide a "grammar" for XML documents. The document type declaration can point to an external DTD, contain the markup declarations directly, or both. The DTD for a document consists of both subsets taken together. Here's an example of a document type declaration:

```
<!DOCTYPE book SYSTEM "docbookx.dtd">
```

This document type declaration has the name `book` and points to an external DTD named `docbookx.dtd`. It has no inline DTD.

If a document contains the full DTD and no external entities, it's a called a *stand-alone document* and marked as such in the XML declaration:

```
<?xml version="1.0" standalone='yes'?>
```

This can be useful for some applications; for example, for delivery of documents over a network, when you want to open only a single document stream. Note that even XML documents with external DTDs can be converted to stand-alone documents by importing the DTD and external entities into the document prologue.

Document Structure

Now you know all the pieces that form an XML document: elements (with attributes), processing instructions, entities, comments, and CDATA sections. But how are these pieces grouped together to form a meaningful XML document?

The XML specification only defines a very generic document structure. It says that each well-formed document has these qualities (more about what "well-formed" means later):

- May have a document prologue identifying the XML version and DTD.
- Must have exactly one root element and an arbitrary number of elements below the root.
- May have miscellaneous stuff after that.

The last part, "miscellaneous stuff," is referenced in a wry tone here—it's considered by many people to be a design error of XML. It makes parsing XML documents potentially much harder, because you can't rely on the document end being the closing root element. When parsing a document over a network connection, for example, you can't close the connection after having received the closing root element—you must wait until the server closes the connection on its own, as there may still be more "miscellaneous" content to consider.

But nothing was said yet about the syntax and structure of the thing that supposedly is responsible for the whole magic of XML: the Document Type Definition. Indeed, it's the DTD that gives meaning to an XML document; it defines its syntax, the sequence and nesting of tags, possible element attributes, entities—in short, the whole grammar. Writing complex DTDs is no easy task and whole books have been written to cover the subject. Because as an XML user you usually don't need to deal with this task directly, we won't cover this topic here. Instead, we'd like to look at another XML concept that may be more important in your daily work.

XML Namespaces

You've seen some different XML applications (Document Type Definitions) and what they're used for. But what if you want to create a single XML document containing elements from two different DTDs? For example, the `<part>` element could mean a book part in one DTD and a manufacturing part in another. Without a way to separate these two namespaces, the two element names would clash. How could these distinct elements be identified? You need to associate an identifier with the element, for example `<part namespace = "book">` or, if you want to avoid attributes, `<book:part>` and `<manufacturing:part>`.

The W3C learned early about this shortcoming in XML and introduced a new specification: Namespaces in XML, published as a Recommendation on January 14, 1999.

XML namespaces provide a method for having multiple namespaces, identified by Uniform Resource Identifiers (URI), in one XML document. The Resource Description Framework DTD uses this method. Look at the following example from the RDF specification:

```
<?xml version="1.0"?>
<rdf:RDF   xmlns:rdf="http://www.w3.org/1999/02/22-rdf-syntax-ns#"
           xmlns:s="http://description.org/schema/">
    <rdf:Description about="http://www.w3.org/Home/Lassila">
        <s:Creator>Ora Lassila</s:Creator>
    </rdf:Description>
</rdf:RDF>
```

This defines two namespaces, one named `rdf` and one named `s`. After the definition, a namespace is referenced by prefixing it (concatenated with a colon) to an element name, thus effectively avoiding the collision of different logical meanings and syntactical definitions.

Note: The URI in a namespace identifier is not a DTD. It would of course be nice to be able to point to different DTDs using XML namespaces, but there are currently many technical problems with this approach—this is being addressed by the W3C in the XML Schema definition, which is under development at the time of this writing.

EBNF—Or "What the Heck Is That Again?"

As a Web developer, you'll frequently be faced with the task of reading specifications—whether project specs, formal language definitions, or standards whitepapers. When reading some of the specifications from the W3C (the most well-known are the HTML and XML documents, probably), you'll stumble across a strange mixture of characters that presumably form a grammar definition.

```
document ::= prolog element Misc*
```

This is the very first syntax definition in the XML specification and defines the basic structure of an XML document. The notation used is called *Extended Backus-Naur Form*, or *EBNF* for short. Understanding the formal specifications will get a lot easier once you understand the basics of EBNF.

EBNF is a formal way to define the syntax of a programming language so that there's no ambiguity left as to what's valid or allowed. It's also used in many other standards, such as protocol or data formats and markup languages like XML and SGML. As EBNF makes for a very rigorous grammar definition, there are software tools available that automatically transform a set of EBNF rules into a parser. Programs that do this are called *compiler compilers*. The most famous of these is YACC (Yet Another Compiler Compiler), but there are of course many more.

You can see EBNF as a set of rules, called *productions* or *production rules*. Every rule describes a part of the overall syntax. You start with one start symbol (called S, by tradition) and then you define rules for what you can replace this symbol with. Gradually, this will form a complex language grammar composed by the set of strings you can produce when following these rules.

If you look at the example from above again, you see that this is an assignment; there's a symbol on the left, an assignment operator (which can also be written as :=), and a list of values on the right. You play the game by following the symbol definition down to the last occurrence—then on the right side of the assignment no symbols are given, but a final string called *terminal*, which is an atomic value.

EBNF defines three operators, which will look familiar to you from regular expressions:

Operator	Meaning
?	Optional
+	Must occur one or more times
*	Must occur zero or more times

To define the grammar of language, which allows you to express floating-point numbers, this EBNF notation would be used:

```
S   := SIGN? D+ (. D+)?
D   := [0-9]
SIGN := "+"¦"-"
```

The first line defines the start symbol, with the following sequence:

- An optional sign, consisting either of + or -
- One or more elements of the D production
- Optionally, a dot, and again one or more elements of D production

Notice that EBNF allows operators to work on groups of symbols: (. D+)? means that this expression is optional.

The second line lists the finals (atoms) for the D production, the digits 0 to 9 in this case. The syntax used is the same as with regular expressions; a set is defined in a bracket expression. The third line defines the two possible signs. The pipe character (¦) is used to denote alternatives: A¦B means "A or B but not both."

That's a very basic explanation of EBNF. The XML specification defines additional syntax; for example, validity constraints and well-formedness constraints—it's explained in the Notation section of the spec, so we won't go into details here. More information about EBNF can be found in any modern compiler book.

Validity and Well-Formedness

There are two types of compliant XML documents: *valid* documents and *well-formed* documents. Any XML document is well-formed if it matches XML's basic syntax guidelines:

- It contains one root element and an arbitrary number of elements below that element.

- Elements are properly nested.

- Attributes appear only once per element and are enclosed by single or double quotes. They cannot contain direct or indirect entity references to external entities. Nor can they contain an opening tag (<).

- Entities must be declared before they're used, except for the standard entities.

- Entities must not refer to themselves recursively.

For example, the following is a well-formed XML document:

```
<greeting>Hello world.</greeting>
```

But it's not a valid document. The XML specification defines it this way: *An XML document is valid if it has an associated document type declaration and if the document complies with the constraints expressed in it.* This means that any valid XML document is also well-formed. A well-formed document may be invalid if it doesn't adhere to the syntax laid out in the associated DTD. An ill-formed document can never be valid. An ill-formed document is not an XML document: It contains fatal errors and XML parsers are instructed to stop processing at this point. The distinction between valid and well-formed has two very important connotations to XML. First, it brings along two classes of XML parsers: those that care about validity of an XML document and those that don't: that is, *validating* and *non-validating* parsers. The XML specification lists ease of use for developers as a design goal, and indeed it's quite easy for any medium-level programmer to write a non-validating parser. Writing a validating parser is a different matter, through.

Second, the validity versus well-formedness concept divides XML applications into two categories. One range of applications treats XML as an extended data-storage format. Well-formed documents are used for data storage and display. For this task, a DTD is not necessary; a well-formed document is sufficient. You would achieve some level of code reuse with this approach; for example, you could reuse the code for parsing data and generating tags in later applications. But as soon as you want to exchange information as information (as opposed to treating it as pure data), you need to give the document a meaning and associate it with a DTD. In applications dealing with information processing and exchange, only valid documents are appropriate.

Now that you've learned about the basics of XML and related topics, let's put the gained knowledge into practice by looking at Expat, a non-validating parser built into PHP.

PHP and Expat

Expat is the parser that is responsible for XML processing in Mozilla, Apache, Perl, and many other projects. It can be compiled into PHP since version 3.0.6 and is part of the official Apache distribution since Apache 1.3.9. Since Expat is a non-validating parser, it's fast and small—well suited for Web applications.

Event–Based API

There are two types of XML parser APIs: tree-based parsers that usually provide an interface to the Document Object Model (more about this later) and those that process XML documents with an event-based approach. Expat makes an event-based API available.

Event-based parsers have a data-centric view of XML documents. They parse the document from top to bottom and report events—such as the start of an element, the end of an element, starting of character data, etc.—to the application, usually through callback functions. The "Hello World" example document from earlier in the chapter would be reported by an event-based parser as a series of these events:

1. Open Element: greeting
2. Open CDATA section, value: Hello World
3. Close Element: greeting

Unlike tree-based parsers, they don't create a structure representation of the document. This provides for a lower-level access and is much more efficient in terms of speed and resource usage. There's no need to hold the entire document in memory; indeed, documents can be much larger than your system's memory. Of course, it's still completely possible to create a native tree structure if you need to do so. Prior to parsing a document, event-based parsers generally require you to register callback functions that will get invoked when a certain event occurs. Expat is no exception. It defines six possible events plus one default handler:

Target	Function	Description
elements	xml_set_element_handler()	Opening and closing of elements
character data	xml_set_character_data_handler()	Beginning of character data
external entities	xml_set_external_entity_ref_handler()	Occurrence of an external entity
unparsed external entities	xml_set_unparsed_entity_decl_handler	Occurrence of an unparsed external entity
processing instructions	xml_set_processing_instruction_handler()	Occurrence of a processing instruction
notation declarations	xml_set_notation_decl_handler()	Occurrence of a notation declaration
default	xml_set_default_handler()	All events that have no assigned handler

Let's start with a really basic example. The source code in Listing 7.2 forms a program to extract all comments from an XML document (remember, comments have the form <!-- ... -->). The example registers only one handler that gets called for all events during the parsing. If you register another handler, for example using `xml_set_character_data_handler()`, the default handler would not be invoked for this specific event—the default handler processes only "free" events with no assigned handler.

Listing 7.2 **Extracting comments from an XML document.**

```php
require("xml.php3");

function default_handler($p, $data)
{
    global $count;  // count of comments found

    // Check if the current contains a comment
    if (ereg("!--", $data, $matches))
    {
        $line = xml_get_current_line_number($p);

        // Insert a tab before new lines
        $data = str_replace("\n", "\n\t", $data);

        // Output line number and comment
        print "$line:\t$data\n";

        // Increase count of comments found
        $count++;
    }

}

// Process the file passed as first argument to the script
$file = $argv[1];

$count = 0;

// Create the XML parser
$parser = xml_parser_create();

// Set the default handler for all events
xml_set_default_handler($parser, "default_handler");

// Parse file and check the return code
$ret = xml_parse_from_file($parser, $file);
if(!$ret)
{
    // Print error message and die
```

```
        die(sprintf("XML error: %s at line %d",
                    xml_error_string(xml_get_error_code($parser)),
                    xml_get_current_line_number($parser)));
    }

    // Free the parser instance
    xml_parser_free($parser);
```

The example works in a pretty straightforward way. First, the XML parser instance is created using `xml_parser_create()`. In all subsequent functions, you'll use the parser identifier you created this way—in a similar fashion to the result-identifier in the MySQL functions. Then the default handler is registered and the file is parsed. `xml_parse_from_file()` is a custom function we provide in a library; this function simply opens the file specified as the argument and parses it in blocks of 4KB. PHP's original XML functions `xml_parse()` and `xml_parse_into_struct()` operate on strings—by using wrappers for opening, reading, and closing a file and passing its contents to the respective functions, you can save time and code.

The default handler checks whether the current data section is a comment and outputs it if this is the case. Along with each comment, the current line number (returned by `xml_get_current_line_number()`) is also printed.

Now, while this example shows off the basic concepts of invoking the XML parser, registering callback functions, and processing data, it doesn't exactly demonstrate the common usage of an XML parser. It doesn't process information; raw data is just read in and scanned for a string—nothing that couldn't be done with traditional regular expressions. In most situations where you process XML, you'll want to keep at least a basic representation of the document structure.

Stacks, Depths, and Lists

Our second example illustrates how to remember the element depth the parser is currently processing. In the start-element handler the global `$depth` variable is increased by four; in the stop-element handler it's decreased by the same figure. This is the most reduced case of a parser stack—no structure other than depth information is being kept. As an XML pretty printer, the example uses the depth to properly indent code. The handler functions simply apply a Cascading Style Sheet to the current data to produce nicely formatted output. The only other noteworthy part of the code is this line:

```
    xml_parser_set_option($parser, XML_OPTION_CASE_FOLDING, 0);
```

This disables case folding for the parser, telling it that the case of element names should be preserved. If this option is enabled, all element names are transformed to uppercase. Usually, you'll want to turn this off, as case is important for element names in XML.

We won't print the source code of the example here because of its simplicity; you can find it on the CD-ROM. Figure 7.4 shows a screen shot of the output.

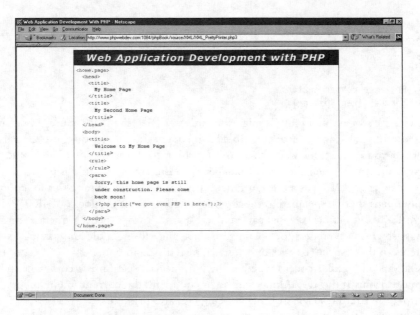

Figure 7.4   Output of the XML pretty printer.

Usually, this naive approach of maintaining just one depth variable is not enough. With event-based parsers, you'll usually end up using your own stacks or lists to maintain information about the document's structure. This is evidenced quite well by the next example, shown in Listing 7.3.

Listing 7.3   *XMLStats—collecting statistical information about an XML document.*

```php
require("xml.php3");

// The first argument is the file to process
$file = $argv[1];

// Initialize variables
$elements = $stack = array();
$total_elements = $total_chars = 0;

// The base class for an element
class element
{
    var $count = 0;
    var $chars = 0;
    var $parents = array();
    var $childs = array();
}

// Utility function to print a message in a box
```

```php
function print_box($title, $value)
{
    printf("\n+%'-60s+\n", "");
    printf("|%20s", "$title:");
    printf("%14s", $value);
    printf("%26s|\n", "");
    printf("+%'-60s+\n", "");
}

// Utility function to print a line
function print_line($title, $value)
{
    printf("%20s", "$title:");
    printf("%15s\n", $value);
}

// Sort function for usasort()
function my_sort($a, $b)
{
    return(is_object($a) && is_object($b) ? $b->count - $a->count: 0);
}

function start_element($parser, $name, $attrs)
{
    global $elements, $stack;

    // Does this element already exist in the global $elements array?
    if(!isset($elements[$name]))
    {
        // No - add a new instance of class element
        $element = new element;
        $elements[$name] = $element;
    }

    // Increase this element's count
    $elements[$name]->count++;

    // Is there a parent element?
    if(isset($stack[count($stack)-1]))
    {
        // Yes - set $last_element to the parent
        $last_element = $stack[count($stack)-1];

        // If there is no entry for the parent element in the current
        // element's parents array, initialize it to 0
        if(!isset($elements[$name]->parents[$last_element]))
        {
            $elements[$name]->parents[$last_element] = 0;
        }

        // Increase the count for this element's parent
```

continues

Listing 7.3 **Continued**

```php
        $elements[$name]->parents[$last_element]++;

        // If there is no entry for this element in the parent's
        // elements' child array, initialize it to 0
        if(!isset($elements[$last_element]->childs[$name]))
        {
            $elements[$last_element]->childs[$name] = 0;
        }

        // Increase the count for this element parent in the parent's
        // childs array
        $elements[$last_element]->childs[$name]++;
    }

    // Add current element to the stack
    array_push($stack, $name);
}

function stop_element($parser, $name)
{
    global $stack;

    // Remove last element from the stack
    array_pop($stack);
}

function char_data($parser, $data)
{
    global $elements, $stack, $depth;

    // Increase character count for the current element
    $elements[$stack[count($stack)-1]]->chars += strlen(trim($data));
}

// Create Expat parser
$parser = xml_parser_create();

// Set handler functions
xml_set_element_handler($parser, "start_element", "stop_element");
xml_set_character_data_handler($parser, "char_data");
xml_parser_set_option($parser, XML_OPTION_CASE_FOLDING, 0);

// Parse the file
$ret = xml_parse_from_file($parser, $file);
if(!$ret)
{
    die(sprintf("XML error: %s at line %d",
                xml_error_string(xml_get_error_code($parser)),
                xml_get_current_line_number($parser)));
```

```php
    }

    // Free parser
    xml_parser_free($parser);

    // Free helper elements
    unset($elements["current_element"]);
    unset($elements["last_element"]);

    // Sort $elements array by element count
    uasort($elements, "my_sort");

    // Loop through all elements collected in $elements
    while(list($name, $element) = each($elements))
    {
        print_box("Element name", $name);

        print_line("Element count", $element->count);
        print_line("Character count", $element->chars);

        printf("\n%20s\n", "* Parent elements");

        // Loop through the parents of this element, output them
        while(list($key, $value) = each($element->parents))
        {
            print_line($key, $value);
        }
        if(count($element->parents) == 0)
        {
            printf("%35s\n", "[root element]");
        }

        // Loop through the childs of this element, output them
        printf("\n%20s\n", "* Child elements");
        while(list($key, $value) = each($element->childs))
        {
            print_line($key, $value);
        }
        if(count($element->childs) == 0)
        {
            printf("%35s\n", "[no childs]");
        }

        $total_elements += $element->count;
        $total_chars += $element->chars;
    }

    // Final summary
    print_box("Total elements", $total_elements);
    print_box("Total characters", $total_chars);
```

This application uses Expat to collect statistical data about an XML document. For each element, it prints a bunch of information:

- How many times it occurred within the document
- How much character data was found within this element
- All parent elements encountered
- All child elements

To achieve this, the script needs at the very least to know the parent element for the current element. This is not possible using the normal XML parser—you only get events for the current element, and no contextual information is recorded. Thus we needed to set up our own stack structure. We could have used a FIFO stack (First In, First Out) with two elements, but to give you a better example of keeping element nesting information within a data structure, we voted for a FILO (First In, Last Out) stack. This stack, which is a normal array, holds all currently open elements. In the open-element handler, the current element is pushed on top of the stack using `array_push()`. Accordingly, the end-element handler function removes the top element with `array_pop()`.

A note on `array_pop()` and `array_push()`. These and many other useful functions dealing with arrays have been added only in PHP 4.0. We wanted to port them over to PHP 3.0, but it's difficult to implement them efficiently in native PHP (to backport it to PHP 3.0) because of the way `unset()` works. To pop an element off the stack, you would use a snippet like this:

```
unset($array[count($array) - 1]);
```

If this would work well, it would be trivial to implement `array_pop()`- however, it doesn't work well. With PHP, `unset()` leaves holes in the array—it doesn't reset the "index counter." You can easily verify this yourself:

```
$array = array("a");
unset($array[0]);
$array[] = "a";
var_dump($array);
```

The element a will now have the key 1, instead of the expected 0. This leads to fragmented arrays—unsuitable for a stack. This behavior has its reasons with every other element in the array: If the hole was eliminated, the array would need to be reorganized, which would be undesirable in many situations. To work around this problem, we'd need an `array_compact()` version—which doesn't exist in PHP at the time of this writing. The only conclusion to draw is this: Use PHP 4.0. In the PHP 3.0 implementation of the example (see the CD-ROM), we had to use the `$depth` variable to keep track of the element nesting manually. This introduces another global variable and is not as elegant as `array_pop()` and `array_push()`, but it works.

To collect information about each element, the scripts needs to remember all occurrences of each element. We use a global array variable, $elements, to hold all distinct elements of the document. The array entries are instances of the element class, which has four properties (class variables):

Property	Description
count	The number of times the element was found in the document.
chars	Bytes of character data within this element.
parents	Parent elements.
childs	Child elements.

As you see, it's no problem to keep class instances within an array.

Tip: A peculiar language feature of PHP is that you can traverse class structures just like you would traverse associative arrays, using the while(list() = each()) loop shown in Chapter 1, "Development Concepts." It will show you all class variables and method names as strings.

Each time an element is found, the count element in the corresponding elements array item is incremented. In the parent's entry (*parent* meaning the last opened element tag), the current element's name is appended to the childs array entry. The parent element is added to the array entry with the key parents. The rest of the code loops through the elements array and its subarrays to display the statistics. While this produces a nice output, the code *per se* is neither of particular elegance nor does it consist of clever tricks: It's a loop like you probably use every day simply to get the job done.

DOM—Document Object Model

The other main family of XML parsers are those that enable access to a Document Object Model (DOM) structure. As you've seen, with event-based parsers you often have to set up your own data structures. The DOM approach avoids that requirement by building its own structure in main memory. Rather than responding to specific events, you work with this structure to process the document. While event-based parsers read an XML document in small chunks, reducing parsing memory usage and increasing performance, DOM parsers need to create an in-memory representation of the whole document. This uses more memory—keep this in mind when working with large documents.

The DOM Level 1.0 was defined as a standard (W3C Recommendation) in October 1998 by the (by now probably well known) W3C organization. You may have heard of the DOM standard already in another context: The term is also commonly used to describe the object model of HTML pages that can be accessed with JavaScript. For example, to read the value of a form field, you could use the following JavaScript snippet:

```
fieldvalue = document.myform.myfield.value;
```

Notice the hierarchy expressed in the statement. `document` is the root element and `myform` denotes an HTML form, within which `myfield` is a text field. Indeed, the HTML DOM is an extension of the core Document Object Model defined by the W3C. The DOM core represents the functionality used for XML documents, and also serves as the basis for the HTML DOM. It's a collection of objects that you use to access and manipulate the data and markup stored in an XML document. It defines the following:

- A set of objects for representing the complete structure of an XML document
- A model of how these objects can be combined
- An interface for accessing and manipulating these objects

By abstracting the document, the DOM exposes a tree, with parent and child nodes, and methods like `getAttribute()` for the nodes. Put short, DOM provides you with a standard, object-oriented and tree-like interface to XML documents.

The DOM specification is programming-language-independent. The specification recommends an object-oriented implementation, thus requiring a language with at least basic object-orientation features. It defines a set of node types (interfaces), which taken together form the complete document. Some types of nodes may have child nodes, others are leaf nodes that cannot have anything below them. We'll continue by describing these node types, as they're outlined in the original W3C specification. Please refer to the specification for a detailed description of all methods and attributes of each instance.

Document

The `Document` interface is the root node of the structure tree. This interface can contain only one element, which is the XML document's root element. It can also contain the document type declaration associated with this document (organized in a `DocumentType` interface), and, if available, processing instructions or comments from outside the root element.

Since the other nodes are all placed below the `Document` node, the `Document` interface contains a number of methods to create subnodes. Using these functions, it's possible to construct a complete XML document programmatically. The specification also defines a method `getElementsByTagName()` to retrieve all elements with a given tag name in the document.

DocumentFragment

A DocumentFragment node is a portion of a complete XML document. It's often necessary to rearrange parts of a document or to extract part of it; for this, a lightweight object is needed to hold the resulting fragment. For example, imagine you want to construct a single book file out of many different chapter files—each chapter could be read into the DocumentFragment object and inserted into the book's document structure. Without a way to organize fragments of documents, you'd have to add each element of each chapter one by one to the book document.

To make it even easier, the specification defines that when DocumentFragment is inserted into a node, only the children of the DocumentFragment and not the DocumentFragment itself are inserted into the node.

DocumentType

The DocumentType node holds the document type declaration of a document, if present. This interface is read-only; it cannot be altered through the DOM at this time.

Element

Each element in a document is represented by an Element node. To get the name of the element, the tagName property can be used. This interface also defines a series of functions to set and get element attributes, and to access sub-elements.

Attr

An Attr node represents an element attribute in an Element object. Name and value of the attribute can be read for the name and value properties of the interface. The specified property tells you whether the user specified a value for this Attr or the value is the default string specified in the DTD.

EntityReference

This node represents an entity reference found in the XML document. Note that character references (for example, <) are expanded by the XML parser and are thus not made available as EntityReference nodes.

Entity

This node represents an entity, either parsed or unparsed.

ProcessingInstruction

The ProcessingInstruction node represents a processing instruction (PI) in a document. It has only two attributes, namely target (the PI target) and data (the contents).

Comment

This CharacterData interface represents the content of a comment, i.e. all the characters between <!-- and -->. It has no further attributes or methods.

Text

The Text CharacterData interface represents the character data (textual content) of an Element or Attr note. The Text interface has no attributes, and only one method, namely splitText(). This method splits one Text node into two, which can be useful for rearranging content.

CDATASection

The CDATASection interface inherits the Text interface (and with it the CharacterData interface) and holds the CDATA section.

Notation

This node represents a notation declared in the document type declaration.

Basic Interfaces

All these objects inherit the Node interface, which is the primary basic datatype for the DOM. It represents a single node in the document tree structure. The Node interface defines the attributes and methods you'll use most often when dealing with the DOM. To traverse a document, for example, you would use the childNodes attribute containing all children and the nextSibling attribute containing the next node on the same level. Methods like appendChild() and removeChild() can be used to alter the tree structure.

The only objects not directly derived from a Node interface are CDATASection, Text, and Comment. Text and Comment are derived from the CharacterData interface; CDATASection inherits Text. The CharacterData interface extends Node with a set of attributes and methods for accessing character data. For example, you can use substringData() to extract part of the character data.

Example: Analyzing a Short Document with the DOM

The easiest way to get an idea about the concrete implementation of the DOM is by seeing how a sample XML document would be handled by a DOM-compliant processor. Let's create a short book document:

```
<?xml version="1.0"?>
<!DOCTYPE book SYSTEM "docbookx.dtd">
<book>
    <title>
        Cutting-Edge Applications
    </title>
    <para language="en">
```

```
        Sample paragraph.
    </para>
</book>
```

A DOM representation of this document will be organized in a hierarchical structure like the one shown in Figure 7.5. In a DOM–compliant API, code could be similar to the following pseudocode:

```
// Construct Document class instance
$doc = new Document("file.xml");

// Output the root element's name
printf("Root element: %s<p>", $doc->documentElement->tagName);

// Get all elements below the root node
$node_list = $doc->getElementsbyTagName("*");

// Traverse the returned node list
for($i=0; $i<$node_list->length; $i++)
{
    // Create node
    $node = $node_list->item($i);

    // Output node name and value
    printf("Node name: %s<br>", $node->nodeName);
    printf("Node value: %s<br>", $node->nodeValue);
}
```

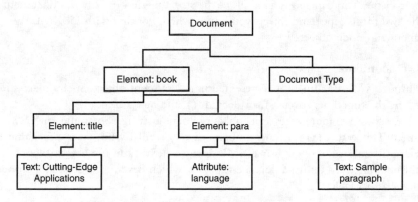

Figure 7.5 DOM structure.

LibXML—A DOM-Based XML Parser

Since version 4.0, a new XML parser is built into PHP: LibXML. Daniel Veillard originally created this parser for the Gnome project to offer a DOM-ready parser for managing complex data exchange, and Uwe Steinman integrated it into PHP.

While LibXML's internal document representation is very close to the DOM interfaces, it's misleading to call LibXML a DOM parser: Parsing and DOM usage really happen at different times in a document's life. It would be feasible to create an API above Expat to provide a DOM interface. The LibXML library makes this much easier, though—it's merely a matter of changing the API to match the DOM specification. Indeed, there is a GDome module in Gnome, which implements a DOM interface for LibXML.

Note: At the time of this writing, the LibXML API in PHP was being finalized. It was unstable and contained bugs—nonetheless it already showed the tremendous benefits the finished LibXML API will offer. Therefore, we decided to document the basic principles here and provide some examples; if changes occur, we'll document them on the book's Web site.

Overview

Most developers will agree that an XML document is best represented in a tree structure. LibXML provides a nice API to construct trees and DOM-like data structures from an XML file. When you parse a document with LibXML, PHP constructs a set of classes, and you'll work with them directly. By invoking functions on these classes, you can access all levels of the structure and modify the document.

The two most important objects you'll spot when working with LibXML are document and node objects.

XML Documents

The abstract XML document is represented in a document object. Such objects are created by the functions `xmldoc()`, `xmldocfile()`, and `new_xmldoc()`.

The function `xmldoc()` takes as its only argument a string containing an XML document. The `xmldocfile()` function behaves very similarly, but takes a filename as argument. To construct a new, blank XML document, you can use `new_xmldoc()`.

All three functions return a document object, which has four associated methods and one class variable:

- `root()`
- `add_root()`
- `dtd()`
- `dumpmem()`
- `version`

The function root() returns a node object containing the root element of the document. On empty documents as created by new_xmldoc(), you can add a root element using add_root(), which will return a node object as well. The function add_root() expects the name of the element as first argument when called as class method. You can also call it as global function, but then you need to pass a document class instance as first argument, and the name of the root element as second argument.

The dtd() function returns a DTD object with no methods, and the class variables name, sysid, and extid. The name of a DTD is always the name of the root element. The variable sysid contains the system identifier (for example, doobookx.dtd); the extid variable contains the external or public identifier. To convert the in-memory structure to a string, you can use the dumpmem() function. The version class variable contains the document's XML version, usually 1.0 today.

With these explanations, you're ready for a first, simple example. Let's construct a Hello World XML document with LibXML:

```
$doc = new_xmldoc("1.0");
$root = $doc->add_root("greeting");
$root->content = "Hello World!";
print(htmlspecialchars($doc->dumpmem()));
```

This will result in a well-formed XML document:

```
<?xml version="1.0"?>
<greeting>Hello World!</greeting>
```

The example also shows one property you don't know yet—accessing the contents of a node object.

Nodes

The Tao Te King says everything is Tao. In XML parsing, everything is a node. Elements, attributes, text, PIs, and so forth—from a programmer's point of view, you can treat them all in a very similar way, because they're nodes.

As we've already mentioned, nodes can be the most basic, atomic structure in an XML document. A node object has the following associated functions and variables:

- parent()
- children()
- new_child()
- getattr()
- setattr()
- attributes()
- type
- name
- if available, content

With these functions and properties, you can get all available information about a node. You can access its attributes, child nodes (if any), and parent node. And you can modify the tree by adding children or setting attributes. Listing 7.4 shows the functions in action. This is the XML pretty printer mentioned earlier in the Expat section, ported to LibXML—instead of registering handler functions, it applies different formatting according to the node's type. Each node has an associated type. The type identifier is a PHP constant, and you can see the complete list in the example's source. Using the `children()` function, which returns the node's child elements (as node objects), it's easy to loop through the document. The example performs the loop recursively by calling the `output_node()` function again.

Listing 7.4 **XML pretty printer—example using the LibXML functions.**

```
// Define tab width
define("INDENT", 4);

function output_node($node, $depth)
{
    // Different action per node type
    switch($node->type)
    {
        case XML_ELEMENT_NODE:
            for($i=0; $i<$depth; $i++) print(" ");

            // Print start element
            print("<span class='element'>&lt;");
            print($node->name);

            // Get attribute names and values
            $attribs = $node->attributes();
            if(is_array($attribs))
            {
                while(list($key, $value) = each($attribs))
                {
                    print(" $key = <span class='attribute'>$value</span>");
                }
            }

            print("&gt;</span><br>");

            // Process children, if any
            $children = $node->children();
            for($i=0; $i < count($children); $i++)
            {
                output_node($children[$i], $depth+INDENT);
            }

            // Print end element
            for($i=0; $i<$depth; $i++) print(" ");
```

```php
                print("<span class='element'>&lt;/");
                print($node->name);
                print("&gt;</span><br>");
                break;
        case XML_PI_NODE:
                for($i=0; $i<$depth; $i++) print(" ");
                printf("<span class='pi'>&lt;?%s %s?&gt;</span><br>", $node->name,
                ↦$node->content);
                break;
        case XML_COMMENT_NODE:
                for($i=0; $i<$depth; $i++) print(" ");
                print("<span class='element'>&lt;!-- </span>");
                print($node->content);
                print("<span class='element'> --&gt;</span><br>");
                break;
        case XML_TEXT_NODE:
        case XML_ENTITY_REF_NODE:
        case XML_ENTITY_REF_NODE:
        case XML_DOCUMENT_NODE:
        case XML_DOCUMENT_TYPE_NODE:
        case XML_DOCUMENT_FRAG_NODE:
        case XML_CDATA_SECTION_NODE:
        case XML_NOTATION_NODE:
        case XML_GLOBAL_NAMESPACE:
        case XML_LOCAL_NAMESPACE:
        default:
                for($i=0; $i<$depth; $i++) print(" ");
                printf("%s<br>", isset($node->content) ? $node->content : "");
    }
}

// Output stylesheet
?>
<style type="text/css">
<!--
.xml {  font-family: "Courier New", Courier, mono;
        font-size: 10pt; color: #000000}
.element {  color: #0033CC}
.attribute {  color: #000099}
.pi {  color: #990066}
-->
</style>
<span class="xml">
<?

// Process the file passed as first argument to the script
$file = "test.xml";

// Initial indenting
$depth = 0;
```

continues

Listing 7.4 **Continued**

```
// Check if file exists
if(!file_exists($file))
{
    die("Can't find file \"$file\".");
}

// Create xmldoc object from file
$doc = xmldocfile($file) or die("XML error while parsing file \"$file\"");

// Access root node
$root = $doc->root();

// Start traversal
output_node($root, $depth);

// End stylesheet span
print("</span>");
```

One of the great advantages of LibXML over Expat is that you can also use it to construct XML documents. This avoids messing around with custom XML creation routines and frees you from tasks like remembering the nesting level to properly close tags. Listing 7.5 takes our earlier Hello World example a step further and constructs a complete RSS document (RSS stands for Rich Site Summary, an XML format to provide content information for Web sites). It uses `setattr()` to add attributes to an element and `new_child()` to add elements to a node. Have you noted the way `new_child()` is used? The function returns a node object, and you can simply discard that return value if you don't need it—you only need to assign it to a variable if you want to add child elements to the note you've just created.

Listing 7.5 **Using LibXML routines to construct XML documents.**

```
$doc = new_xmldoc("1.0");

$root = $doc->add_root("rss");
$root->setattr("version", "0.91");

$channel = $root->new_child("channel", "");
$channel->new_child("title", "XML News and Features from XML.com");
$channel->new_child("description", "XML.com features a rich mix of information and
➥services for the XML community.");
$channel->new_child("language", "en-us");
$channel->new_child("link", "http://xml.com/pub");
$channel->new_child("copyright", "Copyright 1999, O'Reilly and Associates and
➥Seybold Publications");
$channel->new_child("managingEditor", "dale@xml.com (Dale Dougherty)");
$channel->new_child("webMaster", "peter@xml.com (Peter Wiggin)");
```

```
$image =$channel->new_child("image", "");
$image->new_child("title", "XML News and Features from XML.com");
$image->new_child("url", "http://xml.com/universal/images/xml_tiny.gif");
$image->new_child("link", "http://xml.com/pub");
$image->new_child("width", "88");
$image->new_child("height", "31");

print(htmlspecialchars($doc->dumpmem()));
```

XML Trees

The methods outlined above construct separate objects for the document and for each node. While this is great for looping through the document as shown in the XML pretty printer, accessing single elements tends to get a bit cumbersome. Do you remember our sample Hello World document from earlier in the chapter?

```
<?xml version="1.0"?>
<greeting>Hello World!</greeting>
```

To access the contents of the root element, you'd have to use the following code:

```
// Create xmldoc object from file
$doc = xmldocfile("test.xml") or die("XML error while parsing file \"$file\"");

// Access root node
$root = $doc->root();

// Access root's children
$children = $root->children();

// Print first child's content
print($children[0]->content);
```

And that's for a depth of one; imagine how you'd have to continue with deeper nested elements. If you think that this is a bit too much work, we agree. Fortunately, Uwe Steinman agrees too, and has provided a more elegant method of random access to document elements: xmltree(). This function creates a structure of PHP objects, representing the whole XML document. When you pass it a string containing an XML document as first argument, the function returns a document object. The object is a bit different from the one described earlier, though: It doesn't allow functions to be called, but sets up properties of the same. Instead of getting a list of child elements with a children() call, the children are already present in the structure (in the children class variable)—making it easy to access elements in every depth. Accessing the contents of the greeting element would therefore be done with the following call:

```
// Create xmldoc object from file
$doc = xmldocfile(join("", file($file)) or die("XML error while parsing
⇒file \"$file\"");

        print($doc->root->ohildren[0]->content);
```

That looks infinitely better now. When you dump the structure returned by xmltree() with var_dump(), you get the following output:

```
object(Dom document)(2) {
  ["version"]=>
  string(3) "1.0"

  ["root"]=>
  object(Dom node)(3) {
    ["type"]=>
    int(1)

    ["name"]=>
    string(8) "greeting"

    ["children"]=>
    array(1) {
      [0]=>
      object(Dom node)(3) {
        ["name"]=>
        string(4) "text"

        ["content"]=>
        string(12) "Hello World!"

        ["type"]=>
        int(3)
      }
    }
  }
}
```

You see that this is one large structure, with the whole document ready in place. The actual parts of the structure are still document or object nodes; indeed, internally the same class definitions are used. In contract to objects created with xmldoc() and friends, though, you can't invoke functions on these structures. Consequently, the structure returned by xmltree() is read-only at this time—to construct XML documents, you need to use the other methods.

Interchanging Data with WDDX

Now that you've learned how to create and process XML documents, it's time to introduce you to a real application of this technology. You've heard that XML is cross-platform, vendor-independent, and supported well by PHP and other programming languages. What about using XML to communicate between different platforms, or between different programming languages? WDDX does exactly that.

The Web Distributed Data eXchange (WDDX)

WDDX is an open technology proposed by Allaire Corporation; it's an XML vocabulary for describing basic and complex data structures such as strings, arrays, and recordsets in a generic fashion, so that they can be moved between different Web scripting platforms using only HTTP. PHP supports WDDX, and so do most other prominent Web scripting languages; for example, Perl, ASP, and ColdFusion.

The Challenge

As Web applications play an ever-increasing role in the software world, one of the most important challenges is data exchange between different programming environments. The new Web promotes distributed, networked applications. First, there were simple Web sites with static information. They grew into more advanced dynamic Web applications, and now these Web applications are beginning to work together, to exchange data, to offer additional, programmable services. It was only recently that open standards like XML emerged and gained widespread use, and that the market forced vendors to adopt these standards in their products.

By extending Web applications to implement open programming interfaces for data exchange and modification, the intelligence of the Web experiences a huge increase. Suddenly, applications can talk to each other—they evolve from closed, proprietary Web sites to a new generation of wired business applications.

Web applications can expose an API or make data structures available: Data exchanges between distributed servers becomes possible. WDDX offers one possible solution for exchanging structured data. WDDX consists of two parts; one part deals with abstracting data into an XML representation called *WDDX packets*; the other part translates data structures to and from the scripting environment and WDDX packets.

WDDX is not a remote procedure call facility: There is no way in pure WDDX to invoke a function on a server, which then returns a WDDX packet. How to transfer packets is completely up to you. For this reason, WDDX has no provision for security—it's your task to select a communications channel of appropriate security and allow only authorized parties to access the WDDX part of your system.

Possible Scenarios

Whether for synchronizing data, centralizing data serving, or performing business-to-business communications, structured data exchange opens a new dimension in distributed computing. For example, imagine that you operate an e-commerce Web site. Wouldn't it be great if you could provide customers with package tracking during the shipment? This could be implemented easily if UPS or FedEx provided a way to query for a shipped item programmatically. By opening formed customer-centric services (most couriers do allow tracking packages for their customers) to distributed computing (package tracking as programmable API), a new form of application interaction is made possible.

In another scenario, WDDX could be used in server-to-server interaction. Certain services may work best on a Windows NT platform; for example, querying an SAP back end using a COM connector. You could use ASP for this, and hand over the query results as WDDX packets to your PHP application on a UNIX Web server. There the packets would be turned into PHP data structures, such as arrays, transparently and without any further work.

Abstracting Data with WDDX

The most important fact up front: WDDX is XML. The possible WDDX structures are defined in an XML DTD, and therefore valid WDDX packets are always well-formed and potentially valid XML. The specification doesn't require WDDX packets to be valid, as they don't need to include a document type declaration in the document prologue.

The basic idea is that WDDX lets you transform any standard data structure—integers, strings, arrays, etc.—into an XML representation, which conforms to the WDDX DTD. This data can then be transferred over any communications channel capable of transferring XML: HTTP, FTP, email, etc. At any time, the data can be read from the WDDX format back into exactly the same structure as before. During this whole conversion process, datatypes are preserved. If you serialize an array as WDDX packet, it will be an array again at deserialization time.

Now, if this was all, it wouldn't be very exciting. After all, you can serialize any data structure in PHP into a proprietary form using `serialize()` and bring it back with `deserialize()` as many times as you like. The interesting aspect of WDDX is that the serialized representation is in XML, and the serializer and deserializer modules are cleanly separated from it. Each of the programming languages supporting WDDX will be able to serialize and deserialize WDDX packets. Serialize a PHP array to a WDDX packet, deserialize the packet in ASP—and you've got an array again! The actual implementation of the serializer/deserializer is not important; in PHP, you've got the `wddx_*()` functions; in ColdFusion, you use the `CFWDDX` tag; in ASP, a COM component is available.

Sure, all this could be done without WDDX. Doing so would be pretty complicated, though, especially when you think of preserving datatypes across different programming environments. The advantage of WDDX is that it frees you from this undertaking and provides a flexible, open, and pragmatic way for exchanging structured application data.

WDDX Datatypes

Most programming languages share a common set of datatypes; for example, strings or arrays. Accessing these structures may vary from language to language, but the general idea remains: A string is a series of characters, and whether you enclose them with a single quote, double quotes, or not at all doesn't matter from a conceptual point of view.

WDDX supports these generic datatypes. In version 1.0 of the specification, the following types are defined:

- Null values: `null` element
- Boolean values: `bool`
- Numbers (with no distinction between integers and floating-point numbers): `number`
- Strings: `string`
- Date/time values: `dateTime`
- Indexed arrays: `array`
- Associative arrays: `struct`
- Collections of associative arrays, a set of named fields with the same number of rows of data: `recordset`
- Binary objects, at this time encoded with Base64: `binary`

All WDDX packets follow a common XML format. The root element is `wddxPacket`, with an optional version attribute specifying the version of the WDDX DTD. The version number, currently `1.0`, is bound to and defined in the DTD. This means that any WDDX packet with a version of `1.0` is valid *only* when used with the WDDX DTD 1.0, and not with 2.0 or 0.9.

The `header` element must follow right below the root `wddxPacket` element. The header can contain only one comment element, and nothing else.

The next required element is `data`, denoting the body of the packet. Within this element, exactly one `null`, `boolean`, `number`, `dateTime`, `string`, `array`, `struct`, `recordset`, or `binary` element must appear. A sample WDDX packet is shown in Listing 7.6.

Listing 7.6 **A sample WDDX packet.**

```
<wddxPacket version='1.0'>
    <header/>
    <data>
        <struct>
            <var name='string'>
                <string>This is a 'string'.</string>
            </var>
            <var name='int'>
                <number>42</number>
            </var>
            <var name='float'>
                <number>42.5</number>
            </var>
            <var name='bool'>
                <boolean value='true'/>
            </var>
```

continues

Listing 7.6 **Continued**

```
                <var name='array'>
                    <array length='3'>
                        <number>1</number>
                        <number>2</number>
                        <number>3</number>
                    </array>
                </var>
                <var name='hash'>
                    <struct>
                        <var name='foo'>
                            <string>bar</string>
                        </var>
                        <var name='baz'>
                            <string>fubar</string>
                        </var>
                    </struct>
                </var>
            </struct>
        </data>
</wddxPacket>
```

PHP and WDDX

Because WDDX uses XML for the representation of data structures, you need to compile PHP with both XML and WDDX in order to use it. If you've done that, the following functions are at your disposal:

- `wddx_serialize_value()`
- `wddx_serialize_vars()`
- `wddx_packet_start()`
- `wddx_add_vars()`
- `wddx_packet_end()`
- `wddx_deserialize()`

Using these functions, you can serialize PHP variables into WDDX packets and deserialize WDDX packets.

The WDDX Functions

Using the WDDX functions, there are three different ways to construct a packet. The most basic method is to use `wddx_serialize_value()`. This function takes one variable plus an optional comment, and creates a WDDX packet out of it:

```
$var = "This is a string.";
print(wddx_serialize_value($var, "This is a comment."));
```

And that's it. This snippet will output the following WDDX packet:

```
<wddxPacket version='1.0'>
    <header>
        <comment>This is a comment.</comment>
    </header>
    <data>
        <string>This is a string.</string>
    </data>
</wddxPacket>
```

Note: Actually, this packet has been manually edited for clarity: The original packet as created by PHP doesn't contain whitespace or indentation.

The two other methods serialize multiple PHP variables into a WDDX struct element, similar to the one shown in Listing 7.6. The wddx_serialize_vars() function takes an arbitrary number of string arguments containing the names of PHP variables. The function's return value is the WDDX packets as string. The advantage of this is that it lets you serialize multiple PHP variables into one WDDX packet; but note that when fed to the deserializer, it will result in an associative array (of course—the original distinct PHP variable has earlier been converted to a WDDX struct tag). In code, a basic example for wddx_serialize_vars() could look like the following snippet:

```
$string = "This is a string.";
$int = 42;
print(wddx_serialize_vars("string", "int"));
```

The trio wddx_packet_start(), wddx_add_vars(), and wddx_packet_end() works in basically the same way: Multiple PHP variables are transformed into a WDDX struct as well. The difference is that it works as a transaction with three steps, having the advantage that you can add PHP variables to a WDDX packet over a longer run—for example, during a complex calculation. By contrast, the function wddx_serialize_vars() works in an atomic way. You start assembling a packet by calling the wddx_packet_start() function, which takes one optional argument, the header comment for the WDDX packet. This function returns a packet identifier, similar to file identifiers returned with fopen(). The identifier is used as the first argument in the wddx_add_vars() function. The remaining arguments are exactly the same as with wddx_serialize_vars(): an arbitrary number of strings, containing the names of PHP variables. A basic example:

```
$i1 = $i2 = $i3 = "Foo";
$packet_id = wddx_packet_start("This is a comment");
for($i=1; $i<=3; $i++)
{
    wddx_add_vars($packet_id, "i$i");
}
print(wddx_packet_end($packet_id));
```

The example simply adds three string variables to a WDDX packet in a `for()` loop and produces the following output (again, edited for clarity by adding proper indentation):

```
<wddxPacket version='1.0'>
    <header>
        <comment>This is a comment</comment>
    <data>
        <struct>
            <var name='i1'>
                <string>Foo</string>
            </var>
            <var name='i2'>
                <string>Foo</string>
            </var>
            <var name='i3'>
                <string>Foo</string>
            </var>
        </struct>
    </data>
</wddxPacket>
```

Summary

This chapter has taught you everything you need to know about today's cutting-edge applications. You have learned how to design, create, and set up a knowledge repository, store data appropriately in the repository, and retrieve it efficiently. We have presented common data formats and open standards for data exchange, remote procedure calling, and platform-independent data storage. Having read and understood these techniques will enable you to implement key features of today's high-performance applications.

8

Case Studies

Knowing others is intelligence;
Knowing yourself is true wisdom.

THE FOLLOWING SECTIONS FEATURE THREE CASE STUDIES on the use of PHP on large-scale Web sites and in commercial products. These case studies describe companies that have chosen PHP after careful evaluation of competing technologies, and that depend on PHP for a great part of their daily business. Much of the text has been provided by the companies profiled, and therefore shows concrete insight into their development processes and technical facts. The case studies prove that PHP is a reliable, cutting-edge solution for server-side Web application development; we hope that they can help you to convince management and colleagues of PHP's advantages.

BizChek.com

You probably knew that HotMail, a Microsoft company, uses FreeBSD on its servers. While it would be nice if we had a case study revealing that Microsoft uses PHP for its Web-based mail, we have something at least equivalent: BizChek.com (`www.bizchek.com`), the leading Web-based email provider for businesses, does use PHP. With customers like Budweiser and Micro Warehouse and over 2 million registered users, BizChek.com is one of the key players in the industry.

Not only that—Mark Musone, CTO of Chek Inc., BizChek.com's parent company, is an active PHP developer. He has written or co-written such useful modules for PHP as IMAP and MCAL, which are part of PHP's standard distribution.

Web Mail

With more than 70 employees, 8 of whom are programmers, BizChek is an important market player in the Web-based e-communication/intranet market. When BizChek is combined with the rest of the Chek Network, Chek.com consistently ranks within the top 20 of the Internet's 100hot listing (www.100hot.com).

BizChek occupies a unique position in the area of email business solutions. Though the main application is a stand-alone Web-based email product, BizChek also offers a suite of productivity tools that add cohesion to the individual business while at the same time increasing the organization's overall effectiveness and productivity. BizChek is more than an email product. Under a private-label arrangement, BizChek can help a company establish an electronic identity. The company can brand itself with its employees and the general business market by having a mail address with its company name instead of a generic address (AOL, HotMail, and so on). Once a business understands the tangible and intangible benefits derived from a Web-based e-communication solution, the conversion or initiation of service is easy. Business owners and managers alike are becoming aware of the benefits that an outsourced Web-based e-communication product can bring.

BizChek offers a number of features including email, document/file sharing and revision, task manager, calendar service, a company bulletin board, and many more. When a financial comparison is done, outsourcing will dramatically lower a company's costs over time in almost every case. With no investment in hardware or software, and no maintenance required from an IT standpoint, the savings become real and measurable. Outsourcing can also translate to lower risk by providing a professional, reliable solution in which virus monitoring and spam prevention are all centrally administered and controlled. This also points to the added intangible benefits an outsourced Web-based communication product offers.

Choosing PHP

BizChek developers have used PHP since incorporation in early 1998, using PHP 2.0. Although BizChek was built from the ground up around PHP, this doesn't mean that no other solutions were discussed or evaluated. The company's experts spent several months evaluating and challenging various ideas: ASP, Mod_Perl, and Cold Fusion. They found that PHP was the best choice for BizChek, and since the beginning PHP has been their primary focus. As a startup dot-com company with limited funds and nothing but tons of hard work to offer initially, they found the Open Source community very attractive. Although PHP, like many Open Source products, is not backed or supported commercially by large companies, recent market studies have shown an enormous increase in site use and overall involvement in PHP. Netcraft's Web server survey, for example, found that PHP was used on over 1.4 million domains in February, 2000, of 11 million total analyzed servers.[1] The BizChek developers believe that if you compare these results, it's not hard to see that PHP and other Open Source products top their respective fields, even against commercial contenders from established companies.

In their search for a scripting language, the BizChek developers evaluated many viable options that might have produced a solution to fit their needs. The first two options were Perl and various CGI scripting languages. Next was Microsoft's powerhouse ASP. Finally, two dark horses were recommended: Cold Fusion and PHP. With their primary needs being server-side scripting and database connectivity, BizChek developers could exclude any client-side scripting engines. Although they liked Perl as an excellent general-purpose language, they felt that it was never truly optimized for Web use, and fell short when dealing with heavy traffic across multiple Web sites; CGI and Perl scripts can quickly saturate memory and CPU, resulting in performance problems. Because ASP, Cold Fusion, and PHP work in conjunction with the Web server without having to spawn extra processes, these became the logical choices for further evaluation by BizChek. Although Cold Fusion might have been an acceptable choice, it was still a newer product at this time—little was known about it, and this made BizChek drop it as an option. BizChek figured that if Apache were chosen as the Web server, Mod_Perl, which embeds the Perl interpreter directly into the Web server, would produce results near to those of the PHP and ASP choices. Although Mod_Perl might have been a great choice, the BizChek developers felt that it might be lacking in dealing with high-volume Web applications. It was too much a general-purpose language for them, whereas they saw PHP as very simple, yet very powerful, and made specifically for the Web. There was no need to jump through any hoops to get PHP to "work with the Web."

ASP offered a wide variety of third-party components, but the initial and upkeep costs were a large concern. The fact that ASP was also restricted to only Internet Information Server and Microsoft's Windows platforms further degraded it as an option for BizChek. While ASP relies primarily on ODBC to make database connections, which could prove useful if you switch databases once a month, PHP and Perl have native database connections, giving them a slight advantage. Debugging—which every programmer knows can take a majority of a project's time and be a true nightmare if accuracy is not preserved—was also harder under ASP. PHP offers precise error messages that can effectively help to solve a problem.

Other advantages of PHP were seen in its clear C-like language syntax, the ease with which it can be added to plain HTML, its extensibility, database connectivity, and price. The final advantage was the support that the PHP community provides. An extensive mailing list, one of the best online documentation centers, numerous online and hardcopy tutorials, as well as a friendly sharing of knowledge between gurus and beginners, make up this support chain.

Another great aspect that many people overlook about Open Source products is that development occurs continually and in some cases new versions are released monthly. If you need a particular function you can add it yourself, if you have the time and knowledge. This means that you no longer have to wait for the next release to see whether your needs will be meet. Some of BizChek's programmers belong to the PHP development team and have contributed code that resulted from their own needs. Although most work on PHP projects is done outside the office, it occasionally occurs during company time; BizChek actively supports this activity, since most of the code created will be plugged right back into its system. The BizChek developers have been a contributing factor in a number of PHP modules, including MCAL, IMAP, FTP, and Aspell. Originally these modules were created to support BizChek, but because other programmers could benefit from the modules, and because the developers felt a compelling urge to give something back to the community, the extensions were added to PHP's core code. Some BizChek employees are also involved in small developments with Apache and Linux.

Eager for Updates

BizChek was previously upgraded from PHP 2.0 to version 3.0, and is ready to be migrated to PHP 4.0 as soon as it's out of beta. Migration from 2.0 to 3.0 and from 3.0 to 4.0 betas was accomplished without any serious difficulties and only needed a couple of small alterations.

Growing daily, the total system consists of about 200 files and 25,000–30,000 lines of code. Seeing that only about 20 lines of code needed to be changed for each upgrade, the BizChek developers were very happy with the exceptional backward support offered by PHP.

BizChek's ambition to run PHP 4.0, already tested internally, is matched only by the concern of using a beta on a production server. They already like the upgrades in array manipulation, installation, and the new modules in PHP 4.0 betas. The upgraded session-support system for PHP 4.0 was one of the major features BizChek was looking for, especially since PHPLib didn't exist during BizChek creation and they have never switched to using it. While their in-house session-management system works reliably, they'll convert to using PHP 4.0's built-in session support.

Conclusion

"PHP has worked wonderfully to meet our needs," says CTO Mark Musone. "It has worked in conjunction with Apache, MySQL, and Oracle, to name a few, very reliably and with highest performance, resulting in efficient dynamic Web content with limited problems and near 100% uptime. PHP is a clear advantage for our business, and we are glad we can use it!"

SixCMS

Professional content-management systems have traditionally been the domain of large companies and have been very cost-intensive, with standard products typically selling for six-figure sums. How would you like a full-featured content-management system (CMS) written in PHP? Six Open Systems (`www.six.de`) has one in its back pocket.

Company Background

Founded eight years ago, Six Offene Systeme GmbH (translated as Six Open Systems, Inc., and referred to simply as "Six" in this case study) has been developing and delivering sophisticated database applications using Open Source–based Internet and intranet technologies for diverse sectors of industry. Six specializes in developing individual solutions tailored to the goal of the enterprise, with an emphasis on the targeted market, the product range, and the customer's technical requirements. The scope of the Six consulting services and tailored solutions include the development of effective business models for the online presence, the definition of milestones with a differentiated strategy for implementation, assistance with identifying mid- and long-term profitability plans, utilizing business-process modeling for optimal resource utilization, formulating technical requirements, and the development of detailed requirement specifications. By applying the accumulated experience and know-how that has resulted from more than four years of development experience, Six has now released two standardized commercial solutions utilizing PHP: SixCMS (Content Management System) and SixAIM (Account and Invoice Management). Six currently employs 27 people as well as providing an excellent environment and opportunity for students from various fields involved with IT and "new media" to research and fulfill their practical semester and thesis requirements.

Of the 27 Six employees, 20 are directly involved in developing and programming applications. One of the advantages Six has realized is based on the diverse educational and experience backgrounds of its developers, who come from such fields as computer science, physics, printing and publishing, cartography, agriculture, philosophy, and systems management.

Open Source Business

Six still sees distinct advantages in the Open Source/System approach versus many of the more proprietary technology approaches. Ranked as a market leader and provider of world-class solutions throughout Germany and western Europe, Six opened an office in New York City, New York, USA, in January, 2000.

The SixCMS application is recognized by many people as being the number one content-management system application in Europe. The application's support of multiple languages for the interface and its extensive functionality makes it an optimal solution for managing dynamic content-driven sites.

The corporate Web site (`http://www.six.de`) and the SixCMS-specific URL (`http://sixcms.com`) provide additional information about the company, its customers, and its solutions. These Web sites provide an excellent vehicle for the company to disburse information about the company and its solutions; but word-of-mouth publicity from satisfied customers currently results in nearly half the leads and new customers. The Web presentation also provides an opportunity to showcase SixCMS in action and create customer-specific demo and test sites.

Why PHP?

Ease of use and low licensing costs were naturally critical criteria in the selection of PHP for Six. Cost and licensing requirements are a non-issue with PHP, while other options would have cost thousands of dollars per development or active server. This is a considerable advantage of employing Open Source technology as a solution provider. You don't get tied up with the customer discussing intricate scaled licensing fees, and can therefore discuss total solution costs with respect to functionality of the application alone. Performance of PHP also played a role, however, and the ability to embed PHP as a module into the Apache Web server provided performance benefits over other CGI methods. From a business standpoint, it made "just plain good sense" to use PHP, ensuring cost-effective and high-performance applications. Six developers have additionally considered, tested, and in some cases used Hexbase, WebSQL, WebObjects, Cold Fusion, Oracle Web Application Server, CGI, embperl, Java, C, and Perl. Although PHP is not the only development platform used at Six (Perl is still being applied in some situations), well over 90% of its applications have been done using PHP—a decision Six still supports today. All of the PHP applications were built and developed using PHP first.

Additionally, the Open Source aspects of PHP contributed to its selection. In an environment where Linux, Apache, and MySQL are being utilized, PHP fits very nicely in this mix. The widespread use and growing acceptance of the Open Source/System approach allows Six to use this environment very effectively for its commercial solutions, such as SixCMS. It's a very viable approach to take in this market and provides an excellent method to deliver valuable intellectual capital in a cost-effective manner. Open Source technologies have gained and most likely will continue to gain respect and support from industry, especially as its use becomes more widespread and more solutions based on this technology become available. One of the advantages of using Open Source solutions is that, if something isn't working as expected, you can at least have a look at the source code yourself. It has been the experience at Six that it's much easier and more timely to get support, changes, and fixes for the Open Source components than the commercial ones. A simple posting to one of the newsgroups or mailing lists often results in a number of qualified and help-ful responses…in a matter of hours, if not minutes. Commercial and proprietary appli-cations and environments are complicated and often "less than ideal" with respect to both costs and proprietary mechanisms.

Meanwhile, Six supports the development of PHP both directly and indirectly. One Six employee, Dr. Egon Schmid, is a PHP Documentation Group member and a con-tributor to and coauthor of the PHP Book *PHP. Dynamische Webauftritte professionell realisieren* (Markt u. Technik, Haar; 1999). Additionally, Six developers contribute with recommendations and opinions as participants in PHP mailing lists and user groups. These efforts are both supported and encouraged on company time as well as privately.

Technology Considerations

Six recommends using PHP in many situations and uses PHP for most of its applica-tions, including SixCMS. Particularly for layout-oriented sites with light-to-middle traffic loads, or in situations in which an application needs to be built quickly from the bottom up, PHP is an excellent platform. Naturally, it all boils down to the scope of the project. As with any platform, PHP has limitations; in very large projects or sites with extremely high activity, PHP can present a problem, especially if script runtime is taken into consideration. If performance issues arise with respect to system load with PHP, caching and preprocessing of code to create static pages should be implemented. Generally speaking (this depends on a number of factors), it's most likely necessary to generate static pages if a site is getting somewhere around 500,000 fully dynamic page views a month, or 5–10 queries concurrently for one page.

In specific situations, Six also uses Mod_Perl, but server configuration and kernel-tuning requirements admittedly become more significant issues with this method. Perl is very well thought out and has been around a long time; therefore it has a very con-sistent language scheme and syntax. Additionally, because Mod_Perl is compiled and held in memory, a Web site can be created from distinct components that have their own named space and can be compiled separately from each other. It's also possible with Mod_Perl to directly intervene with the Apache handler, which makes it a very fitting supplement to PHP and other scripting languages for the implementation of proxies, specific rewrite-rules, and post-transaction handlers, for example. Six has also tested both server-side and client-side Java, and although there have been some perfor-mance and compatibility issues, server-side Java seems promising for specific future applications. When compared to other technologies such as Mod_Perl, Java, Cold Fusion, and ASP, generally speaking PHP is less costly, with fast performance, integrates well with other technologies, and is very stable when embedded within Apache. But are there problems with it? Basically, the PHP platform is good, but developers should be aware of the limitations and the sometimes subtle changes in the programming language or function calls between versions. Additional considerations such as memory-handling problems—especially with strings that can literally waste megabytes of server memory (a problem that hopefully will be addressed in PHP 4.0)—and poor

Oracle integration needs to be recognized. The lack of consistency of the language syntax and design, and implicit typecasting have also been noted as deficits by Six developers.

Another issue with PHP is the simple fact that you have to pass the full source code of your application to the customer or partner. The value of your applications as intellectual property and capital, and the need to protect them, can be a significant issue. Six has worked with a number of advertising and design agencies as partners for Web site design, who, after having open access to Six's code, began adding programming ability to their graphic design skills...to become "competitors." These are companies who want to try to be a "one-stop shop" for Web solutions—unlike Six, which focuses on its core competence of application development. One can certainly argue that technology is developing so quickly that having your code open for all to see is not a definitive critical problem in the long term. The ability to utilize a bytecode compiler with PHP when it becomes available will improve this situation considerably, and Six currently encapsulates substantial functions as compiled code in the database itself to limit the effect of PHP code exposure or local changes being made by third parties.

PHP in Real Life

The two previously mentioned commercial products, SixCMS and SixAIM, are examples of Six applications that have been realized with PHP 3.0. In its 3.0 version, SixCMS has 283 files containing 25,000 lines of code and requires 1.2MB of disk space. The application uses a MySQL database containing 40 tables. In comparison, SixAIM has about 71,000 lines of PHP 3.0 code (plus another 10,000 lines of code written in Oracle's PL/SQL language code) and takes up 2MB of disk space. The Oracle database includes nearly 200 objects: 65 tables, 25 database functions, 15 procedures, and 8 packets, which incorporate an additional 45 functions and 30 procedures (not including any special customer-specific functionality). Six has been and is currently using the standard or basic version of PHP; specifically versions 3.0.6, 3.0.7, 3.0.12, and for testing purposes 4.0b3. Six is planning to make the switch to the 4.0 version for new projects as soon as it's no longer "beta" and runs stable. Although Six has migrated a number of solutions from the 2.x to 3.x versions of PHP, it's a time-consuming task that's also open to human error, even when automated with scripts. Syntax and language changes plus functional variations, such as with array handling and variable declaration, add migration time and testing requirements.

PHP has performed well for Six and its customers, but is not necessarily ideal for higher-traffic sites, as mentioned earlier. Certain caching concepts have helped, and Six has also used a reverse-proxy technique, so that the PHP-enabled server doesn't get tied up serving graphics and static pages. Six handles session issues with its own developed mechanisms and often utilizes cookies for session-dependent parameters. They haven't made much use of the PHPLib until now, but have identified a number of excellent features and ideas in it. XML has also been incorporated into a number of customer-specific applications when required, and additional open standards such as LDAP, SMTP, and X509 have been applied in various projects. Six has recently instituted version control for some of its development projects using CVS, and plans to extend its use to all development work in the future. The increase in programmers and the opening of a branch office in Berlin have necessitated a reevaluation of managing distributed development teams and projects. To this end, Six has also created a number of its own tools (with PHP) to assist in the management of project and development resources. Six has done solutions with a number of databases, including Oracle, MySQL, postgres, Microsoft SQL Server, and Sybase. Again, due to its Open Source philosophy and cost considerations, Six prefers using MySQL for most non-transaction-based applications, and Oracle for transaction-based applications such as SixAIM.

PHP has played and will continue to play a significant role in the success of Six and its solutions, as well as its customers. The selection and utilization of PHP for Six began in December 1996 with the PHP 2.0 beta, and currently is still a central component for the SixCMS application. Utilization of PHP not only has supported the company's Open Source philosophy, but has provided a comfortable and expedient environment for high-end application development.

PHP: A Business Advantage

Many of the functional and performance advantages of Six applications can be attributed directly to PHP, as well as the advantages of rapid development, the ability to make modifications quickly and without recompiling, plus the ease of understanding and using PHP effectively without previous knowledge or experience. These advantages increase proficiency as well as reduce development overhead costs. This industry dictates very short development and implementation time schedules, and PHP provides a reliable middleware or application-server component to support these turnaround time requirements.

MarketPlayer.com

Eric B. Schorvitz, Ph.D., and John E. Joganic from MarketPlayer.com provided this detailed case study about a company implementing PHP in real life on a high-traffic server farm.

Company Background

MarketPlayer.com offers real-life financial training to the individual investor who wants to learn how to make money in the stock market. MarketPlayer.com's institutional-quality stock screening and charting tools help investors build their own investment strategies, and its risk-free, fun, and exciting stock competitions enable investors to test and trade an investment portfolio.

MarketPlayer.com's products are available for free at its own Web site, www.marketplayer.com, and through strategic content alliances with leading media, ISP, and financial services partners including AOL, CNBC, E★TRADE, money.com, CompuServe, ESEC (Pan-European partner), internet.com, and others.

MarketPlayer.com employs 24 people in the areas of marketing, product development, customer service, and programming. Three of the programmers are highly skilled in C and PHP; two others are talented PHP programmers.

The PHP Products

MarketPlayer.com's product offerings fall into two basic categories: quantitative financial applications and online stock market trading-simulation software. To keep competitive in these industries, MarketPlayer.com must continually determine how to improve applications and content in order to remain one step ahead of the competition. For example, MarketPlayer.com is the only site on the Web allowing investors to screen and chart stocks based on a 12-month forward Constant Time Horizon Earnings Estimate methodology—a technique favored by institutional money managers. MarketPlayer.com has submitted multiple patent applications to protect the unique way in which the online stock tournaments operate. MarketPlayer.com also has an expert staff of product developers and programmers whose goal is to come up with new and useful Web-based financial tools to assist the individual investor in obtaining the knowledge and experience necessary to be successful in the investment community.

Why PHP?

MarketPlayer.com uses PHP because of its ability to provide a rapid product-development environment. Using PHP, MarketPlayer.com can take conceptual designs from the blackboard and bring them into a beta environment in a matter of days. They can then take the pieces of the application that need to be optimized (for speed), write them in C, and include those functions in a custom PHP library.

MarketPlayer.com began using PHP in October of 1999 after deciding to expand the product development group. Before PHP, MarketPlayer.com was using a server-side include approach to generate dynamic pages. Thus, most of the company was comfortable using WYSIWYG applications for Web development. PHP made it possible for MarketPlayer.com to build sophisticated, dynamic Web pages while still using the talents of the existing group comfortable with WYSIWYG approaches to Web development. The company had implemented solutions prior to PHP using Perl and Java, but once PHP was introduced these other languages soon fell by the wayside.

The fact that PHP is Open Source provides many advantages for MarketPlayer.com over other scripting languages:

- MarketPlayer.com can easily optimize applications by adding modules and functions to the PHP source code that are MarketPlayer.com-specific.
- The number of places that you can go to get support is growing daily.
- Many individuals provide top-notch PHP applications to the general community, with GNU licensing making the development of key products faster.

Advantages of PHP in MarketPlayer.com Product Development

MarketPlayer.com uses PHP over other technologies because of its simplicity in design, the availability and extensibility of the source code, the tight integration with the Apache Web server, and—perhaps most importantly—its similarity to the C programming language. Perl may have been a second choice; however, lack of familiarity with the language was a barrier to MarketPlayer.com programmers, and extensions for databases and proprietary algorithms would have been costly. Cold Fusion was not evaluated, and ASP's reliance on a Windows platform made it a non-contender. Until recently, MarketPlayer.com relied on server-side Java for specific user-configurable requests. Over time, the code became too voluminous to maintain and was replaced with a solution written entirely in PHP and C. The beta implementation is running five times faster than the Java production system, with plenty of room for optimization.

No fundamental flaws have been identified in the system, but relative paths in the `include()` statement have caused quite a bit of frustration, specifically when nesting includes. C source and header files use their own directory as the base for relative paths, whereas the PHP `include` statement uses the directory of the originally invoked file. As such, maintaining a directory of source specifically for `includes` and referencing those files from within a hierarchical directory structure can be complicated. The workaround was to create a variable for the `include` directory and use only absolute paths when including.

Additionally, integrating custom extensions has been complicated under PHP 3.0. MarketPlayer.com has tested PHP 4.0 and is happier with that model, but until it's out of beta, deployment to production servers can't be justified. Currently MarketPlayer.com is running 3.0.12.

All things considered, MarketPlayer.com has not been constrained by any missing components in PHP. There's certainly an interest in a debugging tool that caters to PHP if someone produces one; however, immediate needs call for a simple mechanism for extending the functionality without invoking the overhead of a `dl()` call or modifying PHP source directly.

PHP Battling in Real Life

MarketPlayer.com's applications vary in size from single scripts to entire site-management packages. All told, there are at least 10,000 lines of code currently in PHP and another 40,000 forecasted for the next quarter. As part of the development process, common functionality is moved to inline functions, those functions are moved to C, and the C code is ultimately incorporated into libraries for use by low-level integrators. This strategy of top-down programming guarantees that focus stays on product delivery rather than code production, as is necessary in the Web content industry.

PHP has proven scalable and fast as MarketPlayer.com uses it on high-traffic sites without hassle. If constraints were encountered, migration to faster machines or a change in network topography would be more likely than a pursuit for a different technology. Constant profiling identifies bottlenecks and helps prioritize which PHP code needs to be rewritten in C and linked in natively.

Sessioning

MarketPlayer.com uses two techniques for managing sessions. In the first case, the user's credentials are encrypted and stored on the client's machine in the form of a cookie. The immediate drawback is the requirement that every server providing dynamic content be capable of decrypting the cookie. In the development environment, new features have been stalled, waiting for this functionality.

The second and more portable case involves a database table that maps unique, random session identifiers to authenticated users. When the user authenticates using a valid name and password, a new session identifier is generated and stored in the user table along with IP address, time, and username. The user needs only a valid session identifier and a connection from the originally authenticated IP address to connect. From the point of view of security, a session identifier can be invalidated or expired by removing it from the database. Additionally, using it from a different IP address is silently ignored. Finally, credentials are sent only once. As for performance, only one database call must be made, and all of the user's information can be gathered via the session identifier by joining tables.

The session identifier is provided to the user in two ways. In the first case, it's inserted into all the URLs on the page so that on-site links retain this information. URLs are generated using a function that takes into account whether the user is authenticated or not, and outputs the correct HTML. Additionally, it's sent to the user as a cookie. This has the effect of guaranteeing that any incorrectly defined links don't cause the client to "forget" the identifier. Moreover, browsers that either don't support or actively reject cookies can still log into the site. Cookie variables override GET variables, so if the user bookmarks a page, the current session will override whatever identifier may be specified in the bookmarked URL. Finally, if the user leaves the site and returns before the session identifier expires, he or she remains authenticated.

PHP Server Integration

Because MarketPlayer.com's PHP library is modified constantly, they have compiled Apache for loadable modules and built a shared-object implementation for PHP. XML is not used for content, but is used for internal configuration files. The GNU autoconf and configure mechanism is used for deploying across the varied platforms of development and production equipment. Virtually all MarketPlayer.com's source is either proprietary legacy code or Open Source. The database infrastructure is a composite of MySQL for prototyping and minor chores, and Velocis for core functionality. The efficacy of Velocis over other database solutions has yet to be fully demonstrated; however, to date, with existing code, the network organizational model appears to outperform relational models. This may change as migration to new technology continues.

Code Management

MarketPlayer.com's content developers currently work under Windows NT with Source Safe handling version control. However, all of the new technology code is appropriately stored in CVS. When the content department has the necessary tools to work entirely under Linux, the aim is to pull them back into CVS.

Product directors manage MarketPlayer.com teams and design and organize the code while overseeing the implementation by team members. Prototype code is developed to alpha release and checked into CVS. These components are then distributed to other developers and audited by the directors for security, efficiency, and design. Subsequent releases alternate between feature additions, bug fixes, and design improvements. Design teams are specialized and highly focused, allowing immediate responsiveness to the company's needs.

PHP allows component interfaces to be relatively vague during the prototyping phase, since functionality is normally implemented inline. As modules come together, parameter order and function nomenclature can be finalized without forcing massive rewrites. Using PHP, pending functionality can easily be simulated or bypassed in the development environment; delivered functionality merges into PHP seamlessly. This narrows the design to prototype interval and prevents delivery delays from affecting other developers.

The Future

MarketPlayer.com is moving toward becoming a 100% PHP site. With over 8 million page views a month across all of its sites, MarketPlayer.com finds PHP to have absolutely no problems in handling the traffic, and they believe there is no traffic frequency PHP couldn't handle.

Summary

As you can see, PHP has changed from its origins. Even though it has had a tremendous impact on the Open Source community, in its early days PHP was still being looked at as an amateur's solution and mostly considered a new "toy." Of course, the "Pretty Hip People" (as PHP users sometimes title themselves) were fully convinced of their own tool, yet had to admit that it sometimes simply didn't stand up to the competition. Throughout the development of version 3, PHP kept attacking the old giants such as ASP, Cold Fusion, et al.—winning the battle more and more often.

In this chapter you have seen three examples in which PHP successfully kicked its combatants out of the ring, proving its fitness for real-life, cutting-edge usage. Considering the vastly growing amount of servers on which PHP is now running, and taking a look at the huge step PHP made from version 3 to version 4, we believe that PHP has become what it has been aiming at: a great tool for rapid development of stable and fast scripting solutions.

References

[1] The survey can be found at www.netcraft.com/survey/.

III

Beyond PHP

9

Extending PHP 4.0: Hacking the Core of PHP

Those who know don't talk.
Those who talk don't know.

SOMETIMES, PHP "AS IS" SIMPLY ISN'T ENOUGH. Although these cases are rare for the average user, professional applications will soon lead PHP to the edge of its capabilities, in terms of either speed or functionality. New functionality cannot always be implemented natively due to language restrictions and inconveniences that arise when having to carry around a huge library of default code appended to every single script, so another method needs to be found for overcoming these eventual lacks in PHP.

As soon as this point is reached, it's time to touch the heart of PHP and take a look at its core, the C code that makes PHP go.

Note: This chapter only deals with the extension of PHP 4.0. Although a lot of the information is relevant to PHP 3.0, none of the examples are designed to be compatible with PHP 3.0. We believe that, if someone makes the effort to extend PHP, PHP 4.0 will be installed anyway. (Recompiling old PHP 3.0 servers doesn't make sense, considering the benefits of the new PHP version.)

Also, at the time of this writing, quite a few things in PHP 4.0 were not completely finished and working yet (one of the major things is the thread-safe version of Zend).

Updates of this chapter can be found at `www.phpwizard.net`.

Overview

"Extending PHP" is easier said than done. PHP has evolved to a full-fledged tool consisting of a few megabytes of source code, and to hack a system like this quite a few things have to be learned and considered. When structuring this chapter, we finally decided on the "learn by doing" approach. This is not the most scientific and professional approach, but the method that's the most fun and gives the best end results. In the following sections, you'll learn quickly how to get the most basic extensions to work almost instantly. After that, you'll learn about Zend's advanced API functionality. The alternative would have been to try to impart the functionality, design, tips, tricks, etc. as a whole, all at once, thus giving a complete look at the big picture before doing anything practical. Although this is the "better" method, as no dirty hacks have to be made, it can be very frustrating as well as energy- and time-consuming, which is why we've decided on the direct approach.

Note that even though this chapter tries to impart as much knowledge as possible about the inner workings of PHP, it's impossible to really give a complete guide to extending PHP that works 100% of the time in all cases. PHP is such a huge and complex package that its inner workings can only be understood if you make yourself familiar with it by practicing, so we encourage you to work with the source.

What Is Zend? and What Is PHP?

The name *Zend* refers to the language engine, PHP's core. The term *PHP* refers to the complete system as it appears from the outside. This might sound a bit confusing at first, but it's not that complicated (see Figure 9.1). To implement a Web script interpreter, you need three parts:

- The *interpreter* part analyzes the input code, translates it, and executes it.
- The *functionality* part implements the functionality of the language (its functions, etc.).
- The *interface* part talks to the Web server, etc.

Zend takes part 1 completely and a bit of part 2, PHP takes parts 2 and 3. Together they form the complete PHP package. Zend itself really forms only the language core, implementing PHP at its very basics with some predefined functions. PHP contains all the modules that actually create the language's outstanding capabilities.

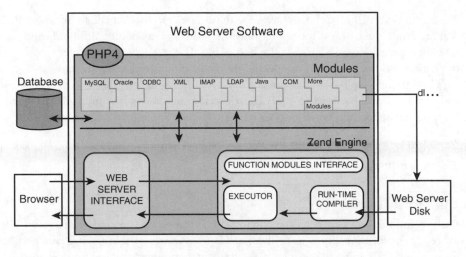

Figure 9.1 The internal structure of PHP.

The following sections discuss where PHP can be extended and how it's done.

Extension Possibilities

As shown in Figure 9.1 above, PHP can be extended primarily at three points: external modules, built-in modules, and the Zend engine. The following sections discuss these options.

External Modules

External modules can be loaded at script runtime using the function `dl()`. This function loads a shared object from disk and makes its functionality available to the script to which it's being bound. After the script is terminated, the external module is discarded from memory. This method has both advantages and disadvantages, as described in the following table:

Advantages	Disadvantages
External modules don't require recompiling of PHP.	The shared objects need to be loaded every time a script is being executed (every hit), which is very slow.
The size of PHP remains small by "outsourcing" certain functionality.	External additional files clutter up the disk.
	Every script that wants to use an external module's functionality has to specifically include a call to `dl()`, or the `extension` tag in `php.ini` needs to be modified (which is not always a suitable solution).

To sum up, external modules are great for third-party products, small additions to PHP that are rarely used, or just for testing purposes. To develop additional functionality quickly, external modules provide the best results. For frequent usage, larger implementations, and complex code, the disadvantages outweigh the advantages.

Third parties might consider using the `extension` tag in `php.ini` to create additional external modules to PHP. These external modules are completely detached from the main package, which is a very handy feature in commercial environments. Commercial distributors can simply ship disks or archives containing only their additional modules, without the need to create fixed and solid PHP binaries that don't allow other modules to be bound to them.

Built-in Modules

Built-in modules are compiled directly into PHP and carried around with every PHP process; their functionality is instantly available to every script that's being run. Like external modules, built-in modules have advantages and disadvantages, as described in the following table:

Advantages	Disadvantages
No need to load the module specifically; the functionality is instantly available.	Changes to built-in modules require recompiling of PHP.
No external files clutter up the disk; everything resides in the PHP binary.	The PHP binary grows and consumes more memory.

Built-in modules are best when you have a solid library of functions that remains relatively unchanged, requires better than poor-to-average performance, or is used frequently by many scripts on your site. The need to recompile PHP is quickly compensated by the benefit in speed and ease of use. However, built-in modules are not ideal when rapid development of small additions is required.

The Zend Engine

Of course, extensions can also be implemented directly in the Zend engine. This strategy is good if you need a change in the language behavior or require special functions to be built directly into the language core. In general, however, modifications to the Zend engine should be avoided. Changes here result in incompatibilities with the rest of the world, and hardly anyone will ever adapt to specially patched Zend engines. Modifications can't be detached from the main PHP sources and are overridden with the next update using the "official" source repositories. Therefore, this method is generally considered bad practice and, due to its rarity, is not covered in this book.

Source Layout

Before we start discussing code issues, you should familiarize yourself with the source tree to be able to quickly navigate through PHP's files. This is a must-have ability to implement and debug extensions.

After extracting the PHP archive, you'll see a directory layout similar to that in Figure 9.2.

Figure 9.2   Main directory layout of the PHP source tree.

Prerequisites

Prior to working through the rest of this chapter, you should retrieve clean, unmodified source trees of your favorite Web server. We're working with Apache (available at www.apache.org) and, of course, with PHP (available at www.php.net—does it need to be said?).

Alternatively, you can use the provided source archives on the CD-ROM accompanying this book. All the examples in this book work with the source archives on the CD-ROM; we can't guarantee this for every version retrieved from the Net. However, as Open Source software develops extremely rapidly, chances are that the versions on the CD-ROM are already outdated and don't have all the functionality you need. If you can't get the official archives from the corresponding Web sites to work, experiment with the CD-ROM archives and then try to go on from there.

Make sure that you can compile a working PHP environment by yourself! We won't go into this issue here, however, as you should already have this most basic ability when studying this chapter.

The following table describes the contents of the major directories.

Directory	Contents
php-4	Main PHP source files and main header files; here you'll find all of PHP's API definitions, macros, etc. (important).
dl	Repository for dynamic loadable modules; contains special header file phpdl.h as well as required files for automating the make process. This is a leftover from the previous PHP build system and this directory is planned for removal from the source tree. Its usage is deprecated.
ext	Repository for dynamic and built-in modules; by default, these are the "official" PHP modules that have been integrated into the main source tree. In PHP 4.0, it's possible to compile these standard extensions as dynamic loadable modules (at least, those that support it).
pear	Directory for the PHP class repository. At the time of this writing, this is still in the design phase, but it's being tried to establish something similar to CPAN for Perl here.
sapi	Contains the code for the different server abstraction layers.
TSRM	Location of the "Thread Safe Resource Manager" (TSRM) for Zend and PHP.
Zend	Location of Zend's file; here you'll find all of Zend's API definitions, macros, etc. (important).

Discussing all the files included in the PHP package is beyond the scope of this chapter. However, you should take a close look at the following files:

- php.h, located in the main PHP directory. This file contains most of PHP's macro and API definitions.
- zend.h, located in the main Zend directory. This file contains most of Zend's macros and definitions.
- zend_API.h, also located in the Zend directory, which defines Zend's API.

You should also follow some sub-inclusions from these files; for example, the ones relating to the Zend executor, the PHP initialization file support, and such. After reading these files, take the time to navigate around the package a little to see the interdependencies of all files and modules—how they relate to each other and especially how they make use of each other. This also helps you to adapt to the coding style in which PHP is authored. To extend PHP, you should quickly adapt to this style.

Extension Conventions

Zend is built using certain conventions; to avoid breaking its standards, you should follow the rules described in the following sections.

Macros

For almost every important task, Zend ships predefined macros that are extremely handy. The tables and figures in the following sections describe most of the basic functions, structures, and macros. The macro definitions can be found mainly in `zend.h` and `zend_API.h`. We suggest that you take a close look at these files after having studied this chapter. (Although you can go ahead and read them now, not everything will make sense to you yet.)

Memory Management

Resource management is a crucial issue, especially in server software. One of the most valuable resources is memory, and memory management should be handled with extreme care. Memory management has been partially abstracted in Zend, and you should stick to this abstraction for obvious reasons: Due to the abstraction, Zend gets full control over all memory allocations. Zend is able to determine whether a block is in use, automatically freeing unused blocks and blocks with lost references, and thus prevent memory leaks. The functions to be used are described in the following table:

Function	Description
emalloc()	Serves as replacement for malloc().
efree()	Serves as replacement for free().
estrdup()	Serves as replacement for strdup().
estrndup()	Serves as replacement for strndup(). Faster than estrdup() and binary-safe. This is the recommended function to use if you know the string length prior to duplicating it.
ecalloc()	Serves as replacement for calloc().
erealloc()	Serves as replacement for realloc().

emalloc(), estrdup(), estrndup(), ecalloc(), and erealloc() allocate internal memory; efree() frees these previously allocated blocks. Memory handled by the e*() functions is considered local to the current process and is discarded as soon as the script executed by this process is terminated.

> **Warning**
> To allocate resident memory that survives termination of the current script, you
> can use malloc() and free(). This should only be done with extreme care,
> however, and only in conjunction with demands of the Zend API; otherwise,
> you risk memory leaks.

Zend also features a thread-safe resource manager to provide better native support for
multithreaded Web servers. This requires you to allocate local structures for all of your
global variables to allow concurrent threads to be run. Because the thread-safe mode
of Zend is not finished yet, we could not include coverage in this book.

Directory and File Functions

The following directory and file functions should be used in Zend modules (they
behave exactly like their C counterparts):

Zend Function	Regular C Function
V_GETCWD()	getcwd()
V_FOPEN()	fopen()
V_CHDIR()	chdir()
V_GETWD()	getwd()
V_CHDIR_FILE()	Takes a file path as an argument and changes the current working directory to that file's directory.
V_STAT()	stat()
V_LSTAT()	lstat()

String Handling

Strings are handled a bit differently by the Zend engine than other values such as
integers, Booleans, etc., which don't require additional memory allocation for storing
their values. If you want to return a string from a function, introduce a new string
variable to the symbol table, or do something similar, you have to make sure that the
memory the string will be occupying has previously been allocated, using the
aforementioned e*() functions for allocation. (This might not make much sense to
you yet; just keep it somewhere in your head for now—we'll get back to it shortly.)

Complex Types

Complex types such as arrays and objects require different treatment. Zend features a single API for these types—they're stored using hash tables.

Note: To reduce complexity in the following source examples, we're only working with simple types such as integers at first. A discussion about creating more advanced types follows later in this chapter.

PHP's Automatic Build System

PHP 4.0 features an automatic build system that's very flexible. All modules reside in a subdirectory of the `ext` directory. In addition to its own sources, each module consists of an `M4` file (for example, see `www.gnu.org/manual/m4/html_mono/m4.html`) for configuration and a `Makefile.in` file, which is responsible for compilation (the results of autoconf and automake; for example, see `http://sourceware.cygnus.com/` `autoconf/autoconf.html` and `http://sourceware.cygnus.com/automake/` `automake.html`).

Both files are generated automatically, along with `.cvsignore`, by a little shell script named `ext_skel` that resides in the `ext` directory. As argument it takes the name of the module that you want to create. The shell script then creates a directory of the same name, along with the appropriate `config.m4` and `Makefile.in` files.

Step by step, the process looks like this:

```
root@dev:/usr/local/src/php4/ext > ./ext_skel my_module
Creating directory
Creating basic files: config.m4 Makefile.in .cvsignore [done].

To use your new extension, you will have to execute the following steps:

    $ cd ..
    $ ./buildconf
    $ ./configure                    (your extension is automatically enabled)
    $ vi ext/my_module/my_module.c
    $ make

Repeat the last two steps as often as necessary.
```

This instruction creates the aforementioned files. To include the new module in the automatic configuration and build process, you have to run `buildconf`, which regenerates the `configure` script by searching through the `ext` directory and including all found `config.m4` files.

Finally, running `configure` parses all configuration options and generates a makefile based on those options and the options you specify in `Makefile.in`.

Listing 9.1 shows the previously generated `Makefile.in`:

Listing 9.1 **The default** *Makefile.in.*

```
# $Id: Extending_Zend.xml,v 1.22 2000/05/22 20:02:58 till Exp $

LTLIBRARY_NAME        = libmy_module.la
LTLIBRARY_SOURCES     = my_module.c
LTLIBRARY_SHARED_NAME = my_module.la

include $(top_srcdir)/build/dynlib.mk
```

There's not much to tell about this one: It contains the names of the input and output files. You could also specify build instructions for other files if your module is built from multiple source files.

The default `config.m4` shown in Listing 9.2 is a bit more complex:

Listing 9.2 **The default** *config.m4.*

```
dnl $Id: Extending_Zend.xml,v 1.22 2000/05/22 20:02:58 till Exp $
dnl config.m4 for extension my_module
dnl don't forget to call PHP_EXTENSION(my_module)

dnl If your extension references something external, use with:

PHP_ARG_WITH(my_module, for my_module support,
dnl Make sure that the comment is aligned:
[  --with-my_module          Include my_module support])

dnl Otherwise use enable:

PHP_ARG_ENABLE(my_module, whether to enable my_module support,
dnl Make sure that the comment is aligned:
[  --enable-my_module        Enable my_module support])

if test "$PHP_MY_MODULE" != "no"; then
  dnl Action..
  PHP_EXTENSION(my_module, $ext_shared)
fi
```

If you're unfamiliar with M4 files (now is certainly a good time to get familiar), this might be a bit confusing at first; but it's actually quite easy.

Note: Everything prefixed with `dnl` is treated as a comment and is not parsed.

The `config.m4` file is responsible for parsing the command-line options passed to `configure` at configuration time. This means that it has to check for required external files and do similar configuration and setup tasks.

The default file creates two configuration directives in the configure script: `--with-my_module` and `--enable-my_module`. Use the first option when referring external files (such as the `--with-apache` directive that refers to the Apache directory). Use the second option when the user simply has to decide whether to enable your extension. Regardless of which option you use, you should uncomment the other, unnecessary one; that is, if you're using `--enable-my_module`, you should remove support for `--with-my_module`, and vice versa.

By default, the `config.m4` file created by `ext_skel` accepts both directives and automatically enables your extension. Enabling the extension is done by using the `PHP_EXTENSION` macro. To change the default behavior to include your module into the PHP binary when desired by the user (by explicitly specifying `--enable-my_module` or `--with-my_module`), change the test for `$PHP_MY_MODULE` to `== "yes"`:

```
if test "$PHP_MY_MODULE" == "yes"; then
dnl Action..
PHP_EXTENSION(my_module, $ext_shared)
fi
```

This would require you to use `--enable-my_module` each time when reconfiguring and recompiling PHP.

Note: Be sure to run `buildconf` every time you change `config.m4`!

We'll go into more details on the M4 macros available to your configuration scripts later in this chapter. For now, we'll simply use the default files. The sample sources on the CD-ROM all have working `config.m4` files. To include them into the PHP build process, simply copy the source directories to your PHP ext directory, run `buildconf`, and then include the sample modules you want by using the appropriate `--enable-*` directives with `configure`.

Creating Extensions

We'll start with the creation of a very simple extension at first, which basically does nothing more than implement a function that returns the integer it receives as parameter. Listing 9.3 shows the source.

Listing 9.3 **A simple extension.**

```
/* include standard header */
#include "php.h"

/* declaration of functions to be exported */
ZEND_FUNCTION(first_module);

/* compiled function list so Zend knows what's in this module */
zend_function_entry firstmod_functions[] =
{
    ZEND_FE(first_module, NULL)
    {NULL, NULL, NULL}
```

continues

Listing 9.3 **Continued**

```
};

/* compiled module information */
zend_module_entry firstmod_module_entry =
{
    "First Module",
    firstmod_functions,
    NULL, NULL, NULL, NULL, NULL,
    STANDARD_MODULE_PROPERTIES
};

/* implement standard "stub" routine to introduce ourselves to Zend */
#if COMPILE_DL
DLEXPORT zend_module_entry *get_module(void) { return(&firstmod_module_entry); }
#endif

/* implement function that is meant to be made available to PHP */
ZEND_FUNCTION(first_module)
{
    zval **parameter;

    if((ZEND_NUM_ARGS() != 1) || (zend_get_parameters_ex(1, &parameter)
    ↪!= SUCCESS))
    {
        WRONG_PARAM_COUNT;
    }

    convert_to_long_ex(parameter);

    RETURN_LONG((*parameter)->value.lval);
}
```

This code contains a complete PHP module. We'll explain the source code in detail shortly, but first we'd like to discuss the build process. (This will allow the impatient to experiment before we dive into API discussions.)

Compiling Modules

There are basically three ways to compile modules:

- Use the provided "make" mechanism in the dl directory.
- Use the provided "make" mechanism in the ext directory, which also allows building of dynamic loadable modules.
- Compile the sources manually.

The second method should definitely be favored, since, as of PHP 4.0, this has been standardized into a sophisticated build process. The fact that it is so sophisticated is also its drawback, unfortunately—it's hard to understand at first. We'll provide a more detailed introduction to this later in the chapter, but first let's work with the default files.

The make process contained in the `dl` directory is a bit of a dirty hack, outdated and planned for removal from the source tree. To be honest, it's much simpler to use this at first to build dynamic extensions, but because it doesn't have the possibilities of the `ext` directory and it's scheduled for deletion anyway, usage of the `dl` directory is deprecated.

The third method is good for those who (for some reason) don't have the full PHP source tree available, don't have access to all files, or just like to juggle with their keyboard. These cases should be extremely rare, but for the sake of completeness we'll also describe this method.

Compiling Using *Make*

To compile the sample sources using the standard mechanism, copy all their subdirectories to the `ext` directory of your PHP source tree. Then run `buildconf`, which will create a new `configure` script containing appropriate options. By default, all the sample sources are disabled, so you don't have to fear breaking your build process.

After you run `buildconf`, `configure --help` shows the following additional modules:

`--enable-array_experiments`	Enables array experiments
`--enable-call_userland`	Enables userland module
`--enable-cross_conversion`	Enables cross-conversion module
`--enable-firstmodule`	Enables first module
`--enable-infoprint`	Enables infoprint module
`--enable-reference_test`	Enables reference test module
`--enable-resource_test`	Enables resource test module
`--enable-variable_creation`	Enables variable-creation module

The module shown earlier in Listing 9.3 can be enabled with `--enable-first_module` or `--enable-first_module=yes`.

Compiling Manually

To compile your modules manually, you need the following commands:

Action	Command
Compiling	`cc -fpic -DCOMPILE_DL=1 -I/usr/local/include -I. -I.. -I../Zend -c -o <your_object_file> <your_c_file>`
Linking	`cc -shared -L/usr/local/lib -rdynamic -o <your_module_file> <your_object_file(s)>`

The command to compile the module simply instructs the compiler to generate position-independent code (`-fpic` shouldn't be omitted) and additionally defines the constant `COMPILE_DL` to tell the module code that it's compiled as a dynamically loadable module (the test module above checks for this; we'll discuss it shortly). After these options, it specifies a number of standard include paths that should be used as the minimal set to compile the source files.

Note: All include paths in the example are relative to the directory `ext`. If you're compiling from another directory, change the pathnames accordingly. Required items are the PHP directory, the `Zend` directory, and (if necessary) the directory in which your module resides.

The link command is also a plain vanilla command instructing linkage as a dynamic module.

You can include optimization options in the compilation command, although these have been omitted in this example (but some are included in the `makefile` template described in an earlier section).

Note: Compiling and linking manually as a static module into the PHP binary involves very long instructions and thus is not discussed here. (It's not very efficient to type all those commands.)

Using Extensions

Depending on the build process you selected, you should either end up with a new PHP binary to be linked into your Web server (or run as CGI), or with an `.so` (shared object) file. If you compiled the example file `first_module.c` as a shared object, your result file should be `first_module.so`. To use it, you first have to copy it to a place from which it's accessible to PHP. For a simple test procedure, you can copy it to your `htdocs` directory and try it with the source in Listing 9.4. If you compiled it into the PHP binary, omit the call to `dl()`, as the module's functionality is instantly available to your scripts.

Warning

For security reasons, you *should not* put your dynamic modules into publicly accessible directories. Even though it *can* be done and it simplifies testing, you should put them into a separate directory in production environments.

Listing 9.4 **A test file for *first_module.so*.**

```php
<?php

//dl("first_module.so");

$param = 2;
$return = first_module($param);

print("We sent \"$param\" and got \"$return\"");

?>
```

Calling this PHP file in your Web browser should give you the output shown in Figure 9.3.

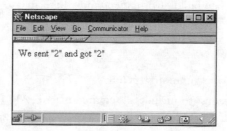

Figure 9.3 Output of `first_module.php`.

If required, the dynamic loadable module is loaded by calling the `dl()` function. This function looks for the specified shared object, loads it, and makes its functions available to PHP. The module exports the function `first_module()`, which accepts a single parameter, converts it to an integer, and returns the result of the conversion.

If you've gotten this far, congratulations! You just built your first extension to PHP.

Troubleshooting

Actually, not much troubleshooting can be done when compiling static or dynamic modules. The only problem that could arise is that the compiler will complain about missing definitions or something similar. In this case, make sure that all header files are available and that you specified their path correctly in the compilation command. To be sure that everything is located correctly, extract a clean PHP source tree and use the automatic build in the ext directory with the fresh files from the CD-ROM; this will guarantee a safe compilation environment. If this fails, try manual compilation.

PHP might also complain about missing functions in your module. (This shouldn't happen with the sample sources if you didn't modify them.) If the names of external functions you're trying to access from your module are misspelled, they'll remain as "unlinked symbols" in the symbol table. During dynamic loading and linkage by PHP, they won't resolve because of the typing errors—there are no corresponding symbols in the main binary. Look for incorrect declarations in your module file or incorrectly written external references. Note that this problem is specific to dynamic loadable modules; it doesn't occur with static modules. Errors in static modules show up at compile time.

Source Discussion

Now that you've got a safe build environment and you're able to include the modules into PHP files, it's time to discuss how everything works.

Module Structure

All PHP modules follow a common structure:

- Header file inclusions (to include all required macros, API definitions, etc.)
- C declaration of exported functions (required to declare the Zend function block)
- Declaration of the Zend function block
- Declaration of the Zend module block
- Implementation of get_module()
- Implementation of all exported functions

Header File Inclusions

The only header file you really have to include for your modules is php.h, located in the PHP directory. This file makes all macros and API definitions required to build new modules available to your code.

Tip: It's good practice to create a separate header file for your module that contains module-specific definitions. This header file should contain all the forward definitions for exported functions and also include `php.h`.

Declaring Exported Functions

To declare functions that are to be exported (i.e., made available to PHP as new native functions), Zend provides a set of macros. A sample declaration looks like this:

```
ZEND_FUNCTION(my_function);
```

`ZEND_FUNCTION` declares a new C function that complies with Zend's internal API. This means that the function is of type `void` and accepts `INTERNAL_FUNCTION_PARAMETERS` (another macro) as parameters. Additionally, it prefixes the function name with `zend_if`. The immediately expanded version of the above definition would look like this:

```
void zend_if_my_function(INTERNAL_FUNCTION_PARAMETERS);
```

Expanding `INTERNAL_FUNCTION_PARAMETERS` results in the following:

```
void zend_if_my_function(int ht, zval *return_value,
                    ↪zval *this_ptr, int return_value_used,
                    ↪zend_executor_globals *executor_globals);
```

Since the interpreter and executor core have been separated from the main PHP package, a second API defining macros and function sets has evolved: the Zend API. As the Zend API now handles quite a few of the responsibilities that previously belonged to PHP, a lot of PHP functions have been reduced to macros aliasing to calls into the Zend API. The recommended practice is to use the Zend API wherever possible, as the old API is only preserved for compatibility reasons. For example, the types `zval` and `pval` are identical. `zval` is Zend's definition; `pval` is PHP's definition (actually, `pval` is an alias for `zval` now). As the macro `INTERNAL_FUNCTION_PARAMETERS` is a Zend macro, the above declaration contains `zval`. When writing code, you should always use `zval` to conform to the new Zend API.

The parameter list of this declaration is very important; you should keep these parameters in mind (see Table 9.1 for descriptions).

Table 9.1 **Zend's Parameters to Functions Called from PHP**

Parameter	Description
ht	The number of arguments passed to the Zend function. You should not touch this directly, but instead use `ZEND_NUM_ARGS()` to obtain the value.
return_value	This variable is used to pass any return values of your function back to PHP. Access to this variable is best done using the predefined macros. For a description of these see below.

continues

Table 9.1   **Continued**

this_ptr	Using this variable, you can gain access to the object in which your function is contained, if it's used within an object. Use the function getThis() to obtain this pointer.
return_value_used	This flag indicates whether an eventual return value from this function will actually be used by the calling script. 0 indicates that the return value is not used; 1 indicates that the caller expects a return value. Evaluation of this flag can be done to verify correct usage of the function as well as speed optimizations in case returning a value requires expensive operations (for an example, see how array.c makes use of this).
executor_globals	This variable points to global settings of the Zend engine. You'll find this useful when creating new variables, for example (more about this later). The executor globals can also be introduced to your function by using the macro ELS_FETCH().

Declaration of the Zend Function Block

Now that you have declared the functions to be exported, you also have to introduce them to Zend. Introducing the list of functions is done by using an array of zend_function_entry. This array consecutively contains all functions that are to be made available externally, with the function's name as it should appear in PHP and its name as defined in the C source. Internally, zend_function_entry is defined as shown in Listing 9.5.

Listing 9.5   **Internal declaration of *zend_function_entry*.**

```
typedef struct _zend_function_entry {
    char *fname;
    void (*handler)(INTERNAL_FUNCTION_PARAMETERS);
    unsigned char *func_arg_types;
} zend_function_entry;
```

The following table describes the entries.

Entry	Description
fname	Denotes the function name as seen in PHP (for example, fopen, mysql_connect, or, in our example, first_module).
handler	Pointer to the C function responsible for handling calls to this function. For example, see the standard macro INTERNAL_FUNCTION_PARAMETERS discussed earlier.
func_arg_types	Allows you to mark certain parameters so that they're forced to be passed by reference. You usually should set this to NULL.

In the example above, the declaration looks like this:

```
zend_function_entry firstmod_functions[] =
{
    ZEND_FE(first_module, NULL)
    {NULL, NULL, NULL}
};
```

You can see that the last entry in the list always has to be {NULL, NULL, NULL}. This marker has to be set for Zend to know when the end of the list of exported functions is reached.

Note: You *cannot* use the predefined macros for the end marker, as these would try to refer to a function named "NULL"!

The macro ZEND_FE simply expands to a structure entry in zend_function_entry. Note that these macros introduce a special naming scheme to your functions—your C functions will be prefixed with zend_if_, meaning that ZEND_FE(first_module) will refer to a C function zend_if_first_module(). If you want to mix macro usage with hand-coded entries (not a good practice), keep this in mind.

Tip: Compilation errors that refer to functions named zend_if_*() relate to functions defined with ZEND_FE.

Table 9.2 shows a list of all the macros you can use to define functions.

Table 9.2 **Macros for Defining Functions**

Macro Name	Description
ZEND_FE(name, arg_types)	Defines a function entry of the name *name* in zend_function_entry. Requires a corresponding C function. *arg_types* needs to be set to NULL. This function uses automatic C function name generation by prefixing the PHP function name with zend_if_. For example, ZEND_FE("first_module", NULL) introduces a function first_module() to PHP and links it to the C function zend_if_first_module(). Use in conjunction with ZEND_FUNCTION.

continues

Table 9.2 **Continued**

Macro Name	Description
ZEND_NAMED_FE (*php_name*, *name*, *arg_types*)	Defines a function that will be available to PHP by the name *php_name* and links it to the corresponding C function *name*. *arg_types* needs to be set to NULL. Use this function if you don't want the automatic name prefixing introduced by ZEND_FE. Use in conjunction with ZEND_NAMED_FUNCTION.
ZEND_FALIAS (*name*, *alias*, *arg_types*)	Defines an alias named *alias* for *name*. *arg_types* needs to be set to NULL. Doesn't require a corresponding C function; refers to the alias target instead.
PHP_FE(*name*, *arg_types*)	Old PHP API equivalent of ZEND_FE.
PHP_NAMED_FE(*runtime_name*, *name*, *arg_types*)	Old PHP API equivalent of ZEND_NAMED_FE.

Note: You can't use ZEND_FE in conjunction with PHP_FUNCTION, or PHP_FE in conjunction with ZEND_FUNCTION. However, it's perfectly legal to mix ZEND_FE and ZEND_FUNCTION with PHP_FE and PHP_FUNCTION when staying with the same macro set for each function to be declared. But mixing is *not* recommended; instead, you're advised to use the ZEND_* macros only.

Declaration of the Zend Module Block

This block is stored in the structure zend_module_entry and contains all necessary information to describe the contents of this module to Zend. You can see the internal definition of this module in Listing 9.6.

Listing 9.6 **Internal declaration of *zend_module_entry*.**

```
typedef struct _zend_module_entry zend_module_entry;

struct _zend_module_entry {
    char *name;
    zend_function_entry *functions;
    int (*module_startup_func)(INIT_FUNC_ARGS);
    int (*module_shutdown_func)(SHUTDOWN_FUNC_ARGS);
    int (*request_startup_func)(INIT_FUNC_ARGS);
    int (*request_shutdown_func)(SHUTDOWN_FUNC_ARGS);
    void (*info_func)(ZEND_MODULE_INFO_FUNC_ARGS);
    int (*global_startup_func)(void);
    int (*global_shutdown_func)(void);

[ Rest of the structure is not interesting here ]

};
```

The following table describes the entries.

Entry	Description
name	Contains the module name (for example, "File functions", "Socket functions", "Crypt", etc.). This name will show up in phpinfo(), in the section "Additional Modules."
functions	Points to the Zend function block, discussed in the preceding section.
module_startup_func	This function is called once upon module initialization and can be used to do one-time initialization steps (such as initial memory allocation, etc.) To indicate a failure during initialization, return FAILURE; otherwise, SUCCESS. To mark this field as unused, use NULL. To declare a function, use the macro ZEND_MINIT.
module_shutdown_func	This function is called once upon module shutdown and can be used to do one-time deinitialization steps (such as memory deallocation). This is the counterpart to module_startup_func(). To indicate a failure during deinitialization, return FAILURE; otherwise, SUCCESS. To mark this field as unused, use NULL. To declare a function, use the macro ZEND_MSHUTDOWN.
request_startup_func	This function is called once upon every page request and can be used to do one-time initialization steps that are required to process a request. To indicate a failure here, return FAILURE; otherwise, SUCCESS. *Note:* As dynamic loadable modules are loaded only on page requests, the request startup function is called right after the module startup function (both initialization events happen at the same time). To mark this field as unused, use NULL. To declare a function, use the macro ZEND_RINIT.
request_shutdown_func	This function is called once after every page request and works as counterpart to request_startup_func(). To indicate a failure here, return FAILURE; otherwise, SUCCESS. *Note:* As dynamic loadable modules are loaded only on page requests, the request shutdown function is immediately followed by a call to the module shutdown handler (both deinitialization events happen at the same time). To mark this field as unused, use NULL. To declare a function, use the macro ZEND_RSHUTDOWN.

continues

Entry	Description
info_func	When phpinfo() is called in a script, Zend cycles through all loaded modules and calls this function. Every module then has the chance to print its own "footprint" into the output page. Generally this is used to dump environmental or statistical information. To mark this field as unused, use NULL. To declare a function, use the macro ZEND_MINFO.
global_startup_func	The global startup functions are rarely used. You should usually skip through the rest of this structure by placing the macro STANDARD_MODULE_PROPERTIES. To mark this field as unused, use NULL. To declare a function, use the macro ZEND_GINIT.
global_shutdown_func	To mark this field as unused, use NULL. To declare a function, use the macro ZEND_GSHUTDOWN.
Remaining structure elements	These are used internally and can be prefilled by using the macro STANDARD_MODULE_PROPERTIES_EX. You should not assign any values to them. Use STANDARD_MODULE_PROPERTIES_EX only if you use global startup and shutdown functions; otherwise, use STANDARD_MODULE_PROPERTIES directly.

In our example, this structure is implemented as follows:

```
zend_module_entry firstmod_module_entry =
{
    "First Module",
    firstmod_functions,
    NULL, NULL, NULL, NULL, NULL,
    STANDARD_MODULE_PROPERTIES
};
```

This is basically the easiest and most minimal set of values you could ever use. The module name is set to First Module, then the function list is referenced, after which all startup and shutdown functions are marked as being unused.

For reference purposes, you can find a list of the macros involved in declared startup and shutdown functions in Table 9.3. These are not used in our basic example yet, but will be demonstrated later on. You should make use of these macros to declare your startup and shutdown functions, as these require special arguments to be passed (INIT_FUNC_ARGS and SHUTDOWN_FUNC_ARGS), which are automatically included into the function declaration when using the predefined macros. If you declare your functions manually and the PHP developers decide that a change in the argument list is necessary, you'll have to change your module sources to remain compatible.

Table 9.3 **Macros to Declare Startup and Shutdown Functions**

Macro	Description
ZEND_MINIT(*module*)	Declares a function for module startup. The generated name will be zend_minit_<*module*> (for example, zend_minit_first_module). Use in conjunction with ZEND_MINIT_FUNCTION.
ZEND_MSHUTDOWN(*module*)	Declares a function for module shutdown. The generated name will be zend_mshutdown_<*module*> (for example, zend_mshutdown_first_module). Use in conjunction with ZEND_MSHUTDOWN_FUNCTION.
ZEND_RINIT(*module*)	Declares a function for request startup. The generated name will be zend_rinit_<*module*> (for example, zend_rinit_first_module). Use in conjunction with ZEND_RINIT_FUNCTION.
ZEND_RSHUTDOWN(*module*)	Declares a function for request shutdown. The generated name will be zend_rshutdown_<*module*> (for example, zend_rshutdown_first_module). Use in conjunction with ZEND_RSHUTDOWN_FUNCTION.
ZEND_GINIT(*module*)	Declares a function for global startup. The generated name will be zend_ginit_<*module*> (for example, zend_ginit_first_module). Use in conjunction with ZEND_GINIT_FUNCTION.
ZEND_GSHUTDOWN(*module*)	Declares a function for global shutdown. The generated name will be zend_gshutdown_<*module*> (for example, zend_gshutdown_first_module). Use in conjunction with ZEND_GSHUTDOWN_FUNCTION.
ZEND_MINFO(*module*)	Declares a function for printing module information, used when phpinfo() is called. The generated name will be zend_info_<*module*> (for example, zend_info_first_module). Use in conjunction with ZEND_MINFO_FUNCTION.

Implementation of *get_module()*

This function is special to all dynamic loadable modules. Take a look at the implementation first:

```
#if COMPILE_DL
DLEXPORT zend_module_entry *get_module(void) { return(&firstmod_module_entry); }
#endif
```

The function implementation is surrounded by a conditional compilation statement. This is needed since the function get_module() is only required if your module is built as a dynamic extension. By specifying a definition of COMPILE_DL in the compiler command (see above for a discussion of the compilation instructions required to build a dynamic extension), you can instruct your module whether you intend to build it as a dynamic extension or as a built-in module. If you want a built-in module, the implementation of get_module() is simply left out.

get_module() is called by Zend at load time of the module. You can think of it as being invoked by the dl() call in your script. Its purpose is to pass the module information block back to Zend in order to inform the engine about the module contents.

If you don't implement a get_module() function in your dynamic loadable module, Zend will compliment you with an error message when trying to access it.

Implementation of All Exported Functions

Implementing the exported functions is the final step. The example function in first_module looks like this:

```
ZEND_FUNCTION(firstmodule)
{
    zval **parameter;

    if((ZEND_NUM_ARGS() != 1) || (zend_get_parameters_ex(1, &parameter)
    != SUCCESS))
    {
        WRONG_PARAM_COUNT;
    }

    convert_to_long_ex(parameter);

    RETURN_LONG((*parameter)->value.lval);
}
```

The function declaration is done using ZEND_FUNCTION, which corresponds to ZEND_FE in the function entry table (discussed earlier).

After the declaration, code for checking and retrieving the function's arguments, argument conversion, and return value generation follows (more on this later).

Summary

That's it, basically—there's nothing more to implementing PHP modules. Built-in modules are structured similarly to dynamic modules, so, equipped with the information presented in the previous sections, you'll be able to fight the odds when encountering PHP module source files.

Now, in the following sections, read on about how to make use of PHP's internals to build powerful extensions.

Accepting Arguments

One of the most important issues for language extensions is accepting and dealing with data passed via arguments. Most extensions are built to deal with specific input data (or require parameters to perform their specific actions), and function arguments are the only real way to exchange data between the PHP level and the C level. Of course, there's also the possibility of exchanging data using predefined global values (which is also discussed later), but this should be avoided by all means, as it's extremely bad practice. For details, refer to Chapter 1, "Development Concepts."

PHP doesn't make use of any formal function declarations; this is why call syntax is always completely dynamic and never checked for errors. Checking for correct call syntax is left to the user code. For example, it's possible to call a function using only one argument at one time and four arguments the next time—both invocations are syntactically absolutely correct.

Determining the Number of Arguments

Since PHP doesn't have formal function definitions with support for call syntax checking, and since PHP features variable arguments, sometimes you need to find out with how many arguments your function has been called. You can use the ZEND_NUM_ARGS macro in this case. In previous versions of PHP, this macro retrieved the number of arguments with which the function has been called based on the function's hash table entry, ht, which is passed in the INTERNAL_FUNCTION_PARAMETERS list. As ht itself now contains the number of arguments that have been passed to the function, ZEND_NUM_ARGS has been stripped down to a dummy macro (see its definition in zend_API.h). But it's still good practice to use it, to remain compatible with future changes in the call interface. *Note:* The old PHP equivalent of this macro is ARG_COUNT.

The following code checks for the correct number of arguments:

```
if(ZEND_NUM_ARGS() != 2)
    WRONG_PARAMETER_COUNT;
```

If the function is not called with two arguments, it exits with an error message. The code snippet above makes use of the tool macro WRONG_PARAMETER_COUNT, which can be used to generate a standard error message (see Figure 9.4).

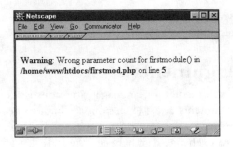

Figure 9.4   `WRONG_PARAMETER_COUNT` in action.

This macro prints a default error message and then returns to the caller. Its definition can also be found in `zend_API.h` and looks like this:

```
ZEND_API void wrong_param_count(void);
```

```
#define WRONG_PARAM_COUNT { wrong_param_count(); return; }
```

As you can see, it calls an internal function named `wrong_param_count()` that's responsible for printing the warning. For details on generating customized error messages, see the later section "Printing Information."

Retrieving Arguments

After having checked the number of arguments, you need to get access to the arguments themselves. This is done with the help of `zend_get_parameters_ex()`:

```
zval **parameter;
```

```
if(zend_get_parameters_ex(1, &parameter) != SUCCESS)
    WRONG_PARAMETER_COUNT;
```

All arguments are stored in a `zval` container, which needs to be pointed to *twice*. The snippet above tries to retrieve one argument and make it available to us via the `parameter` pointer.

`zend_get_parameters_ex()` accepts at least two arguments. The first argument is the number of arguments to retrieve, which should match the number of arguments with which the function has been called; this is why it's important to check for correct call syntax. The second argument (and all following arguments) are pointers to pointers to pointers to `zval`s. (Confusing, isn't it?) All these pointers are required because Zend works internally with `**zval`; to adjust a local `**zval` in our function, `zend_get_parameters_ex()` requires a pointer to it.

The return value of zend_get_parameters_ex() can either be SUCCESS or FAILURE, indicating (unsurprisingly) success or failure of the argument processing. A failure is most likely related to an incorrect number of arguments being specified, in which case you should exit with WRONG_PARAMETER_COUNT.

To retrieve more than one argument, you can use a similar snippet:

```
zval **param1, **param2, **param3, **param4;

if(zend_get_parameters_ex(4, &param1, &param2, &param3, &param4) != SUCCESS)
    WRONG_PARAMETER_COUNT;
```

zend_get_parameters_ex() only checks whether you're trying to retrieve too many parameters. If the function is called with five arguments, but you're only retrieving three of them with zend_get_parameters_ex(), you won't get an error but will get the first three parameters instead. Subsequent calls of zend_get_parameters_ex() won't retrieve the remaining arguments, but will get the same arguments again.

Dealing with a Variable Number of Arguments/Optional Parameters

If your function is meant to accept a variable number of arguments, the snippets just described are sometimes suboptimal solutions. You have to create a line calling zend_get_parameters_ex() for every possible number of arguments, which is often unsatisfying.

For this case, you can use the function zend_get_parameters_array_ex(), which accepts the number of parameters to retrieve and an array in which to store them:

```
zval **parameter_array[4];

/* get the number of arguments */
argument_count = ZEND_NUM_ARGS();

/* see if it satisfies our minimal request (2 arguments) */
/* and our maximal acceptance (4 arguments) */
if(argument_count < 2 || argument_count > 5)
    WRONG_PARAMETER_COUNT;

/* argument count is correct, now retrieve arguments */
if(zend_get_parameters_array_ex(argument_count, parameter_array) != SUCCESS)
    WRONG_PARAMETER_COUNT;
```

First, the number of arguments is checked to make sure that it's in the accepted range. After that, zend_get_parameters_array_ex() is used to fill parameter_array with valid pointers to the argument values.

A very clever implementation of this can be found in the code handling PHP's fsockopen() located in ext/standard/fsock.c, as shown in Listing 9.7. Don't worry if you don't know all the functions used in this source yet; we'll get to them shortly.

Listing 9.7   **PHP's implementation of variable arguments in** *fsockopen( )*.

```
pval **args[5];
int *sock=emalloc(sizeof(int));
int *sockp;
int arg_count=ARG_COUNT(ht);
int socketd = -1;
unsigned char udp = 0;
struct timeval timeout = { 60, 0 };
unsigned short portno;
unsigned long conv;
char *key = NULL;
FLS_FETCH();

if (arg_count > 5 || arg_count < 2 ||
➥zend_get_parameters_array_ex(arg_count,args)==FAILURE) {
    CLOSE_SOCK(1);
    WRONG_PARAM_COUNT;
}

switch(arg_count) {
    case 5:
        convert_to_double_ex(args[4]);
        conv = (unsigned long) ((*args[4])->value.dval * 1000000.0);
        timeout.tv_sec = conv / 1000000;
        timeout.tv_usec = conv % 1000000;
        /* fall-through */
    case 4:
        if(!ParameterPassedByReference(ht,4)) {
            php_error(E_WARNING,"error string argument to fsockopen not passed by
            ➥reference");
        }
        pval_copy_constructor(*args[3]);
        (*args[3])->value.str.val = empty_string;
        (*args[3])->value.str.len = 0;
        (*args[3])->type = IS_STRING;
        /* fall-through */
    case 3:
        if(!ParameterPassedByReference(ht,3)) {
            php_error(E_WARNING,"error argument to fsockopen not passed by
            ➥reference");
        }
        (*args[2])->type = IS_LONG;
        (*args[2])->value.lval = 0;
        break;
}

convert_to_string_ex(args[0]);
convert_to_long_ex(args[1]);
portno = (unsigned short) (*args[1])->value.lval;

key = emalloc((*args[0])->value.str.len + 10);
```

`fsockopen()` accepts two, three, four, or five parameters. After the obligatory variable declarations, the function checks for the correct range of arguments. Then it uses a fall-through mechanism in a `switch()` statement to deal with all arguments. The `switch()` statement starts with the maximum number of arguments being passed (five). After that, it automatically processes the case of four arguments being passed, then three, by omitting the otherwise obligatory `break` keyword in all stages. After having processed the last case, it exits the `switch()` statement and does the minimal argument processing needed if the function is invoked with only two arguments.

This multiple-stage type of processing, similar to a stairway, allows convenient processing of a variable number of arguments.

Accessing Arguments

To access arguments, it's necessary for each argument to have a clearly defined type. Again, PHP's extremely dynamic nature introduces some quirks. Because PHP never does any kind of type checking, it's possible for a caller to pass any kind of data to your functions, whether you want it or not. If you expect an integer, for example, the caller might pass an array, and vice versa—PHP simply won't notice.

To work around this, you have to use a set of API functions to force a type conversion on every argument that's being passed (see Table 9.4).

Note: All conversion functions expect a `**zval` as parameter.

Table 9.4 **Argument Conversion Functions**

Function	Description
`convert_to_boolean_ex(value)`	Forces conversion to a Boolean type. Boolean values remain untouched. Longs, doubles, and strings containing **0** as well as NULL values will result in Boolean **0** (FALSE). Arrays and objects are converted based on the number of entries or properties, respectively, that they have. Empty arrays and objects are converted to FALSE; otherwise, to TRUE. All other values result in a Boolean 1 (TRUE).
`convert_to_long_ex(value)`	Forces conversion to a long, the default integer type. NULL values, Booleans, resources, and of course longs remain untouched. Doubles are truncated. Strings containing an integer are converted to their corresponding numeric representation, otherwise resulting in **0**. Arrays and objects are converted to **0** if empty, 1 otherwise.

continues

Table 9.4 **Continued**

Function	Description
convert_to_double_ex(*value*)	Forces conversion to a double, the default floating-point type. NULL values, Booleans, resources, longs, and of course doubles remain untouched. Strings containing a number are converted to their corresponding numeric representation, otherwise resulting in 0.0. Arrays and objects are converted to 0.0 if empty, 1.0 otherwise.
convert_to_string_ex(*value*)	Forces conversion to a string. Strings remain untouched. NULL values are converted to an empty string. Booleans containing TRUE are converted to "1", otherwise resulting in empty string. Longs and doubles are converted to their corresponding string representation. Arrays are converted to the string "Array" and objects to the string "Object".
convert_to_array_ex(*value*)	Forces conversion to an array. Arrays remain untouched. Objects are converted to an array by assigning all their properties to the array table. All property names are used as keys, property contents as values. NULL values are converted to an empty array. All other values are converted to an array that contains the specific source value in the element with the key 0.
convert_to_object_ex(*value*)	Forces conversion to an object. Objects remain untouched. NULL values are converted to an empty object. Arrays are converted to objects by introducing their keys as properties into the objects and their values as corresponding property contents in the object. All other types result in an object with the property scalar, having the corresponding source value as content.
convert_to_null_ex(*value*)	Forces the type to become a NULL value, meaning empty.

Note: You can find a demonstration of the behavior in cross_conversion.php on the accompanying CD-ROM. Figure 9.5 shows the output.

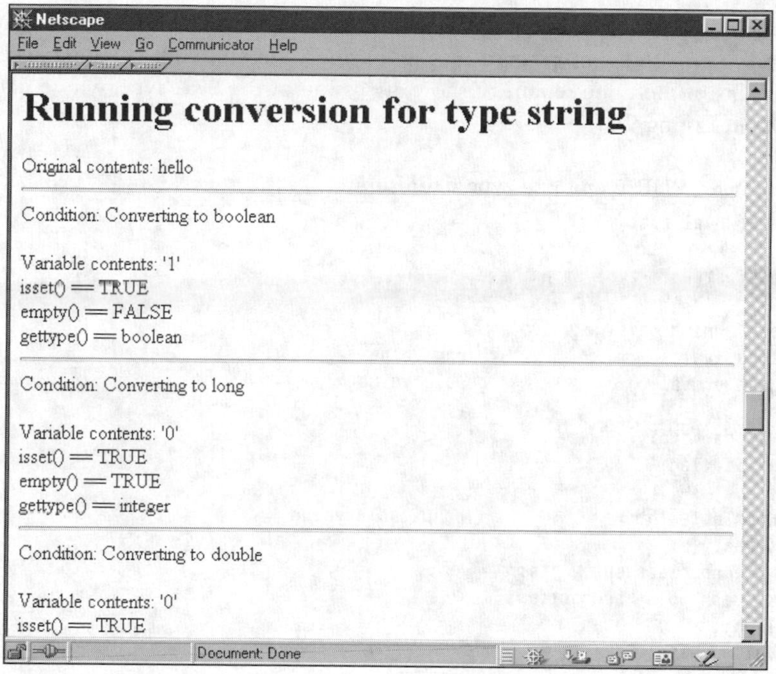

Figure 9.5   Cross-conversion behavior of PHP.

Using these functions on your arguments will ensure type safety for all data that's passed to you. If the supplied type doesn't match the required type, PHP forces dummy contents on the resulting value (empty strings, arrays, or objects, 0 for numeric values, FALSE for Booleans) to ensure a defined state.

Following is a quote from the sample module discussed previously, which makes use of the conversion functions:

```
zval **parameter;

if((ZEND_NUM_ARGS() != 1) || (zend_get_parameters_ex(1, &parameter) != SUCCESS))
{
    WRONG_PARAM_COUNT;
}

convert_to_long_ex(parameter);

RETURN_LONG((*parameter)->value.lval);
```

After retrieving the parameter pointer, the parameter value is converted to a long (an integer), which also forms the return value of this function. Understanding access to the contents of the value requires a short discussion of the zval type, whose definition is shown in Listing 9.8.

Listing 9.8   **PHP/Zend *zval* type definition.**

```
typedef pval zval;

typedef struct _zval_struct zval;

typedef union _zvalue_value {
    long lval;                  /* long value */
    double dval;                /* double value */
    struct {
        char *val;
        int len;
    } str;
    HashTable *ht;                  /* hash table value */
    struct {
        zend_class_entry *ce;
        HashTable *properties;
    } obj;
} zvalue_value;

struct _zval_struct {
    /* Variable information */
    zvalue_value value;         /* value */
    unsigned char type;    /* active type */
    unsigned char is_ref;
    short refcount;
};
```

Actually, pval (defined in php.h) is only an alias of zval (defined in zend.h), which in turn refers to _zval_struct. This is a most interesting structure. _zval_struct is the "master" structure, containing the value structure, type, and reference information. The substructure zvalue_value is a union that contains the variable's contents. Depending on the variable's type, you'll have to access different members of this union. For a description of both structures, see Tables 9.5, 9.6, and 9.7.

Table 9.5   **Zend *zval* Structure**

Entry	Description
value	Union containing this variable's contents. See Table 9.6 for a description.
type	Contains this variable's type. For a list of available types, see Table 9.7.

Entry	Description
is_ref	0 means that this variable is not a reference; 1 means that this variable is a reference to another variable.
refcount	The number of references that exist for this variable. For every new reference to the value stored in this variable, this counter is increased by 1. For every lost reference, this counter is decreased by 1. When the reference counter reaches 0, no references exist to this value anymore, which causes automatic freeing of the value.

Table 9.6 **Zend *zvalue_value* Structure**

Entry	Description
lval	Use this property if the variable is of the type IS_LONG, IS_BOOLEAN, or IS_RESOURCE.
dval	Use this property if the variable is of the type IS_DOUBLE.
str	This structure can be used to access variables of the type IS_STRING. The member len contains the string length; the member val points to the string itself. Zend uses C strings; thus, the string length contains a trailing 0x00.
ht	This entry points to the variable's hash table entry if the variable is an array.
obj	Use this property if the variable is of the type IS_OBJECT.

Table 9.7 **Zend Variable Type Constants**

Constant	Description
IS_NULL	Denotes a NULL (empty) value.
IS_LONG	A long (integer) value.
IS_DOUBLE	A double (floating point) value.
IS_STRING	A string.
IS_ARRAY	Denotes an array.
IS_OBJECT	An object.
IS_BOOL	A Boolean value.
IS_RESOURCE	A resource (for a discussion of resources, see the appropriate section below).
IS_CONSTANT	A constant (defined) value.

To access a long you access `zval.value.lval`, to access a double you use `zval.value.dval`, and so on. Because all values are stored in a union, trying to access data with incorrect union members results in meaningless output.

Accessing arrays and objects is a bit more complicated and is discussed later.

Dealing with Arguments Passed by Reference

If your function accepts arguments passed by reference that you intend to modify, you need to take some precautions.

What we didn't say yet is that under the circumstances presented so far, you don't have write access to any `zval` containers designating function parameters that have been passed to you. Of course, you can change any `zval` containers that you created within your function, but you mustn't change any `zvals` that refer to Zend-internal data!

We've only discussed the so-called `*_ex()` API so far. You may have noticed that the API functions we've used are called `zend_get_parameters_ex()` instead of `zend_get_parameters()`, `convert_to_long_ex()` instead of `convert_to_long()`, etc. The `*_ex()` functions form the so-called new "extended" Zend API. They give a minor speed increase over the old API, but as a tradeoff are only meant for providing read-only access.

Because Zend works internally with references, different variables may reference the same value. Write access to a `zval` container requires this container to contain an isolated value, meaning a value that's not referenced by any other containers. If a `zval` container were referenced by other containers and you changed the referenced `zval`, you would automatically change the contents of the other containers referencing this `zval` (because they'd simply point to the changed value and thus change their own value as well).

`zend_get_parameters_ex()` doesn't care about this situation, but simply returns a pointer to the desired `zval` containers, whether they consist of references or not. Its corresponding function in the traditional API, `zend_get_parameters()`, immediately checks for referenced values. If it finds a reference, it creates a new, isolated `zval` container, copies the referenced data into this newly allocated space, and then returns a pointer to the new, isolated value.

This action is called *zval separation* (or `pval` separation). Because the `*_ex()` API doesn't perform `zval` separation, it's considerably faster, while at the same time disabling write access.

To change parameters, however, write access is required. Zend deals with this situation in a special way: Whenever a parameter to a function is passed by reference, it performs automatic `zval` separation. This means that whenever you're calling a function like this in PHP, Zend will automatically ensure that $parameter is being passed as an isolated value, rendering it to a write-safe state:

```
my_function(&$parameter);
```

But this *is not* the case with regular parameters! All other parameters that are not passed by reference are in a read-only state.

This requires you to make sure that you're really working with a reference— otherwise you might produce unwanted results. To check for a parameter being passed by reference, you can use the function `ParameterPassedByReference()`. This function accepts two parameters. The first is the function's `ht` value, and the second is the argument number that you want to test, counted from left to right, as shown in Listing 9.9 and Figure 9.6 (see the CD-ROM for the full source).

Listing 9.9 **Testing for referenced parameter passing.**

```
zval **parameter;

if((ZEND_NUM_ARGS() != 1) || (zend_get_parameters_ex(1, &parameter) != SUCCESS))
{
    WRONG_PARAM_COUNT;
}

/* check for parameter being passed by reference */
if(!ParameterPassedByReference(ht, 1))
{
    zend_error(E_WARNING, "Parameter wasn't passed by reference");
    RETURN_NULL();
}

/* make changes to the parameter */
(*parameter)->type = IS_LONG;
(*parameter)->value.lval = 10;
```

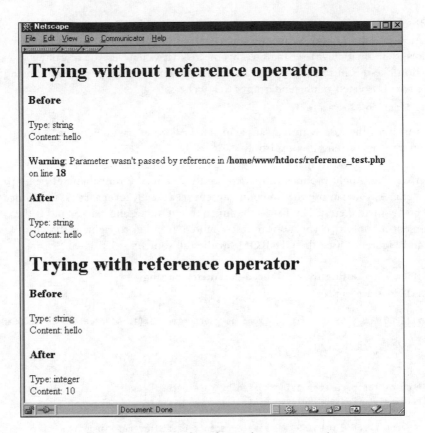

Figure 9.6 Testing for referenced parameter passing.

Assuring Write Safety for Other Parameters

You might run into a situation in which you need write access to a parameter that's retrieved with `zend_get_parameters_ex()` but not passed by reference. For this case, you can use the macro `SEPARATE_ZVAL`, which does a `zval` separation on the provided container. The newly generated `zval` is detached from internal data and has only a local scope, meaning that it can be changed or destroyed without implying global changes in the script context:

```
zval **parameter;

/* retrieve parameter */
zend_get_parameters_ex(1, &parameter);

/* at this stage, <parameter> still is connected */
/* to Zend's internal data buffers */
```

```
/* make <parameter> write-safe */
SEPARATE_ZVAL(parameter);

/* now we can safely modify <parameter> */
/* without implying global changes
*/
```

SEPARATE_ZVAL uses `emalloc()` to allocate the new `zval` container, which means that even if you don't deallocate this memory yourself, it will be destroyed automatically upon script termination. However, doing a lot of calls to this macro without freeing the resulting containers will clutter up your RAM.

Note: As you can easily work around the lack of write access in the "traditional" API (with `zend_get_parameters()` and so on), this API seems to be obsolete, and is not discussed further in this chapter.

Creating Variables

When exchanging data from your own extensions with PHP scripts, one of the most important issues is the creation of variables. This section shows you how to deal with the variable types that PHP supports.

Overview

To create new variables that can be seen "from the outside" by the executing script, you need to allocate a new `zval` container, fill this container with meaningful values, and then introduce it to Zend's internal symbol table. This basic process is common to all variable creations:

```
zval *new_variable;

/* allocate and initialize new container */
MAKE_STD_ZVAL(new_variable);

/* set type and variable contents here, see the following sections */

/* introduce this variable by the name "new_variable_name" into the symbol
↪table */
ZEND_SET_SYMBOL(EG(active_symbol_table), "new_variable_name", new_variable);

/* the variable is now accessible to the script by using $new_variable_name */
```

The macro `MAKE_STD_ZVAL` allocates a new `zval` container using `ALLOC_ZVAL` and initializes it using `INIT_ZVAL`. As implemented in Zend at the time of this writing, `initializing` means setting the reference count to 1 and clearing the `is_ref` flag, but this process could be extended later—this is why it's a good idea to keep using `MAKE_STD_ZVAL` instead of only using `ALLOC_ZVAL`. If you want to optimize for speed (and you don't have to explicitly initialize the `zval` container here), you can use `ALLOC_ZVAL`, but this is not recommended because it doesn't ensure data integrity.

ZEND_SET_SYMBOL takes care of introducing the new variable to Zend's symbol table. This macro checks whether the value already exists in the symbol table and converts the new symbol to a reference if so (with automatic deallocation of the old zval container). This is the preferred method if speed is not a crucial issue and you'd like to keep memory usage low.

Note that ZEND_SET_SYMBOL makes use of the Zend executor globals via the macro EG. By specifying EG(active_symbol_table), you get access to the currently active symbol table, dealing with the active, local scope. The local scope may differ depending on whether the function was invoked from within a function.

If you need to optimize for speed and don't care about optimal memory usage, you can omit the check for an existing variable with the same value and instead force insertion into the symbol table by using zend_hash_update():

```
zval *new_variable;

/* allocate and initialize new container */
MAKE_STD_ZVAL(new_variable);

/* set type and variable contents here, see the following sections */

/* introduce this variable by the name "new_variable_name" into the symbol
➥table */
zend_hash_update(EG(active_symbol_table), "new_variable_name",
➥strlen("new_variable_name") + 1, &new_variable, sizeof(zval *), NULL);
```

This is actually the standard method used in most modules.

The variables generated with the snippet above will always be of local scope, so they reside in the context in which the function has been called. To create new variables in the global scope, use the same method but refer to another symbol table:

```
zval *new_variable;

// allocate and initialize new container
MAKE_STD_ZVAL(new_variable);

//
// set type and variable contents here
//

// introduce this variable by the name "new_variable_name" into the global
➥symbol table
ZEND_SET_SYMBOL(&EG(symbol_table), new_variable);
```

The macro ZEND_SET_SYMBOL is now being called with a reference to the main, global symbol table by referring EG(symbol_table).

Note: The active_symbol_table variable is a pointer, but symbol_table is not. This is why you have to use EG(active_symbol_table) and &EG(symbol_table) as parameters to ZEND_SET_SYMBOL—it requires a pointer.

Similarly, to get a more efficient version, you can hardcode the symbol table update:

```
zval *new_variable;

// allocate and initialize new container
MAKE_STD_ZVAL(new_variable);

//
// set type and variable contents here
//

// introduce this variable by the name "new_variable_name" into the global
⮕symbol table
zend_hash_update(&EG(symbol_table), "new_variable_name",
⮕strlen("new_variable_name") + 1, &new_variable, sizeof(zval *), NULL);
```

Listing 9.10 shows a sample source that creates two variables—local_variable with a local scope and global_variable with a global scope (see Figure 9.7). The full example can be found on the CD-ROM.

Note: You can see that the global variable is actually not accessible from within the function. This is because it's not imported into the local scope using global $global_variable; in the PHP source.

Listing 9.10   **Creating variables with different scopes.**

```
ZEND_FUNCTION(variable_creation)
{
    zval *new_var1, *new_var2;

    MAKE_STD_ZVAL(new_var1);
    MAKE_STD_ZVAL(new_var2);

    new_var1->type = IS_LONG;
    new_var1->value.lval = 10;

    new_var2->type = IS_LONG;
    new_var2->value.lval = 5;

    ZEND_SET_SYMBOL(EG(active_symbol_table), "local_variable", new_var1);
    ZEND_SET_SYMBOL(&EG(symbol_table), "global_variable", new_var2);

    RETURN_NULL();

}
```

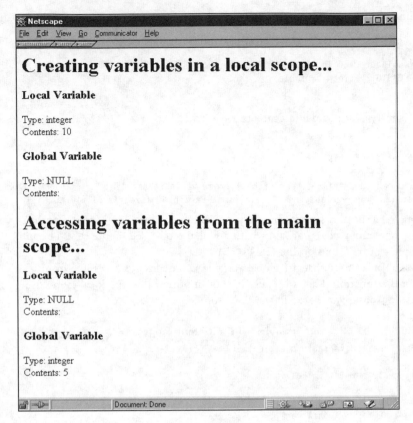

Figure 9.7   Variables with different scopes.

Longs (Integers)

Now let's get to the assignment of data to variables, starting with longs. Longs are PHP's integers and are very simple to store. Looking at the zval.value container structure discussed earlier in this chapter, you can see that the long data type is directly contained in the union, namely in the lval field. The corresponding type value for longs is IS_LONG (see Listing 9.11).

Listing 9.11   **Creation of a long.**

```
zval *new_long;

MAKE_STD_ZVAL(new_long);

new_long->type = IS_LONG;
new_long->value.lval = 10;
```

Alternatively, you can use the macro ZVAL_LONG:

```
zval *new_long;

MAKE_STD_ZVAL(new_long);
ZVAL_LONG(new_long, 10);
```

Doubles (Floats)

Doubles are PHP's floats and as easy to assign as longs, because their value is also contained directly in the union. The member in the zval.value container is dval; the corresponding type is IS_DOUBLE.

```
zval *new_double;

MAKE_STD_ZVAL(new_double);

new_double->type = IS_DOUBLE;
new_double->value.dval = 3.45;
```

Alternatively, you can use the macro ZVAL_DOUBLE:

```
zval *new_double;

MAKE_STD_ZVAL(new_double);
ZVAL_DOUBLE(new_double, 3.45);
```

Strings

Strings need slightly more effort. As mentioned earlier, all strings that will be associated with Zend's internal data structures need to be allocated using Zend's own memory-management functions. Referencing of static strings or strings allocated with standard routines is not allowed. To assign strings, you have to access the structure str in the zval.value container. The corresponding type is IS_STRING:

```
zval *new_string;
char *string_contents = "This is a new string variable";

MAKE_STD_ZVAL(new_string);

new_string->type = IS_STRING;
new_string->value.str.len = strlen(string_contents);
new_string->value.str.val = estrdup(string_contents);
```

Note the usage of Zend's estrdup() here. Of course, you can also use the predefined macro ZVAL_STRING:

```
zval *new_string;
char *string_contents = "This is a new string variable";

MAKE_STD_ZVAL(new_string);
ZVAL_STRING(new_string, string_contents, 1);
```

ZVAL_STRING accepts a third parameter that indicates whether the supplied string contents should be duplicated (using estrdup()). Setting this parameter to 1 causes the string to be duplicated; 0 simply uses the supplied pointer for the variable contents. This is most useful if you want to create a new variable referring to a string that's already allocated in Zend internal memory.

If you want to truncate the string at a certain position or you already know its length, you can use ZVAL_STRINGL(*zval, string, length, duplicate*), which accepts an explicit string length to be set for the new string. This macro is faster than ZVAL_STRING and also binary-safe.

To create empty strings, set the string length to 0 and use empty_string as contents:

```
new_string->type = IS_STRING;
new_string->value.str.len = 0;
new_string->value.str.val = empty_string;
```

Of course, there's a macro for this as well (ZVAL_EMPTY_STRING):

```
MAKE_STD_ZVAL(new_string);
ZVAL_EMPTY_STRING(new_string);
```

Booleans

Booleans are created just like longs, but have the type IS_BOOL. Allowed values in lval are 0 and 1:

```
zval *new_bool;

MAKE_STD_ZVAL(new_bool);

new_bool->type = IS_BOOL;
new_bool->value.lval = 1;
```

The corresponding macros for this type are ZVAL_BOOL (allowing specification of the value) as well as ZVAL_TRUE and ZVAL_FALSE (which explicitly set the value to TRUE and FALSE, respectively).

Arrays

Arrays are stored using Zend's internal hash tables, which can be accessed using the zend_hash_*() API. For every array that you want to create, you need a new hash-table handle, which will be stored in the ht member of the zval.value container.

There's a whole API solely for the creation of arrays, which is extremely handy. To start a new array, you call `array_init()`:

```
zval *new_array;

MAKE_STD_ZVAL(new_array);

if(array_init(new_array) != SUCCESS)
{
    // do error handling here
}
```

If `array_init()` fails to create a new array, it returns FAILURE.

To add new elements to the array, you can use numerous functions, depending on what you want to do. Tables 9.8, 9.9, and 9.10 describe these functions. All functions return FAILURE on failure and SUCCESS on success.

Note: The functions in Table 9.8 all operate on the array *array* with the key *key*. The key string doesn't have to reside in Zend internal memory; it will be duplicated by the API.

Table 9.8 **Zend's API for Associative Arrays**

Function	Description
add_assoc_long (*zval *array, char *key, long n*);	Adds an element of type long.
add_assoc_unset (*zval *array, char *key*);	Adds an unset element.
add_assoc_bool (*zval *array, char *key, int b*);	Adds a Boolean element.
add_assoc_resource (*zval *array, char *key, int r*);	Adds a resource to the array.
add_assoc_double (*zval *array, char *key, double d*);	Adds a floating-point value.
add_assoc_string (*zval *array, char *key, char *str, int duplicate*);	Adds a string to the array. The flag duplicate specifies whether the string contents have to be copied to Zend internal memory.
add_assoc_stringl(*zval *array, char *key, char *str, uint length, int duplicate*);	Adds a string with the desired length *length* to the array. Otherwise, behaves like `add_assoc_string()`

Note: The functions in Table 9.9 all operate on the array *array* with the index *idx*. The index is always an integer.

Table 9.9   **Zend's API for Indexed Arrays, Part 1**

Function	Description
add_index_long (*zval *array*, *uint idx*, *long n*);	Adds an element of type long.
add_index_unset (*zval *array*, *uint idx*);	Adds an unset element.
add_index_bool (*zval *array*, *uint idx*, *int b*);	Adds a Boolean element.
add_index_resource (*zval *array*, *uint idx*, *int r*);	Adds a resource to the array.
add_index_double (*zval *array*, *uint idx*, *double d*);	Adds a floating-point value.
add_index_string(*zval *array*, *uint idx*, *char *str*, int duplicate);	Adds a string to the array. The flag duplicate specifies whether the string contents have to be copied to Zend internal memory.
add_index_stringl(*zval *array*, *uint idx*, *char *str*, *uint length*, int duplicate);	Adds a string with the desired length *length* to the array. This function is faster and binary-safe. Otherwise, behaves like add_index_string().

Note: The functions in Table 9.10 all operate on the array *array*. These functions automatically generate a new index based on the highest index found in the array.

Table 9.10   **Zend's API for Indexed Arrays, Part 2**

Function	Description
add_next_index_long (*zval *array*, *long n*);	Adds an element of type long.
add_next_index_unset(*zval *array*);	Adds an unset element.
add_next_index_bool (*zval *array*, *int b*);	Adds a Boolean element.
add_next_index_resource (*zval *array*, *int r*);	Adds a resource to the array.
add_next_index_double (*zval *array*, *double d*);	Adds a floating-point value.
add_next_index_string(*zval *array*, *char *str*, int duplicate);	Adds a string to the array. The flag duplicate specifies whether the string contents have to be copied to Zend internal memory.
add_next_index_stringl(*zval *array*, *char *str*, *uint length*, int duplicate);	Adds a string with the desired length *length* to the array. This function is faster and binary-safe. Otherwise, behaves like add_index_string().

All these functions provide a handy abstraction to Zend's internal hash API. Of course, you can also use the hash functions directly—for example, if you already have a zval container allocated that you want to insert into an array. This is done using zend_hash_update() for associative arrays (see Listing 9.12) and zend_hash_index_update() for indexed arrays (see Listing 9.13):

Listing 9.12 **Adding an element to an associative array.**

```
zval *new_array, *new_element;
char *key = "element_key";

MAKE_STD_ZVAL(new_array);
MAKE_STD_ZVAL(new_element);

if(array_init(new_array) == FAILURE)
{
    // do error handling here
}

ZVAL_LONG(new_element, 10);

if(zend_hash_update(new_array->value.ht, key, strlen(key) + 1,
➥(void *)&new_element, sizeof(zval *), NULL) == FAILURE)
{
    // do error handling here
}
```

Listing 9.13 **Adding an element to an indexed array.**

```
zval *new_array, *new_element;
int key = 2;

MAKE_STD_ZVAL(new_array);
MAKE_STD_ZVAL(new_element);

if(array_init(new_array) == FAILURE)
{
    // do error handling here
}

ZVAL_LONG(new_element, 10);

if(zend_hash_index_update(new_array->value.ht, key, (void *)&new_element,
➥sizeof(zval *), NULL) == FAILURE)
{
    // do error handling here
}
```

To emulate the functionality of add_next_index_*(), you can use this:

```
zend_hash_next_index_insert(ht, zval **new_element, sizeof(zval *), NULL)
```

Note: To return arrays from a function, use array_init() and all following actions on the predefined variable return_value (given as argument to your exported function; see the earlier discussion of the call interface). You do not have to use MAKE_STD_ZVAL on this.

Tip: To avoid having to write new_array->value.ht every time, you can use HASH_OF(new_array), which is also recommended for compatibility and style reasons.

Objects

Since objects can be converted to arrays (and vice versa), you might have already guessed that they have a lot of similarities to arrays in PHP. Objects are maintained with the same hash functions, but there's a different API for creating them.

To initialize an object, you use the function object_init():

```
zval *new_object;

MAKE_STD_ZVAL(new_object);

if(object_init(new_object) != SUCCESS)
{
    // do error handling here
}
```

You can use the functions described in Table 9.11 to add members to your object.

Note: All functions in Table 9.11 work on the object *object* with the key *key*. The key forms the member name, so the resulting member can be accessed via $object->key.

Table 9.11 **Zend's API for Object Creation**

Function	Description
add_property_long (*zval *object, char *key, long l*);	Adds a long to the object.
add_property_unset (*zval *object, char *key*);	Adds an unset property to the object.
add_property_bool (*zval *object, char *key, int b*);	Adds a Boolean to the object.
add_property_resource (*zval *object, char *key, int r*);	Adds a resource to the object.
add_property_double (*zval *object, char *key, double d*);	Adds a double to the object.
add_property_string(*zval *object, char *key, char *str*, int duplicate);	Adds a string to the object.

Function	Description
add_property_stringl(*zval *object, char *key, char *str, uint length*, int duplicate);	Adds a string of the specified length to the object. This function is faster than add_property_string and also binary-safe.

Resources

Resources are a special kind of data type in PHP. The term *resources* doesn't really refer to any special kind of data, but to an abstraction method for maintaining any kind of information. Resources are kept in a special resource list within Zend. Each entry in the list has a corresponding type definition that denotes the kind of resource to which it refers. Zend then internally manages all references to this resource. Access to a resource is never possible directly—only via a provided API. As soon as all references to a specific resource are lost, a corresponding shutdown function is called.

For example, resources are used to store database links and file descriptors. The *de facto* standard implementation can be found in the MySQL module, but other modules such as the Oracle module also make use of resources.

To get a handle for your special resource, you have to register the resource type prior to using it:

```
int resource_handle = register_list_destructors(destructor_handler, NULL);
```

This call gives you a handle that you can use whenever adding entries to the resource list. The specified function (here named destructor_handler) will always be called whenever all references to a certain resource are lost and Zend tries to kill it. This function has to take care of proper resource freeing and deallocation. It must be of type void and as argument it only has to accept a pointer to the type that you want to insert into the list.

```
typedef struct
{
    int resource_link;
    int resource_type;
} my_resource;

void destructor_handler(my_resource *resource)
{

    // do all deallocation relating to the resource here

    // free container
    efree(resource);

}
```

Now, to add a resource to the list, use `zend_list_insert()`:

```
my_resource *resource;

// allocate resource here and fill it with values
resource = (my_resource *)emalloc(sizeof(my_resource));

resource_value = zend_list_insert(resource, resource_handle);
```

The function accepts two arguments: The first is the pointer to the resource that you want to add to the list, and the second is the type of the resource (for which you previously registered a destructor). You can now use the return value of this call to `zend_list_insert()` as the `value` field in your corresponding `IS_RESOURCE` zval container.

For example, to use the resource allocated above as return value, do this:

```
RETURN_RESOURCE(resource_value);
```

Or, more elaborately:

```
return_value->type = IS_RESOURCE;
return_value->value.lval = resource_value;
```

You can see that resources are stored in the `lval` field.

Zend now keeps track of all references to this resource. As soon as all references to the resource are lost, the destructor that you previously registered for this resource is called. The nice thing about this setup is that you don't have to worry about memory leakages introduced by allocations in your module—just register all memory allocations that your calling script will refer to as resources. As soon as the script decides it doesn't need them anymore, Zend will find out and tell you.

To force removal of a resource from the list, use the function `zend_list_delete()`. You can also force the reference count to increase if you know that you're creating another reference for a previously allocated value (for example, if you're automatically reusing a default database link). For this case, use the function `zend_list_addref()`. To search for previously allocated resource entries, use `zend_list_find()`. The complete API can be found in `zend_list.h`.

For a little example showing how to make use of resources, see the demonstration on the CD-ROM.

Macros for Automatic Global Variable Creation

In addition to the macros discussed earlier, a few macros allow easy creation of simple global variables. These are nice to know in case you want to introduce global flags, for example. This is somewhat bad practice, but Table 9.12 describes macros that do exactly this task. They don't need any `zval` allocation; you simply have to supply a variable name and value.

Note: All macros in Table 9.12 create a global variable of the name *name* with the value *value*.

Table 9.12 **Macros for Global Variable Creation**

Macro	Description
SET_VAR_STRING(*name*, *value*)	Creates a new string.
SET_VAR_STRINGL(*name*, *value*, *length*)	Creates a new string of the specified length. This macro is faster than SET_VAR_STRING and also binary-safe.
SET_VAR_LONG(*name*, *value*)	Creates a new long.
SET_VAR_DOUBLE(*name*, *value*)	Creates a new double.

Creating Constants

Zend supports the creation of true constants (as opposed to regular variables). Constants are accessed without the typical dollar sign ($) prefix and are available in all scopes. Examples include TRUE and FALSE, to name just two.

To create your own constants, you can use the macros in Table 9.13. All the macros create a constant with the specified name and value.

You can also specify flags for each constant:

- CONST_CS—This constant's name is to be treated as case sensitive.
- CONST_PERSISTENT—This constant is persistent and won't be "forgotten" when the current process carrying this constant shuts down.

To use the flags, combine them using a binary OR:

```
// register a new constant of type "long"
REGISTER_LONG_CONSTANT("NEW_MEANINGFUL_CONSTANT", 324, CONST_CS |
➥CONST_PERSISTENT);
```

There are two types of macros—REGISTER_*_CONSTANT and REGISTER_MAIN_*_CONSTANT. The first type creates constants bound to the current module. These constants are dumped from the symbol table as soon as the module that registered the constant is unloaded from memory. The second type creates constants that remain in the symbol table independently of the module.

Table 9.13 **Macros for Creating Constants**

Macro	Description
REGISTER_LONG_CONSTANT (*name*, *value*, *flags*)	Registers a new constant of type long.
REGISTER_MAIN_LONG_CONSTANT (*name*, *value*, *flags*)	

continues

Table 9.13 **Continued**

Macro	Description
REGISTER_DOUBLE_CONSTANT (*name*, *value*, *flags*)	Register a new constant of type double.
REGISTER_MAIN_DOUBLE_CONSTANT (*name*, *value*, *flags*)	
REGISTER_STRING_CONSTANT (*name*, *value*, *flags*) REGISTER_MAIN_STRING_CONSTANT (*name*, *value*, *flags*)	Registers a new constant of type string. The specified string must reside in Zend's internal memory.
REGISTER_STRINGL_CONSTANT (*name*, *value*, *length*, *flags*) REGISTER_MAIN_STRINGL_CONSTANT (*name*, *value*, *length*, *flags*)	Registers a new constant of type string. The string length is explicitly set to *length*. The specified string must reside in Zend's internal memory

Duplicating Variable Contents: The Copy Constructor

Sooner or later, you may need to assign the contents of one zval container to another. This is easier said than done, since the zval container doesn't contain only type information, but also references to places in Zend's internal data. For example, depending on their size, arrays and objects may be nested with lots of hash table entries. By assigning one zval to another, you avoid duplicating the hash table entries, using only a reference to them (at most).

To copy this complex kind of data, use the *copy constructor*. Copy constructors are typically defined in languages that support operator overloading, with the express purpose of copying complex types. If you define an object in such a language, you have the possibility of overloading the = operator, which is usually responsible for assigning the contents of the lvalue (result of the evaluation of the left side of the operator) to the rvalue (same for the right side).

Overloading means assigning a different meaning to this operator, and is usually used to assign a function call to an operator. Whenever this operator would be used on such an object in a program, this function would be called with the lvalue and rvalue as parameters. Equipped with that information, it can perform the operation it intends the = operator to have (usually an extended form of copying).

This same form of "extended copying" is also necessary for PHP's zval containers. Again, in the case of an array, this extended copying would imply re-creation of all hash-table entries relating to this array. For strings, proper memory allocation would have to be assured, and so on.

Zend ships with such a function, called `zend_copy_ctor()` (the previous PHP equivalent was `pval_copy_constructor()`).

A most useful demonstration is a function that accepts a complex type as argument, modifies it, and then returns the argument:

```
zval **parameter;

if((ZEND_NUM_ARGS() != 1) || (zend_get_parameters_ex(1, &parameter) != SUCCESS))
{
    WRONG_PARAM_COUNT;
}

// do modifications to the parameter here

// now we want to return the modified container:
*return_value == **parameter;
zval_copy_ctor(return_value);
```

The first part of the function is plain-vanilla argument retrieval. After the (left out) modifications, however, it gets interesting: The container of `parameter` is assigned to the (predefined) `return_value` container. Now, in order to effectively duplicate its contents, the copy constructor is called. The copy constructor works directly with the supplied argument, and the standard return values are `FAILURE` on failure and `SUCCESS` on success.

If you omit the call to the copy constructor in this example, both `parameter` and `return_value` would point to the same internal data, meaning that `return_value` would be an illegal additional reference to the same data structures. Whenever changes occurred in the data that `parameter` points to, `return_value` might be affected. Thus, in order to create separate copies, the copy constructor must be used.

The copy constructor's counterpart in the Zend API, the destructor `zval_dtor()`, does the opposite of the constructor. The corresponding alias in the PHP API is `pval_destructor()`.

Returning Values

Returning values from your functions to PHP was described briefly in an earlier section; this section gives the details. Return values are passed via the `return_value` variable, which is passed to your functions as argument. The `return_value` argument consists of a `zval` container (see the earlier discussion of the call interface) that you can freely modify. The container itself is already allocated, so you don't have to run `MAKE_STD_ZVAL` on it. Instead, you can access its members directly.

To make returning values from functions easier and to prevent hassles with accessing the internal structures of the `zval` container, a set of predefined macros is available (as usual). These macros automatically set the corresponding type and value, as described in Tables 9.14 and 9.15.

Note: The macros in Table 9.14 automatically return from your function.

Table 9.14   **Predefined Macros for Returning Values from a Function**

Macro	Description
RETURN_RESOURCE(*resource*)	Returns a resource.
RETURN_BOOL(*bool*)	Returns a Boolean.
RETURN_NULL()	Returns nothing (a NULL value).
RETURN_LONG(*long*)	Returns a long.
RETURN_DOUBLE(*double*)	Returns a double.
RETURN_STRING(*string*, duplicate)	Returns a string. The duplicate flag indicates whether the string should be duplicated using estrdup().
RETURN_STRINGL(*string*, *length*, duplicate)	Returns a string of the specified *length*; otherwise, behaves like RETURN_STRING. This macro is faster and binary-safe, however.
RETURN_EMPTY_STRING()	Returns an empty string.
RETURN_FALSE	Returns Boolean false.
RETURN_TRUE	Returns Boolean true.

Note: The macros in Table 9.15 only *set* the return value; they don't return from your function.

Table 9.15   **Predefined Macros for Setting the Return Value of a Function**

Macro	Description
RETVAL_RESOURCE(*resource*)	Sets the return value to the specified *resource*.
RETVAL_BOOL(*bool*)	Sets the return value to the specified Boolean value.
RETVAL_NULL()	Sets the return value to NULL.
RETVAL_LONG(*long*)	Sets the return value to the specified long.
RETVAL_DOUBLE(*double*)	Sets the return value to the specified double.
RETVAL_STRING(*string*, duplicate)	Sets the return value to the specified string and duplicates it to Zend internal memory if desired (see also RETURN_STRING).

Macro	Description
RETVAL_STRINGL(*string*, *length*, duplicate)	Sets the return value to the specified *string* and forces the length to become *length* (see also RETVAL_STRING). This macro is faster and binary-safe, and should be used whenever the string length is known.
RETVAL_EMPTY_STRING()	Sets the return value to an empty string.
RETVAL_FALSE	Sets the return value to Boolean false.
RETVAL_TRUE	Sets the return value to Boolean true.

Complex types such as arrays and objects can be returned by using array_init() and object_init(), as well as the corresponding hash functions on return_value. Since these types cannot be constructed of trivial information, there are no predefined macros for them.

Printing Information

Often it's necessary to print messages to the output stream from your module, just as print() would be used within a script. PHP offers functions for most generic tasks, such as printing warning messages, generating output for phpinfo(), and so on. The following sections provide more details. Examples of these functions can be found on the CD-ROM.

zend_printf()

zend_printf() works like the standard printf(), except that it prints to Zend's output stream.

zend_error()

zend_error() can be used to generate error messages. This function accepts two arguments; the first is the error type (see zend_errors.h) and the second is the error message:

```
zend_error(E_WARNING, "This function has been called with empty arguments");
```

Table 9.16 shows a list of possible values (see Figure 9.8). These values are also referred to in php.ini. Depending on which error type you choose, your messages will be logged.

Table 9.16 **Zend's Predefined Error Messages**

Error	Description
E_ERROR	Signals an error and terminates execution of the script immediately.
E_WARNING	Signals a generic warning. Execution continues.
E_PARSE	Signals a parser error. Execution continues.
E_NOTICE	Signals a notice. Execution continues. Note that by default the display of this type of error messages is turned off in php.ini.
E_CORE_ERROR	Internal error by the core; shouldn't be used by user-written modules.
E_COMPILE_ERROR	Internal error by the compiler; shouldn't be used by user-written modules.
E_COMPILE_WARNING	Internal warning by the compiler; shouldn't be used by user-written modules.

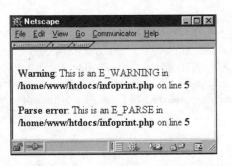

Figure 9.8 Display of warning messages in the browser.

Including Output in *phpinfo()*

After creating a real module, you'll want to show information about the module in phpinfo() (in addition to the module name, which appears in the module list by default). PHP allows you to create your own section in the phpinfo() output with the ZEND_MINFO() function. This function should be placed in the module descriptor block (discussed earlier) and is always called whenever a script calls phpinfo().

PHP automatically prints a section in phpinfo() if you specify the ZEND_MINFO function, including the module name in the heading. Everything else must be formatted and printed by you.

Typically, you can print an HTML table header using
`php_info_print_table_start()` and then use the standard functions
`php_info_print_table_header()` and `php_info_print_table_row()`. As arguments,
both take the number of columns (as integers) and the column contents (as strings).
Listing 9.14 shows a source example; Figure 9.9 shows the output. To print the table
footer, use `php_info_print_table_end()`.

Listing 9.14 **Source code and output in** *phpinfo().*

```
php_info_print_table_start();
php_info_print_table_header(2, "First column", "Second column");
php_info_print_table_row(2, "Entry in first row", "Another entry");
php_info_print_table_row(2, "Just to fill", "another row here");
php_info_print_table_end();
```

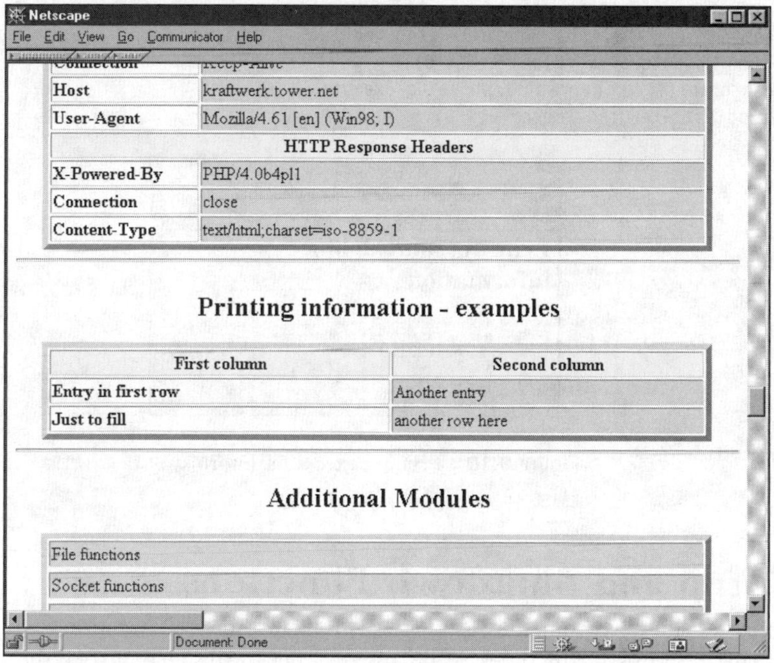

Figure 9.9   Output from `phpinfo()`.

Execution Information

You can also print execution information, such as the current file being executed. The
name of the function currently being executed can be retrieved using the function
`get_active_function_name()`. This function returns a pointer to the function name
and doesn't accept any arguments. To retrieve the name of the file currently being

executed, use `zend_get_executed_filename()`. This function accesses the executor globals, which are passed to it using the `ELS_C` macro. The executor globals are automatically available to every function that's called directly by Zend (they're part of the `INTERNAL_FUNCTION_PARAMETERS` described earlier in this chapter). If you want to access the executor globals in another function that doesn't have them available automatically, call the macro `ELS_FETCH()` once in that function; this will introduce them to your local scope.

Finally, the line number currently being executed can be retrieved using the function `zend_get_executed_lineno()`. This function also requires the executor globals as arguments. For examples of these functions, see Listing 9.15 and Figure 9.10. Of course, all the examples are also available on the CD-ROM.

Listing 9.15 **Printing execution information.**

```
zend_printf("The name of the current function is %s<br>",
➥get_active_function_name());
zend_printf("The file currently executed is %s<br>",
➥zend_get_executed_filename(ELS_C));
zend_printf("The current line being executed is %i<br>",
➥zend_get_executed_lineno(ELS_C));
```

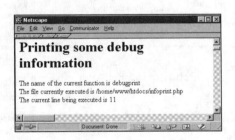

Figure 9.10 Printing execution information.

Startup and Shutdown Functions

Startup and shutdown functions can be used for one-time initialization and deinitialization of your modules. As discussed earlier in this chapter (see the description of the Zend module descriptor block), there are global, module, and request startup and shutdown events.

The global startup functions are called once when PHP starts up, similarly the global shutdown functions are called once when PHP shuts down. Please note that they're really only called *once*, not when a new Apache process is being created!

The module startup and shutdown functions are called whenever a module is loaded and needs initialization; the request startup and shutdown functions are called every time a request is processed (meaning that a file is being executed).

For dynamic extensions, module and request startup/shutdown events happen at the same time.

Declaration and implementation of these functions can be done with macros; see the earlier section "Declaration of the Zend Module Block" for details.

Calling User Functions

You can call user functions from your own modules, which is very handy when implementing callbacks - for example, for array walking, searching, or simply for event-based programs.

User functions can be called with the function `call_user_function_ex()`. It requires a hash value for the function table you want to access, a pointer to an object (if you want to call a method), the function name, return value, number of arguments, argument array, and a flag indicating whether you want to perform `zval` separation:

```
ZEND_API call_user_function_ex(HashTable *function_table, zval *object,
                        ➥zval *function_name, zval **retval_ptr_ptr,
                        ➥int param_count, zval **params[]
                        ➥int no_separation);
```

Notice that you don't have to specify both *function_table* and *object*; either will do. If you want to call a method, you have to supply the object that contains this method, in which case `call_user_function()` automatically sets the function table to this object's function table. Otherwise, you only need to specify *function_table* and can set *object* to NULL.

Usually, the default function table is the "root" function table containing all function entries. This function table is part of the compiler globals and can be accessed using the macro `CG`. To introduce the compiler globals to your function, call the macro `CLS_FETCH` once.

The function name is specified in a `zval` container. This might be a bit surprising at first, but is quite a logical step, since most of the time you'll accept function names as parameters from calling functions within your script, which in turn are contained in `zval` containers again. Thus, you only have to pass your arguments through to this function. This `zval` must be of type `IS_STRING`.

The next argument consists of a pointer to the return value. You don't have to allocate memory for this container; the function will do so by itself. However, you have to destroy this container (using `zval_dtor()`) afterward!

Next is the parameter count as integer and an array containing all necessary parameters. The last argument specifies whether the function should perform `zval` separation—this should always be set to `0`. If set to `1`, the function consumes less memory but fails if any of the parameters need separation.

Listing 9.16 and Figure 9.11 show a small demonstration of calling a user function. The code calls a function that's supplied to it as argument and directly passes this function's return value through as its own return value. Note the use of the constructor and destructor calls at the end—it might not be necessary to do it this way here (since they should be separate values, the assignment might be safe), but this is bulletproof.

Listing 9.16 **Calling user functions.**

```
zval **function_name;
zval *retval;

if((ZEND_NUM_ARGS() != 1) || (zend_get_parameters_ex(1, &function_name)
➥!= SUCCESS))
{
    WRONG_PARAM_COUNT;
}

if((*function_name)->type != IS_STRING)
{
    zend_error(E_ERROR, "Function requires string argument");
}

CLS_FETCH();

if(call_user_function_ex(CG(function_table), NULL, *function_name, &retval,
➥0, NULL, 0) != SUCCESS)
{
    zend_error(E_ERROR, "Function call failed");
}

zend_printf("We have %i as type<br>", retval->type);

*return_value = *retval;
zval_copy_ctor(return_value);
zval_dtor(retval);

<?php

dl("call_userland.so");

function test_function()
{

    print("We are in the test function!<br>");

    return("hello");

}

$return_value = call_userland("test_function");
```

```
print("Return value: \"$return_value\"<br>");
?>
```

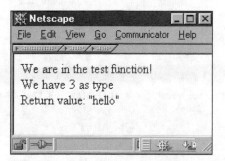

Figure 9.11   Calling user functions.

Initialization File Support

PHP 4.0 features a redesigned initialization file support. It's now possible to specify default initialization entries directly in your code, read and change these values at runtime, and create message handlers for change notifications.

To create an .ini section in your own module, use the macros PHP_INI_BEGIN() to mark the beginning of such a section and PHP_INI_END() to mark its end. In between you can use PHP_INI_ENTRY() to create entries.

```
PHP_INI_BEGIN()
    PHP_INI_ENTRY("first_ini_entry",  "has_string_value", PHP_INI_ALL, NULL)
    PHP_INI_ENTRY("second_ini_entry", "2",                PHP_INI_SYSTEM,
                                                          ➥OnChangeSecond)
    PHP_INI_ENTRY("third_ini_entry",  "xyz",              PHP_INI_USER, NULL)
                                                          ➥PHP_INI_END()
```

The PHP_INI_ENTRY() macro accepts four parameters: the entry name, the entry value, its change permissions, and a pointer to a change-notification handler. Both entry name and value must be specified as strings, regardless of whether they really are strings or integers.

The permissions are grouped into three sections: PHP_INI_SYSTEM allows a change only directly in the php3.ini file; PHP_INI_USER allows a change to be overridden by a user at runtime using additional configuration files, such as .htaccess); and PHP_INI_ALL allows changes to be made without restrictions. There's also a fourth level, PHP_INI_PERDIR, for which we couldn't verify its behavior yet.

The fourth parameter consists of a pointer to a change-notification handler. Whenever one of these initialization entries is changed, this handler is called. Such a handler can be declared using the `PHP_INI_MH` macro:

```
PHP_INI_MH(OnChangeSecond);                    // handler for ini-entry
                                              ⇒"second_ini_entry"


// specify ini-entries here

PHP_INI_MH(OnChangeSecond)
{

    zend_printf("Message caught, our ini entry has been changed to %s<br>",
            ⇒new_value);

    return(SUCCESS);

}
```

The new value is given to the change handler as string in the variable `new_value`. When looking at the definition of `PHP_INI_MH`, you actually have a few parameters to use:

```
#define PHP_INI_MH(name) int name(php_ini_entry *entry, char *new_value,
                          ⇒uint *new_value_length, void *mh_arg1,
                          ⇒void *mh_arg2, void *mh_arg3)
```

All these definitions can be found in `php_ini.h`. Your message handler will have access to a structure that contains the full entry, the new value, its length, and three optional arguments. These optional arguments can be specified with the additional macros `PHP_INI_ENTRY1` (allowing one additional argument), `PHP_INI_ENTRY2` (allowing two additional arguments), and `PHP_INI_ENTRY3` (allowing three additional arguments).

The change-notification handlers should be used to cache initialization entries locally for faster access or to perform certain tasks that are required if a value changes. For example, if a constant connection to a certain host is required by a module and someone changes the hostname, automatically terminate the old connection and attempt a new one.

Access to initialization entries can also be handled with the macros shown in Table 9.17.

Table 9.17   **Macros to Access Initialization Entries in PHP**

Macro	Description
INI_INT(*name*)	Returns the current value of entry *name* as integer (long).
INI_FLT(*name*)	Returns the current value of entry *name* as float (double).
INI_STR(*name*)	Returns the current value of entry *name* as string. *Note:* This string is not duplicated, but instead points to internal data. Further access requires duplication to local memory.

Macro	Description
INI_BOOL(*name*)	Returns the current value of entry *name* as Boolean (defined as `zend_bool`, which currently means unsigned char).
INI_ORIG_INT(*name*)	Returns the original value of entry *name* as integer (long).
INI_ORIG_FLT(*name*)	Returns the original value of entry *name* as float (double).
INI_ORIG_STR(*name*)	Returns the original value of entry *name* as string. Note: This string is not duplicated, but instead points to internal data. Further access requires duplication to local memory.
INI_ORIG_BOOL(*name*)	Returns the original value of entry *name* as Boolean (defined as zend_bool, which currently means unsigned char).

Finally, you have to introduce your initialization entries to PHP. This can be done in the module startup and shutdown functions, using the macros `REGISTER_INI_ENTRIES()` and `UNREGISTER_INI_ENTRIES()`:

```
ZEND_MINIT_FUNCTION(mymodule)
{

    REGISTER_INI_ENTRIES();

}

ZEND_MSHUTDOWN_FUNCTION(mymodule)
{

    UNREGISTER_INI_ENTRIES();

}
```

Where to Go from Here

You've learned a lot about PHP. You now know how to create dynamic loadable modules and statically linked extensions. You've learned how PHP and Zend deal with internal storage of variables and how you can create and access these variables. You know quite a set of tool functions that do a lot of routine tasks such as printing informational texts, automatically introducing variables to the symbol table, and so on.

Even though this chapter often had a mostly "referential" character, we hope that it gave you insight on how to start writing your own extensions. For the sake of space, we had to leave out a lot; we suggest that you take the time to study the header files and some modules (especially the ones in the `ext/standard` directory and the MySQL module, as these implement commonly known functionality). This will give you an idea of how other people have used the API functions—particularly those that didn't make it into this chapter.

Reference: Some Configuration Macros

config.m4

The file config.m4 is processed by buildconf and must contain all the instructions to be executed during configuration. For example, these can include tests for required external files, such as header files, libraries, and so on. PHP defines a set of macros that can be used in this process, the most useful of which are described in Table 9.18.

Table 9.18 **M4 Macros for *config.m4***

Macro	Description
AC_MSG_CHECKING(*message*)	Prints a checking *<message>* text during configure.
AC_MSG_RESULT(*value*)	Gives the result to AC_MSG_CHECKING; should specify either yes or no as *value*.
AC_MSG_ERROR(*message*)	Prints *message* as error message during configure and aborts the script.
AC_DEFINE(*name, value, description*)	Adds #define to php_config.h with the value of *value* and a comment that says *description* (this is useful for conditional compilation of your module).
AC_ADD_INCLUDE(*path*)	Adds a compiler include path; for example, used if the module needs to add search paths for header files.
AC_ADD_LIBRARY_WITH_PATH (*libraryname, librarypath*)	Specifies an additional library to link.
AC_ARG_WITH(*modulename, description, unconditionaltest, conditionaltest*)	Quite a powerful macro, adding the module with *description* to the configure --help output. PHP checks whether the option --with-*<modulename>* is given to the configure script. If so, it runs the script *unconditionaltest* (for example, --with-myext=yes), in which case the value of the option is contained in the variable $withval. Otherwise, it executes *conditionaltest*.
PHP_EXTENSION(*modulename*, [shared])	This macro is a *must* to call for PHP to configure your extension. You can supply a second argument in addition to your module name, indicating whether you intend compilation as a shared module. This will result in a definition at compile time for your source as COMPILE_DL_*<modulename>*.

Additional API Macros

Shortly before the release of this book, a new set of macros was introduced into Zend's API that simplify access to zval containers (see Table 9.19). However, we chose not to use them in the example sources, as they don't make many accesses to zval containers, and the macros would have resulted in source code that was more difficult to read.

Table 9.19   **New API macros for Accessing *zval* Containers**

Macro	Refers to
Z_LVAL(*zval*)	(*zval*).value.lval
Z_DVAL(*zval*)	(*zval*).value.dval
Z_STRVAL(*zval*)	(*zval*).value.str.val
Z_STRLEN(*zval*)	(*zval*).value.str.len
Z_ARRVAL(*zval*)	(*zval*).value.ht
Z_LVAL_P(*zval*)	(*zval*).value.lval
Z_DVAL_P(*zval*)	(*zval*).value.dval
Z_STRVAL_P(*zval_p*)	(*zval*).value.str.val
Z_STRLEN_P(*zval_p*)	(*zval*).value.str.len
Z_ARRVAL_P(*zval_p*)	(*zval*).value.ht
Z_LVAL_PP(*zval_pp*)	(**zval*).value.lval
Z_DVAL_PP(*zval_pp*)	(**zval*).value.dval
Z_STRVAL_PP(*zval_pp*)	(**zval*).value.str.val
Z_STRLEN_PP(*zval_pp*)	(**zval*).value.str.len
Z_ARRVAL_PP(*zval_pp*)	(**zval*).value.ht

Updates of this chapter can be found at www.phpwizard.net.

Index

L

Q–R

S

Open Source Resource

In MySQL, Paul DuBois provides you with a comprehensive guide to one of the most popular relational database systems, MySQL. As an important contributor to the online documentation for MySQL, Paul uses his day-to-day experience answering questions users post on the MySQL mailing list
to pinpoint the problems most users and administrators encounter. Through two sample databases that run throughout the book, he gives you solutions to problems you'll likely face, including integratin MySQL efficiently with third-party tools like PHP and Perl, enabling you to generate dynamic Web pages through database queries.

ISBN: 0-7357-0921-1

The goal of the Python Essential Reference is to concisely describe the Python programming language and its large library of standard modules, collectively known as the Python programming "environment." This book is for the professional who has experience with other systems programming language such as C or C++, and is looking for content that is not embellished with basic introductory material on the Python programming environment.

ISBN: 0-7357-09017

This book details the security steps that a small, non-enterprise business user might take to protect his system. These steps include packet-level firewall filtering, IP masquerading, proxies, tcp wrappers, system integrity checking, and system security monitoring with an overall emphasis on filtering and protection. The goal of the book is to help people get their Internet security measures in place quickly, without the need to become experts in security of firewalls.

ISBN: 0-7357-0900-9

Advanced Information on Networking Technologies

New Riders Books Offer Advice and Experience

LANDMARK

Rethinking Computer Books

We know how important it is to have access to detailed, solution-oriented information on core technologies. *Landmark* books contain the essential information you need to solve technical problems. Written by experts and subjected to rigorous peer and technical reviews, our *Landmark* books are hard-core resources for practitioners like you.

ESSENTIAL REFERENCE

Smart, Like You

The *Essential Reference* series from New Riders provides answers when you know what you want to do but need to know how to do it. Each title skips extraneous material and assumes a strong base of knowledge. These are indispensable books for the practitioner who wants to find specific features of a technology quickly and efficiently. Avoiding fluff and basic material, these books present solutions in an innovative, clean format—and at a great value.

CIRCLE SERIES

The *Circle Series* is a set of reference guides that meet the needs of the growing community of advanced, technical-level networkers who must architect, develope, and administer operating systems like UNIX, Linux, Windows NT, and Windows 2000. These books provide network designers and programmers with detailed, proven solutions to their problems.

New Riders\ Books for Networking Professionals

Open Source Titles

MySQL
By Paul DuBois
1st Edition
$49.99
ISBN: 0-7357-0921-1

MySQL teaches readers how to use the tools provided by the MySQL distribution, covering installation, setup, daily use, security, optimization, maintenance, and troubleshooting. It also discusses important third-party tools, such as the Perl DBI and Apache/PHP interfaces that provide access to MySQL.

Python Essential Reference
By David Beazley
1st Edition
$34.95
ISBN: 0-7357-0901-7

Avoiding the dry and academic approach, the goal of Python Essential Reference is to concisely describe the Python programming language and its large library of standard modules, collectively known as the Python programming environment. This is an informal reference that covers Python's lexical conventions, datatypes, control flow, functions, statements, classes and execution model. A truly essential reference for any Python programmer.

Linux Firewalls
By Robert Ziegler
$39.99

ISBN: 0-7357-0900-9

A Linux machine connected to the Internet is in a high-risk situation. This book details security steps that a small, non-enterprise business user might take to protect himself. These steps include packet-level firewall filtering, IP masquerading, proxies, tcp wrappers, system integrity checking, and system security monitoring with an overall emphasis on filtering and protection. The goal is to help people get their Internet security measures in place quickly, without the need to become experts in security or firewalls.

KDE Application Development
By Uwe Thiem
$39.99 US / $59.95 CAN

ISBN: 1-57870-201-1

KDE Application Development offers a head start on KDE and Qt. The book covers the essential widgets available in KDE and Qt, and offers a strong start without the "first try" annoyances which sometimes make strong developers and programmers give up.

DCE/RPC over SMB: Samba and Windows NT Domain Internals
By Luke Leighton
$45.00
ISBN: 1-57870-150-3

Security people, system and network administrators, and the folks writing tools for them all need to be familiar with the packets flowing across their networks. Authored by a key member of the SAMBA team, this book describes how Microsoft has taken DCE/RPC and implemented it over SMB and TCP/IP.

Grokking the GIMP
By Carey Bunks

$39.99
ISBN: 0-7357-0924-6

Grokking the GIMP is a technical reference that covers the intricacies of the GIMP's functionality. The material gives the reader the ability to get up to speed quickly and start creating great graphics using the GIMP. Included as a bonus are step-by-step cookbook features used entirely for advanced effects.

GIMP Essential Reference
By Alex Harford
$24.95

ISBN: 0-7357-0911-4

As the use of the Linux OS gains steam, so does the use of the GIMP. Many Photoshop users are starting to use the GIMP, recognized for its power and versatility. Taking this into consideration, GIMP Essential Reference has shortcuts exclusively for Photoshop users and puts the power of this program into the palm of the reader's hand.

UNIX/Linux Titles

Solaris Essential Reference
By John P. Mulligan
1st Edition
300 pages, $24.95
ISBN: 0-7357-0023-0

Looking for the fastest and easiest way to find the Solaris command you need? Need a few pointers on shell scripting? How about advanced administration tips and sound, practical expertise on security issues? Are you looking for trustworthy information about available third-party software packages that will enhance your operating system? Author John Mulligan—creator of the popular "Unofficial Guide to The Solaris™ Operating Environment" Web site (sun.icsnet.com)—delivers all that and more in one attractive, easy-to-use reference book. With clear and concise instructions on how to perform important administration and management tasks, and key information on powerful commands and advanced topics, *Solaris Essential Reference* is the book you need when you know what you want to do and only need to know how.

Linux System Administration
By M. Carling, Stephen Degler, and James Dennis
1st Edition
450 pages, $29.99
ISBN: 1-56205-934-3

As an administrator, you probably feel that most of your time and energy is spent in endless firefighting. If your network has become a fragile quilt of temporary patches and work-arounds, this book is for you. Have you had trouble sending or receiving email lately? Are you looking for a way to keep your network running smoothly with enhanced performance? Are your users always hankering for more storage, services, and speed? *Linux System Administration* advises you on the many intricacies of maintaining a secure, stable system. In this definitive work, the authors address all the issues related to system administration, from adding users and managing file permissions, to Internet services and Web hosting, to recovery planning and security. This book fulfills the need for expert advice that will ensure a trouble-free Linux environment.

GTK+/Gnome Application Development
By Havoc Pennington
1st Edition
492 pages, $39.99
ISBN: 0-7357-0078-8

This title is for the reader who is conversant with the C programming language and UNIX/Linux development. It provides detailed and solution-oriented information designed to meet the needs of programmers and application developers using the GTK+/Gnome libraries. Coverage complements existing GTK+/Gnome documentation, going into more depth on pivotal issues such as uncovering the GTK+ object system, working with the event loop, managing the Gdk substrate, writing custom widgets, and mastering GnomeCanvas.

Developing Linux Applications with GTK+ and GDK

By Eric Harlow
1st Edition
490 pages, $34.99
ISBN: 0-7357-0021-4

We all know that Linux is one of the most powerful and solid operating systems in existence. And as the success of Linux grows, there is an increasing interest in developing applications with graphical user interfaces that take advantage of the power of Linux. In this book, software developer Eric Harlow gives you an indispensable development handbook focusing on the GTK+ toolkit. More than an overview of the elements of application or GUI design, this is a hands-on book that delves into the technology. With in-depth material on the various GUI programming tools and loads of examples, this book's unique focus will give you the information you need to design and launch professional-quality applications.

Linux Essential Reference

By Ed Petron
1st Edition
350 pages, $24.95
ISBN: 0-7357-0852-5

This book is all about getting things done as quickly and efficiently as possible by providing a structured organization for the plethora of available Linux information. We can sum it up in one word—value. This book has it all: concise instructions on how to perform key administration tasks, advanced information on configuration, shell scripting, hardware management, systems management, data tasks, automation, and tons of other useful information. This book truly provides groundbreaking information for the growing community of advanced Linux professionals.

Lotus Notes and Domino Titles

Domino System Administration

By Rob Kirkland, CLP, CLI
1st Edition
850 pages, $49.99
ISBN: 1-56205-948-3

Your boss has just announced that you will be upgrading to the newest version of Notes and Domino when it ships. How are you supposed to get this new system installed, configured, and rolled out to all of your end users? You understand how Lotus Notes works—you've been administering it for years. What you need is a concise, practical explanation of the new features and how to make some of the advanced stuff work smoothly by someone like you, who has worked with the product for years and understands what you need to know. *Domino System Administration* is the answer—the first book on Domino that attacks the technology at the professional level with practical, hands-on assistance to get Domino running in your organization.

Lotus Notes & Domino Essential Reference

By Tim Bankes, CLP
and Dave Hatter, CLP, MCP
1st Edition
650 pages, $45.00
ISBN: 0-7357-0007-9

You're in a bind because you've been asked to design and program a new database in Notes for an important client who will keep track of and itemize a myriad of inventory and shipping data. The client wants a user-friendly interface that won't sacrifice speed or functionality. You are experienced (and could develop this application in your sleep), but feel you need something to facilitate your creative and technical abilities—something to perfect your programming skills. The answer is waiting for you: *Lotus Notes & Domino Essential Reference*. It's compact and simply designed. It's loaded with information. All of the objects, classes, functions, and methods are listed. It shows you the object hierarchy and the relationship between each one. It's perfect for you. Problem solved.

Network Intrusion Detection: An Analyst's Handbook

By Stephen Northcutt
1st Edition
267 pages, $39.99
ISBN: 0-7357-0868-1

Get answers and solutions from someone who has been in the trenches. The author, Stephen Northcutt, original developer of the Shadow intrusion detection system and former director of the United States Navy's Information System Security Office at the Naval Security Warfare Center, gives his expertise to intrusion detection specialists, security analysts, and consultants responsible for setting up and maintaining an effective defense against network security attacks.

Understanding Data Communications, Sixth Edition

By Gilbert Held
6th Edition
600 pages, $39.99
ISBN: 0-7357-0036-2

Updated from the highly successful fifth edition, this book explains how data communications systems and their various hardware and software components work. More than an entry-level book, it approaches the material in textbook format, addressing the complex issues involved in internetworking today. A great reference book for the experienced networking professional that is written by the noted networking authority, Gilbert Held.

Other Books By New Riders

Microsoft Technologies

APPLICATION PROGRAMMING

Delphi COM Programming
1-57870-221-6 • $45.00 US/$67.95 CAN
Windows NT Applications: Measuring and
Optimizing Performance
1-57870-176-7 • $40.00 US/$59.95 CAN
Applying COM+
ISBN 0-7357-0978-5 • $49.99 US/$74.95
CAN
Available August 2000

WEB PROGRAMMING

Exchange & Outlook: Constructing
Collaborative Solutions
ISBN 1-57870-252-6 • $40.00 US/$59.95
CAN

SCRIPTING

Windows Script Host
1-57870-139-2 • $35.00 US/$52.95 CAN
Windows NT Shell Scripting
1-57870-047-7 • $32.00 US/$45.95 CAN
Windows NT Win32 Perl Programming:
The Standard Extensions
1-57870-067-1 • $40.00 US/$59.95 CAN
Windows NT/2000 ADSI Scripting for System
Administration
1-57870-219-4 • $45.00 US/$67.95 CAN
Windows NT Automated Deployment and
Customization
1-57870-045-0 • $32.00 US/$45.95 CAN

Open Source

MySQL
0-7357-0921-1 • $49.99 US/$74.95 CAN
Web Application Development with PHP
0-7357-0997-1 • $45.00 US/$67.95 CAN
Available June 2000
PHP Functions Essential Reference
0-7357-0970-X • $35.00 US/$52.95 CAN
Available August 2000
Python Essential Reference
0-7357-0901-7 • $34.95 US/$52.95 CAN
Autoconf, Automake, and Libtool
1-57870-190-2 • $35.00 US/$52.95 CAN
Available August 2000

Linux/Unix

ADMINISTRATION

Linux System Administration
1-56205-934-3 • $29.99 US/$44.95 CAN
Linux Firewalls
0-7357-0900-9 • $39.99 US/$59.95 CAN
Linux Essential Reference
0-7357-0852-5 • $24.95 US/$37.95 CAN
UnixWare 7 System Administration
1-57870-080-9 • $40.00 US/$59.99 CAN

DEVELOPMENT

Developing Linux Applications with GTK+ and
GDK
0-7357-0021-4 • $34.99 US/$52.95 CAN
GTK+/Gnome Application Development
0-7357-0078-8 • $39.99 US/$59.95 CAN
KDE Application Development
1-57870-201-1 • $39.99 US/$59.95 CAN

GIMP

Grokking the GIMP
0-7357-0924-6 • $39.99 US/$59.95 CAN
GIMP Essential Reference
0-7357-0911-4 • $24.95 US/$37.95 CAN

SOLARIS

Solaris Advanced System Administrator's Guide,
Second Edition
1-57870-039-6 • $39.99 US/$59.95 CAN
Solaris System Administrator's Guide, Second
Edition
1-57870-040-X • $34.99 US/$52.95 CAN
Solaris Essential Reference
0-7357-0023-0 • $24.95 US/$37.95 CAN

Networking

STANDARDS & PROTOCOLS

Cisco Router Configuration & Troubleshooting,
Second Edition
0-7357-0999-8 • $34.99 US/$52.95 CAN
Understanding Directory Services
0-7357-0910-6 • $39.99 US/$59.95 CAN

Understanding the Network: A Practical Guide to
Internetworking
0-7357-0977-7 • $39.99 US/$59.95 CAN
Understanding Data Communications, Sixth
Edition
0-7357-0036-2 • $39.99 US/$59.95 CAN
LDAP: Programming Directory Enabled
Applications
1-57870-000-0 • $44.99 US/$67.95 CAN
Gigabit Ethernet Networking
1-57870-062-0 • $50.00 US/$74.95 CAN
Supporting Service Level Agreements
on IP Networks
1-57870-146-5 • $50.00 US/$74.95 CAN
Directory Enabled Networks
1-57870-140-6 • $50.00 US/$74.95 CAN
Differentiated Services for the Internet
1-57870-132-5 • $50.00 US/$74.95 CAN
Quality of Service on IP Networks
1-57870-189-9 • $50.00 US/$74.95 CAN
Designing Addressing Architectures for
Routing and Switching
1-57870-059-0 • $45.00 US/$69.95 CAN
Understanding & Deploying LDAP Directory
Services
1-57870-070-1 • $50.00 US/$74.95 CAN
Switched, Fast and Gigabit Ethernet, Third

Edition
1-57870-073-6 • $50.00 US/$74.95 CAN
Wireless LANs: Implementing Interoperable
Networks
1-57870-081-7 • $40.00 US/$59.95 CAN
Wide Area High Speed Networks
1-57870-114-7 • $50.00 US/$74.95 CAN
The DHCP Handbook
1-57870-137-6 • $55.00 US/$81.95 CAN
Designing Routing and Switching Architectures
for Enterprise Networks
1-57870-060-4 • $55.00 US/$81.95 CAN
Local Area High Speed Networks
1-57870-113-9 • $50.00 US/$74.95 CAN
Available June 2000
Network Performance Baselining
1-57870-240-2 • $50.00 US/$74.95 CAN
Economics of Electronic Commerce
1-57870-014-0 • $49.99 US/$74.95 CAN

SECURITY

Intrusion Detection
1-57870-185-6 • $50.00 US/$74.95 CAN
Understanding Public-Key Infrastructure
1-57870-166-X • $50.00 US/$74.95 CAN
Network Intrusion Detection: An Analyst's
Handbook
0-7357-0868-1 • $39.99 US/$59.95 CAN
Linux Firewalls
0-7357-0900-9 • $39.99 US/$59.95 CAN

LOTUS NOTES/DOMINO

Domino System Administration
1-56205-948-3 • $49.99 US/$74.95 CAN
Lotus Notes & Domino Essential Reference
0-7357-0007-9 • $45.00 US/$67.95 CAN

Software Architecture & Engineering

Designing for the User with OVID
1-57870-101-5 • $40.00 US/$59.95 CAN
Designing Flexible Object-Oriented Systems
with UML
1-57870-098-1 • $40.00 US/$59.95 CAN
Constructing Superior Software
1-57870-147-3 • $40.00 US/$59.95 CAN
A UML Pattern Language
1-57870-118-X • $45.00 US/$67.95 CAN

New Riders

We Want to Know What You Think

To better serve you, we would like your opinion on the content and quality of this book. Please complete this card and mail it to us or fax it to 317-581-4663.

Name _____

Address _____

City_____State_____Zip _____

Phone _____

Email Address _____

Occupation _____

Operating System(s) that you use _____

What influenced your purchase of this book?
- ❑ Recommendation
- ❑ Cover Design
- ❑ Table of Contents
- ❑ Index
- ❑ Magazine Review
- ❑ Advertisement
- ❑ New Rider's Reputation
- ❑ Author Name

How would you rate the contents of this book?
- ❑ Excellent
- ❑ Very Good
- ❑ Good
- ❑ Fair
- ❑ Below Average
- ❑ Poor

How do you plan to use this book?
- ❑ Quick reference
- ❑ Self-training
- ❑ Classroom
- ❑ Other

What do you like most about this book?
Check all that apply.
- ❑ Content
- ❑ Writing Style
- ❑ Accuracy
- ❑ Examples
- ❑ Listings
- ❑ Design
- ❑ Index
- ❑ Page Count
- ❑ Price
- ❑ Illustrations

What do you like least about this book?
Check all that apply.
- ❑ Content
- ❑ Writing Style
- ❑ Accuracy
- ❑ Examples
- ❑ Listings
- ❑ Design
- ❑ Index
- ❑ Page Count
- ❑ Price
- ❑ Illustrations

What would be a useful follow-up book to this one for you?_____

Where did you purchase this book? _____

_____

Can you name a similar book that you like better than this one, or one that is as good? Why?

_____

How many New Riders books do you own? _____

What are your favorite computer books?_____

_____

What other titles would you like to see us develop? _____

_____

Any comments for us? _____

_____

_____

_____

Web Application Development with PHP 4.0,
0-7357-0997-1

www.newriders.com   •   Fax   317-581-4663

Fold here and tape to mail

- -

New Riders Publishing
201 W. 103rd St.
Indianapolis, IN 46290

New Riders How to Contact Us

Visit Our Web Site

www.newriders.com

On our web site you'll find information about our other books, authors, tables of contents, indexes, and book errata listings, and more.

Email Us

Contact us at this address:

nrfeedback@newriders.com

- If you have comments or questions about this book
- To report errors that you have found in this book
- Opportunities @ newriders.com
- If you have a book proposal to submit or are interested in writing for New Riders
- If you would like to have an author kit sent to you
- If you are an expert in a computer topic or technology and are interested in being a technical editor who reviews manuscripts for technical accuracy

international@mcp.com

- To find a distributor in your area, please contact our international department at this address.

nrmedia@newriders.com

- For instructors from educational institutions who want to preview New Riders books for classroom use. Email should include your name, title, school, department, address, phone number, office days/hours, text in use, and enrollment, along with your request for desk/examination copies and/or additional information.
- For members of the media who are interested in reviewing copies of New Riders books. Send your name, mailing address, and email address, along with the name of the publication or Web site you work for.

Write to Us

New Riders Publishing

201 W. 103rd St.

Indianapolis, IN 46290-1097

Call Us

Toll-free (800) 571-5840 + 9 + 7477

If outside U.S. (317) 581-3500. Ask for New Riders.

Fax Us

(317) 581-4663

Dear Reader:

While the Web development community knows the power and superiority of PHP and promotes its use, commercial backing and the availability of reference materials will continue to be the two keys to making PHP become *the* standard in Web scripting. Zend Technologies was founded to promote PHP via its Web site and to provide commercial backing for PHP, giving it the "rubber stamp" that companies need to adopt Open Source software.

Other ways to promote PHP include the Zend API documentation in this book (Chapter 9, "Extending PHP 4.0: Hacking the Core of PHP"). It will encourage the community and its developers to help extend PHP to fit their needs.

The May 2000 release of PHP 4.0, which incorporates the Zend engine, is much faster and more powerful in every respect. Some of the highlights of this version are support of multithreaded Web server environments, including an ISAPI module (Microsoft's IIS), a new Web server abstraction layer, Java connectivity, and a much-improved build process for better PHP configuration.

PHP 4.0 also includes a new, high-performance API for extension module authors. This API allows PHP to pass parameters to internal functions much more efficiently by avoiding the duplication of values unless absolutely necessary. The new API usually requires no additional programming by the module authors, though additional logic is sometimes necessary. Most of the modules included in the PHP distribution were already converted to use this high-performance API. Chapter 9 describes the new API in depth.

We'd like to take this opportunity to thank everyone who has contributed to making PHP the superior software that it is. We hope that we can continue to join forces to make it the best it can be.

Andi Gutmans
Zeev Suraski
Zend Technologies, Ltd.

OPEN PUBLICATION LICENSE

I. REQUIREMENTS ON BOTH UNMODIFIED AND MODIFIED VERSIONS

The Open Publication works may be reproduced and distributed in whole or in part, in any medium physical or electronic, provided that the terms of this license are adhered to, and that this license or an incorporation of it by reference (with any options elected by the author(s) and/or publisher) is displayed in the reproduction.

Proper form for an incorporation by reference is as follows:

Copyright (c) 2000 by Zend Technologies, Ltd. This material may be distributed only subject to the terms and conditions set forth in the Open Publication License, v1.0 or later (the latest version is presently available at http://www.opencontent.org/openpub/).

The reference must be immediately followed with the following terms:

A. Distribution of substantively modified versions of this document is prohibited without the explicit permission of the copyright holder. "Substantive modification" is defined as a change to the content of the document, and excludes mere changes in format or typographical corrections.

B. Commercial distribution of the work or derivative of the work in any standard (paper) book form is prohibited unless prior permission is obtained from the copyright holder.

Other than as otherwise set forth herein, commercial redistribution of Open Publication-licensed material is permitted.

Any publication in standard (paper) book form shall require the citation of the original publisher and author. The publisher and author's names shall appear on all outer surfaces of the book. On all outer surfaces of the book the original publisher's name shall be as large as the title of the work and cited as possessive with respect to the title.

II. COPYRIGHT

The copyright to each Open Publication is owned by its author(s) or designee.

III. SCOPE OF LICENSE

The following license terms apply to all Open Publication works, unless otherwise explicitly stated in the document.

Mere aggregation of Open Publication works or a portion of an Open Publication work with other works or programs on the same media shall not cause this license to apply to those other works. The aggregate work shall contain a notice specifying the inclusion of the Open Publication material and appropriate copyright notice.

SEVERABILITY. If any part of this license is found to be unenforceable in any jurisdiction, the remaining portions of the license remain in force.

NO WARRANTY. Open Publication works are licensed and provided "as is" without warranty of any kind, express or implied, including, but not limited to, the implied warranties of merchantability and fitness for a particular purpose or a warranty of non-infringement.

IV. REQUIREMENTS ON MODIFIED WORKS

All modified versions of documents covered by this license, including translations, anthologies, compilations and partial documents, must meet the following requirements:

1) The modified version must be labeled as such.
2) The person making the modifications must be identified and the modifications dated.

3) Acknowledgement of the original author and publisher if applicable must be retained according to normal academic citation practices.

4) The location of the original unmodified document must be identified.

5) The original author's (or authors') name(s) may not be used to assert or imply endorsement of the resulting document without the original author's (or authors') permission.

V. GOOD-PRACTICE RECOMMENDATIONS

In addition to the requirements of this license, it is requested from and strongly recommended of redistributors that:

1) If you are distributing Open Publication works on hardcopy or CD-ROM, you provide email notification to the authors of your intent to redistribute at least thirty days before your manuscript or media freeze, to give the authors time to provide updated documents. This notification should describe modifications, if any, made to the document.

2) All substantive modifications (including deletions) be either clearly marked up in the document or else described in an attachment to the document.

Finally, while it is not mandatory under this license, it is considered good form to offer a free copy of any hardcopy and CD-ROM expression of an Open Publication-licensed work to its author(s).

VI. ADDITIONAL LICENSE TERMS

A. Distribution of "substantively modified" versions of this document is prohibited without the explicit permission of the copyright holder. "Substantive modification" is defined as a change to the content of the document, and excludes mere changes in format or typographical corrections.

B. Commercial distribution of the work or derivative of the work in any standard (paper) book form is prohibited unless prior permission is obtained from the copyright holder.

CD-ROM Licensing Agreement

By opening this package, you are agreeing to be bound by the following agreement:

- The source code contained on this CD-ROM is under the copyright of the authors and is licensed for your private use only. Individual programs and other items on the CD-ROM are copyrighted or are under GNU license, or licensed for this book by their various authors or other copyright holders.

- This software is sold as-is without warranty of any kind, either expressed or implied, including but not limited to the implied warranties of merchantability and fitness for a particular purpose. Neither the publisher nor its dealers or distributors assumes any liability for any alleged or actual damages arising from the use of this program. (Some states do not allow for the exclusion of implied warranties, so the exclusion may not apply to you.)

For some third-party software read this Important Note:

Important Note: Some of the Software on this CD-ROM has a "time-out" feature so that it expires within thirty (30) days after you load the Software on your system. The "time-out" feature may install hidden files on your system which, if not deleted, might remain on your computer after the Software has been removed. The purpose of the "time-out" feature is to ensure that the software is not used beyond its intended use.

Additional Note: This CD-ROM uses long and mixed-case filenames requiring the use of a protected-mode CD-ROM driver.